Business Survival Analysis Using SAS®

An Introduction to Lifetime Probabilities

Jorge Ribeiro

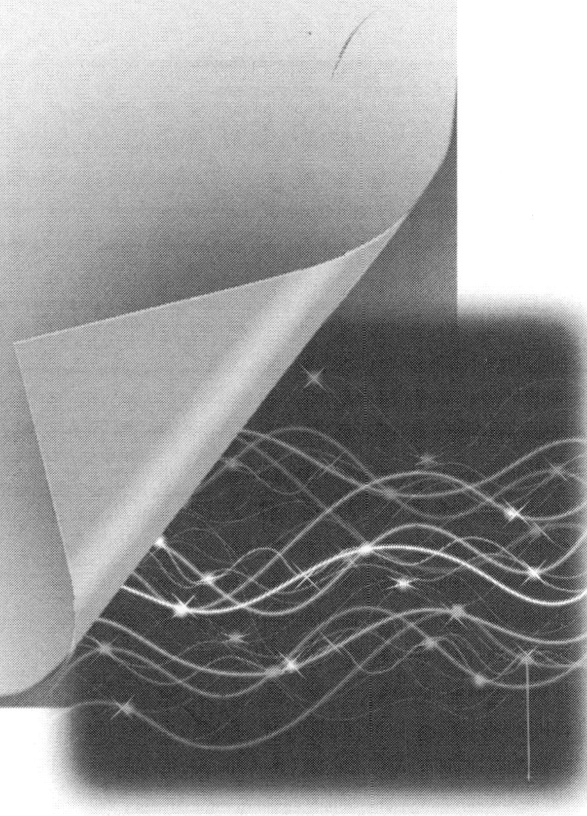

sas.com/books

The correct bibliographic citation for this manual is as follows: Ribeiro, Jorge. 2017. *Business Survival Analysis Using SAS®: An Introduction to Lifetime Probabilities*. Cary, NC: SAS Institute Inc.

Business Survival Analysis Using SAS®: An Introduction to Lifetime Probabilities

ISBN 978-1-62960-483-1 (Hard copy)
ISBN 978-1-62960-519-7 (EPUB)
ISBN 978-1-62960-520-3 (MOBI)
ISBN 978-1-62960-521-0 (PDF)

SAS Institute Inc., SAS Campus Drive, Cary, NC 27513-2414

July 2017

Contents

About This Book

What Does This Book Cover?

The primary purpose of this book, beyond introducing underlying survival analysis theories, methods, and requirements, is to illustrate how to build a time-to-next-purchase survival model in SAS Enterprise Miner. It explains each step with regard to statistics and to Base SAS and SAS/STAT (with which the reader might be more familiar with than SAS Enterprise Miner). It addresses the development and application of survival analysis techniques to common scenarios faced by financial services, insurance companies, marketing, and the telecommunications industry. These scenarios include the following:

- Time-to-next-purchase for marketing
- Employer turnover for human resources
- Small business portfolio macroeconomic stress test for banks
- Mortgage International Financial Reporting Standard (IFRS 9) lifetime probability of default for building societies
- Churn or attrition models for mobile and insurance industries

Business Concepts

This book emphasizes business problems involving time-to-next-purchase and churn.

Time-to-Next-Purchase

The objective of a time-to-next-purchase model is to predict the time until the next purchase for customers of a retail outlet. Thereby, the model addresses common business concerns, including the following:

- When and for how long to undertake an advertising campaign
- Resource planning for staff distribution, call centers, and the like, on the basis of anticipated demand
- Required stock of products subject to seasonality effects
- Customer churn (change and turn)—the proportion of customers who leave each month

Two primary objectives in marketing are to know which products to offer next to a customer and when to send targeted advertisements to customers who are likely to be responsive during certain months of the year. By targeting an appropriate subset of customers, a marketing department can reduce the amount of wasted time, effort, and costs of marketing on customers who are unlikely to respond.

The emphasis is on *which customers* make a second purchase through a web page, catalog, or branch, and the *duration* between the first and second purchase. Accordingly, the focus of the model is on *time to event*, which, in this case, is the time to repurchase. Survival analysis differs from logistic regression in that beyond looking at a binary outcome (such as whether a customer makes another purchase in a fixed period), it looks at the time to event: namely, when a second purchase will occur.

Churn

In this progressively more digital age, a retail outlet has to have an efficient marketing strategy as competition intensifies from new entrants in catalogs and online. The market is saturated and aggressive, and new customers are both hard and expensive to find. To be competitive, the company requires a strategy for long-term retention of customers and to avoid churn. Equally, it needs to track the impact of initiatives to persuade new customers to repurchase.

Overview of Chapters

This book teaches survival analysis using its first principles. It highlights its relevance to real-world business cases. It leads the reader through an actual example to contextualize the statistical methods and coding while understanding that this is an introduction to survival analysis models.

To facilitate learning, a single example is discussed throughout the book. The example illustrates, using minimum statistical theory, how to create a survival analysis model to predict time-to-next-purchase (or repurchase for customers who have already made a first purchase in the past). The book emphasizes survival analysis techniques that can be easily implemented, rather than delving into the heavy detail of the underlying mathematics. As such, it serves as a fundamentals course for understanding problems and techniques that are usually described only in more advanced books and papers.

This book is an introduction to survival analysis. But, unlike other books, this one is focused on business applications using data mining and regression, not on pharmaceutical or medical research. The following elements are presented in detail:

- Continuous and discrete time-to-event definitions
- Censor variables
- Survival function
- Hazard function
- Time-dependent variables and expanded data sets
- Cubic spline function and logistic regression models
- Specific sample methods for survival analysis
- Statistics for validation, such as the following:
    - Depth
    - Lift
    - Benefit
    - Concentration curve
    - Gini Concentration Ratio
    - Kolmogorov-Smirnov Statistic
- Customer scoring

The chapters in this book lead you through the steps to build a time-to-next-purchase survival model, specifically, and survival models, more generally. By following the steps shown in the following flowchart, you can develop any survival analysis model:

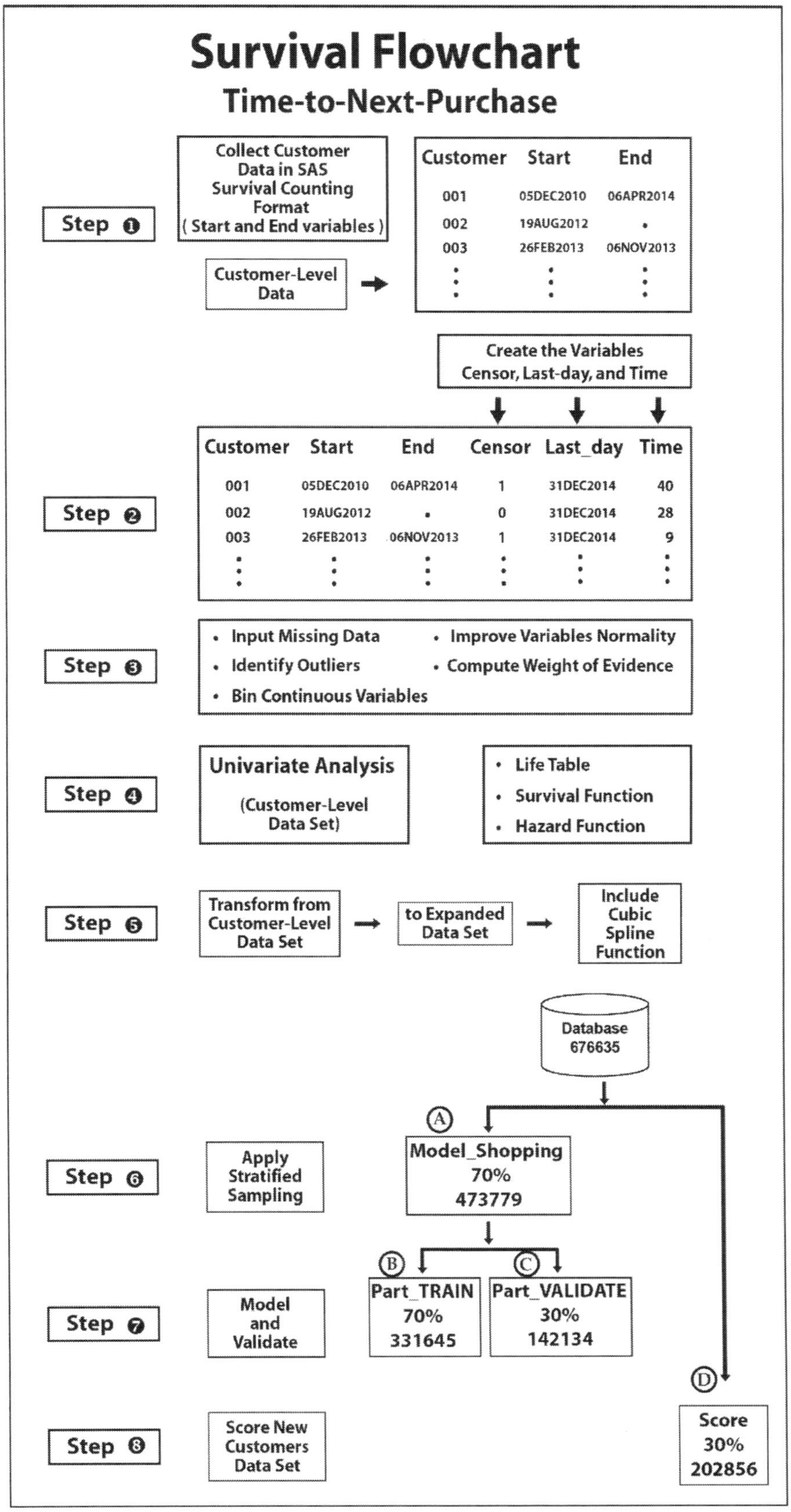

Chapter 1: Data Preparation for Survival Models

Chapter 1 focuses on the problems addressed by survival analysis: objectives, notation, and terminology. The Garden data set and creation of the required variables Censor and Time are presented. Issues such as defining the target (or dependent) variable are explained. The process starts with data sample collection. Next is the Time definition, which includes discussion of important considerations for univariate analysis.

Chapter 2: Exploratory Data Analysis and Basic Statistical Concepts

Chapter 2 introduces the logistic regression model and teaches basic statistical theory concerning the Survival and Hazard functions. This crucial chapter demonstrates the link between the Hazard and Survival functions and the logistic regression model.

Chapter 3: Stratified Sampling Method for Survival Analysis

Chapter 3 shows you how to create the unbiased stratified samples required for developing a survival analysis model.

Chapter 4: SAS Enterprise Miner Use from Source to Customer-Level Model Output

Chapter 4 shows you how to navigate, start a new project, create a data source, and complete other tasks in SAS Enterprise Miner. The focus is on creating the relevant process flow in SAS Enterprise Miner to develop, in detail, a model using the Survival node.

Chapter 5: The Cubic Spline Regression and Model Interpretation

Chapter 5 presents the cubic spline basis variables, which consist of a function joined at points called *knots*. The chapter shows you how the incorporation of the splines improves the survival model by adding flexibility to the Hazard function. The focus is on the interpretation of the coefficients and the cubic spline basis variables within the logistic survival model. You learn how to interpret SAS Enterprise Miner survival model output for continuous and categorical variables and about methods of checking the adequacy of a fitted model. By the end of the chapter, you will understand the meaning of the Hazard function and splines, as well as their relationships in the modeling process of survival analysis.

Chapter 6: The Fully Expanded Data Set Model

Chapter 6 shows you how to create a model using a fully expanded data set format. This model is compared to the customer-level model created in Chapter 4.

Chapter 7: Statistics for Performance and Validation

Chapter 7 is devoted to all the statistical measures necessary to assess the performance and validation of survival models:

- Depth
- Lift
- Benefit
- Concentration curve
- Gini Concentration Ratio
- Kolmogorov-Smirnov Statistic

Chapter 8: The Scoring of New and Old Customers

In Chapter 8, you develop an algorithm to score and validate new customers for a different date or time period.

Is This Book for You?

This book is intended for the following:

- Graduates of economics, business, and marketing programs
- Analysts who want to create statistical models and are working in areas such as credit risk

The examples in this book show people with limited modeling experience how to apply models. They present techniques in a way that avoids high-level theoretical considerations and detailed advanced topics.

What Are the Prerequisites for This Book?

Ideally, the reader should be familiar with linear regression, but statistics is kept at a minimum level to focus on the interpretation of SAS output at each stage of the modeling process.

Familiarity with statistical modeling is beneficial, but it is not a *must-have* condition for the reader. Basic knowledge of SAS 9.4 is recommended, but not of SAS macros. Minimum knowledge of SAS Enterprise Miner enables the reader to understand each of the steps presented in the flowchart.

It is assumed that the reader is familiar with Base SAS, including the following:

- Assigning a SAS library
- Basic DATA steps such as creating SAS data sets and SAS variables
- SAS functions
- Procedures (statements and options)

What Should You Know about the Examples?

This book includes tutorials for you to follow to gain hands-on experience with SAS.

Software Used to Develop the Book's Content

The book covers the use of SAS statistical programming (Base SAS, SAS 9.4, SAS/STAT 14.1, and SAS Enterprise Miner 14.1).

The large volume and granularity of data, combined with the complexity of the survival model calculations applied to the data to score customers' probabilities to repurchase, create substantial pressure on the delivery of output (in essence, a list of customers likely to repurchase in the next month). Marketing managers simply will not be able to wait 10 days, for example, to run a full recalculation based on scoring codes that change every month. As a result, marketing departments and banks need new, high-performance technology that can scale to meet business needs.

SAS Enterprise Miner can achieve optimal results with minimal human intervention to develop and implement survival data mining models. It provides an environment that supports efficient documentation, a strong sample process, flexibility to change time periods, model management, traceability, workflow, and audit trails. The modeler needs only to understand how to rerun calculations and analyses.

For this reason, it is important that the underlying end-to-end Survival Flowchart be traceable (for finance and audit purposes). The Survival Flowchart needs to be usable by marketing analysts so that they can perform this work themselves, rather than having to rely on data miners or consultants to implement a new monthly advertising campaign.

Example Code and Data

The depth and guidance of this book are sufficient to begin developing any business- or finance-related survival analysis model. The book is designed to be read linearly, from Chapter 1 through to Chapter 8, gradually demystifying the complexity of survival analysis. However, this book should be *applied* rather than just *read*. The same can be said about cookbooks, whose practical requirements educate you through trial and error. Consequently, to succeed, run the SAS code of each example. To understand the necessary modification at each step, open the respective SAS data set. Think about any mistakes, and try again.

The Garden data set and all variables are explained in detail in Chapter 1.

You can access the example code and data for this book by linking to its author page at https://support.sas.com/authors.

SAS University Edition

If you are using SAS University Edition to access data and run programs, then check the SAS University Edition page to ensure that the software contains the product or products that you need to run the code: www.sas.com/universityedition.

Output and Graphics

All the output and graphics in this book were created by SAS Enterprise Miner 14.1 or by the SAS 9.4 SGPLOT procedure. Some graphics were modified using Adobe Photoshop and Adobe Illustrator for pedagogical reasons. The respective Adobe Photoshop (PSD) and Adobe Illustrator (AI) files are available from the author by request. These graphics can be useful for model validation documentation, validation reports, or PowerPoint presentations.

We Want to Hear from You

SAS Press books are written *by* SAS users *for* SAS users. We welcome your participation in their development and your feedback on SAS Press books that you are using. Please visit https://support.sas.com/publishing to do the following:

- Sign up to review a book
- Recommend a topic
- Request authoring information
- Provide feedback on a book

Do you have questions about a SAS Press book that you are reading? Contact the author through saspress@sas.com or https://support.sas.com/author_feedback.

SAS has many resources to help you find answers and expand your knowledge. If you need additional help, see our list of resources: https://support.sas.com/publishing.

About The Author

Jorge Ribeiro currently works in the area of econometric model management and development in the retail credit risk industry. He has worked previously as a stress test methodology manager at Yorkshire Bank, head of modeling at Direct Line Group Insurance, Vice President of Barclays Bank in the internal validation unit, head of modeling at HML Mortgages (IFRS 9), and principal data mining and modeler consultant at JD Williams & Co. in the United Kingdom. As a former professor of mathematics, he has more than 20 years of academic experience in advanced econometric techniques, such as vector autoregressive and Bayesian analyses, as well as rational expectations and brand awareness with latent variables using factor analysis and constraint optimization for call center management. He has used SAS since 1986 and has attended more than 50 SAS training courses and has presented at conferences worldwide over the past 25 years. Jorge holds a master's degree in economics from the Fluminense Federal University in Rio de Janeiro. He completed postgraduate work in financial modeling using SAS, and he attended the doctoral program in financial econometrics at the Université de Nantes.

Learn more about this author by visiting his author page at http://support.sas.com/ribeiro_j. There you can download free book excerpts, access example code and data, read the latest reviews, get updates, and more.

Acknowledgments

This book is in large measure the achievement of two extraordinary men who changed my life and, sadly, did not live long enough to see the book's publication.

Robert Tartarin (1947–2001)

Robert Tartarin was my professor at the Université de Nantes in France. Beyond expertly guiding me throughout my master's program, he inspired my post-graduation commitment to the field of econometrics. When my doctoral grant was cut because of a last-minute change in government policy regarding the age of applicants, I asked him to help me make some decision about my future.

Jorge: The government has cut my doctoral grant. What do you suggest I do to find a SAS job?

Prof. Tartarin: You should go work in England.

Jorge: I cannot, because I do not speak English.

Prof. Tartarin: Do not worry. English banks will finance English courses for you. Econometricians able to deliver an econometric stress test in England by using SAS/ETS are in short supply, and a stress test is a fundamental tool for measuring the impact of a coming crisis on banks' and building societies' economic capital and losses.

Jorge: But how will I be able to tell when such a crisis is about to occur?

Prof. Tartarin: You are an econometrician: Examine the Kondratiev Cycle. When the British economy is expected to soon be at its peak, depart for England because the crisis will follow. Depart and you will never return.

Jon Benjamin Thomas (1976–2011)

In 2006, just two years before the global economic crisis, the phone rings. It is a manager from Provident Financial who is keen on interviewing me after seeing the curriculum vitae that I have posted to a European job search page in pursuit of Robert Tartarin's advice.

Jon: I would like to schedule you for an interview for a position as a SAS modeler.

Jorge: I do not speak English. I speak French, Portuguese, and Spanish.

Some minutes later he calls again, this time with a French translator on the line.

Jon: We are looking for a SAS modeler. How can someone with your SAS skills and CV be unemployed?

Jorge: It is because I do not speak English.

Jon: Here, the only prerequisite language that you need is SAS. Don't worry. If you come to work with us, the company will provide a professional English course and give you a translator until you learn to speak and write. Do you have family?

Jorge: Yes, I have family.

Jon: Bring your family. I will give you a new life in England. You will never return to where you are now.

Because of Jon, my family and I came to England. I started to study English. We became friends. Jon's sincerity and disposition to help was essential to the commencement of my career in finance and the change in my life.

As both Jon and Professor Tartarin predicted, it is eleven years later, and we never returned.

I also thank Patrick Ribeiro, John Peter Smith, and Daniel Carden for their hard work in reviewing the book and making edits. I thank the following Publications staff at SAS Institute: Jenny Jennings Foerst for developmental editing and project management; Monica McClain for production, Robert Harris for figure revisions and cover design; John West for editing of the cover; and Kathy Underwood and Amy Wolfe for final copyedit of the full manuscript. Thanks also goes to the following for their technical review of the content: Robert Lucas, Mike Patetta, and two anonymous reviewers at SAS Institute.

I especially thank my dear wife, Peggy Ribeiro, for all of her love and support while I dedicated myself to producing this book.

Chapter 1: Data Preparation for Survival Models

Introduction

Development of any survival analysis model requires that input data be prepared in a specific way. This chapter introduces a Garden data set that contains real data from an anonymous company selling products across six main departments. This is the input data on which you will build the time-to-next-purchase survival model. In addition, this chapter explains general items of relevance to survival analysis, such as the following:

- Variables required (Start, End, Censor, Last_day, and Time)
- Missing data
- Outliers or extreme values
- Non-normality
- Binning of categorical and continuous variables

If you have little experience in data mining or modeling, then for context and additional detail in data preparation, see Svolba (2006) and Refaat (2007).

The chapter highlights how SAS Enterprise Miner handles data preparation:

- Specific nodes designed for data preparation such as Filter and Interactive Binning are used.
- Advanced knowledge of Base SAS or the SAS Macro Language is less critical to implementing and validating models, making the process more transparent and accessible. Where this knowledge is required, SAS Enterprise Miner allows procedures and macros to be isolated in SAS code nodes.
- Whole end-to-end projects from source databases to final model output can be set up quickly with standardized folder names and processes, allowing for easy comparison of different data manipulation scenarios.

The Garden data set contains 676,635 customers who were observed over a four-year period. Their start time is when they make their first purchase. They are monitored until the end of the four-year period.

The aim of the model is to predict the time, in months, to the next purchase of a product. Analysis is centered on whether and when the second purchase (repurchase) occurs. To address this, the database must contain the relevant variables for the model.

In this chapter, the event called *Target* by the SAS Enterprise Miner node is repurchase or second purchase. To model the Target variable, SAS Enterprise Miner analyzes different input variables such as Age, Scorecard, Behavior, and channel (Internet, Telephone, and Catalog) to explain and predict the time elapsed until the customer makes a second purchase. Only variables available at the time of the first purchase are considered as input variables (predictors).

Figure 1.1 shows a step-by-step process to perform a systematic data preparation before model development.

Figure 1.1: Data Preparation Flowchart for Time-to-Next-Purchase Models

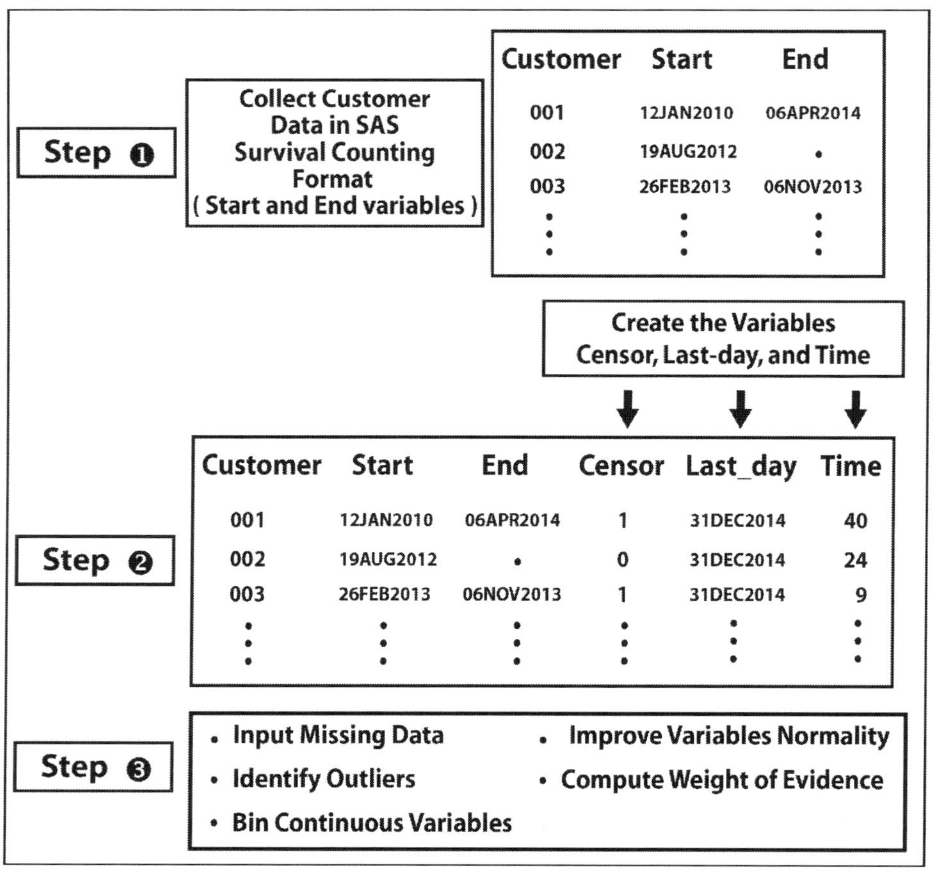

The information in the variables in steps 1 and 2 is universal to survival analysis. These variables are needed for the time to event and so that you can know whether an event occurs for an entity. These variables are also used in the input data for advanced models. After the discussion in this chapter, they are not discussed again. In contrast, the input variables are model-specific and selected based on the analysis required and stakeholder proposals—in this case, the variables to predict time-to-next-purchase. There are considerations in step 3 (such as missing data, outliers, and binning) that must be addressed when using these predictor variables to produce the right survival analysis model. SAS Enterprise Miner has a number of nodes for handling predictor variables.

Step 1: Collect Three Raw Variables

Collect three raw variables:

- *Customer* is a numeric variable with a unique ID number for each customer.
- *Start* is a numeric variable that represents the SAS date when an event occurred in the study period. In this case, the event is a customer's first purchase in the study period 2010 to 2014. The variable is always populated (nonmissing) because customers making no purchases in the study period are out of the scope of the model.
- *End* is a numeric variable that represents the SAS date when a second event occurred in the study period. Its value can be greater than the value of Start or missing if no second event occurs. In this case, the event is a customer making a second purchase (repurchase) in the study period 2010 to 2014.

The information contained in these variables can be displayed in a standard (cross-sectional) data format or in an expanded data format. The Standard format shown in Figure 1.1 consists of one row per entity (in this case, one row per customer). The expanded format has one row per entity per time period. Both formats are covered in more detail in Chapter 2.

Step 2: Create Three Required Variables

Create three required variables:

- *Censor* is a numeric variable equal either to 0 or 1. The value is 1 if the End variable is populated and 0 if it is missing.
- *Last_day* is a numeric variable that represents the SAS date of the end of the study period. In this case, it is 31DEC2014 throughout the database.
- *Time* is a numeric variable that contains the number of interval time periods between Start and End if End is populated, or between Start and Last_day if it is not.

Step 3: Collect and Process Many Predictor Variables

Collect many raw variables containing customer information to predict time to event as denoted by the Time variable. Process these variables by imputing missing values, identifying outliers, and binning, as appropriate.

Data Set Structure

The Garden data set is used throughout Chapter 1 to demonstrate survival analysis data preparation. It consists of data from an anonymous company, which sells across six main departments:

- Garden Tools
- Electrical Tools and Supplies
- Security and Safety
- Computer Accessories
- Car Accessories
- Art and Decoration

Characteristics of the Data Set Used in This Book

The Garden data set consists of customer-level transaction data. Each of the 676,635 rows represents a customer who made their purchase between 1 January 2011 and 31 December 2014.

Some of these customers are new to the business. Others have made purchases prior to 1 January 2011. In the rest of the book, *first purchase* refers to the first purchase made by the customer during the study period 1 January 2011 to 31 December 2014. *Second purchase* refers to the subsequent purchase.

The Garden data set has one record per customer, with 29 columns containing internal data collected through the company's data warehouse. The variables include details of transactions and purchased products.

Special Considerations for Survival Analysis Data Input

You first need to understand how the structure required for data input into a survival analysis model differs from that of other techniques such as linear, logistic regression, or time series. Blossfeld et al. (1989) comment that, because of the difficulty of data preparation and the complexity of dealing with censoring data, most inexperienced modelers avoid survival analysis. The complexities are related to the representativeness, quantity, and quality of the input variables.

It is important to consider what input variables are appropriate and necessary for the creation of a time-to-next-purchase survival analysis model. There are many possible variables that could be of interest. The most important fields for this particular model are as follows:

- Details about the customer at and previous to the first purchase
- Buyers' channels
- Internal family and income information about the customer.
- Products

With regard to buyers' channels, because segmenting the buyers is typically complex, this has been determined before starting the modeling process. You need to have as much information as you can to deliver a model with a high predictive ability, focused exclusively on a company's current customer database, supposing that new customers have the same profile as current customers.

Plan for the Collection of the Required Variables

You should develop a detailed plan of how to collect the required variables. Remember that, no matter how thoroughly defined and logical your database, the results of survival analysis are not credible unless your variables perform well with the validation data set.

The collection of data and its availability for modeling purposes should be agreed on before the model-building process begins. It is good practice for a consensus to be reached among all stakeholders so that everyone can commit to the methodology from the beginning of the project. Creating and implementing models is somewhat of a political issue within some companies.

Five Fundamental Questions for Time-to-Next-Purchase Survival Models

The model presented in this book was created to answer the five fundamental questions normally addressed by time-to-next-purchase survival models. In Figure 1.2, these questions are indicated next to the Variable column. In the following paragraphs, each question is reviewed in more detail.

Figure 1.2: Variables and the Questions That They Answer

		Variable	Type	Label
	1	Id_number	Numeric	Customer Unique ID Number
	2	Start	Numeric	Day of the First Purchase
	3	End	Numeric	Day of the Second Purchase or Missing if Censored
When? ❶	4	Censor	Numeric	Second Purchase(Censor =1) -- Censored (Censor = 0)
	5	Last_day	Numeric	Last Day of Sample Selection 31/12/2014
	6	Time	Numeric	Time Elapsed after First Purchase
	7	Garden	Numeric	Garden Tools
	8	Decorating	Numeric	Art, Craft and Decorating
	9	Car	Numeric	Car Accessories
	10	Electrical	Numeric	Electrical Tools
	11	Safety	Numeric	Security and Safety Products
	12	Computer	Numeric	Computer and Accessories
How much? ❷	13	**Prev**_Garden	Numeric	Previous Spent in Garden Tools
	14	**Prev**_Decorating	Numeric	Previous Spent in Art, Craft and Decorating
	15	**Prev**_Car	Numeric	Previous Spent in Car Accessories
	16	**Prev**_Electrical	Numeric	Previous Spent in Electrical Tools
	17	**Prev**_Safety	Numeric	Previous Spent in Security and Safety Products
	18	**Prev**_Computer	Numeric	Previous Spent in Computer and Accessories
	19	Amount_CLV	Numeric	Total amount spent in Customer Lifetime Value
How many? ❸ →	20	Strata	**Character**	Strata Total Orders
How? ❹	21	Account_Origin	**Character**	Account Origin
	22	Order	**Character**	Origin Purchase Order
	23	Age	**Character**	Binned Age
	24	Credit_score	**Character**	Binned Credit Scorecard
	25	Behavior	**Character**	Binned Behavior
Who? ❺	26	Mosaic	**Character**	Mosaic Bureau Data
	27	Credicard	**Character**	Credicard Brand - Method of Payment
	28	Family	Numeric	Family Bureau Data
	29	Income	Numeric	Income Bureau Data

> **Key Tip**: Include a label preceded by a number for any model created by SAS Enterprise Miner. The labels will be important later in the modeling process.

Question 1: When Were the Purchases Made?

The When? ❶ variables address the question of when a customer (or group of customers) buys a specific product. The dates are required for survival analysis models created in SAS/STAT or SAS Enterprise Miner. The variables record the time of each purchase for each customer in the data set. The preparation of these variables for modeling purposes is discussed in detail in the section "Data Set Creation."

Question 2: How Much of What Was Purchased?

The primary goal of survival analysis is to model the Hazard function, assessing the relationship between the hazard and a set of variables (predictors) to determine whether they are statistically significant, controlling for other variables. The How much? ❷ variables numbered 7 to 12 represent the cost of the first purchase. The How much? ❷ variables numbered 13 to 18 represent the costs of previous purchases. They have the prefix (Prev_) added to their original names.

You want to measure the impact of these characteristics on the time to the second purchase and to predict which customers are most likely to make a second purchase. In addition, you want to establish when the purchase is likely to occur.

The input variables 7 to 19 represent the amount of money spent on each product by each customer. A customer can buy multiple products from each department at one time. These variables represent the monetary relationship between the customer and the company. By including this information, you can quantify the relationship between past and current purchases in terms of profit per customer and customer lifetime value (CLV).

Question 3: How Many Purchases?

For the How many? ❸ variable, the categorical variable Strata segments customers according to the total number of purchases they made since their first purchase, which for some customers was 20 years ago. It is one of the most important input variables for time-to-next-purchase models and is discussed in greater depth in the section "Strata by Previous Purchases."

Question 4: How Were the Purchases Made?

The How? ❹ variables record the channel through which the customer made their purchase.

Account_Origin

The variable Account_Origin tells you how the customers made their first purchase. It has the following categories:

- **Branch**. Customers who made their first purchase through a branch. A plausible hypothesis is that these customers are likely to purchase larger items from the Garden Tools department.
- **Internet**. Customers who made their first purchase on the company's website. Another hypothesis is that customers who use this channel are younger than those using other channels.
- **Post**. Customers who made their first purchase through mail-order by using a product reference number from the company's catalog and sending the order by post.
- **Telephone**. Customers who made their first purchase by telephone. A plausible hypothesis is that these customers tend to be older with no access to the Internet or who do not trust online shopping.

Output 1.1 shows that 46.64% of customers over the past made their first purchase using the Internet. The Account_Origin variable could be useful if management wants to review channel strategy (for example, to assess how important branches are as a way of servicing customers). For example, management might be considering closing the least profitable stores (branches) and dispatching the products via other channels instead.

Output 1.1: Descriptive Statistics: Account_Origin

Account_Origin	Frequency	Percent	Cumulative Frequency	Cumulative Percent
Branch	100830	14.90	100830	14.90
Internet	315575	46.64	416405	61.54
Post	108914	16.10	525319	77.64
Telephone	151316	22.36	676635	100.00

Order

Another important variable for marketing purposes is Order, which represents how a customer made his or her first purchase. Suppose that the marketing department is interested only in customers purchasing through one of the following three channels:

- Internet
- Post
- Telephone

This might be because the business is considering moving away from selling through the branch network and would like to assess the impact of this decision on total sales by creating a forecast without this channel of business.

Output 1.2 shows that 43.49% of customers made their first purchase through the Internet. Both Order and Account_Origin could be used as a stratus, to categorize these customers.

Output 1.2: Descriptive Statistics: Order

Order	Frequency	Percent	Cumulative Frequency	Cumulative Percent
Internet	294259	43.49	294259	43.49
Post	126287	18.66	420546	62.15
Telephone	256089	37.85	676635	100.00

Question 5: Who Are the Purchasers?

The Who? ❺ variables numbered 23 to 29 were selected by the marketing department to describe a customer's profile. The real problem is that there is no easy way to describe a perfect customer, and all available information (AAI) is limited to what is captured in a company's database. Sometimes, customer-context variables that have an emphasis on income, gender, internal scorecard, behavior score, and type of credit card are enough to provide a reasonable prediction of time-to-next-purchase.

Data Set Creation

In this section, the process of data set creation and preparation is discussed in depth. This topic is of paramount importance because data preparation for a typical survival analysis project represents up to 80% of the project timeline. A minor mistake in univariate analysis or absence of a critical part of univariate analysis can substantially reduce the predictive ability of the model.

For the moment, concentrate on only the first five variables:

- **Id_number**. A unique numeric variable that allows the identification of the 676,635 customers. It is a mandatory variable in the modeling, sampling, and validation process.
- **Start**. The variable Start is, by definition, when the analysis time is 0—that is, the time at which the customer completes his or her first purchase.
- **End**. The variable End indicates the time of the second purchase. This variable is missing if the customer does not make a second purchase, so it is intrinsically linked to the Censor variable.
- **Censor**. This is a binary target that indicates whether the customer made a second purchase in the time period after the first purchase was made.
  - Censor = 1 if the outcome is New Purchase in the period of study.
  - Censor = 0 if the outcome is No Purchase in the period of study.

In terms of modeling, the most difficult requirement is often precisely defining the Censor variable. In this model, it is a transition stage when the customer makes the second purchase.

(Start, End) Calendar Timeline

Output 1.3 presents two required variables in survival analysis data—Start and End. These variables are in the calendar timeline format SAS DATE9. The variable Start marks the beginning of the contractual relationship between the supplier and the customer. This is also known as the starting point of the modeling process—the "beginning of the time" or the moment when the customer made the first purchase.

Output 1.3: Variables Start and End

Start	End
01JAN2011	04JAN2011
02JAN2011	05JAN2011
03JAN2011	17FEB2011
04JAN2011	06JAN2011
05JAN2011	18FEB2011
01JAN2011	08JAN2011
15JAN2011	25JAN2011
11JAN2011	19JAN2011
14JAN2011	16JAN2011
01JAN2011	27JAN2011

Modelers often encounter problems when defining the beginning of data collection. This can be attributed to a range of business-related issues such as merges between databases (when the company loses some customers), the implementation of new systems, or the acquisition of other businesses. The best solution for these types of problems is to design a timeline that coincides with how far back the oldest employees can give you accurate information about the historic problems faced by the company.

If there is an issue with the data prior to a certain month or period, modelers can choose an arbitrary Start time. This approach was adopted with the Garden data set. Following the completion of univariate analysis, it was decided that only customers purchasing after 1 January 2011 would be included in the final data set. Hence, the starting point of the study period is fixed to 01/JAN/2011, and the latest observation of the data set is fixed to 31/DEC/2014. SAS Enterprise Miner scans the database and creates a variable representing the censoring date based on the maximum date for the End variable and the interval time that you select (quarter, month, or day).

In Figure 1.3, the modeling period spans four years, which, in total, gives 48 observation points. This enables you to verify that the final model performs well throughout the course of the year, taking into account trends and seasonality such as purchases made for Christmas and Mother's Day.

Figure 1.3: Calendar Time for Variables Start and End

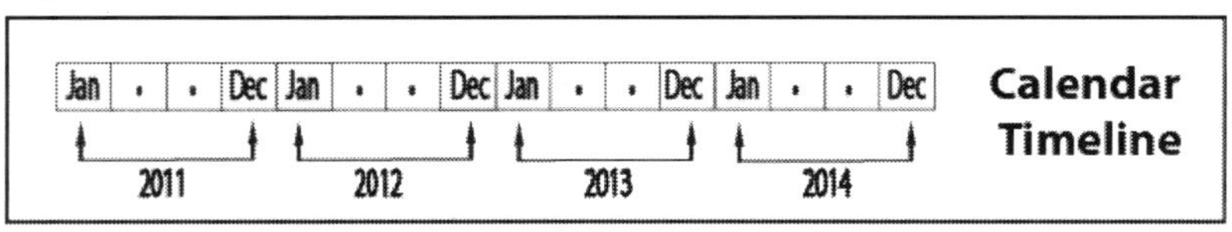

The variables Start and End are prerequisites for SAS Enterprise Miner and serve as a basis for the creation of the model's validation and performance graph in Figure 1.4.

Figure 1.4: Validation and Performance of Survival Analysis Model

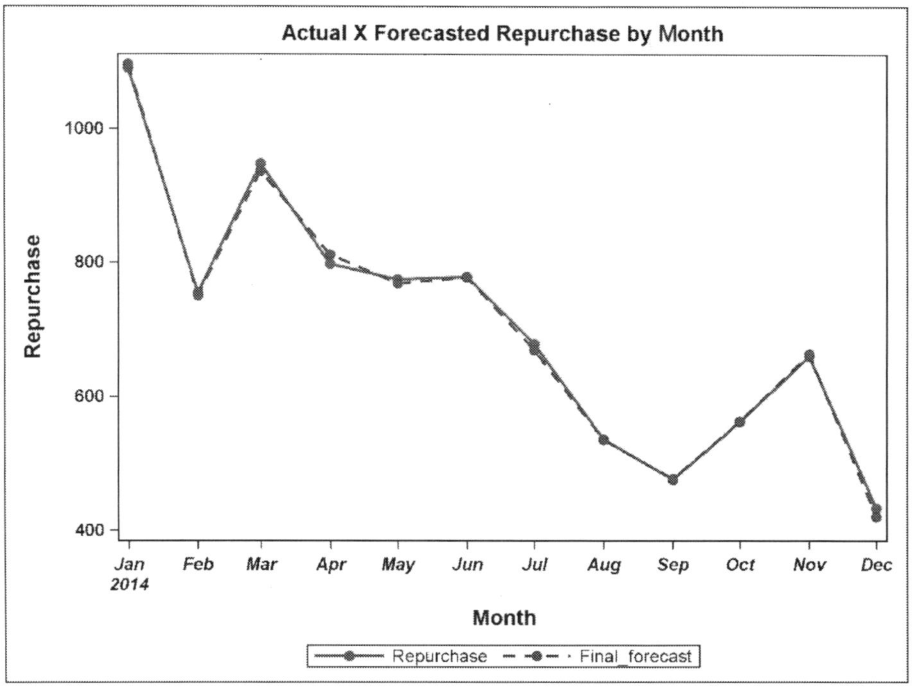

Time and Censor Variables

Time is the most important variable because it is the outcome variable of interest. Time is the number of months from the first purchase to the event (event being second purchase) or until the end of the period if the customer does not purchase again. Program 1.1 demonstrates how this variable is derived.

Program 1.1: Computing the Time Variable

```
Data Time;
Set  Garden (keep = Id_number Start End Censor);
Last_day = input ("31DEC2014" ❶, anydtdte10.);
Time  ❸   = Intck ❷ ("MONTH", Start, Min(End, Last_day));
Format Last_day Date9.;
run;
```

Before you create a predictive model using SAS Enterprise Miner, PROC LIFEREG, PROC PHREG, or any other procedure, you should first create the Time variable that represents the elapsed time between Start and the censoring date (Last_day)—that is, the last day of data collection ❶.

Although the data is collected daily, the Intck function ❷ creates the Time variable ❸ by using a monthly interval. Therefore, the final model is created by month. The parameters of the Intck function can be summarized as follows: Intck ("INTERVAL", Start date, End date).

The Intck function returns the number of intervals (in months) between two dates, counting the number of months from the first value (Start) to the second (End).

One important feature of the Time variable is illustrated in Figure 1.5. Customers can start at any point during the data collection (study) period. Therefore, the Time variable needs to reflect the period when each customer is considered in the model.

Figure 1.5: Time Values for Different Customers

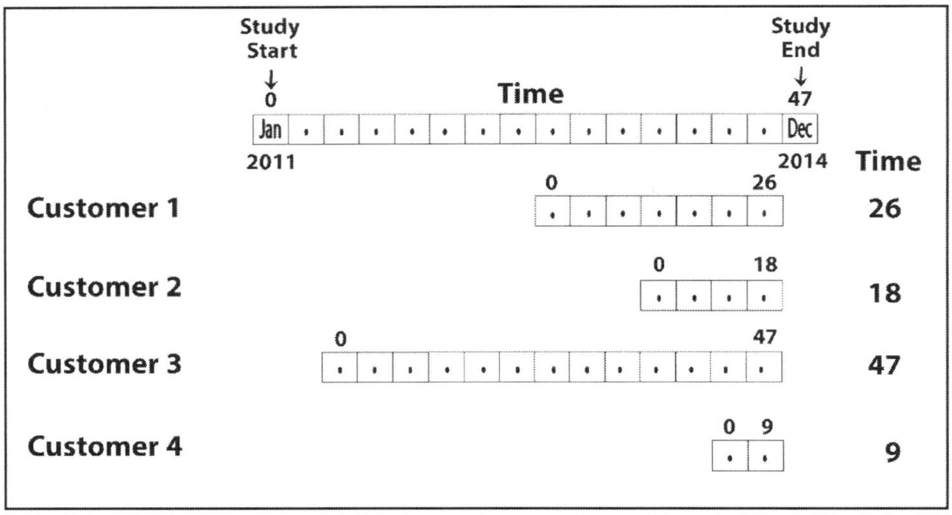

In Program 1.1, the function Min ensures that the results are correct for customers that are censored, which occurs when the End variable is missing (End = .). The function determines the smallest nonmissing value between the variables End and Last_day. Last_day represents the last day of data collection, also known as the censoring date. The Last_day variable is used as a boundary in the modeling process, and SAS Enterprise Miner calculates it automatically for any survival model created.

Output 1.4 shows some selected customers from the data set named Time created by Program 1.1 to explain how they are processed in data preparation for modeling. The data was sorted by the variable Time starting in 01JAN2011.

Output 1.4: Selected Customers' Time to Purchase

Id_number	Start	End	❼ Censor	Last_day	Time
40	01JAN2011	.	0	31DEC2014	❸ 47
41	01JAN2011	.	0	31DEC2014	47
42	01JAN2011	.	0	31DEC2014	47
43	01JAN2011	04JAN2011	1	31DEC2014	❹ 0
44	01JAN2011	04JAN2011	1	31DEC2014	0
45	01JAN2011	05JAN2011	1	31DEC2014	0
46	01JAN2011	05JAN2011	1	31DEC2014	0
47	01JAN2011	06JAN2011	1	31DEC2014	0
48	01JAN2011	07JAN2011	1	31DEC2014	0
49	01JAN2011	08JAN2011	1	31DEC2014	0
50	01JAN2011	10JAN2011	1	31DEC2014	0
51	01JAN2011	12JAN2011	1	31DEC2014	0
52	01JAN2011	16JAN2011	1	31DEC2014	0
53	01JAN2011	27JAN2011	1	31DEC2014	0
54	01JAN2011	27JAN2011	1	31DEC2014	0
55	01JAN2011	16FEB2011	1	31DEC2014	❺ 1
56	01JAN2011	17FEB2011	1	31DEC2014	1
57	01JAN2011	20FEB2011	1	31DEC2014	1

Id_number	Start	End	❼ Censor	Last_day	Time
58	01JAN2011	03APR2011	1	31DEC2014	❻ 3
59	01JAN2011	11APR2011	1	31DEC2014	3
60	01JAN2011	11APR2011	1	31DEC2014	3

Customers 40 to 42

Time has a computed value of 47, which was created by the Intck function ❸. You see that customers 40, 41, and 42 made their first purchase on 01JAN2011 as indicated by the Start variable. Because the End variable is set to missing (End = .), you conclude that by the last day of the study period, these customers did not make a second purchase. These customers are still present in the data set at the end of the period of data collection, but they have not made a second purchase. So, these customers are referred to as censored, and the variable Censor is set to 0 ❼.

You do not know how long it will take these customers to make a second purchase. This is an important feature of this data set.

Customers 43 to 54

These customers are significantly different when they are compared to the first group of customers. Here, Time is the difference between Start and End, and its calculated value is 0 ❹ because the customers made another purchase before the end of January 2011, the month in which they made their first purchase. These customers are not censored, and the variable Censor is set to 1. This value represents death in terms of survival analysis. Customers who make a second purchase do not come back and they are treated as new. The irreversibility of the event of death is an essential feature of survival analysis.

Customers 55 to 57

These customers made a second purchase in February 2011. The Time variable is calculated as 1 ❺.

Customers 58 to 60

These customers made a second purchase in April 2011. Therefore, the Time variable is calculated as 3 ❻. Of the customers whose first purchase occurred in January, no one made a purchase in March 2011. Therefore, Time is not equal to 2 within this subset of customers.

Censor and Time Variables for Selected Customers

To clarify the relationship between the Time and Censor variables, Figure 1.6 illustrates four customers. The graphic displays the experience of each customer even though you do not know when they made their first purchase.

Figure 1.6: Censor and Time for Four Customers

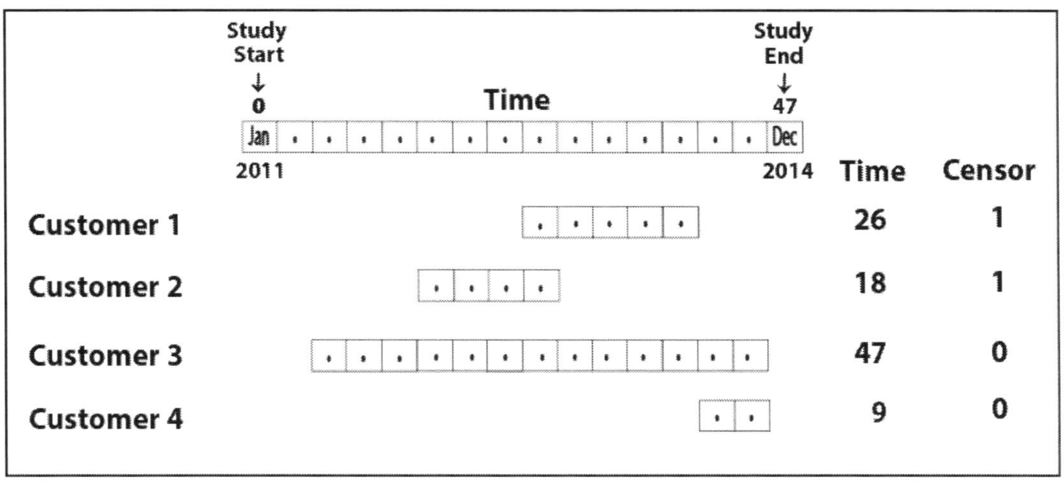

Customers 1 and 2, for example, both made a first purchase at different starting points. They are uncensored (Censor = 1) because they made a second purchase after 26 and 18 months, respectively.

Customer 3 made a first purchase in January 2011 (Time = 47). Customer 4 made a first purchase in March 2014 (Time = 9). They are censored (Censor = 0) because they did not make a second purchase after 47 and 9 months, respectively, until the end of the study in 12/31/2014.

The Time variable should be created using Program 1.1 at an early stage of the analysis. This program was created to match the SAS Enterprise Miner requirement. The Time variable is the basis of the construction of the Hazard function, which is discussed in detail in the next section.

Strata by Previous Purchases

The Strata variable segments customers into categories based on specific criteria. For the Garden data set, the Strata variable is based on the number of historic purchases made by the customer. When a new customer makes their first purchase, they are assigned to the customer strata as “01”, “02”, “03”, and so on, depending on the number of purchases that they have made previously. Care must be taken when tracking each purchase made by the customer because each new purchase makes the initial state (first purchase) change to a second state (second purchase). Each period between purchases starts when the last purchase happens. In summary, each purchase is a new time (0). Every time that a customer repurchases, they start as a new customer.

Key Tip: Create a categorical variable based on the total number of previous purchases.

To stratify a continuous variable, you need to define the bins based on business experience. This can be challenging because stakeholders from different areas of the business might interpret the data differently. They might have conflicting opinions of how to bin the data. Business experience is a key factor to transform the distribution into a reduced number of bins.

Never create more than six bins. This ensures that there are robust volumes within each bin, as problems of convergence are likely to occur with inadequate volumes in each bin. If you do encounter this problem, PROC PHREG has the Firth’s method to fix it by adding a penalty term to the partial-log-likelihood. See PROC PHREG documentation in the *SAS/STAT User’s Guide* for more details.

A key finding from numerous research papers is that in some segments, customers with fewer purchases can be much more expensive to target when implementing marketing campaigns because they have a higher churn rate. Therefore, a key aspect to consider in the binning process is avoiding these segments of customers and placing emphasis on those customers who are more likely to increase the customer base.

Program 1.2 creates the Strata variable with six bins using a DATA step that can be customized for other models.

Program 1.2: Binning Transformation

```
data   strata;
set    total_orders;
if total_orders in (1,2) and start <"01JAN2014"d then
strata = "01-02-(2011-2013)";❶
else if total_orders in (1,2) and start >= "01JAN2014"d then
strata = "01-02-(2014)"; ❷
else if 3  <= total_orders <=  5 then strata = "03-05";
else if 5  <  total_orders <= 10 then strata = "06-10";
else if 10 <  total_orders <= 20 then strata = "11-20";
else if       total_orders >  20 then strata = "21-High";
run;
```

The first strata, "01-02-(2011-2013)", contains customers that made their first purchase between 01JAN2011 and 31DEC2013, the first three years of the study period ❶. They made a maximum of two purchases (they either had 0, 1, or 2 purchases prior to 1 January 2011). You hypothesize that customers who have not made an additional purchase after this time (more than three years) are the least likely to make any further purchases. You expect the model to allocate to customers in this segment (strata) the smallest probability of a second purchase.

In the second strata, "01-02-(2014)", customers have characteristics similar to those in the first strata ❷. That is, they have less than two total purchases, but they made their first purchase in the last year of the study period, between 01JAN2014 and 31DEC2014. They are potential target customers for a marketing campaign because they are new to the database.

The other four strata represent the total number of purchases made without taking into account a time limit. Thus, the customer's full lifetime is considered.

One popular approach is to create a bin based on the start of each year. But, for time-to-next-purchase models, old customers are less likely to buy again. By creating a specific bin, you can compare old customers (using Survival and Hazard functions) with customers from recent years.

Another approach is one often used in econometrics, when some years perform better than others with respect to the economy. A hypothesis linked to the economy is that a marketing campaign performs better in a specific year. Then, to create a stratus for a specific year, the impact of the campaign on sales would be tracked. However, this approach is limited by the modeler's creativity, business knowledge, and understanding of their database.

Stratification can be created or considered from variables whose value is fixed at time equal to 0, such as gender or region.

Categorical Variables

The variables numbered 23 to 29 in Figure 1.2 attempt to describe a customer's behavior. These variables help identify characteristics that are indicative of good customers. To identify good customers effectively, customers should be ranked by the number of purchases or by using a scorecard. In Output 1.5, consider the internal credit score at the time of application, segmenting the customers into 200-point bins with the best customers in the final bin 800-1000 as follows:

Output 1.5: Credit Score from Bureau Data Binned

Credit_score	Frequency	Cumulative Frequency
0 - 400	157793	157793
400 - 600	73994	231787
600 - 800	118060	349847
800 - 1000	200765	550612
Missing	126023	676635

An interesting approach is to bin the variables Age, Credit_score, and Behavior. This is a typical framework derived from summarizing empirical results from other published models using categorical and binned variables.

Over the past 10 years, there has been an expansion in customer research, specifically marked by some trends such as credit card behavior, postal code for geo-localization, and text mining. Tracking these trends enables you to collect more data about a customer's experience. The collection of this additional data enables you to create internal variables, which could be considered as input variables to predict a customer's behavior.

Although income has previously been considered as a principal variable for predicting customer behavior, recent internal research for web analysis investigates the effect of discount prices on customer behavior. Early results show that this is a more powerful characteristic when considering a customer's behavior.

Binning variables is important for a variety of reasons, but its primary purpose is to provide a framework (structure) for the Hazard function. Once you have established a clear definition of the binning process, you can assess the impact of the binned variable on the model by checking the sensitivity of the model with and without the binned variable.

In Output 1.6, data is binned by the Age variable.

Output 1.6: Age Variable Binned

Age	Frequency	Cumulative Frequency
18 - 31	58902	58902
32 - 43	72487	131389
44 - 56	125824	257213
57 - 68	164404	421617
69 - 81	155015	576632
82 - high	46324	622956
Missing	53679	676635

The goals and output of the model depend on your company's needs. You could have any of the following variables:

- Geographic
- Products
- Gender
- Seasonality
- Price

Without a deep understanding of how the customers are segmented, you will have more difficulty interpreting the coefficients and hazard results.

In summary, segmenting continuous variables and regrouping discrete ones into smaller categories are the key aspects of data preparation in survival analysis.

Data Preparation with Base SAS, Macros, and SAS/STAT

This section presents the different approaches using Base SAS, SAS macros, and SAS/STAT for data preparation. Techniques and strategies are presented.

Multiple Imputation

Multiple imputation for missing data is such a complex technique that SAS published the book *Multiple Imputation of Missing Data Using SAS* by Patricia Berglund and Steven Heeringa. How should missing data values be treated? There is no easy answer. Choosing the "best" missing value replacement technique inherently requires the modeler to make assumptions about the true (missing) data. It is beyond the scope of this book to extend the discussion about these methods.

For further details, read about the MI procedure and the MIANALYZE procedure in the *SAS/STAT User's Guide*. There, you will find a detailed explanation of missing methods. The documentation shows how the MI procedure can create multiple imputed data sets for incomplete multivariate data and how the MIANALYZE procedure can generate valid statistical inferences about parameters by combining results from the imputations.

Winsorization

Winsorization is a technique named after the engineer-biostatistician Charles P. Winsor. This process is sometimes called *trimming* or *truncation.* Winsorization is a method of censoring. It involves replacing the original data by an arbitrary percentile that you believe is an acceptable value. For example, a 95% Winsorization would replace all data above the 95th percentile by the value of the 95th percentile. This process is standard in modeling in financial services and insurance companies. It can be implemented using PROC UNIVARIATE or macros (Löeffler and Poach 2011). Figure 1.7 provides an example of Winsorization.

Figure 1.7: Winsorization

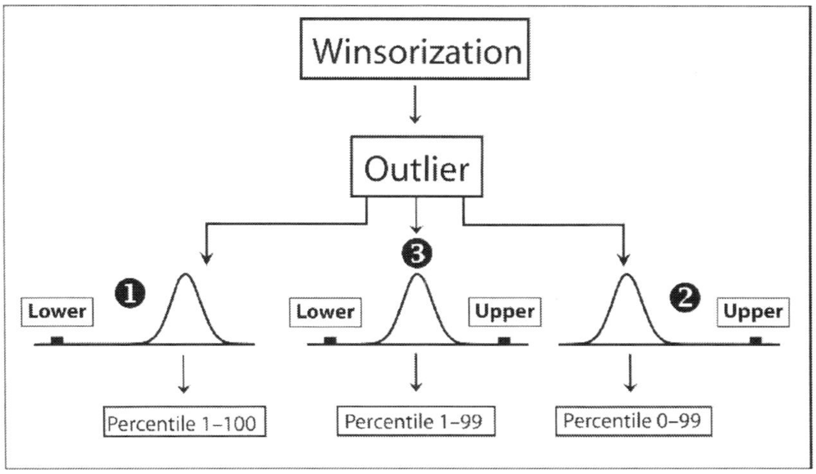

The maximum percentile distribution ranges from 0 to 100 and covers the full distribution of a variable. Winsorization can be used to customize the range of the distribution so that the range of the variable falls between a limited range of percentiles.

In Figure 1.7, you see that the outlier is located in the extreme negative area, called the lower area of the distribution ❶. A 1% Winsorization replaces all data below the 1st percentile by the value of the 1st percentile.

An outlier is also located in the extreme positive area, called the upper area of the distribution ❷. A 99% Winsorization replaces all data above the 99th percentile by the value of the 99th percentile. This technique with the upper and lower outliers is called one-sided Winsorization.

In the first distribution graph in Figure 1.7, you see the percentile values 1 to 100. In other words, you are replacing the outlier from the lower area by the 1st percentile, but you are not replacing the right side. The 100th percentile stays the same value because it is not an outlier. The same reasoning is valid in the third distribution graph, where you see percentile values 0 to 99. You replace the values above the 99th percentile, but the left side stays unchanged. It is represented by 0, the minimum value of the variable.

In the second distribution graph, you apply simultaneously both the 1st percentile and the 99th percentile because the variable has Lower and Upper outliers. This technique is called two-sided Winsorization.

One reason that Winsorization is popular within the financial industry is because when you exclude an observation, you also exclude all the information present in the other variables of that observation, whether they have outliers or not. The main advantage of Winsorization compared to the outright exclusion of an observation is that this information remains available during the modeling process.

Binning Using Macros

Binning continuous variables needs someone who has an expert level of Base SAS programming and who has used the SAS Macro Language. Mamdouh Refaat (2007) implemented these techniques very well using advanced macros:

Equal Width
: creates bounds by dividing the variable into an equal number of ranges of equal width.

Equal Height
: creates upper and lower limits for each bin.

Optimal Binning
: attempts to minimize the frequencies of the observations in the new bins.

Data Preparation with SAS Enterprise Miner

The preparation process with SAS Enterprise Miner can modify the data by creating new variables. Variables can be selected and transformed to improve the model-selection process by techniques such as the stepwise selection. The Modify step, which is one of the SEMMA steps, includes the use of advanced tools and awards algorithms for defining transformations, missing-value handling, values recoding, and interactive binning:

- **S**—Sample
- **E**— Explore
- **M**—Modify
- **M**—Model
- **A**—Assess

Furthermore, advanced visualization tools enable you to quickly and easily examine large amounts of data in multidimensional histograms and to graphically compare different models and transformations. After you have completed the Modify step, you can apply the scoring modeling formula to a new data set without any Base SAS manipulation or macros. You can then select the champion model with the best binning transformation.

The time to select the final model can be reduced from three weeks for a standard survival analysis project to one or two days.

Figure 1.8 shows an example of data preparation using a SAS Enterprise Miner process flow, which will be presented in detail in Chapter 4. Table 1.1 provides details.

Figure 1.8: Data Preparation Process Flow

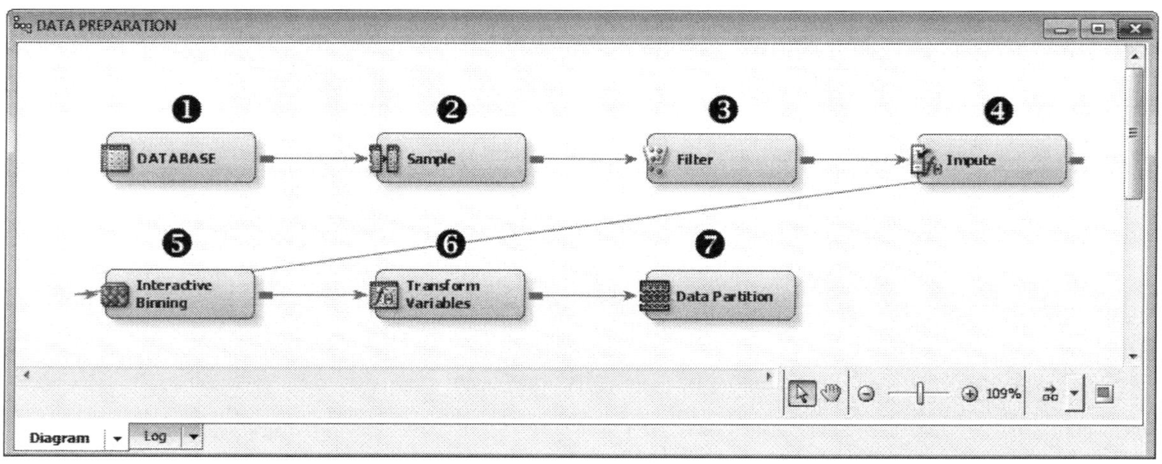

Table 1.1: SAS Enterprise Miner Nodes for Data Preparation

Data Preparation	Node	Description
Input data		The input data node specifies the data set (Garden) used in this project. It is the first node in the process flow diagram.
Sample		The Sample node enables you to extract a sample from the input data source (Garden). The node and the sampling technique are covered in detail in Chapter 4.
Exclude outliers		The Filter node excludes outliers and enables the user to choose cutoffs and different methods.
Replace missing data		The Impute node enables you to replace missing values in the data set before you start the modeling process. The node has more than 12 different imputation techniques to replace missing values.
Bin continuous variables	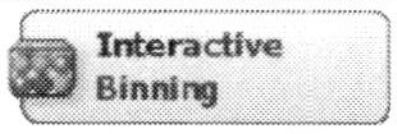	One of the more important tools in data preparation in SAS Enterprise Miner is the Interactive Binning node, which can create bins, buckets, or classes of all input variables. These include both class and interval input variables. You can create bins to reduce the number of unique levels as well as to attempt to improve the predictive power of each input variable. In the Interactive Binning node, the predictive power of a variable (its ability to separate high-risk survival customers from low-risk ones) is assessed by its Gini Concentration Ratio by grouping the selected characteristics based on business considerations. The node is helpful in shaping the data to reduce overfitting. In most cases, binning attributes leads to stronger predictive power and improvement in the survival model without any Base SAS preparation. The code generated by the Interactive Binning node can be saved, exported, and implemented using Base SAS.
Transform variables	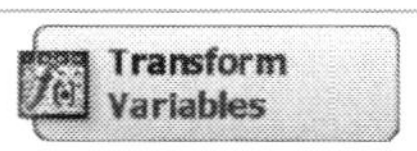	The Transform Variables node transforms variables to improve normality and the fit of the model as presented below: 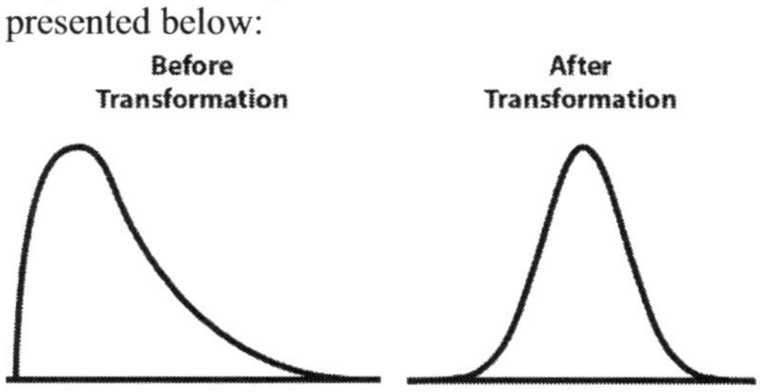
Partition data		A Data Partition node can statistically split a data set into three data sets: one for training, one for validation, and one for scoring. The one for scoring is not used in building the model, but is used as a holdout sample. These data sets are carried along through the process flow and used during the model assessment.

A detailed explanation of each node can be found in SAS Enterprise Miner documentation.

Chapter 2: Exploratory Data Analysis and Basic Statistical Concepts

Introduction

In Chapter 1, you created the required variables to develop a survival analysis model. This chapter explains the relevant terminology and concepts in survival analysis, such as the Survival and Hazard functions and death rate applied to a business context. This knowledge is necessary to understand the key considerations when building a survival analysis model and when interpreting statistical output from SAS Enterprise Miner or SAS/STAT.

Two core components of survival analysis are the Survival and Hazard functions. Their derivation is covered in detail for the varying time formats on which they are dependent. It is worth knowing different ways that data can be formatted and stored because the chosen ways can affect the Survival and Hazard functions. Here are some examples:

- different formats of time: continuous and discrete
- alternate ways the data is stored: Customer-Level data set or Month data set

This chapter uses procedures available in Base SAS. Each step of a calculation is presented and followed by an in-depth interpretation of the results. Where possible, results are related to a business context. Having an understanding of the derivation of the functions enables you to more easily interpret the results.

In survival analysis, tables, graphics, and functions are used to describe raw data—that is, the full database or the sample data used to create the model. The basis of univariate analysis and descriptive statistics of survival analysis are nonparametric counting methods to find the number of customers buying each month. These methods are used to compare different approaches for continuous and discrete time using empirical data.

To illustrate the differences between continuous and discrete time, descriptive analysis is the simplest way because the Survival and Hazard functions are estimated when there are no covariates. A graphical analysis of customer behavior is particularly interesting. Although simple, graphical analysis helps you understand more complex modeling techniques in later chapters.

You cannot build and implement a time-to-next-purchase survival model without first establishing a clear assumption about the continuous or discrete nature of the Hazard function. This understanding serves as the foundation of the research. To be effective, a time-to-next-purchase survival model must be driven by a clearly defined set of objectives and output. To explain survival analysis, the examples in this chapter demonstrate that the most important output in time-to-next-purchase models is the probability of the customer repurchasing in a specific month.

Overview of Continuous and Discrete Distributions

In this section, there are two key objectives:

- Two different versions of the Survival and Hazard functions (continuous and discrete) are presented using the four variables created in Chapter 1 that are required to analyze the distributions: Start, End, Censor, and Time.
- A realistic interpretation (real-life example) of these functions is given, extracting the most relevant information to identify customers who are more likely to make the second purchase and, more importantly, when they will make it.

At the beginning of a survival analysis design project, a modeler needs to decide how to collect or calculate the Time variable. This needs to be decided at the beginning because the statistical methods that are applied to continuous time are not appropriate for discrete time. Therefore, before starting the project, decide which unit of time to use.

The flowchart in Figure 2.1 summarizes the differences between calculating continuous versus discrete Hazard functions. The continuous and discrete formulas are presented later, as is the discrete approach using PROC LIFETEST with actuarial estimates. The purpose of using PROC LIFETEST is to show that with a small adjustment to the LIFETEST output, the discrete empirical hazard can be calculated, and the output from the SAS Enterprise Miner Survival node can be replicated. Thus, you clarify how the Survival node works and why it is so useful. For more information about smoothed hazard, see PROC LIFETEST documentation.

Figure 2.1: Continuous and Discrete Time Flowchart

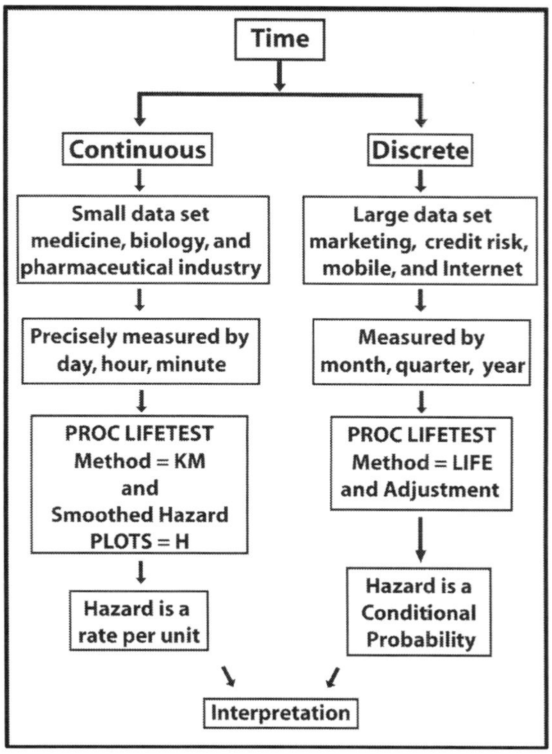

In Figure 2.2, two Hazard functions are presented—the continuous time via kernel smoothing in PROC LIFETEST Hazard function and the discrete time Hazard function. This section provides guidelines to help you decide which is more appropriate for your business situation and how to interpret each graph.

Figure 2.2: Continuous Time and Discrete Time Hazard Functions

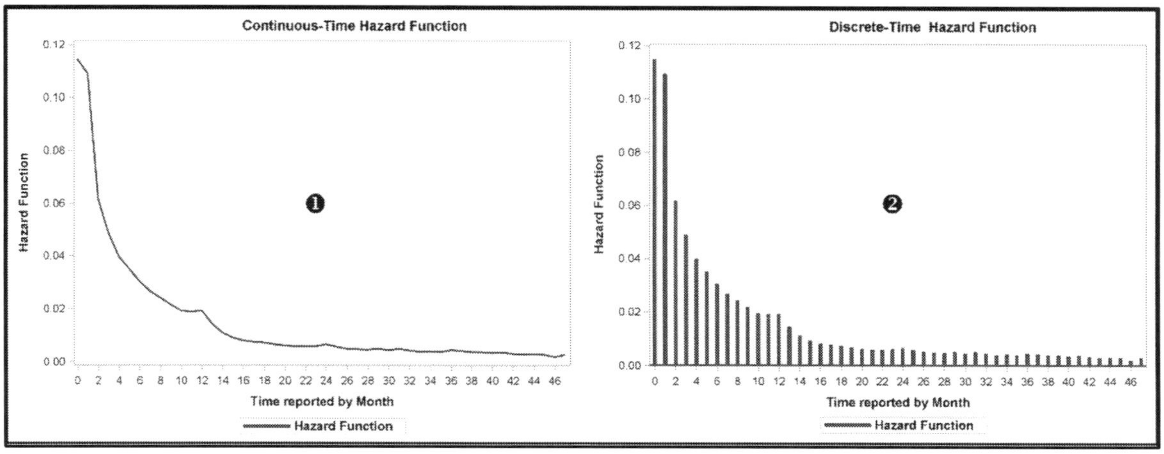

Deciding Whether to Use Continuous Time or Discrete Time

Where data is recorded in a precise unit of time (such as day, hour, and minute), you can create models using continuous time. Otherwise, discrete time is preferred. For this reason, it is worth collecting as large a sample as possible and recording time as accurately as possible, while remaining relevant to the modeling process. Table 2.1 summarizes the units of time commonly used in survival analysis.

There is no general guideline or easy solution for this choice because different degrees of accuracy are required for different business needs. For example, when modeling the number of web page visits, time has to be recorded by hours, minutes, or even smaller units.

An alternative example is in credit risk default analysis for mortgages, where time is recorded in months. A customer might be in default in a certain month, but you might have no information as to when they became default. The number of days before the censoring state changed cannot be known.

In stress test modeling, data needs to be collected by quarter because GDP (gross domestic product) is released every quarter. However, the original GDP by quarter can be transformed into GDP by month using PROC EXPAND.

Table 2.1: Time Units

Unit	Common Applications
Day	Models that forecast web page visits or sales by day grouped by week
Month	Models where annual seasonality plays a key role or where business decisions and recommendations are crucial such as for a marketing campaign or stock replacement
Quarter	Stress test models because some variables such as GDP are available only during a specific quarter of the year
Year	Employee turnover time because it can be recorded by year to track an employee's length of service

With the Garden data set, a model to predict sales by month needs to be developed with data collected daily. Time is computed as the desired unit—month—by using the Intck function.

Every survival analysis model is dependent on the Time variable. The Cox proportional hazards model, the model most common in survival analysis, assumes that time is measured on a continuous scale.

Understanding the Concept of a Customer Tie

There is a substantial difference between creating a statistical model using PROC LIFEREG or PROC PHREG with hundreds of observations and creating a data mining model with hundreds of thousands of customers. This is because of an occurrence known as a *tie*.

A tie occurs when two or more customers buy at the same time (same day or same month). The customers have the same calculated value for the Time variable. In small databases, the probability of customers buying at exactly the same time is small. But, with more than 600,000 customers (as in the Garden data set), ties are more likely. Smaller units of time (such as hours, minutes, and seconds) could be used to reduce this likelihood. But, this increases the size of the data required and processing requirements, and reduces the ease of interpretation. In addition, the unit of time used is primarily decided based on business requirements and the available data. Given the constraints on how accurately time could be or is needed to be recorded when using large data sets, ties are inevitable.

In Output 2.1, customers with Id_number 43 and 44 have the same values for the variables Start, End, and Time. They both made a first purchase on 01JAN2011 and a second purchase on 04JAN2011. This is an example of customers that are tied.

Output 2.1: Tied Customers by Day and Month

Id_number	Start	End	Censor	Last_day	Time
41	01JAN2011	.	0	31DEC2014	47
42	01JAN2011	.	0	31DEC2014	47
43	**01JAN2011**	**04JAN2011**	1	**31DEC2014**	**0**
44	**01JAN2011**	**04JAN2011**	1	**31DEC2014**	**0**
45	01JAN2011	05JAN2011	1	31DEC2014	0

Output 2.2 and Output 2.3 present the total number of tied customers in the Garden data set during January 2011 by day and during all of 2011 by month.

Output 2.2: Total Number of Tied Customers by Day and Month

End (Day of the Second Purchase)		
End	Frequency	Cumulative Frequency
03JAN2011	1	1
04JAN2011	9	10
05JAN2011	9	19
06JAN2011	19	38
07JAN2011	16	54
08JAN2011	12	66
09JAN2011	8	74
10JAN2011	20	94
11JAN2011	31	125
12JAN2011	46	171
13JAN2011	26	197
14JAN2011	29	226
15JAN2011	28	254
16JAN2011	22	276
17JAN2011	31	307
18JAN2011	49	356
19JAN2011	47	403
20JAN2011	47	450
21JAN2011	42	492
22JAN2011	42	534
23JAN2011	26	560
24JAN2011	54	614
25JAN2011	46	660
26JAN2011	61	721
27JAN2011	64	785
28JAN2011	52	837
29JAN2011	35	872
30JAN2011	22	894
31JAN2011	55	❶ 949

Output 2.3: Number of Tied Customers by Month

End (Month of the Second Purchase)		
End	Frequency	Cumulative Frequency
JAN2011	949	❶ 949
FEB2011	1950	2899
MAR2011	2986	5885
APR2011	3291	9176
MAY2011	3823	12999
JUN2011	3757	16756
JUL2011	3661	20417
AUG2011	3916	24333
SEP2011	4171	28504
OCT2011	4556	33060
NOV2011	5173	38233
DEC2011	4499	42732

❶ Verifying the frequency of purchases by day and by month should be the first task of exploratory data analysis after you create a survival analysis data set. In the previous output, the cumulative total frequency of tied customers who made a second purchase in January is in the last row of the table by day and in the first row of the table by month.

If the data set in question has a large proportion of tied customers, then it is more appropriate to construct and analyze the discrete Hazard function. Because the number of customers that are tied in the Garden data set is highly discretized in a month unit, it is appropriate to choose a discrete logistic model using SAS Enterprise Miner. The Survival node in SAS Enterprise Miner uses the same statistical approach as PROC LIFETEST. The discrete Hazard function (as described in this book) is consistent with this. The advantage of SAS Enterprise Miner is that it is easier to use to update and explore models, and it creates a clearer audit trial of the model-building process. The alternative is the continuous Hazard model created by PROC PHREG using the Cox proportional hazards model, which is covered in more advanced books about survival analysis.

Continuous Distribution

Although the continuous distribution is not suitable for the Garden data set, this subsection considers this function.

Let T represent the variable that indicates the customer's survival time in months after the first purchase. T represents the variable Time, and t denotes a specific value of T.

In time-to-next-purchase models, customers who survive are those that do not make a second purchase because the occurrence of the second purchase represents death.

Survival Function for Continuous Time

The definition of the Survival function, denoted by $S(t)$, is the probability of a customer surviving longer than a specific time, t.

For example, if you need to evaluate whether a customer survives for more than three months after the first purchases, let $t = 3$.

This is written as (T = time). Thus, survival for three months is represented as follows:

$$S(3) = P(\text{A customer survives longer than 3 months})$$

Alternatively, it can be represented as follows:

$$S(3) = P(\text{Time} > 3)$$

A customer surviving longer than three months is a customer who does not repurchase within three months of their first purchase. In general, the Survival function gives a probability of a customer surviving longer than a specific time period. It can be represented by the following equation:

$$S(t) = P(\text{A customer survives longer than } t \text{ months})$$

An alternative equation is as follows:

$$S(t) = P(T > t)$$

There are two types of survival graphs when you build time-to-next-purchase models. They are categorized by short and long survival times relative to each other. What would be considered short and long depends on the context. With the Garden data set, you might expect customers typically to make repurchases every six months. In that case, customers buying glue have a shorter survival time, and those buying electrical tools have a longer survival time.

Figure 2.3 shows customers who bought glue and have a shorter survival time.

Figure 2.3: Short Survival Time

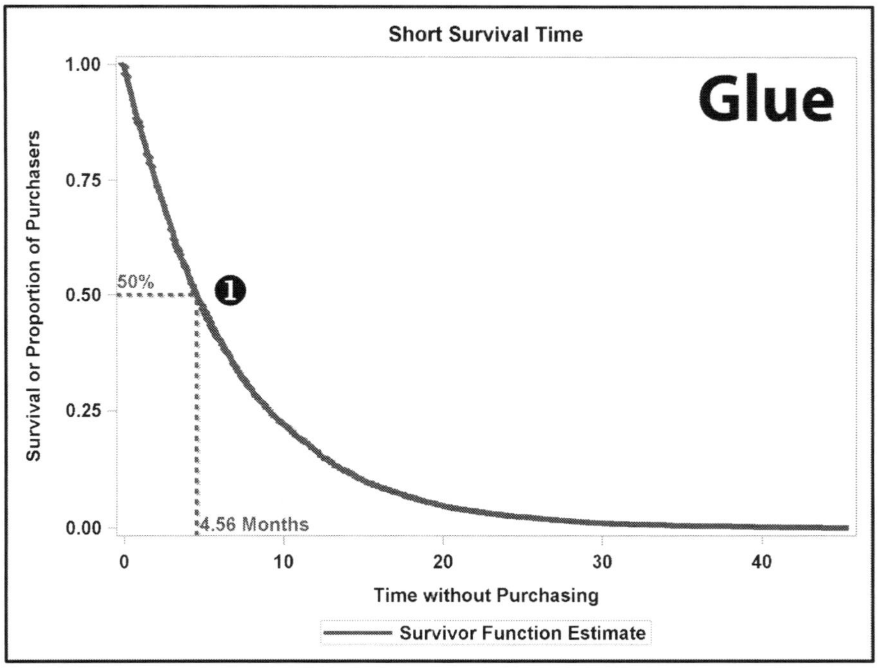

❶ The short survival graph has a half-life of 4.56 months. This means that 50% of customers make a second purchase in less than five months. Customers return to make a second purchase shortly after the first purchase. Glue is an example of a product with a short lifetime.

Figure 2.4 shows customers who bought electrical tools and have a long survival time.

Figure 2.4: Long Survival Time

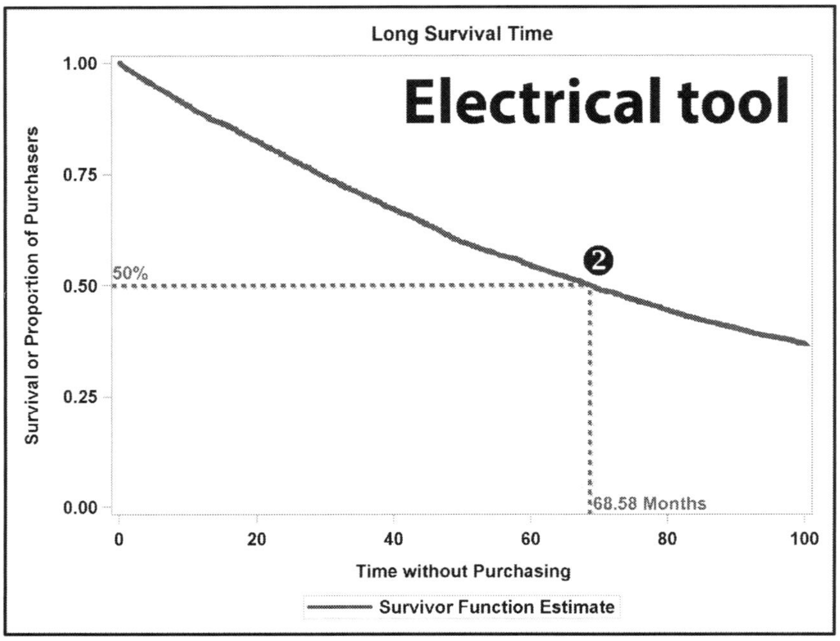

The best way to understand the difference between short and long survival times is to analyze the median lifetime value of the Survival function. The median lifetime value is the month at which half the population makes a second purchase. Remember, a customer survives if they do not make a second purchase.

❷ In the long survival graph, the half-life is 68.58 months. This means that 50% of customers make a second purchase in less than 69 months. It takes a long time for the customer to make the second purchase. In other words, after 69 months, approximately 50% of customers still had not made a second purchase. Both graphs were created using simulated data. Later in the chapter, the half-life of the Survival function of the Garden data set is analyzed. Electrical tools are a good example of products with a long lifetime.

In some published papers, Survival functions are represented differently because in time-to-next-purchase models, the quantity of interest is $1 - S(t)$. This is because surviving is the absence of a second purchase. But, the focus is on those who made a second purchase—that is, those who died. Therefore, the graphs can be presented as $1 - S(t)$ because survival is the probability of not purchasing. Figure 2.5 shows a short survival graph using the cumulative probability of purchasing function.

Figure 2.5: Cumulative = 1 − *S*(*t*) for Short Survival Time

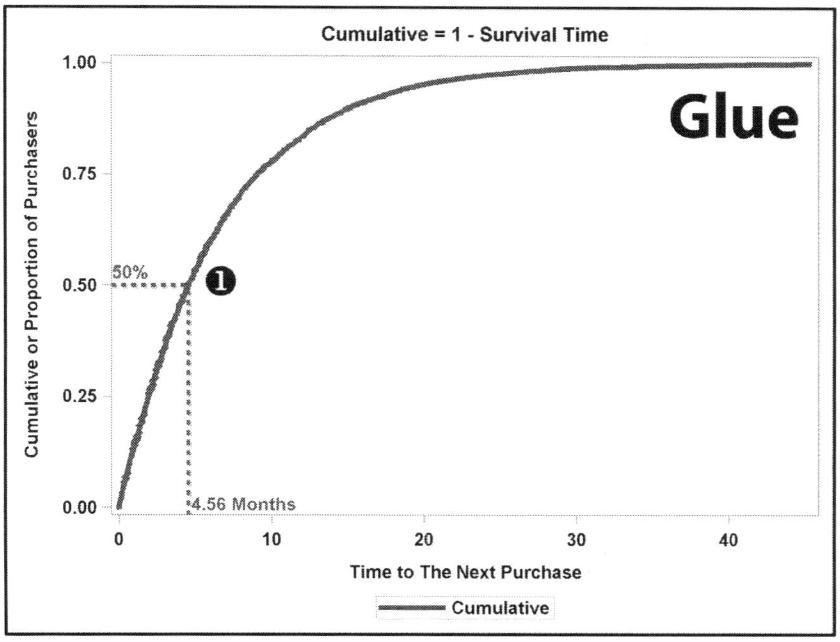

Figure 2.6 shows a long survival graph using the cumulative probability of purchasing function.

Figure 2.6: Cumulative = 1 − *S*(*t*) for Long Survival Time

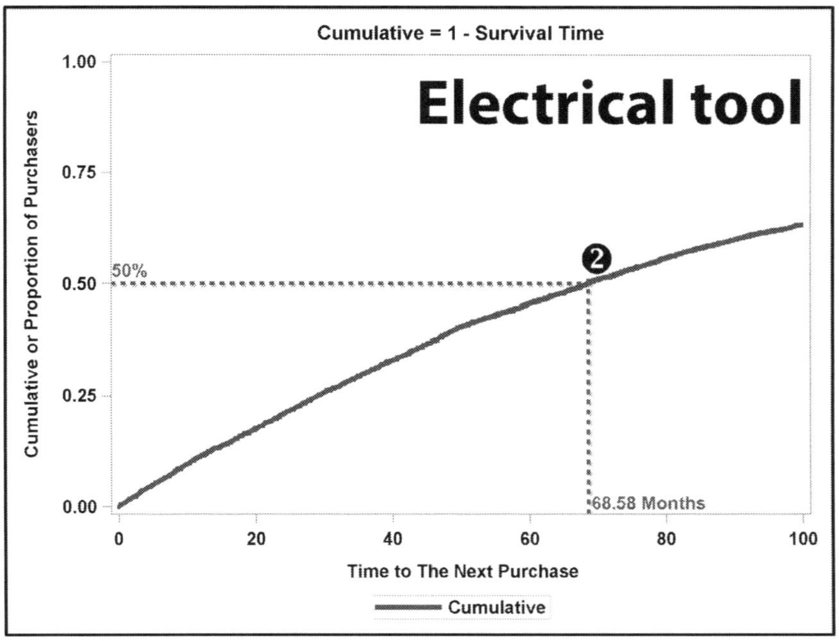

Hazard Function for Continuous Time

Hazard is another fundamental quantity in survival analysis. It is defined as follows:

$$h(t) = \lim_{\Delta t \to 0} \frac{P\left(t \le T \le t + \Delta t \middle| T \ge t\right)}{\Delta t}$$

Remember that in the Cox proportional hazards model, Time (*T*) is continuous. It considers the probability of an event occurring at a small interval of time $(t, t + \Delta t)$. This is assuming that the event (in this case, the second purchase) has not occurred before *t*.

The expression Δt represents a small interval of time. Hazard is the instantaneous potential of a second purchase occurring in the next interval of time (given that the customer has not yet made a second purchase) when the following is the case:

$$\lim_{\Delta t \to 0}$$

The implication of having a small interval Δt in the denominator is that the Hazard function is not a probability, but a rate—a conditional second purchase rate per unit of time, whose value can be greater than one.

The hazard in time-to-next-purchase models is of fundamental interest because it illustrates the instantaneous rate of purchases in any month, over time. However, a specific problem in interpreting the hazard as a rate is related to the need to include the units in which time is measured.

The Hazard function can be expressed in terms of the Survival function as shown below:

$$h(t) = -\frac{d}{dt}\{\log S(t)\}$$

The relationship of these functions is summarized in Table 2.2.

Table 2.2: Continuous Time

Function	Definition in Continuous Time
Survival	$S(t) = P(T > t)$
Hazard	$h(t) = \lim_{\Delta t \to 0} \frac{P(t \le T \le t + \Delta t \mid T \ge t)}{\Delta t}$ or $h(t) = -\frac{d}{dt}\{\log S(t)\}$ Hazard function is a rate.

The first problem for continuous time is that the Hazard function is difficult to estimate because continuous time is infinitely divisible in hours, minutes, and seconds. The implication of this divisibility is that the probability of an event (purchase online) occurring at any specific minute is infinitely small, approaching zero. A consequence of continuous time is that the probability of a tie is also infinitely small. But, there could be thousands of customers making purchases on popular global shopping web pages, such as www.amazon.com, at the same minute or even same second. These distributional assumptions about continuous time do not hold in data mining because business data includes ties, which places this modeling approach—continuous time modeling—as Plan B. Plan A is the SAS Enterprise Miner discrete distribution.

Discrete Distribution

With discrete time, the Time variable period is generally measured in months, quarters, or years, which results in hazard as a conditional probability and not as a rate. This is the fundamental difference between discrete and continuous time.

In the case of a discrete random variable, *T* (time) can take on values such as $t = 0, 1, 2, 3\ldots$ with a probability mass function as follows:

$$p(t_i) = \Pr(T = t_i)$$

The Hazard function for a discrete time variable is defined as follows:

$$h(t) = \frac{\text{Number of events}_t}{\text{Number at risk}_t}$$

The hazard probability is calculated by dividing the number of customers that repurchased during month *t* by the number of customers who were at risk of repurchasing during month *t*. The hazard at month *t* is the conditional probability of a customer purchasing in a specified month, *t*, given that they have not yet repurchased.

The Hazard function formula can be translated into the context of a time-to-next purchase model as follows:

$$h(t) = \frac{\text{Number of customers who purchase this month}_t}{\text{Number of customers at risk of purchasing at the beginning of the month}_t}$$

Because the definition of hazard is different for continuous and discrete time, the two must be interpreted differently.

Data Formats

Two data formats are used in this book. Both are accepted by the Survival node in SAS Enterprise Miner: They are the Standard format and the Expanded format. When you use these different data formats, various statistics are calculated. Detailed examples of the Expanded format are not provided in this chapter. (They are provided in Chapter 8.) A key insight to keep in mind is that the Expanded format can hold time-dependent information or other valuable information for use in the Survival node, while the simpler Standard format cannot.

Customer-Level Data Set (Standard Data Format)

The Customer-Level data set is a table in which each customer has one, and only one, record. All the information known about the customer is condensed into just one row and one observation that resembles the cross-sectional format. The fundamental advantage of the Customer-Level data set is the ease with which each customer's Start, End, Time, and Censor record. All input variables can be quickly and easily examined. The data is compact, and it is easy to quickly assess information about each customer.

The SAS Enterprise Miner Survival node refers to the Customer-Level data set as the Standard data format.

Calculation of the Discrete Hazard—An Example

The calculation of the discrete Hazard and Survival functions are shown using a small sample of 200 customers who made their first purchase in January. They are displayed in the Standard format. For this example, the data set Sample_200 has been kept small to clearly demonstrate the calculations. After this example, the same method is applied to the Garden data set with 676,635 customers.

In Output 2.4, you can see that all customers in the Sample_200 data set made a first purchase of soap in January, and some made a second purchase after 1 January and before 1 July. In the section "Life Table Method," how to use PROC LIFETEST to obtain these results is explained. Here, you learn how to derive the results by hand. The aim is to explain the formulas and demonstrate various approaches to the Hazard and Survival functions without any SAS code. Understanding must come before coding—this is the approach of this book.

Output 2.4: Selected Customers from Sample_200

ID	TIME ❶	Month ❷	Censor ❸
1	0	**January**	**1**
23	1	**February**	**1**
35	2	**March**	**1**
70	3	**April**	**1**
98	4	**May**	**1**
122	5	**June**	**1**
200	5	June	0

❶ Customers identified by ID 1, 23, 35, 70, 98, and 122 all made a second purchase in the months indicated by the variables Time and Month. Time is the number of a month in numeric format. Time in a numeric format is a requirement for creating the Expanded format in the next section.

❷ For customer 1, Time = 0. This indicates that customer 1 repurchased before the end of January and Censor is set to 1. Customer 200 did not make a second purchase before the end of June and Censor is set to 0.

In Output 2.5, the calculations for the Hazard function are defined.

Output 2.5: Hazard Calculation for Discrete Time

Time reported by Month	Purchase (Censor =1)	Customer Number at Risk of Purchase	Hazard Function
January	22	200	0.11000
February	12	178	0.06742
March	35	166	0.21084
April	28	131	0.21374
May	24	103	0.23301
June	23	79	0.29114

$$h(time=0)=\frac{22}{200}=0.1100$$

$$h(time=1)=\frac{12}{178}=0.06742$$

$$h(time=2)=\frac{35}{166}=0.21084$$

$$h(time=3)=\frac{28}{131}=0.21374$$

$$h(time=4)=\frac{24}{103}=0.23301$$

$$h(time=5)=\frac{23}{79}=0.29114$$

The calculation of the Hazard function for January is as follows:

$$\text{Hazard(January)} = \frac{\text{Number of customers who repurchased in January}}{\text{Number of customers at risk of repurchasing at the beginning of January}}$$

The actual calculation is as follows:

$$\text{Hazard(January)} = \frac{22}{200} = .11$$

In the first month (January), 22 of the 200 customers made a second purchase. You calculate the hazard probability by dividing 22 by 200, which equals .11 or 11%. Of all customers making their first purchase in January, 11% repurchased in January and 89% did not.

In February, 12 customers made a second purchase. However, the 22 customers who made a second purchase in January are no longer included in the total because they are considered dead. Now, the total number of customers at risk of repurchase is 200 – 22 = 178. Thus, the calculation of the Hazard function for February is as follows:

$$\text{Hazard(February)} = \frac{\text{Number of customers who repurchase in February}}{\text{Number of customers at risk of repurchasing at the beginning of February}}$$

The actual calculation is as follows:

$$\text{Hazard(February)} = \frac{12}{178} = .06742$$

Interpretation of the Results

The interpretation of the Hazard function is easier when hazard values are presented in a graph. Once the hazard values for every month have been obtained, the values are presented using two different formats of graphs: the time series and the needle. The meaning of both graphs is the same, but the implication of each is subtly different. The time series suggests correlation between the hazard rates. The needle suggests more independence.

Figure 2.7 shows the discrete Hazard function in a time series graph.

Figure 2.7: Discrete Hazard Function—Time Series Graph

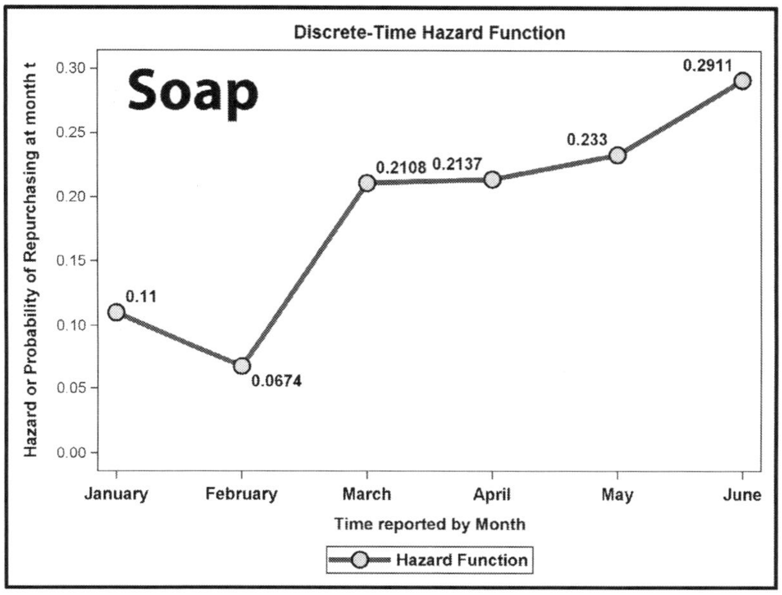

Figure 2.8 shows the discrete Hazard function in a needle graph.

Figure 2.8: Discrete Hazard Function—Needle Graph

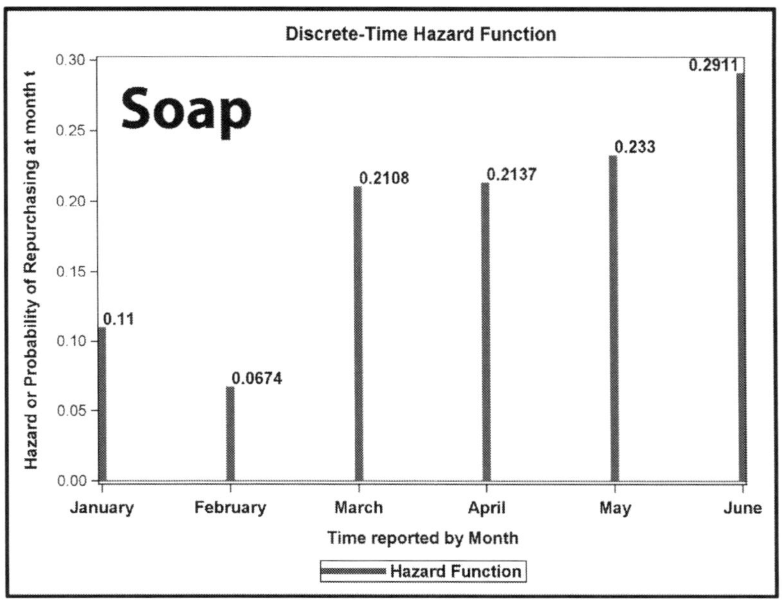

The value of hazard in each month lies between 0 and 1. This indicates the risk of repurchase in that month, where the risk is proportional to the hazard. The greater the hazard, the higher the risk of repurchase.

In Output 2.5, examined the Hazard function for the Sample_200 data set. The output showed that 11% of customers made a second purchase in the first month (January) after their original purchase in January.

A time series graph presents values over time following the recommendation of Miller (1981) and Lee (2013). Plotting probabilities as a time series helps identify the months where seasonality can affect the risk of repurchase.

The needle graph follows the pragmatic approach adopted by Mike Patetta and Will Potts in their SAS training course, *Survival Data Mining: Predictive Hazard Modeling for Customer History: A Programming Approach*.

The choice of a time series or needle graph is key to determine the behavior of hazard and whether it increases, decreases, or remains constant. For soap, it is plausible that the repurchase rate is seasonal. Thus, it might be lower after the end-of-year holidays and higher toward the northern hemisphere summer. Therefore, the time series plot is probably best. Both graphs were constructed using PLOC SGPLOT. (The code is available on the authors' page at http://support.sas.com/authors.)

The graphs show the characteristic hazard of short-term products such as soap that are often replaced within six months of their original purchase. For example, it seems that some customers in January might purchase a quantity of soap and realize quickly that the amount purchased is not enough. So, they repurchase in January. The hazard of 0.11 represents customers in this situation.

In real life, it would be expected that the risk of repurchase drops following an initial purchase because customers should buy a sufficient amount of soap, or any other product for that matter, to meet their immediate needs. However, after a certain time, the risk of a second purchase should increase. This fact can be seen in the previous graphs as the risk of repurchase drops dramatically from January (0.11) to February (0.06742). But, from March to June, the risk begins to rise again as the customer uses up the first purchase and replaces it with a second purchase.

Month Data Set (Expanded Data Format)

An expanded customer data set is a table that has several observations per customer. It can be obtained by converting a Customer-Level data set that has one observation per customer into a data set expanded by month. Each customer has one or more records and one for each month. This can be changed to any period of time depending on the data available.

A new data set is needed with several months and observations per customer. Figure 2.9 shows the differences between the Standard and Expanded data formats.

Figure 2.9: Expanding the Customer Data Set

Standard data set format

Customer Level data set

	ID	TIME	Month	Censor
❶	1	0	January	1
❷	23	1	February	1
❸	35	2	March	1
❹	70	3	April	1
❺	98	4	May	1
❻	122	5	June	1
❼	200	5	June	0

200 observations
(One per customer ID)

Fully Expanded data set format

Customer Expanded month data set

	ID	TIME	Month Numeric	Month	Censor	
❶	1	0	0	January	1	⬅
❷	23	1	0	January	0	
	23	1	1	February	1	⬅
❸	35	2	0	January	0	
	35	2	1	February	0	
	35	2	2	March	1	⬅
❹	70	3	0	January	0	
	70	3	1	February	0	
	70	3	2	March	0	
	70	3	3	April	1	⬅
❺	98	4	0	January	0	
	98	4	1	February	0	
	98	4	2	March	0	
	98	4	3	April	0	
	98	4	4	May	1	⬅
❻	122	5	0	January	0	
	122	5	1	February	0	
	122	5	2	March	0	
	122	5	3	April	0	
	122	5	4	May	0	
	122	5	5	June	1	⬅
❼	200	5	0	January	0	
	200	5	1	February	0	
	200	5	2	March	0	
	200	5	3	April	0	
	200	5	4	May	0	
	200	5	5	June	0	⬅

857 observations
(One or more per customer ID)

In Figure 2.9, the Customer-Level data set presents data from seven selected customers. The third and fourth columns in the Month data set display the month indicator label “Month Numeric” and “Month,” which identify the specific month that the observation row relates to.

Customers ❶ to ❻ are uncensored (they repurchased and Censor = 1). The number of observations increases proportionately to the number of months that it takes for each customer to repurchase. Customer 200 ❼ is censored (did not repurchase), and Censor = 0 for all months. The arrows ⬅ indicate that the last month of the customer in the database is in the Expanded format. The purpose of this transformation is to prepare the data for it to be analyzed by PROC LOGISTIC.

Program 2.1 converts the Customer-Level data set to Expanded format for the Month data set. The book, *Longitudinal Data and SAS: A Programmer’s Guide* by Ron Cody (2001), covers all the necessary features to restructure data sets such as lag, retain, DO loop, and arrays.

Program 2.1: Expanding the Data Set Sample_200

```
data Expanded_200 (rename = (Target = Censor));
set  sample_200;
do Month= 0 to Time ❶;
    Target = Censor *(Time = Month)❷;
    output;
end;
drop Censor;
run;
```

❶ The DO loop increments the number of observations for each customer using Time as a counter.

❷ The Target variable, renamed as Censor in the output data set, indicates whether the customer repurchased (Censor = 1) or not (Censor = 0).

Output 2.6 shows the output from the previous program. It provides the number of observations per customer.

Output 2.6: Number of Observations in the Month Data Set

ID	How many observations?	Repurchase Month	Censor
1	1	January	1
23	2	February	1
35	3	March	1
70	4	April	1
98	5	May	1
122	6	June	1
200	**6**	**--------**	**0**

The original data set Sample_200 has 200 customers (one row per customer). The new Expanded_200 data set has 857 rows (customer * Month). Even though customer 200 did not repurchase, the number of observations is counted from 0 to 5 because customers stay in the data set six months following their first purchase. For all other customers, Censor = 1 in the last month of the observation and is set to 0 elsewhere.

The primary advantage of the Expanded data format is that the time-varying-dependent inputs (predictors) can be handled easily. This is discussed in more detail later. A second advantage is that a Month variable can be created whose values vary over time using a SAS format. This improves the readability of the table.

Creation of Dummy Variables

A *dummy variable* is a numerical variable that is often used to distinguish groups of customers. In a simple example, a (0 – 1) dummy variable would be used where a customer is given a value of 1 if Sex = “Male” or 0 if Sex = “Female”. The dummy variable is useful because separate equation models for each Sex group are not required. In a survival regression model with dummy variables, separate equations for each sex can be created by substituting the dummy values.

A Simple Example

To illustrate dummy variables, suppose that a customer's sex is written as character variable Gender, which is a numeric dummy variable summarized as follows:

$$\begin{cases} \text{Gender} = \mathbf{1} \text{ if Sex} = \text{"Male"} \\ \text{Gender} = \mathbf{0} \text{ if Sex} = \text{"Female"} \end{cases}$$

The most important characteristic of dummy variables is that they can be used to sort or rank the data into mutually exclusive categories such as methods of payment (credit card or cash). Understanding how dummy variables are created is very important in the survival model process because they are particularly useful with qualitative data. Later in the book, the CLASS statement and dummy variables created automatically by SAS Enterprise Miner with PROC LOGISTIC or PROC PHREG is discussed.

A question asked frequently by graduates is, "Which category of dummy variable should I choose to have the value of 1?" The answer depends on which category needs to be tested or explained. For example, if the fact that some customers repurchase in January and other customers do not needs to be accounted for, a dummy variable to indicate January as 1 and all other months of the year as 0 must be created. In other words, a dummy variable must be created that takes the value of 1 if the customer repurchases in a particular month and 0 if the customer does not.

A Time-to-Next-Purchase Example

In this section, the relationship between betas (regression coefficients), odds, hazard calculation, and the months in which customers made their second purchases is demonstrated. Betas are the estimated parameters of the model. A logistic model with every month name as a dummy variable is used to demonstrate the relationship. This can be summarized as follows:

$$\begin{cases} \text{January} = 1 \text{ if Month } = \text{"January"} \\ \text{January} = 0 \text{ if Month } \neq \text{"January"} \end{cases}$$

Dummy variables are important in survival analysis because the coefficients of each dummy variable measure the impact between a category's receiving a value of 1 compared to the category's receiving a value of 0. This means that a parameter can be estimated for the category values. Using dummy variables, the interpretation of the coefficients, odds, Survival, and Hazard functions are straightforward. The decision to add dummy variables can be made for simplification. It is easier to interpret a coefficient from a numeric variable than a coefficient from a categorical variable (for which dummy values have to implicitly be used anyway). Program 2.2 creates six dummy variables, one for each month.

Program 2.2: Creating Dummy Variables for Each Month

```
data Expanded_200;
set  Expanded_200;
     January  = (Month=0); ❶
     February = (Month=1);
     March    = (Month=2);
     April    = (Month=3);
     May      = (Month=4);
     June     = (Month=5);
run;
```

❶ The statement creates a variable called January with a value of 1 if (Month = 0), and 0 otherwise. The code is just a more efficient way of writing an IF/THEN statement for each month as follows:

```
     if Month=0 then January = 1;
else                 January = 0;
```

Output 2.7 shows the updated version of the Expanded_200 data set with the dummy variables (January to June) included. The callout numbers indicate each month and their respective dummy indicator.

Output 2.7: Expanded_200 Data Set with Months as Dummy Variables

ID	TIME	Month	Censor	January	February	March	April	May	June
1	0	⓿ January	1	⓿ 1	0	0	0	0	0
23	1	January	0	1	0	0	0	0	0
23	1	❶ February	1	0	❶ 1	0	0	0	0
35	2	January	0	1	0	0	0	0	0
35	2	February	0	0	1	0	0	0	0
35	2	❷ March	1	0	0	❷ 1	0	0	0
70	3	January	0	1	0	0	0	0	0
70	3	February	0	0	1	0	0	0	0
70	3	March	0	0	0	1	0	0	0
70	3	❸ April	1	0	0	0	❸ 1	0	0
98	4	January	0	1	0	0	0	0	0
98	4	February	0	0	1	0	0	0	0
98	4	March	0	0	0	1	0	0	0
98	4	April	0	0	0	0	1	0	0
98	4	❹ May	1	0	0	0	0	❹ 1	0
122	5	January	0	1	0	0	0	0	0
122	5	February	0	0	1	0	0	0	0
122	5	March	0	0	0	1	0	0	0
122	5	April	0	0	0	0	1	0	0
122	5	May	0	0	0	0	0	1	0
122	5	❺ June	1	0	0	0	0	0	❺ 1
200	5	January	0	1	0	0	0	0	0
200	5	February	0	0	1	0	0	0	0
200	5	March	0	0	0	1	0	0	0
200	5	April	0	0	0	0	1	0	0
200	5	May	0	0	0	0	0	1	0
200	5	June	0	0	0	0	0	0	1

This approach mimics the approach used in SAS Enterprise Miner. In the current example, Censor is the Target variable, and the dummy variables January, February, March, April, May, and June are included as input, enabling you to write the input variables as follows:

$$f(x) = \beta_1\text{January} + \beta_2\text{February} + \beta_3\text{March} + \beta_4\text{April} + \beta_5\text{May} + \beta_6\text{June}$$

The model can be written using odds as follows:

$$\text{Odds} = \frac{\text{Prob(Repurchase)}}{1 - \text{Prob(Repurchase)}}$$

The odds applied in analysis of time-to-next-purchase models is defined as the ratio between the probability that a repurchase occurs and the probability that a repurchase does not occur. (That is, the customer will not repurchase until the end of June.)

The device constraining the probability to be between 0 and 1 can be calculated by equating the logit (log of odds) to the original $Y = f(x)$. This can be expressed as follows:

$$\log(\text{Odds}) = f(x)$$

Alternatively, it can be expressed as follows:

$$\log\left(\frac{\text{Prob(Repurchase)}}{1 - \text{Prob(Repurchase)}}\right) = f(x)$$

Or, you can replace $f(x)$ as follows:

$$f(x) = \beta_1\text{January} + \beta_2\text{February} + \beta_3\text{March} + \beta_4\text{April} + \beta_5\text{May} + \beta_6\text{June}$$

Here is what you now have:

$$\log\left(\frac{\text{Prob(Repurchase)}}{1 - \text{Prob(Repurchase)}}\right) = \beta_1\text{January} + \beta_2\text{February} + \beta_3\text{March} + \beta_4\text{April} + \beta_5\text{May} + \beta_6\text{June}$$

Alternatively, you can have this:

$$\log(\text{Odds}) = \beta_1\text{January} + \beta_2\text{February} + \beta_3\text{March} + \beta_4\text{April} + \beta_5\text{May} + \beta_6\text{June}$$

Applying the exponential function ($e = 2.71828$) to both sides to eliminate the logarithm, we have the following:

$$\text{Odds} = e^{\beta_1\text{January} + \beta_2\text{February} + \beta_3\text{March} + \beta_4\text{April} + \beta_5\text{May} + \beta_6\text{June}}$$

The key point in this relationship is that every single month is a dummy variable. For a particular month, all others months have the value 0.

Next, cancel all other months to realize the calculation of the odds for January because all other months have a value of 0. You see the importance of using dummy variables:

$$\text{Odds} = e^{\beta_1\text{January} + \cancel{\beta_2\text{February}} + \cancel{\beta_3\text{March}} + \cancel{\beta_4\text{April}} + \cancel{\beta_5\text{May}} + \cancel{\beta_6\text{June}}}$$

Alternatively, you can write it as follows:

$$\text{Odds}_{\text{January}} = e^{\beta_1\text{January}}$$

The same is valid for all months:

$$\text{Odds}_{\text{January}} = e^{\beta_1\text{January}}$$

$$\text{Odds}_{\text{February}} = e^{\beta_2\text{February}}$$

$$\text{Odds}_{\text{March}} = e^{\beta_3\text{March}}$$

$$\text{Odds}_{\text{April}} = e^{\beta_4\text{April}}$$

$$\text{Odds}_{\text{May}} = e^{\beta_5\text{May}}$$

$$\text{Odds}_{\text{June}} = e^{\beta_6\text{June}}$$

This relationship demonstrates that, using PROC LOGISTIC, you need only the betas coefficients for every month.

PROC LOGISTIC to Compute Hazard

The only relevant information in the time-to-next-purchase example previously discussed is when a customer buys in January (January = 1). This is because all other months are canceled (the customer drops out of the table and model) because the month values are equal to 0. In this example, PROC LOGISTIC is used to perform the logistic regression, and it estimates the required regression coefficients.

Program 2.3 uses the Expanded_200 data set, not the Customer-Level data set, to run this model:

Program 2.3: Computing Hazard Using PROC LOGISTIC

```
ods output ParameterEstimates = ParameterEstimates ❶ ;
proc logistic data = Expanded_200 ;
model Censor(event='1')= January February March April May June❷/noint❸;
run;
```

❶ This statement produces a SAS data set with parameter estimates of the fitted model.

❷ There are no other input (predictor) variables, only the month effect.

❸ The intercept is excluded using the NOINT option in the MODEL statement to obtain the desired betas estimates. This is necessary because PROC LOGISTIC interprets the intercept as an input variable.

This book is not intended as a tutorial on logistic regression, but the following information must be explained to clarify discussion later in this chapter and to better understand the fundamental relationship between logistic regression and survival analysis.

Output 2.8 shows the Analysis of Maximum Likelihood Estimates table with the required betas.

Output 2.8: Betas Coefficients from PROC LOGISTIC

Analysis of Maximum Likelihood Estimates					
Parameter	**DF**	**Betas Estimate ❶**	**Standard Error**	**Wald Chi-Square**	**Pr > ChiSq**
January	1	**-2.0907**	0.2260	85.5880	<.0001
February	1	**-2.6268**	0.2989	77.2374	<.0001
March	1	**-1.3198**	0.1903	48.1149	<.0001
April	1	**-1.3025**	0.2131	37.3504	<.0001
May	1	**-1.1914**	0.2331	26.1283	<.0001
June	1	**-0.8899**	0.2477	12.9101	0.0003

❶ Using betas, estimate coefficients using PROC LOGISTIC. The principal relationship in the discrete model approach in SAS Enterprise Miner can be calculated. The relationships between betas, odds, and hazard are presented next.

Replacing the betas coefficients, such as $\beta_{1\text{January}} = -2.0907$, you see how to calculate the odds of each month, step by step:

$$\text{Odds}_{\text{January}} = e^{\beta_1 \text{January}} \quad \Rightarrow \quad \text{Odds}_{\text{January}} = e^{-2.0907} = 0.124$$

$$\text{Odds}_{\text{February}} = e^{\beta_2 \text{February}} \quad \Rightarrow \quad \text{Odds}_{\text{February}} = e^{-2.6268} = 0.072$$

$$\text{Odds}_{\text{March}} = e^{\beta_3 \text{March}} \quad \Rightarrow \quad \text{Odds}_{\text{March}} = e^{-1.3198} = 0.267$$

$$\text{Odds}_{\text{April}} = e^{\beta_4 \text{April}} \quad \Rightarrow \quad \text{Odds}_{\text{April}} = e^{-1.3025} = 0.272$$

$$\text{Odds}_{\text{May}} = e^{\beta_5 \text{May}} \quad \Rightarrow \quad \text{Odds}_{\text{May}} = e^{-1.1914} = 0.304$$

$$\text{Odds}_{\text{June}} = e^{\beta_6 \text{June}} \quad \Rightarrow \quad \text{Odds}_{\text{June}} = e^{-0.8899} = 0.411$$

Remember, odds compare the probability that an event will occur with the probability that it will not occur. The relationship between odds and hazard is as follows:

$$\text{Odds} = e^{\text{Betas}}$$

and

$$\text{Hazard} = \frac{1}{1 + e^{-\text{Betas}}}$$

An easy conclusion can be drawn from the above formulas—the betas represent everything needed to calculate the odds and hazard using the Expanded format without needing any other input variables.

Odds Calculation (January)

From Output 2.8, the first beta from January is ($\beta_{1\text{January}} = -2.0907$). From this, the odds value is calculated by using the Odds formula:

$$\text{Odds}_{\text{January}} = e^{\beta_1 \text{January}}$$

The results are:

$$\text{Odds}_{\text{January}} = e^{-2.0907}$$

This, in turn, results in the following:

$$\text{Odds}_{\text{January}} = 0.12360 \cong 0.124$$

The odds results for all months appear in Output 2.9. This table is created by default by PROC LOGISTIC.

Output 2.9: Odds Ratio Estimates from PROC LOGISTIC

Odds Ratio Estimates			
Effect	Point Estimate	95% Wald Confidence Limits	
January	**0.124**	0.079	0.192
February	**0.072**	0.040	0.130
March	**0.267**	0.184	0.388
April	**0.272**	0.179	0.413
May	**0.304**	0.192	0.480
June	**0.411**	0.253	0.667

Even though the odds are a fundamental concept in logistic regression, the hazard for each month is equally important.

Hazard Calculation (January)

Program 2.4 implements all of the necessary calculations using a SAS DATA step:

Program 2.4: Computing Odds and Hazard Function

```
data ParameterEstimates;
set  ParameterEstimates;
Odds ❷ = exp (Betas ❶);
Hazard ❸ = 1 / (1 + exp (- Betas ❶ ));
run;
```

There are two ways to express the hazard in logistic regression. In the following formulas, *h* represents hazard and *t* represents time:

$$\text{Hazard} = h(t) = \frac{\text{odds}}{1+\text{odds}} \qquad \text{Hazard} = h(t) = \frac{1}{1+e^{-\text{Betas}}}$$

❶ For January, $(\beta_{1\text{January}} = -2.0907)$.

❷ Odds = 0.12360.

❸ Substituting values into the two formulas for hazard results in the following:

$$h(\text{January}) = \frac{\text{odds}_{\text{January}}}{1+\text{odds}_{\text{January}}}$$

$$h(\text{January}) = \frac{0.12360}{1+0.12360} \quad ❷$$

$$h(\text{January}) = 0.11000$$

$$h(\text{January}) = \frac{1}{1+e^{-\beta_1 \text{January}}}$$

$$h(\text{January}) = \frac{1}{1+e^{-(-2.0907)}} \quad ❸$$

$$h(\text{January}) = 0.11000$$

Output 2.10 presents the betas, odds, and hazard. The risk of repurchase increases after February as the customer runs out of soap. The hazard probability in June is three times higher than in January. Notice that these hazard values are identical to those calculated in Output 2.5.

Output 2.10: Betas Coefficients, Odds, and Hazard Odds Estimated

Variable	Betas ❶	Odds $\text{Odds} = e^{Betas}$ ❷	Hazard $h(t) = \frac{1}{1+e^{-Betas}}$ ❸
January	**-2.0907**	**0.12360**	**0.11000**
February	-2.6268	0.07231	0.06743
March	-1.3198	0.26718	0.21084
April	-1.3025	0.27184	0.21374
May	-1.1914	0.30380	0.23301
June	-0.8899	0.41071	0.29114

Survival Function

The definition of the Survival function for discrete time is identical to the definition for continuous time. However, now that the Survival function is a non-increasing step function, it is calculated as a sum rather than an integral:

$$S(t) = P(T > t) = \sum_{t_i > t} p(t_i)$$

Figure 2.10 shows an example of the discrete time Survival function for a time-to-next-purchase model.

Figure 2.10: Discrete Survival Time

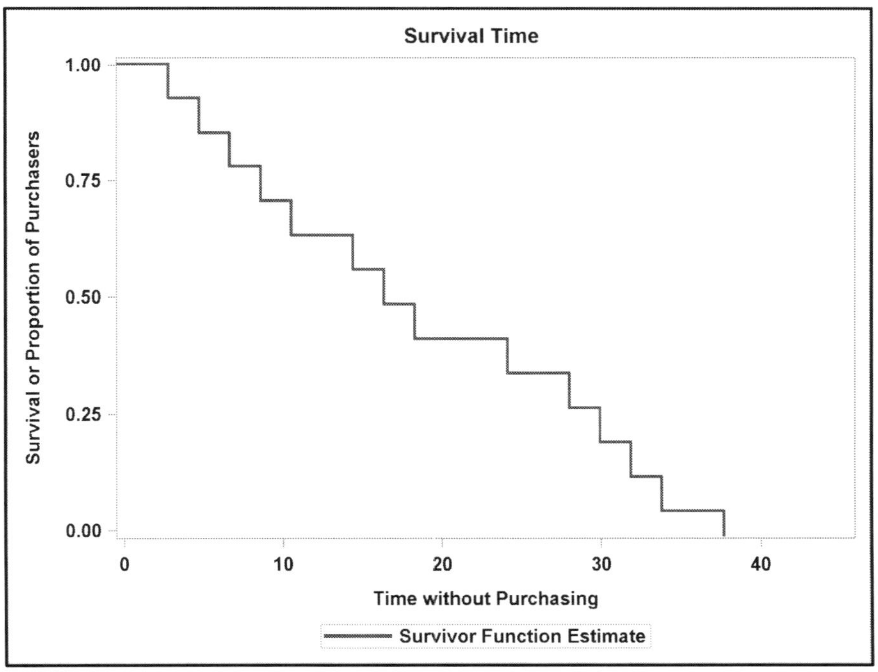

At the beginning of January, when no one has yet made a second purchase, every one of the 200 customers are surviving. Survival, by definition, is 1. As the repurchases occur, the survival declines.

Survival can be expressed as follows:

$$\text{Survival}(t) = \frac{\text{Number of customers who have not repurchased again by the end of the month}}{\text{Total number of customers at risk of repurchasing at the beginning of the month}}$$

The calculation of the Survival function for the first month (January) is as follows:

$$\text{Survival (January)} = \frac{\text{Number of customers who have not repurchased again by the end of January}}{\text{Total number of customers at risk of repurchasing at the beginning of January}}$$

$$\text{Survival (January)} = \frac{178}{200}$$

$$\text{Survival (January)} = 0.89$$

Hazard and Survival Relationship

The reason that hazard was calculated before survival is that the Survival function can be expressed as a function of hazard:

$$\text{Survival} = f(\text{Survival}_{t-1}, \text{Hazard})$$

It is worth noting that it is not possible to calculate survival at time t without knowing the survival of $t - 1$. Once the survival of the previous time period is known and hazard is calculated, the survival of month t can be defined. This is demonstrated in the following equation, where i represents the actual month:

$$S(t_i) = S(t_{i-1}) * [1 - \text{Hazard}(t_i)]$$

For example, the hazard of Month = 3 can be written as follows:

$$S(t_3) = S(t_2) * [1 - \text{Hazard}(t_2)]$$

Using the information from Output 2.5, hazard can be calculated using this relationship. Output 2.11 shows survival for discrete time.

Output 2.11: Survival Calculation for Discrete Time

Time reported by Month	Purchase (Censor =1)	Customer Number at Risk of Purchase	Hazard Function	Survival
December	0	200	0.0000	1.000
January	22	200	0.11000	0.890
February	12	178	0.06742	0.830
March	35	166	0.21084	0.655
April	28	131	0.21374	0.515
May	24	103	0.23301	0.395
June	23	79	0.29114	0.280

Output 2.11 shows the Survival and Hazard functions by discrete time, which in this case is month, calculated in SAS. The following equations provide step-by-step calculations when deriving the survival values by month. The underlying equations are the same as those earlier in this section.

$$S[\text{January}] = S(\text{December}) * [1 - \text{Hazard(January)}] = 1 * [1 - 0.1100] = 0.890$$

$$S[\text{February}] = S(\text{January}) * [1 - \text{Hazard(February)}] = 0.890 * [1 - 0.06742] = 0.830$$

$$S[\text{March}] = S(\text{February}) * [1 - \text{Hazard(March)}] = 0.830 * [1 - 0.21084] = 0.655$$

$$S[\text{April}] = S(\text{March}) * [1 - \text{Hazard(April}] = 0.655 * [1 - 0.21374] = 0.515$$

$$S[\text{May}] = S(\text{April}) * [1 - \text{Hazard(May)}] = 0.515 * [1 - 0.23301] = 0.395$$

$$S[\text{June}] = S(\text{May}) * [1 - \text{Hazard(June)}] = 0.395 * [1 - 0.29114] = 0.280$$

Summary of Distributions

The Hazard function for a discrete time variable can also be defined as a function of the following for time $i = 1, 2, 3...$:

$$h(t) = P\left(T = t_i \middle| T \geq t_{i-1}\right) = 1 - \frac{S(t_i)}{S(t_{i-1})}$$

This demonstration is not in the scope of this book (see Melania Pintilie (2006) instead). Using this relationship by induction, you can derive that the Survival function can be written as follows:

$$S(t_i) = \prod_{t_i \leq t} (1 - h(t_i))$$

The relationship of the functions is summarized in Table 2.3.

Table 2.3: Summary of Distributions for Continuous and Discrete Time

Function	Definition in Continuous Time	Definition in Discrete Time
Survival	$S(t) = P(T > t)$	$S(t) = P(T > t)$ $S(t_i) = S(t_{i-1}) * [1 - \text{Hazard}(t_i)]$ or $S(t_i) = \prod_{t_i \leq t} (1 - h(t_i))$
Hazard	$h(t) = \lim_{\Delta t \to 0} \frac{P\left(t \leq T \leq t + \Delta t \middle| T \geq t\right)}{\Delta t}$ or $h(t) = -\frac{d}{dt}\{\log S(t)\}$	$h(t) = P\left(T = t_i \middle| T \geq t_{i-1}\right) = 1 - \frac{S(t_i)}{S(t_{i-1})}$
Key	Hazard function is a rate.	Hazard function is a conditional probability.

Life Table Method

In this section, the first step in calculating the empirical hazard uses the Life Table. PROC LIFETEST is run with the option Method = Life. Because the Life Table method in PROC LIFETEST does not estimate the discrete Hazard function directly, an adjustment is necessary. The adjustment process is implemented after performing the four steps in Figure 2.11.

Figure 2.11: Empirical Hazard Calculation Flowchart

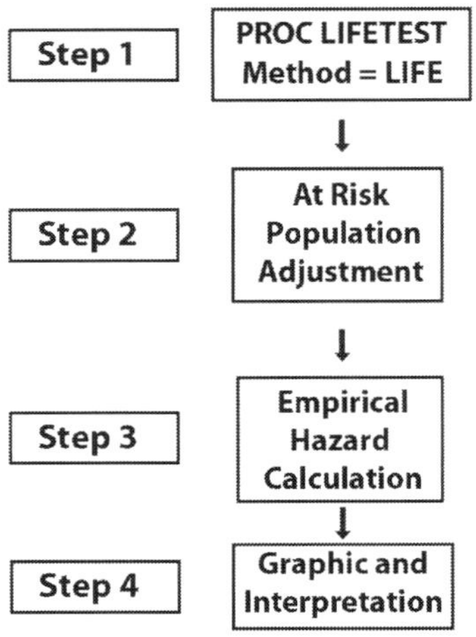

A discrete nonparametric method does not require a specific assumption about the distribution of the survival times. The Life Table (or actuarial) method is not really a nonparametric method because it makes an assumption that censoring occurs uniformly throughout the interval. The direct implication of the actuarial method is that half of the censored customers would no longer be at risk at the month's midpoint. PROC LIFETEST modifies the numbers of customers at risk of purchasing and divides the number of censored customers in the period (month) in half as shown in Figure 2.12:

Figure 2.12: Life Table Method with Midpoint Adjustment

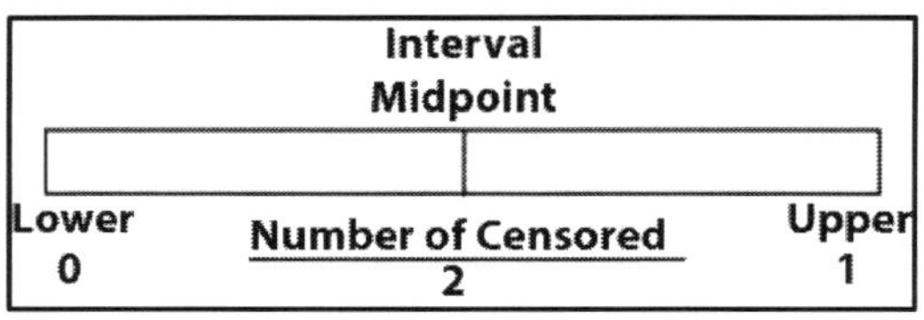

The Life Table method is preferred when the sample size and the number of events (purchases) are large. Their implementation requires the Time variable to be grouped into intervals (years, quarters, months, days, hours, minutes, and seconds).

Step 1: PROC LIFETEST with METHOD = LIFE

In Program 2.5, a Life Table using Method = life is requested and intervals are adjusted with time increasing from 0 to 47 months by one month.

Program 2.5: Computing Hazard Using PROC LIFETEST

```
Ods output lifetableestimates = Lifetable_1 ❶;
Proc lifetest data=Garden
Method = life               ❷
Intervals = 0 to 47 by 1    ❸;
Time Time * Censor(0)       ❹;
run;
```

❶ This statement writes the ODS table lifetableestimates to a SAS data set named Lifetable_1. All of the usual data set options, such as the KEEP= or RENAME= option, can be used in the ODS OUTPUT statement. Thus, to create the Lifetable_1 data set so that it contains only certain columns from the lifetableestimates table, you can use the data set options as follows:

```
Ods output lifetableestimates= Lifetable_1 ❶ ( keep   =  lowertime
effsize censored failed Rename = (lowertime=Time Failed = Purchase));
```

❷ The Method = life option specifies the type of survival and hazard estimate calculated. LIFE, LF, or ACT produces actuarial estimates. If the method is not used, Kaplan-Meier estimates are produced by default. Because Method = life is used, the output includes hazard and density function estimates at the interval midpoint.

❸ Interval specifies the exact number of intervals used to compute the Life Table estimates. They are linked to the Time variable boundaries and are created by 1 because the results are needed in 47 rows. The rows represent every month period after the first purchase of the customer.

❹ The Time statement indicates the purchase Time variable followed by an asterisk. It includes the name of the censoring variable (Censor) that has the value (0), which corresponds to a censored value.

In Output 2.12, PROC LIFETEST constructs 47 intervals, but only a portion of the intervals estimated for the Life Table have been displayed.

Output 2.12: Life Table Using the Method = Life Table

Life Table Survival Estimates															
Interval												Evaluated at the Midpoint of the Interval			
[Lower,	Upper)	❺ Number Failed	❻ Number Censored	❼ Effective Sample Size	❽ Conditional Probability of Failure	Conditional Probability Standard Error	Survival	Failure	Survival Standard Error	Median Residual Lifetime	Median Standard Error	PDF	PDF Standard Error	❾ Hazard	Hazard Standard Error
0	1	77470	7969	**672650.5**	0.1152	0.000389	1.0000	0	0	25.7696	0.2119	0.1152	0.000389	0.122209	0.000438
1	2	64394	13505	**584443.5**	0.1102	0.000410	0.8848	0.1152	0.000389	.	.	0.0975	0.000365	0.116604	0.000459
2	3	31542	11393	**507600.5**	0.0621	0.000339	0.7873	0.2127	0.000501	.	.	0.0489	0.000269	0.064132	0.000361
3	4	22810	8639	**466042.5**	0.0489	0.000316	0.7384	0.2616	0.000541	.	.	0.0361	0.000235	0.050172	0.000332
4	5	17373	8548	**434639.0**	0.0400	0.000297	0.7023	0.2977	0.000565	.	.	0.0281	0.000210	0.040786	0.000309
5	6	14449	8219	**408882.5**	0.0353	0.000289	0.6742	0.3258	0.000581	.	.	0.0238	0.000196	0.035973	0.000299
6	7	11795	10567	**385040.5**	0.0306	0.000278	0.6504	0.3496	0.000593	.	.	0.0199	0.000182	0.03111	0.000286
7	8	9792	8031	**363946.5**	0.0269	0.000268	0.6305	0.3695	0.000603	.	.	0.0170	0.000170	0.027272	0.000276
8	9	8437	8138	**346070.0**	0.0244	0.000262	0.6135	0.3865	0.000610	.	.	0.0150	0.000162	0.02468	0.000269
.	.	.	.	.	.	.	.	.	.	.	.	.	.	.	.
.	.	.	.	.	.	.	.	.	.	.	.	.	.	.	.
.	.	.	.	.	.	.	.	.	.	.	.	.	.	.	.
40	**41**	169	5881	**46772.5**	0.00361	0.000277	0.4695	0.5305	0.000735	.	.	0.00170	0.000130	0.00362	0.000278
41	**42**	154	5329	**40998.5**	0.00376	0.000302	0.4678	0.5322	0.000744	.	.	0.00176	0.000141	0.003763	0.000303
42	**43**	113	5500	**35430.0**	0.00319	0.000300	0.4661	0.5339	0.000755	.	.	0.00149	0.000140	0.003194	0.000301
43	**44**	89	7208	**28963.0**	0.00307	0.000325	0.4646	0.5354	0.000765	.	.	0.00143	0.000151	0.003078	0.000326
44	**45**	72	6267	**22136.5**	0.00325	0.000383	0.4632	0.5368	0.000778	.	.	0.00151	0.000177	0.003258	0.000384
45	**46**	51	8000	**14931.0**	0.00342	0.000477	0.4616	0.5384	0.000795	.	.	0.00158	0.000220	0.003422	0.000479
46	**47**	20	6050	**7855.0**	0.00255	0.000569	0.4601	0.5399	0.000822	.	.	0.00117	0.000262	0.002549	0.00057
47	.	13	4797	**2411.5**	0.00539	0.00149	0.4589	0.5411	0.000861	.	.	.	.	.	.

❺ In the Life Table results, the occurrence of the event (new purchase) is referred to as *Number Failed.*

The most important columns in Output 2.12 are the following:

❺ The number of events (second purchase) that occur in the interval

❻ The number of censored observations that are in the interval

❼ The effective sample size for the interval

❽ The estimated conditional probability of failure in the interval

❾ The hazard estimated at the midpoint of the interval

The Effective Sample Size

In this subsection, the PROC LIFETEST calculation is shown. The same notation used in PROC LIFETEST documentation is maintained.

Output 2.13 displays the summary of censored and uncensored customers and the total number of customers in the Garden data set. Note that 53.89% were censored by the end of the study in 31DEC2014.

Output 2.13: Summary of Censored (No Repurchase) and Uncensored (Repurchase)

Summary of the Number of Censored and Uncensored Values			
Total	Failed	Censored	Percent Censored
⑩ 676635	312009	364626	53.89

One of most important columns back in Output 2.12 is the Effective Sample Size because it is where the actuarial assumption is applied. Below, the values of the first row are defined and demonstrated (that is, the interval between 0 and 1).

The effective sample size is defined as the number of customers who have not yet purchased at the start of the month, assuming that censored customers are at risk of repurchase for only half of the month because the interval is measured in months. This is a major assumption because you have 7,969 customers censored in the first interval. However, only 7969/2 = 3984.5 are considered at risk of repurchase.

This difference in the midpoint interval created by PROC LIFETEST modifies the number of customers at risk of purchasing to only 3984.5, which is the reason that the at-risk adjustment is needed.

Figure 2.13 shows how the at-risk adjustment is applied.

Figure 2.13: Life-Table Method with At-Risk Adjustment for First Interval

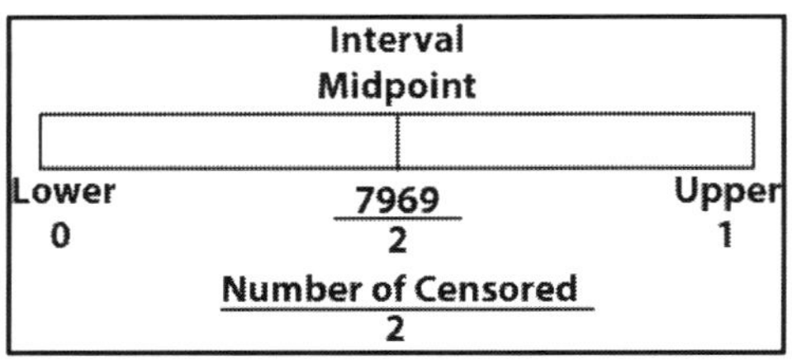

Calculate the effective sample size as follows:

$$n_i - \frac{w_i}{2}$$

The variables are as follows:

- n_i is the number of customers that enter the interval.
- w_i is the number of customers censored in the interval.

For the first interval (Lower = 0 to Upper = 1), there are the following:

- $n_1 = 676635$ is the number of customers (population at risk or repurchase) in the Garden data set.
- $w_1 = 7969$

Thus, you have the following:

$$\text{Effective sample size}_1 = \text{Population at risk}_1 - \frac{\text{Censor}_1}{2}$$

In this example, the formula yields the following:

$$\text{Effective sample size}_1 = 676635 - \frac{7969}{2} = 672650.5$$

The Conditional Probability of Failure

The conditional probability of failure $\hat{q}_i$ of an event is estimated as follows:

$$\hat{q}_i = \frac{d_i}{n_i - \frac{w_i}{2}}$$

The denominator is the already calculated effective sample size, $n_l - w_i/2$. The numerator, d_i, is the number of events or repurchases in each interval.
For the first interval (Lower = 0 to Upper = 1), there is the following:

$$d_1 = 77{,}470$$

Replacing these values in the formula, the conditional probability of failure is as follows:

$$\hat{q}_1 = \frac{\text{Purchase}_1}{\text{Effective sample size}_1}$$

This yields the following:

$$\hat{q}_1 = \frac{77{,}470}{672{,}650.5}$$

This reduces to the following value:

$$\hat{q}_1 = 0.1152$$

The conditional probability of failure $\hat{q}_1$ is as follows:

$$\frac{d_1}{n_1 - \frac{w_1}{2}} = 0.1152$$

The Hazard Estimated at the Midpoint

The hazard $\hat{h}_i$ estimated at the midpoint of the interval is represented by the following formula:

$$\hat{h}_i = \frac{2\hat{q}_i}{b_i(1+\hat{p}_i)}$$

Here, $\hat{p}_i = 1 - \hat{q}_i$. b_i *is* the width of the first interval = 1.

Knowing that $\hat{p}_i = 1 - \hat{q}_i$, for the first interval (Lower = 0 to Upper = 1), replace $\hat{p}_i$. Hazard is as follows:

$$\hat{h}_i = \frac{2\hat{q}_i}{b_i(1+\hat{p}_i)}$$

The result is as follows:

$$\hat{h}_i = \frac{2\hat{q}_i}{b_i(1+1-\hat{q}_i)}$$

This gives the following (Blossfeld 1989):

$$\hat{h}_i = \frac{2\hat{q}_i}{b_i(2-\hat{q}_i)}$$

Replace $\hat{q}_1 = 0.1152$ in the following:

$$\hat{h}_i = \frac{2\hat{q}_i}{b_i(2-\hat{q}_i)}$$

The result is as follows:

$$\hat{h}_i = \frac{2(0.1152)}{1(2-0.1152)}$$

This resolves to $\hat{h}_i = 0.122209$.

This value is an estimator of the average hazard rate at the midpoint of the first interval. The reality is that the probability of repurchasing in an interval is different from an empirical probability calculated and adjusted by SAS Enterprise Miner.

A question asked frequently is, "Why adjust the output from PROC LIFETEST?" The answer is, "If the desire is to understand and to calculate the empirical hazard and replicate the approach followed by SAS Enterprise Miner, one adjustment must be made because the denominator of the effective sample size is an input of the estimated hazard calculation. By correcting the denominator of the formula, exactly the same results presented in the SAS Enterprise Miner graphs are obtained."

Another more important reason is that the size of the sample can make a significant difference in the hazard values. The greater the number of ties and censored customers, the greater the difference between the hazard estimated by the Life Table method and the empirical hazard adjusted by SAS Enterprise Miner.

In a small data set, the difference is very small. But in a data set with more than 600,000 observations (as in the Garden data set), the difference is significant. In the next subsection, the denominator is adjusted.

The Empirical Hazard Function

Unfortunately, there is not an option in PROC LIFETEST to obtain the discrete values automatically. For pedagogical reasons, the adjustment is done by formulas, followed by implementation using Base SAS code.

Remember that the hazard at month t is the conditional probability that a customer will purchase at exactly month t, given that they did not purchase at any earlier time.

Letting the denominator be the number at risk of purchasing at the beginning of the month, you have the following:

$$\hat{h}(t) = \frac{\text{Number of customers who purchase this month}}{\text{Number of customers at risk of purchasing at the beginning of the month}}$$

Because the numerator was not affected by the interval midpoint modification used by PROC LIFETEST to apply the Life Table method, the only adjustment needed is to add back half of the censored customers. In Figure 2.14, the modified interval midpoint is at the top and the adjustment is at the bottom.

Figure 2.14: Empirical Discrete without Midpoint Adjustment

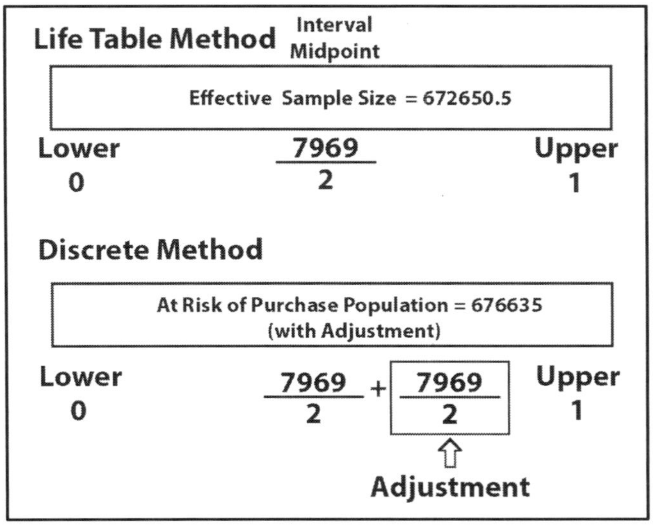

Step 2: At-Risk Adjustment

For the first interval (Lower = 0 to Upper = 1), the adjustment is calculated as follows:

$$\text{Population at risk}_1 = \text{Effective sample size}_1 + \frac{\text{Censor}_1}{2}$$

$$\text{Population at risk}_1 = 672650.5 + \frac{7969}{2} = 676635$$

Step 3: Empirical Hazard Calculation

Hazard for the first period is calculated by replacing the correct adjusted value in the formula:

$$h(t) = \frac{\text{Number of customers who purchase this month}}{\text{Number of customers at risk of purchasing at the beginning of the month}} = \frac{77{,}470}{676{,}635}$$

In our example, this results in the following:

$$h(t) = \frac{77470}{676635} = 0.11449$$

Program 2.6 implements the adjustment and computes the discrete empirical hazard.

Program 2.6: Computing the Empirical Hazard

```
data Lifetable_2;
set  Lifetable_1;
At_risk_population = effsize + censored/2; ❶
Hazard = Purchase /  At_risk_population;    ❷
run;
```

Output 2.14 shows the partial output of the Lifetable_2 data set.

Output 2.14: Lifetable_2 Data Set (Partial Output)

Time reported by Month	Purchase (Censor =1)	NO Purchase (Censor = 0)	At_risk_population	Hazard Function
0	77470	7969	❶ 676635	❷ 0.11449
1	64394	13505	591196	0.10892
2	31542	11393	513297	0.06145
3	22810	8639	470362	0.04849
4	17373	8548	438913	0.03958
5	14449	8219	412992	0.03499
6	11795	10567	390324	0.03022
7	9792	8031	367962	0.02661
8	8437	8138	350139	0.02410
9	7189	10026	333564	0.02155
10	6083	6982	316350	0.01923
11	5731	6123	303285	0.01890
12	5609	5184	291431	0.01925
.	.	.	.	.
.	.	.	.	.
.	.	.	.	.
40	169	5881	49713	0.00340
41	154	5329	43663	0.00353
42	113	5500	38180	0.00296
43	89	7208	32567	0.00273
44	72	6267	25270	0.00285
45	51	8000	18931	0.00269
46	20	6050	10880	0.00184
47	13	4797	4810	0.00270

Step 4: Graphics and Interpretation

Figures 2.15 and 2.16 represent the Empirical Hazard function in continuous and discrete distributions measured by month. The Empirical Hazard function provides a response to one of the most fundamental and strategically important questions asked by a company, “How frequently do customers repurchase new products?”

Figure 2.15: Hazard Function with Time Reported by Month

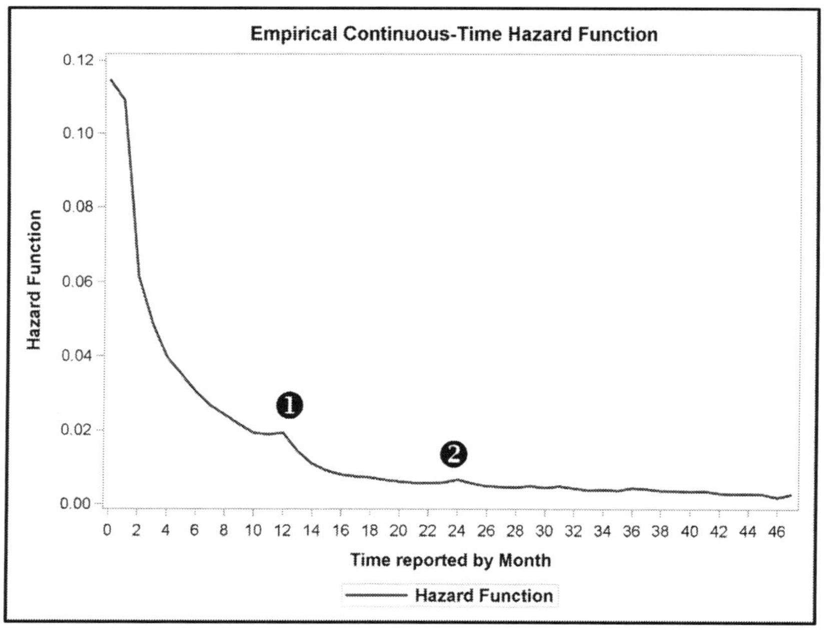

Figure 2.16: Needle Graph of Hazard Function with Time Reported by Month

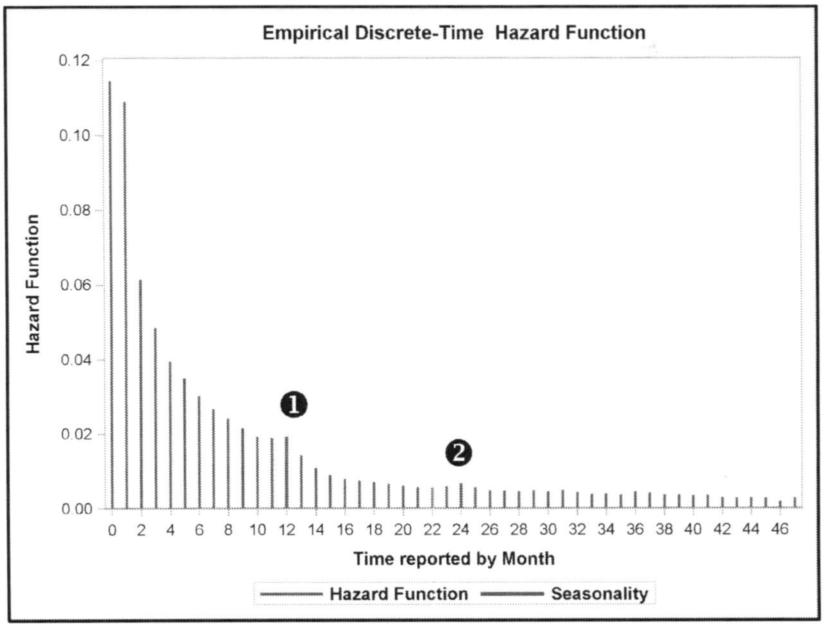

You can see the seasonality effect where customers are more likely to make a second purchase at 12 ❶ or 24 ❷ months after the start date. The business explanation for this pattern could be as follows:

- Some customers purchase every year (in the same month) products for the garden, holidays, Valentine's Day, and so on.
- Products are sold only for one specific period, such as decorations for Halloween or Christmas.
- Safety and security products must be replaced every period, creating an annual demand.
- Car accessories are purchased more in the summer and are linked to holiday demand or in the winter, when customers buy products to deal with snow and ice.

As time goes on, it becomes clear that the probability of the customer repurchasing decreases, especially after two months. This might be interpreted in several ways in terms of marketing initiatives. It might be prudent to advertise or promote to customers to encourage them to repurchase for a short period after an initial purchase. Alternatively, it might be worth designing marketing interventions to revive customer interest after a certain time of inactivity, such as three to six months of no repurchase. This stops them from becoming lost customers. Another option would be to do further research to understand how offerings could be improved to maximize spending from frequently repurchasing customers or to appeal to customers who have not repurchased since their initial purchase.

The peak at the beginning of the month (the month is not necessarily January because the customer can purchase during any month of the year) can suggest several situations. The substantially higher initial hazard values might be explained by customers needing to make second purchases to satisfy their original requirement in situations such as the following:

- Painting an area and determining that the quantity of paint purchased is insufficient.
- A tool does not do the job required. For example, a screwdriver purchased is tiny.
- A bulb is not powerful enough to light up a room.
- A plant is bought and it requires a specific fertilizer.

In these cases, the purchase of the first product creates the need for a second purchase. Additional data mining could confirm the reason for the second purchase, and marketing initiatives could be customized accordingly.

The Hazard function is more intuitive to use in survival analysis than any other tool because it quantifies the likelihood that the customer's second purchase will take place at time t, given that the customer did not purchase before time t. The conclusion derived from the hazard graphics is that as hazard is decreasing, the likelihood of a second purchase decreases each month. It is very plausible in time-to-next-purchase models that some input variables are more important as predictors of repurchase at the beginning (first two months), and then they lose their significance later when the hazard becomes constant.

Once the Empirical Hazard function that captures the likelihood of a second purchase has been developed, the next step is to split the database into a training data set and a validation data set. This is essential because the model is created using the training data set and validated using the validation data set.

Data Storage Formats

Data is stored in various ways. The format in which the data is presented changes the options when you are performing survival analysis using SAS Enterprise Miner.

In this section, data set options in the SAS Enterprise Miner Survival node are explained by referring to and relating them to the data sets and formats presented earlier in this chapter: the Customer-Level data set with the Standard format and the Month data set with the Expanded format.

Understanding the format of your data and having the ability to create a table in the desired format are fundamental when performing survival analysis. Although SAS Enterprise Miner is capable of managing different data formats, a failure to understand the difference between the data formats can lead to producing results that are not interpretable. This makes it impossible to progress to more advanced models such as the stress test or IFRS 9.

Customer-Level Data Set (Standard Format)

The SAS Enterprise Miner Survival node refers to the Customer-Level data set with the Standard data format. The Customer-Level data set contains all the customer information in a single row. Hence, customer IDs are not repeated.

Figure 2.17: SAS Enterprise Miner Train Display in Standard Data Format

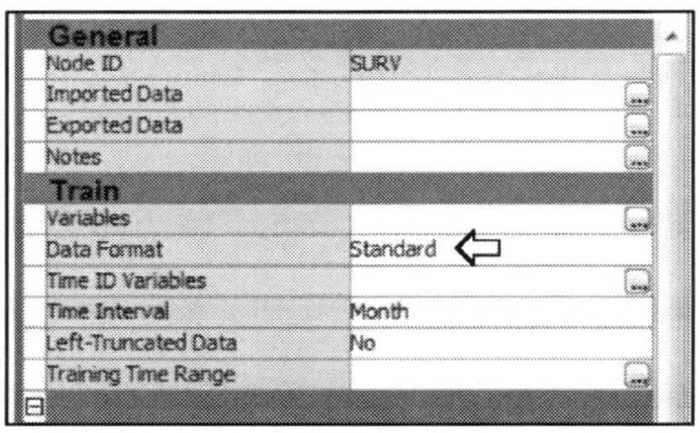

Month Data Set (Expanded Format)

The SAS Enterprise Miner Survival node refers to the Month data set with the Expanded data format. Fully expanded data refers to transactional data where each row is a different transaction. Customer IDs might be repeated. Note that in the Month data set, the ID variable is required and two time ID variables are required. Both must share the same date or date time format, and the _t_ variable is required.

Figure 2.18: SAS Enterprise Miner Train Display in Expanded Data Format

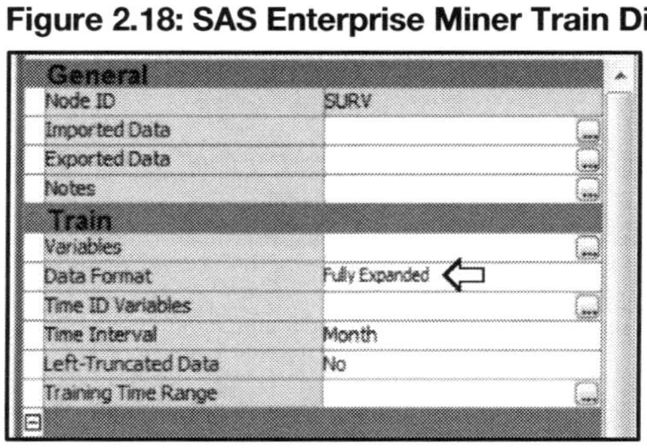

Chapter 3: Stratified Sampling Method for Survival Analysis

Introduction

This chapter demonstrates how to create a stratified sample for a survival analysis model. Stratifying the database—and sampling from all strata at the same rate of a categorical or binary distribution—ensures that the stratum proportions in the sample (model, training, validation, test, and scoring data sets) match the stratum proportions in the database.

For example, if a categorical variable such as Account_Origin has 10% equal to Post in the basis population, stratified sampling should have the same proportion (10%) for Post in each sample.

Survival analysis sampling in the context of time-to-next-purchase requires a flexible approach, one which factors in sub-segments, categories of products, and customers. All existing relevant products and channels should be carefully considered and assessed within the context of the new sample. For this reason, having a solid understanding of a company's commercial business is essential.

The database for survival modeling needs to address all of this information, be relevant, and be flexible enough to quickly adapt to any changes in seasonality demand. This can be achieved only by using a Strata variable to obtain the same proportion of observations from the original Garden data set for both modeling and scoring. In survival data mining with a significant number of observations, sampling reduces the size of the data to improve processing times. Sampling is so important that any mistake at this stage invalidates the whole modeling process.

To address these sampling and modeling challenges, modelers need to have advanced programming skills in Base SAS or experience with SAS/STAT procedures. Or, they need to know how to implement the end-to-end sampling process using SAS Enterprise Miner. SAS Enterprise Miner has the advantage of not requiring advanced Base SAS programming skills. This makes the sampling process more accessible to a wider audience and easier to go through.

The principal reason to develop a sample using PROC SURVEYSELECT is that in many financial service companies, banks, insurance companies, and building societies, sampling is performed before the data is imported into SAS Enterprise Miner. Another reason is that PROC SURVEYSELECT and PROC SQL are more commonly used when data is from multiple sources. In any case, the equivalent SAS Enterprise Miner flowcharts to develop a sample using the Sample node and Data Partition node are provided.

The principal motivation to use the Sample node in SAS Enterprise Miner is that its flowchart can support and handle a large number of models, it ensures auditability, and it can quickly assess the impact of changes in modeling based on variables and their deployment. This process enables modelers to use previous modeling work, adjust models quickly, and easily reuse models for other purposes.

Begin by focusing on the proportion of the variable Start by month and strata. This is a key element of the sampling process.

For analysts with limited experience in sampling, Svolba (2006) and Refaat (2007) have written books about the SAS/STAT and SAS Enterprise Miner environments.

The Sampling Process with PROC SURVEYSELECT

It is critical to develop models and validate them using an established and robust process, even if data mining does not always follow patterns of scientific laws. You must assess the performance of the model on alternative data sets or subsets of customers on which it was not built. This provides confidence that the performance of the model should hold with future populations, while demonstrating that the model is not over-fitted to the model data set. For survival analysis models, you are required to apportion the data into three parts: Model (Part_TRAIN) data set, Validation (Part_VALIDATE), and Scoring.

The ultimate goal of our research and modeling is to determine whether and when a customer makes a second purchase. A key requirement of the model, validation, and scoring data sets is that they must have the same period of time (same months and years) as the full original database.

A stratified sample for survival analysis differs from the stratified sample for a propensity model. This is because in a survival analysis sample, time must be considered as part of the sampling strata. The Time variable does not exist in propensity models. Other variables in the sampling strata are Censor (to maintain the proportion of customers who do and do not make a second purchase) and Strata. The Strata variable determines the number of purchases made over a customer's lifetime.

Although particular variables have been selected as the sampling strata, you are not limited to them. Variables can include any categorical variables that are important. You could have variables such as region, gender, and channel or customer acquisition.

In this section, you learn how to split the Garden data set into a Model_Shopping (70%) data set and Score_Shopping (30%) data set using PROC SURVERYSELECT and PROC SQL in SAS/STAT.

Figure 3.1 illustrates how to create the subsets of data from the full Garden data set.

Figure 3.1: Sampling Process Using PROC SURVEYSLECT and PROC SQL

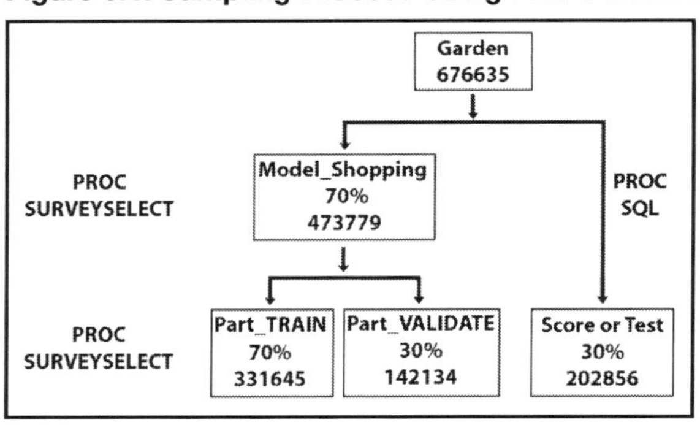

1. From the Garden data set, extract the first sample (Model_Shopping), which contains 70% (473,779 observations) of the available data using PROC SURVEYSELECT.
2. Extract the second sample (Score_Shopping or test), which contains 30% (202,856 observations) of the available data using PROC SQL.
3. Split the Model_Shopping data set into two parts:
   a. Part_TRAIN, which contains 70% (331,645 observations) of the available data using PROC SURVEYSELECT.
   b. Part_VALIDATE, which contains 30% (142,134 observations) of the available data using PROC SQL.

Step 3 is just a repetition of steps 1 and 2. With some knowledge of SAS macros, this process can be improved. However, the focus of this chapter is to present a general method that works for all survival models created in this book.

The Model_Shopping data set is imported into SAS Enterprise Miner later.

Step 1: Analyze Sample Proportion for Strata

The first step of stratified sampling is to understand the proportion of customers in each category of the current strata. Use PROC FREQ with the Strata variable on the full Garden data set.

Remember, the values of the Strata variable were agreed upon before you started the modeling process by consulting with stakeholders from different areas of the business.

Program 3.1 shows the PROC FREQ code run on the Garden data set.

Program 3.1: Strata Percent Code for the Garden Data Set

```
proc freq data=Garden;
   tables Strata;
run;
```

Output 3.1 shows the PROC FREQ results.

Output 3.1: Strata Percent Results for the Garden Data Set

Strata (20-Strata Total Orders)				
Strata	Frequency	Percent	Cumulative Frequency	Cumulative Percent
01-02-(2011-2013)	334685	**49.46**	334685	49.46
01-02-(2014)	130277	**19.25**	464962	68.72
03-04	49094	**7.26**	514056	75.97
05-10	29877	**4.42**	543933	80.39
11-20	111713	**16.51**	655646	96.90
21-High	20989	**3.10**	676635	100.00

All customers fit into one of the defined categories and there are no missing customers. If missing values exist within the Strata variable, the definition of the Strata variable must be modified to ensure that all customers are defined by one of the stratum.

When sampling the population into Model_Shopping and Validation data sets, it is crucial that the percentage distribution (as highlighted by the column Percent in Output 3.1) is maintained in both the Model_Shopping and Validation data sets. If it is not, the sample is biased, and it could nullify the results of the model validation. Moreover, a biased model whose aim is to predict the total number of purchases by month might have a detrimental impact on a business if the strata proportions in the original data set and the samples are not identical.

Another imperative task is to verify that the number of customers making their first purchase in the study period by month is included in the model documentation. This information is important for validating the model. It can be obtained by modifying Program 3.1 to include the variable Start and format monyy7. as shown in Program 3.2.

Program 3.2: Strata Percent Code for the Garden Data Set by Month

```
proc freq data=Garden;
   tables start;
   format start monyy7.;
run;
```

Output 3.2 is generated by Program 3.2.

Output 3.2: Customers' Start by Month

Start – (02-Day of the First Purchase)				
Start	Frequency	Percent	Cumulative Frequency	Cumulative Percent
JAN2011	9610	❶ 1.42	9610	1.42
FEB2011	11409	1.69	21019	3.11
MAR2011	14640	2.16	35659	5.27
APR2011	12237	1.81	47896	7.08
MAY2011	13622	2.01	61518	9.09
JUN2011	10959	1.62	72477	10.71
JUL2011	10388	1.54	82865	12.25
AUG2011	11240	1.66	94105	13.91
SEP2011	12798	1.89	106903	15.80
OCT2011	14368	2.12	121271	17.92
NOV2011	13406	1.98	134677	19.90
DEC2011	9676	1.43	144353	21.33
.....	.....	.....	.....	.....
.....	.....	.....	.....	.....
.....	.....	.....	.....	.....
JAN2014	12255	1.81	495876	73.29
FEB2014	13110	1.94	508986	75.22
MAR2014	18028	2.66	527014	77.89
APR2014	15596	2.30	542610	80.19
MAY2014	16092	2.38	558702	82.57
JUN2014	19117	2.83	577819	85.40
JUL2014	15795	2.33	593614	87.73
AUG2014	15541	2.30	609155	90.03
SEP2014	15410	2.28	624565	92.30
OCT2014	19097	2.82	643662	95.13
NOV2014	21338	3.15	665000	98.28
DEC2014	11635	1.72	❷ 676635	100.00

❶ This value is the percentage of customers making a purchase in January 2011.
❷ This value is the total number of customers in the full database.

Step 2: Create the Model_Shopping Sample

Begin by creating the Model_Shopping data set. It is common for 70% of the available sample to be partitioned as modeling data and 30% for validating the model. This enables you to have robust volumes for the modeling process and, at the same time, to have sufficient volumes for the validation. Some businesses have different preferences. Therefore, the apportionment of the model and validation data sets is another factor that should be agreed upon before starting the modeling process.

The SURVEYSELECT procedure was used to create the Model_Shopping sample. A prerequisite of the SURVEYSELECT procedure is to sort the data by the chosen Strata variable or variables. In this case, these variables are Time, Censor, and Strata. In Program 3.3, this task is accomplished by performing a PROC SORT on the Garden data set, which creates the sorted data as a temporary data set named Sorted.

Program 3.3: Creating the Model_Shopping Data Set

```
proc sort data=Garden out=sorted;
by Time Censor Strata ❺;
run;

proc surveyselect data=sorted
method    = SRS          ❶
samprate  = 0.7          ❷
seed      = 123456789 ❸
out       = Model_Shopping ❹;
strata Time Censor Strata ❺;
run;
```

The SURVEYSELECT procedure uses the temporary sorted data set to create the Model_Shopping ❹ data set. A number of options must be defined for the procedure to sample correctly.

- The statement METHOD=SRS ❶ specifies the selection method to be used. A method of sampling is required to maintain the proportions of the Strata variable. SRS (simple random sampling) is used in this example. You can use any equal-probability, without-replacement selection method. Or, you could use systematic selection (METHOD=SYS) or sequential selection (METHOD=SEQ). The SRS method selects customers with equal probability and without replacement.
- The SAMPRATE= 0.7 ❷ option specifies the sampling rate value, which is defined as 0.7 or 70%. The sampling rate value must always be a positive number and is the sampling rate applied to all strata.
- The statement SEED=123456789 ❸ is the random SEED option. This enables the user to retain the initial seed so that the sample can be re-created at a different date or time. Being able to replicate the samples is useful for companies that work in regulated environments that require re-creation of the model from the documentation. Without specifying the SEED option, this is not possible.
- The output data set is named in the OUT= Model_Shopping ❹ statement. This data set contains the records selected for the sample based on the options specified for the SURVERYSELECT procedure.
- The STRATA Time Censor Strata ❺ statement defines the independent groups of variables from which the procedure creates the sample according to the defined selection method and sampling parameters.

Output 3.3 provides the results from Program 3.3.

Output 3.3: PROC SURVEYSELECT Information

Selection Method	❶ Simple Random Sampling
Strata Variables	❺ Time
	Censor
	Strata
Input Data Set	SORTED
Random Number Seed	❸ 123456789
Stratum Sampling Rate	❷ 0.7
Number of Strata	296
Total Sample Size	473779
Output Data Set	❹ MODEL_SHOPPING

The PROC SURVEYSELECT output is the total sample size, 473,779, which is approximately equal to 70% of the original Garden data set.

Other areas to verify are the selection method ❶ (simple random sampling), the output data set name ❹ (Model_Shopping), and the Strata variables ❺ (Time, Censor, and Strata). As confirmation, you can see that the random number seed ❸ and the stratum sampling rate ❹ are also applied as specified in Program 3.3.

Step 3: Create the Score_Shopping Sample

The Score_Shopping sample represents a subset of the Garden data set that is not a part of the Model_Shopping data set.

In Figure 3.2, customers that are in the Garden data set but not in the Model_Shopping sample belong in the Score_ Shopping data set.

Figure 3.2: PROC SQL Flowchart

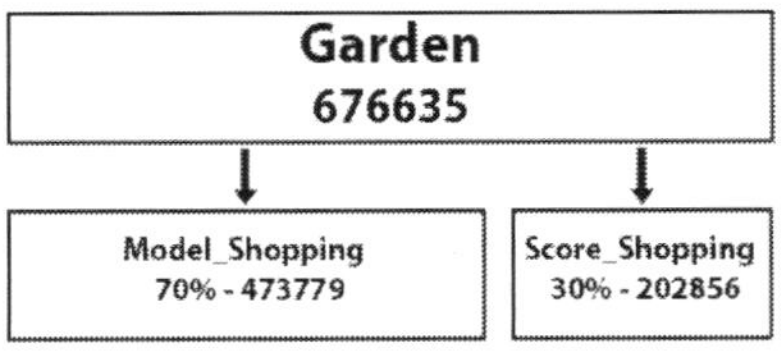

Program 3.4 uses PROC SQL to create the Score_Shopping sample from the Garden data by reducing the rows to customers who are not in the Model_Shopping data set. There are many different ways to create this sample. PROC SQL has been chosen because it is concise and intuitive.

Program 3.4: Creating the Score_Shopping Sample with PROC SQL

```
proc sql;
create table Score_Shopping ❶ as
select  * ❷
from Garden ❸
where id_number not in ❹ (select id_number from Model_Shopping);
quit;
```

❶ The program creates a temporary data set named Score_Shopping.

❷ It selects all variables.

❸ Selections are from the original Garden data set.

❹ Selection is made for an Id_number that is not an Id_number from the Model_Shopping data set.

This correctly limits the number of customers to represent 30% of the total Garden data set.

This PROC SQL program works like an EXCEPT operator, which includes all unique rows (customers) from the first table that are not found in the second table.

The same results could be achieved in the more efficient code in Program 3.5.

Program 3.5: Comparing the Results with PROC FREQ

```
proc surveyselect data=sorted
method    = SRS
samprate = 0.7
seed      = 123456789
out       = Model_Shopping
outall;❶
strata Time Censor Strata;
run;
```

❶ The OUTALL option creates a flag variable that divides the sample into non-overlapping groups as follows:

$$\text{Selected} = \begin{cases} = \ 1 \ \text{ if the Customer is selected (70\%)} \\ = \ 0 \ \text{ if the Customer is not selected (30\%)} \end{cases}$$

Output 3.4 presents the five rows of the output data set Model_Shopping.

Output 3.4: Variable Selected for the Model_Shopping Data Set

Id_number	Selected	Time	Censor	Strata
665001	1	0	0	01-02-(2014)
665002	0	0	0	01-02-(2014)
665003	1	0	0	01-02-(2014)
665004	1	0	0	01-02-(2014)
665005	0	0	0	01-02-(2014)

You can see in the second column of Output 3.4 that PROC SURVEYSELECT created the dummy variable Selected. This indicates whether the specific row or customer was selected. By creating a SAS DATA step, you can split the original Model_Shopping data set into two using an IF/THEN statement as follows:

```
data Model_Shopping (drop=selected)
     Score_Shopping (drop=selected);
 set Model_Shopping;
     if selected=1 then output Model_Shopping;
else if selected=0 then output Score_shopping;
run;
```

The OUTALL option achieves the same results without using PROC SQL. The OUTALL option is more efficient, but SQL is the standard language in database management in the financial world.

Step 4: Compare the Results from the Model_Shopping and Score_Shopping Data Sets

Now that the Model_Shopping and Score_Shopping data sets have been created, we should verify the results by confirming that the proportion of the variable Strata values in these data sets is representative of the Strata variable values in the Garden data set. You achieve this using PROC FREQ in Program 3.6.

Program 3.6: Comparing the Results Using PROC FREQ

```
proc freq data = Model_Shopping ❶;
tables strata;
run;
proc freq data = Score_Shopping ❷;
tables strata;
run;
```

Program 3.6 has been adapted so that PROC FREQ refers to the Model_Shopping ❶ and Score_Shopping ❷ data sets. Both Output 3.5 and Output 3.6 display the proportion of the Strata variable for the Model_Shopping and Score_Shopping data sets.

Output 3.5: PROC FREQ Output for Model_Shopping and Score_Shopping Data Sets: Model_Shopping

20-Strata Total Orders				
Strata	Frequency	❶ Percent	Cumulative Frequency	Cumulative Percent
01-02-(2011-2013)	234317	49.46	234317	49.46
01-02-(2014)	91205	19.25	325522	68.71
03-04	34388	7.26	359910	75.97
05-10	20939	4.42	380849	80.39
11-20	78219	16.51	459068	96.89
21-High	14711	3.11	473779	100.00

Output 3.6: PROC FREQ Output for Model_Shopping and Score_Shopping Data Sets: Score_Shopping

20-Strata Total Orders				
Strata	Frequency	❶ Percent	Cumulative Frequency	Cumulative Percent
01-02-(2011-2013)	100368	49.48	100368	49.48
01-02-(2014)	39072	19.26	139440	68.74
03-04	14706	7.25	154146	75.99
05-10	8938	4.41	163084	80.39
11-20	33494	16.51	196578	96.91
21-High	6278	3.09	202856	100.00

Although the frequencies differ considerably between the two samples, the proportions are similar when you compare the percentages of each category with the Strata variable. This is important because any significant differences in the proportions could result in errors in model validation. For further verification,

Table 3.1 compares the Percent column for the Garden, Model_Shopping, and Score_Shopping data sets from Output 3.5 and Output 3.6. The proportions are very close, which shows that the sampling strategy has worked as intended.

Table 3.1: Comparing Percentages of Strata Variable

Strata	Garden	Model_Shopping	Score_Shopping
01–02-(2011–2013)	49.46	49.46	49.48
01–02-(2014)	19.25	19.25	19.26
03–05	7.26	7.26	7.25
05–10	4.42	4.42	4.41
10–20	16.51	16.51	16.51
21-High	3.10	3.11	3.09

SAS Enterprise Miner Nodes

This section introduces the SAS Enterprise Miner Sample node and Data Partition node and compares them to the sampling process using PROC SURVEYSLECT and PROC SQL.

The Sample Node

Figure 3.3 shows the SAS Enterprise Miner Sample node. The Sample node enables you to extract a sample from the input data source (Garden).

Figure 3.3: Sample Node

The use of sampling nodes in data-intensive applications such as data mining can greatly reduce the amount of processing time. If the sample data is sufficiently representative of the whole data set, patterns in the entire database will be present in the sample data set. This means that no pattern is lost. SAS Enterprise Miner enables you to perform a number of sampling techniques, such as random, stratified, and cluster sampling. The Sample node writes the sampled observations to an output data set and saves the Seed value so that the samples can be replicated.

To tackle the number and frequency of the strata choices, the SAS Enterprise Miner Sample node offers high performance in a controlled customization environment so that modelers can easily adjust and redeploy different sample approaches and compare the performance of many models, each one coming from a different sample.

The Survival node has an outcome-dependent sampling method. There is no need for the Sample node in SAS Enterprise Miner for survival analysis, but the node is useful to extract samples from servers or databases.

The Data Partition Node

The Data Partition node can statistically split a data set into three data sets: one for training, one for validation, and one for scoring, the latter of which is not used in building the model, but is used as a holdout sample. These data sets are carried along through the process flow and used during model assessment.

Figure 3.4 shows the SAS Enterprise Miner Data Partition node.

Figure 3.4: Data Partition Node

The Flowchart

Figure 3.5 has been created specially to illustrate how to sample using PROC SURVEYSELECT in Base SAS and SAS/STAT. A key advantage of SAS Enterprise Miner is that the equivalent of Figure 3.5 is created automatically in a diagram, with standardized names for data sets and the folders that hold them.

SAS Enterprise Miner displays the data set names in a diagram as seen in Figure 3.5, with output that shows data sets with standardized names. With practice, you can quickly discern which output is being entered at each step. For example, a Data Partition node is applied only as a precursor to building a model so that it will read in the main data output by the Sample node.

There are a couple of things to note about PROC SURVEYSELECT compared with SAS Enterprise Miner nodes. First, it should be clear that the same output generated by PROC SURVEYSELECT can be created using the Sample node in SAS Enterprise Miner. The Sample node should be used in situations in which it might not be feasible to process the entire input data set. The Data Partition node partitions all input data, so if the size of the data set is small, then use the Data Partition node. If the data set is large, then use the Sample node. This decision is a function of the hardware limitations of the computer.

Second, using a Data Partition node creates a single step in SAS Enterprise Miner. It is far simpler than the two-step PROC SURVEYSELECT or PROC SQL process.

Figure 3.5: Garden, Model (Part_TRAIN), and Validation (Part_VALIDATE)

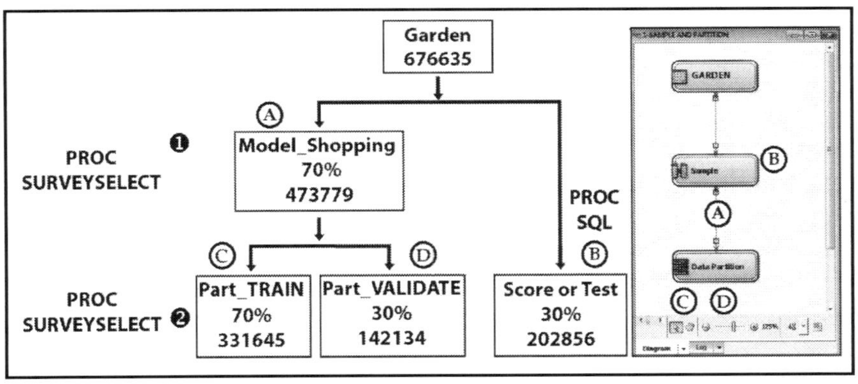

The SAS Enterprise Miner flowchart shown in Figure 3.5 replicates the same strategy as PROC SURVEYSELECT:

❶ The Sample node creates the data sets Ⓐ (Model_Shopping) and Ⓑ (Score_Shopping) by importing the data from the input data node (named Garden). The Sample node is the second node in the process flow diagram.

❷ The Data Partition node splits the Model_Shopping data set into two parts:

- **Part_TRAIN** Ⓒ has 70% (331,645 observations) of the available data set.
- **Part_VALIDATE** Ⓓ has 30% (142134 observations) of the available data set.

By default, the Data Partition node preserves the chronological order (months, quarters, and years) of the observations in the training (Part_TRAIN) and validation (Part_VALIDATE) data sets.

After the samples are obtained and the model is created, hazard calculations for each segment of the portfolio can be performed using a discrete method.

Chapter 4: SAS Enterprise Miner Use from Source to Customer-Level Model Output

Introduction

This chapter shows you how to open SAS Enterprise Miner, start a new project, create a data source, and perform other tasks. The focus is on how to create the required process flow to develop a model using the Survival node. By the end of this chapter, you should have gained enough understanding of the Survival node to be sufficiently prepared for more advanced topics, such as competing risk or IFRS 9 models.

The chapter goes through the required steps in sufficient detail as reference for anyone using SAS Enterprise Miner to create survival models (with the Standard format). The steps allow full traceability from source to final model output, thereby minimizing the effort required for model review, validation, and explanation.

When building a model, it is crucial that the project be managed as a series of specific and fundamental tasks. There should be clarity at each stage about what has to be done. SAS Enterprise Miner provides the means to do this. For each step, SAS Enterprise Miner creates output tables with standardized names. You should be aware of what the input and output tables are for each step.

Creating the Process Flow

Figure 4.1 shows a step-by-step process to create a survival model process flow.

Figure 4.1: Creating a Survival Model Process Flow

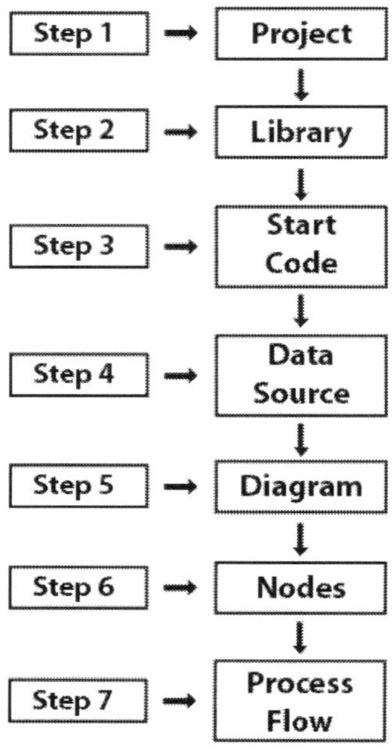

Step 1: Create a new project. SAS Enterprise Miner requires a folder in which the data sources, full code, diagrams, results, and project users are stored. This is advantageous because everything from source data to final model output is stored in one place—in files and folders with distinct standardized names that are created and referenced by SAS Enterprise Miner. This offers a clear audit trail of how grouped analyses such as Customer-Level survival have been generated.

Step 2: Create a new library. These are shortcut locations for data sources that are accessible by the SAS Foundation Server. To use data sources, they must be visible to the SAS Foundation Server via a predefined SAS library. By assigning libraries in SAS Enterprise Miner, the location of data sources can be referenced easily using library references—that is, without the need for full file paths. A library can correspond to a directory on the SAS Foundation Services, a relational database, or even an Excel workbook.

Step 3: Create start code. Start code is run when a project is opened and a node is run. It is used to set up required libraries, SAS options, macro variables, and so on. It offers a flexible way to customize the SAS environment in which SAS Enterprise Miner operates. Start code is distinct from the SAS Code node used within a process flow. The SAS Code node is presented in Chapter 8 in the section, "Analyzing the Optimized Score Code."

Step 4: Create a new data source. SAS Enterprise Miner enables you to set up a metadata source ready for modeling analysis by going through a few steps. Once you complete the steps, all the information associated with the data, including the directory path to the file that creates the data, the name of the data file, and the names and measurement scales of the variables in the data set, is recorded by SAS Enterprise Miner. SAS Enterprise Miner saves all of this metadata as data sets in a folder called Data Sources in the project directory. By requiring this information, SAS Enterprise Miner makes the purpose of input data to the modeling process explicit. It is simple to understand how the source data is being used.

Step 5: Create a process flow diagram. Process flow diagrams map data sources to nodes to final model output. They are visual and enable you to quickly understand the sequence required for multistage analysis. The user can inspect, run, and modify different parts of the process flow as required.

Step 6: Insert the Data Partition node. Nodes are the SAS Enterprise Miner tools available to the user. The nodes used in this chapter are the Data Source node, the Data Partition node, and the Survival node.

Many nodes can be replicated using existing SAS code and procedures. SAS Enterprise Miner offers the SAS Code node to be able to do this. SAS Enterprise Miner nodes minimize the chance of mistakes and ensure code and approaches are consistent. They are easy to visualize within a process flow.

Step 7: Create the survival process flow. The process flow is a logical connection of nodes in a map for the data mining project. For example, in Figure 4.2, you see a process flow with three nodes.

Figure 4.2: Process Flow with Three Nodes

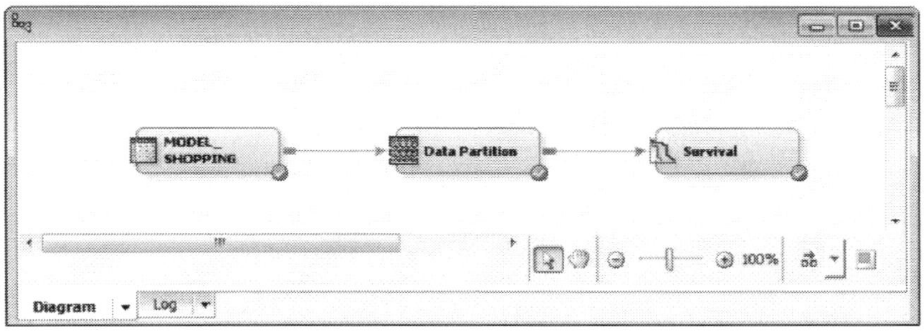

Step 1: Create a New Project

Before opening SAS Enterprise Miner, you need to create a folder such as C:\TheBook. This is where the full project will be stored.

1. Click the SAS Enterprise Miner icon on your desktop. The “Welcome to Enterprise Miner” window appears as shown in Figure 4.3. Click **New Project**.

   Figure 4.3: Opening the SAS Enterprise Miner Welcome Window

   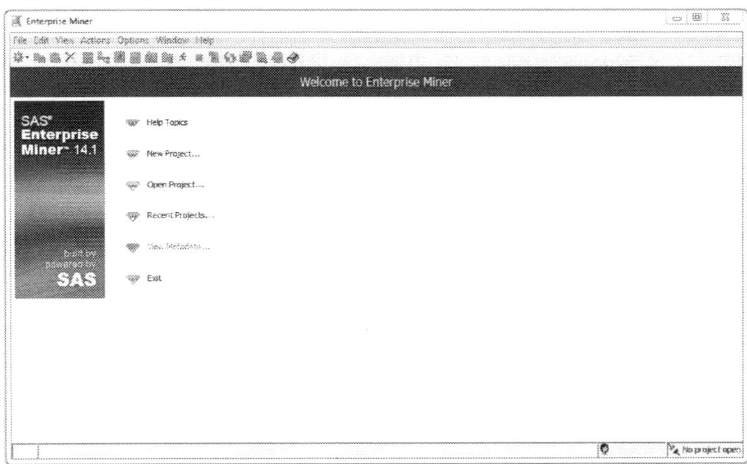

2. To create a SAS Enterprise Miner project, specify a project name and location. Name the new project **Shopping**.

   Figure 4.4: Specifying the Project Name and Location

3. For **SAS Server Directory**, enter **C:\TheBook**.
4. Click **Next**. A new window appears, which shows the new project information. Review the project information. Click **Back** if you need to make changes.
5. Click **Finish** when you are finished. The new project is created. The SAS Enterprise Miner interface now shows the new project.
6. View the four principal components needed to create a survival data mining project.

Figure 4.5: Four Principal Components of a Project

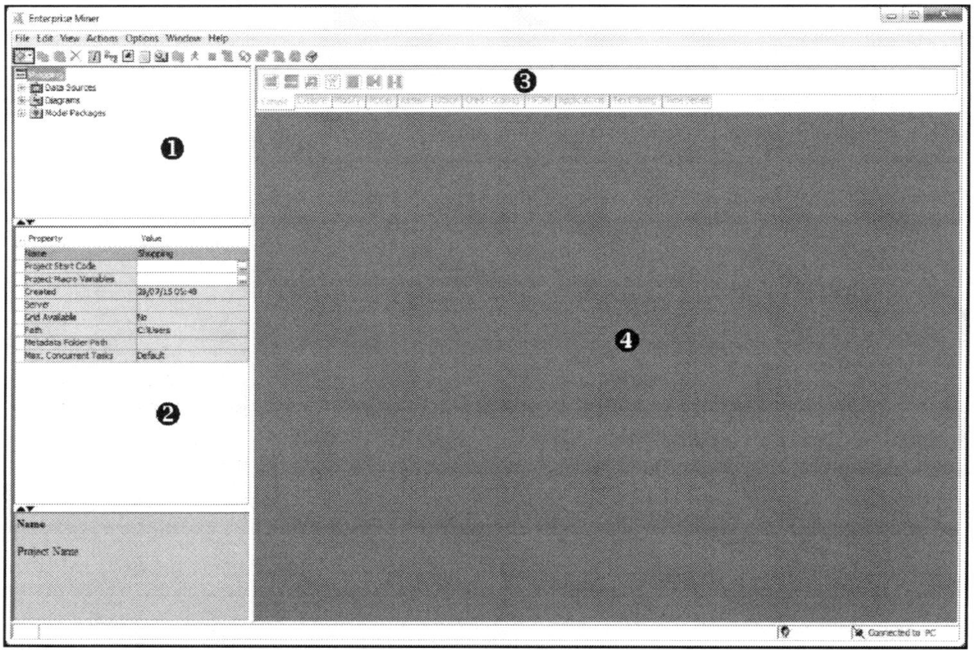

❶ **Project panel**. This panel is for viewing, creating, deleting, and modifying the data sources, diagrams, and model packages.

❷ **Properties panel**. In this panel, the properties of selected projects, data sources, diagrams, nodes, and model packages are shown. You can view and modify the options of each node created.

❸ **Node toolbar and tabs**. The tabs are for selecting different node buttons used to create the process flow diagram in the diagram workspace ❹. The text name of any tool is displayed when you position your mouse pointer over the button. The node toolbar and buttons together are called the *tools palette.*

❹ **Diagram workspace**: This area is for building and running the process flow diagram for the project with nodes of SAS Enterprise Miner.

For details about each component, see *SAS Enterprise Miner: Reference Help.*

Step 2: Create a New Library

A library connects SAS Enterprise Miner to the data sources (SAS data sets), which are the basis of your analysis or model. To create a library, you need to know the name and location of the data that you want to work with.

1. Create a new folder named **Chap4** within **C:\TheBook**. This is the library folder where the Model_Shopping data set needs to be placed.
2. In SAS Enterprise Miner, select **File ▶ New ▶ Library**.
3. Click **Next**. The Data Source Library Wizard—Step 1 of 3 Select Action window, appears.

Figure 4.6: Data Source Library Wizard—Step 1 of 3 Select Action

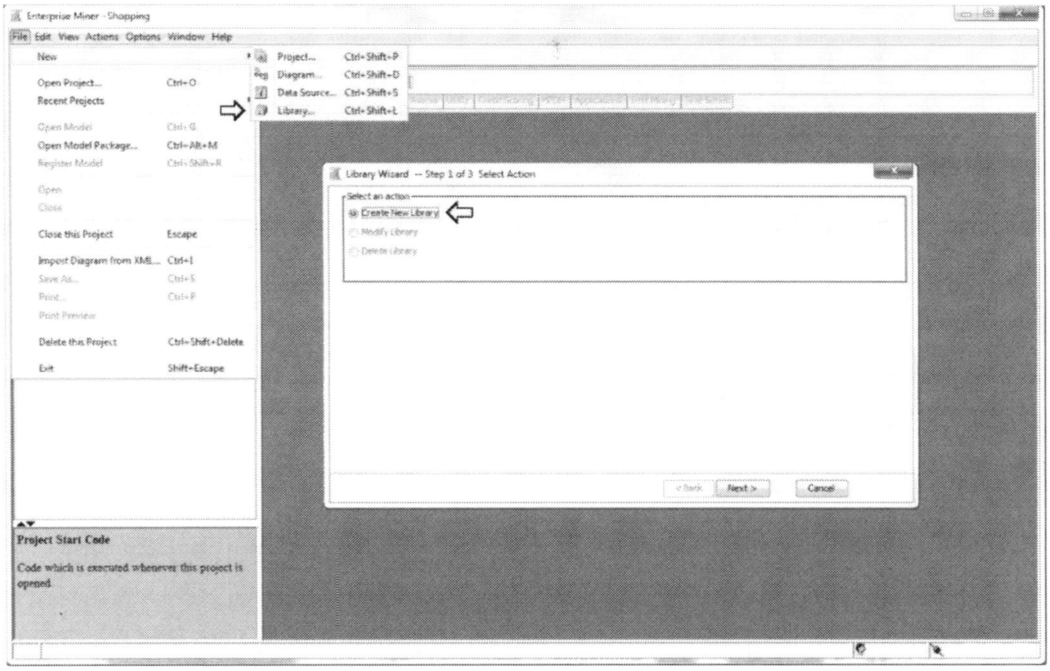

4. Click **Next**. The Data Source Library Wizard—Step 2 of 3 Create or Modify window appears.

Figure 4.7: Data Source Library Wizard

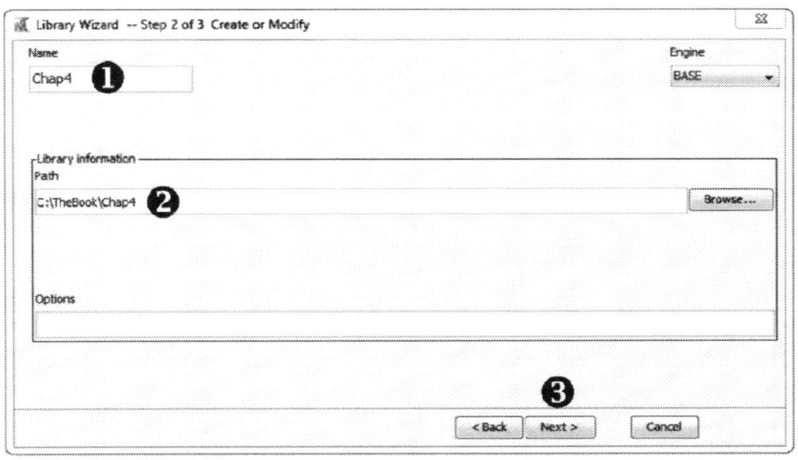

5. For **Name**, enter **Chap4** ❶.
6. For **Path**, enter **C:\TheBook\Chap4** ❷. You can navigate to the folder when defining a library.
7. Click **Next** ❸. The Data Source Library Wizard—Step 3 of 3 Confirm Action window is displayed, showing the name, type, and path of the created SAS library.
8. Click **Finish**. The data set Model_Shopping can now be used in SAS Enterprise Miner.

Step 3: Create Start Code

The principal reason for creating Start Code is to modify the library and the folder where the project is saved. Start Code is used to affect the environment of the SAS code submitted by SAS Enterprise Miner (for example, with OPTIONS, TITLE, and LIBNAME statements). The same strategy can be applied if you are using a server because a server start-up can be included in the same way.

In our example, the Start Code LIBNAME statement is not strictly necessary because the same library has already been assigned using the Data Source Library Wizard. However, you should know how Start Code works for future reference. The SAS code is modified later for pedagogical reasons. For now, complete the following steps:

1. Click **Shopping**.

Figure 4.8: Project Start Code in the Properties Panel

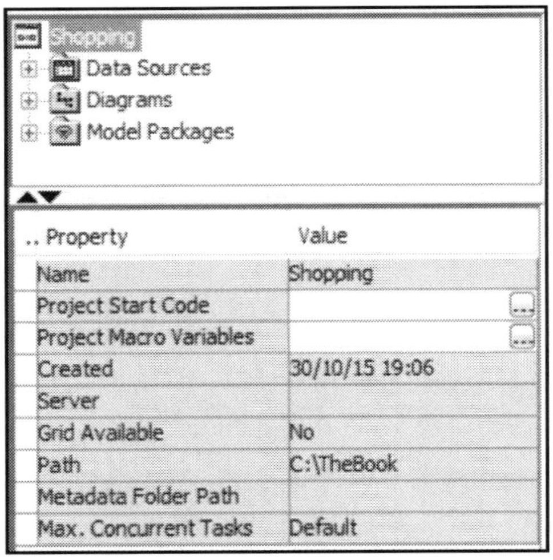

2. In the **Value** column, click the ellipses for the **Project Start Code** row.
3. Enter the SAS code into the Project Start Code dialog box. If you are accessing data in a database that uses a SAS/ACCESS interface, then it is convenient to have those library definitions in the project or server start-up code.

Figure 4.9: Project Start Code Dialog Box

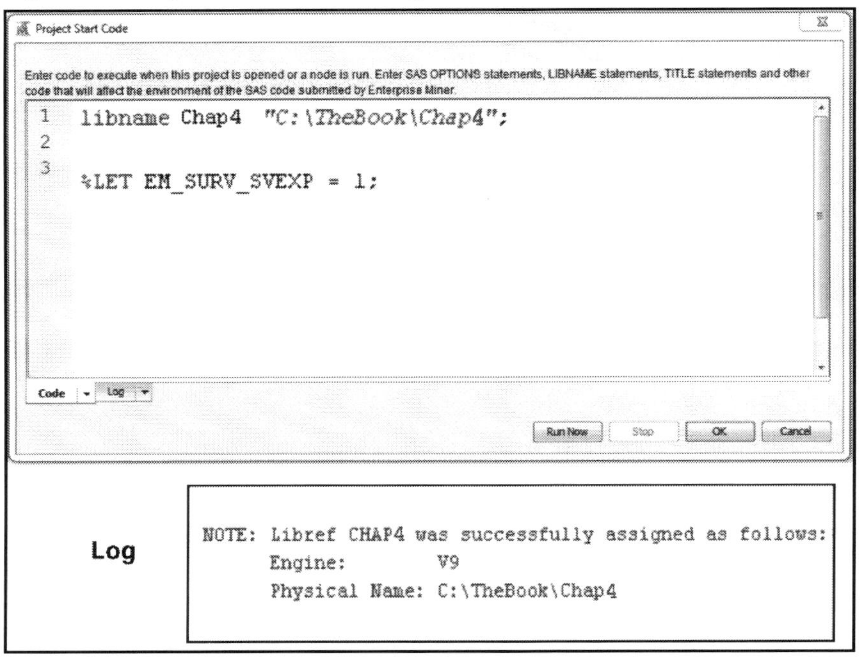

4. Click **Run Now**. The library reference is created.
5. Click the **Log** tab.
6. Check the SAS log. Always check the SAS log when running Start Code for the first time.
7. Add the macro code %LET EM_SURV_SVEXP = 1 to create the data set SURV_EXPCENDATA in the diagram workspace folder. (To explain the power of the SAS Enterprise Miner Survival node, this macro is provided to export the Expanded data set, which is used and explained in detail in Chapter 6.)

Step 4: Create a New Data Source

You must create a data source before working with your SAS Enterprise Miner survival project. The data source contains all the information associated with the data set, such as:

- The directory path to the data set.
- The name of the data set.
- The measurement scale or level of the variables in the data set. (Variables are continuous or categorical. The measurement scales used by SAS Enterprise Miner are interval, ordinal, nominal, and binary.)
- The analysis role of the data set (Raw, Score, and so on).
- The analysis role of each variable (input variable, target variable—all unwanted variables should be rejected).

To create a data source, complete the following steps:

1. Right-click **Data Source** in the project panel. Click **Create Data Source**.

Figure 4.10: Creation of the Data Source

2. The first window of the Data Source Wizard. Select **SAS Table** as the metadata source because Model_Shopping is a SAS data set. Click **Next**.

Figure 4.11: Selection of a Metadata Source

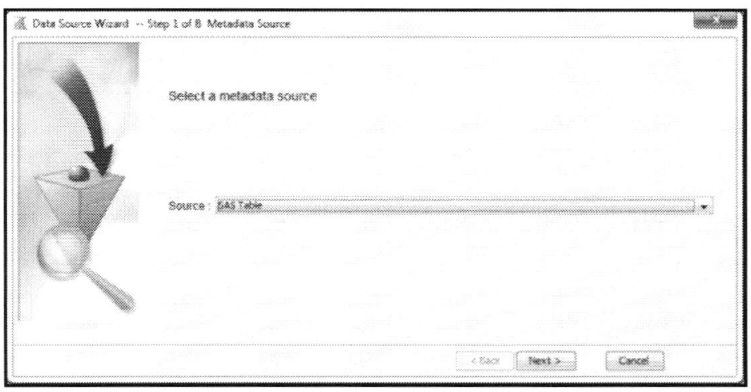

3. The Data Source Wizard -- Step 2 of 8 Select a SAS Table window appears, prompting you to give the location of the SAS data set. Click **Browse**. The **Select a SAS Table** window appears.

Figure 4.12: Selection of the SAS Data Set

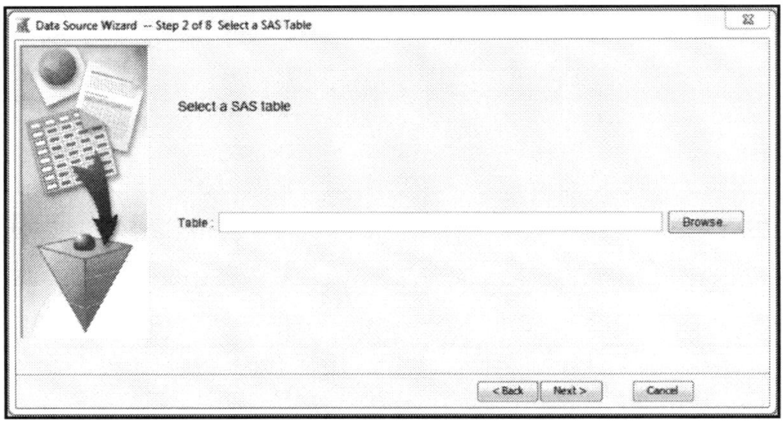

4. Because the data for this project is in the library Chap4, select the library **Chap4**. Select the SAS data set **Model_shopping**. Click **OK**.

Figure 4.13: Selection of the Chap4 Library

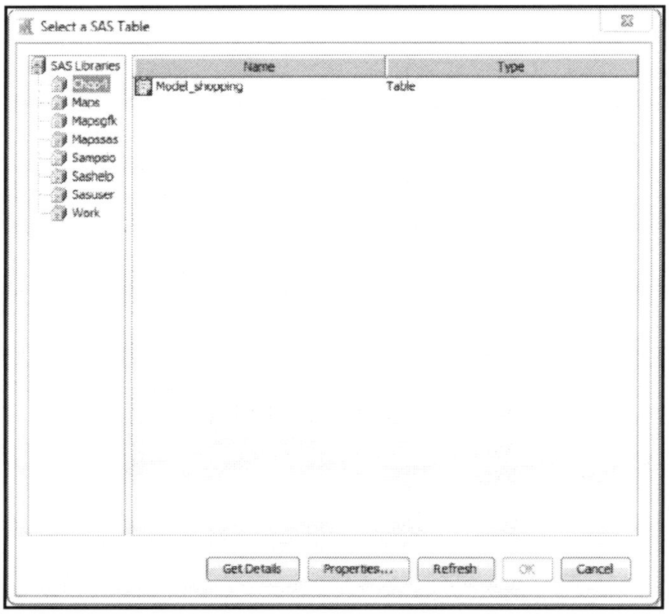

5. The screen in Figure 4.14 appears. Click **Next**.

Figure 4.14: Selection of a Table

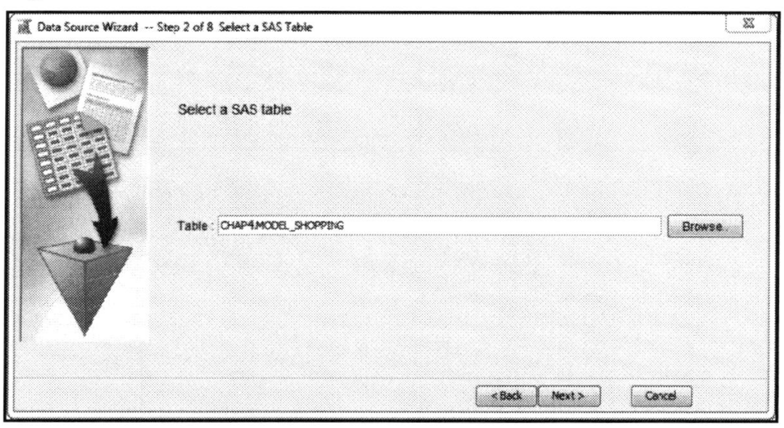

6. The table information is shown. This screen is useful to verify that the number of variables and number of observations are correct. Click **Next**.

Figure 4.15: Table Information

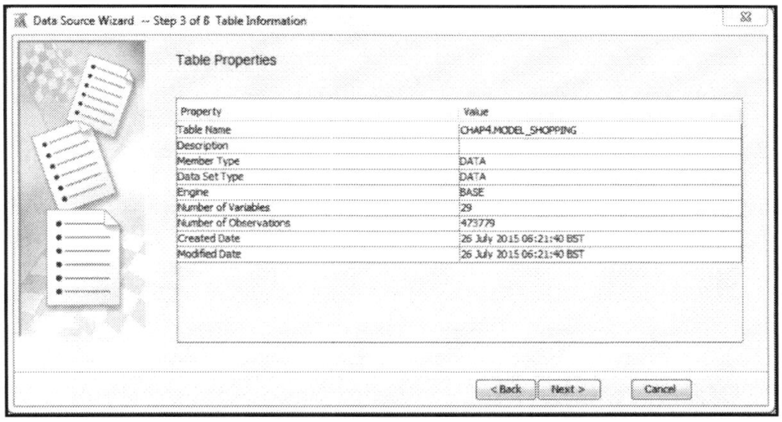

7. Select **Basic**, and click **Next**.

Figure 4.16: Metadata Advisor Options

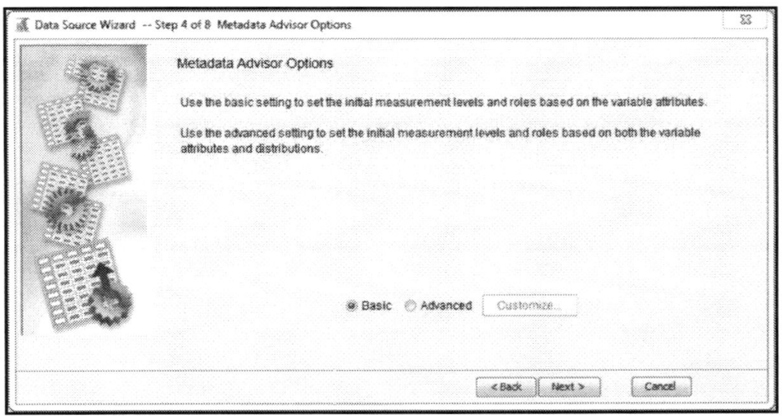

Use the Metadata Advisor Options to specify how each variable is used in the modeling process. If Basic is selected, then the initial measurement scales and roles are based on the variable attributes. All character variables are assigned the measurement scale of nominal. All numeric variables are assigned the measurement scale of interval. If a variable is numeric, its measurement scale is designated to be interval, regardless of how many distinct values the variable has. For example, a numeric binary variable is given an interval scale.

Complete the following steps:

1. Check the **Label** tick box to display variable labels.
2. To re-create the order of variables shown in the Columns row, numbers have been assigned to all variables. Click on the heading **Label** to sort by label name.
3. Drag the label bar wide enough so that even the widest label can be read.
4. Set the variable Censor to have a role of **Target** and a level of **Nominal**. This is an example of a numeric binary variable being assigned a required nominal level using the Basic metadata setting.

Figure 4.17: Column Metadata

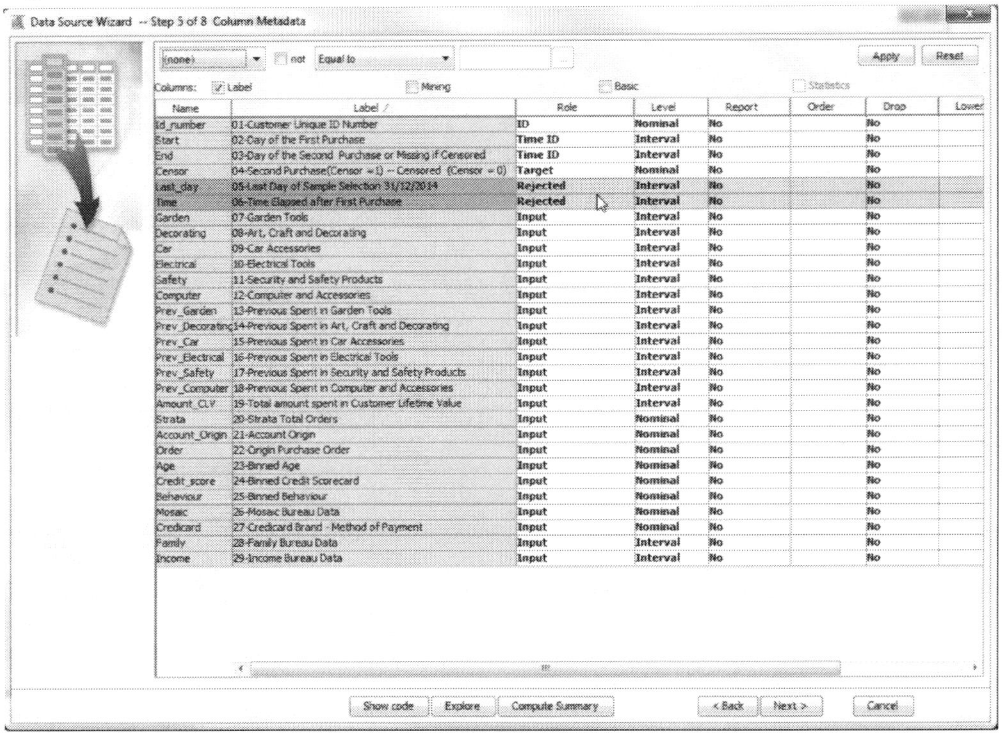

Figure 4.18: Settings of Target and Nominal for the Censor Variable

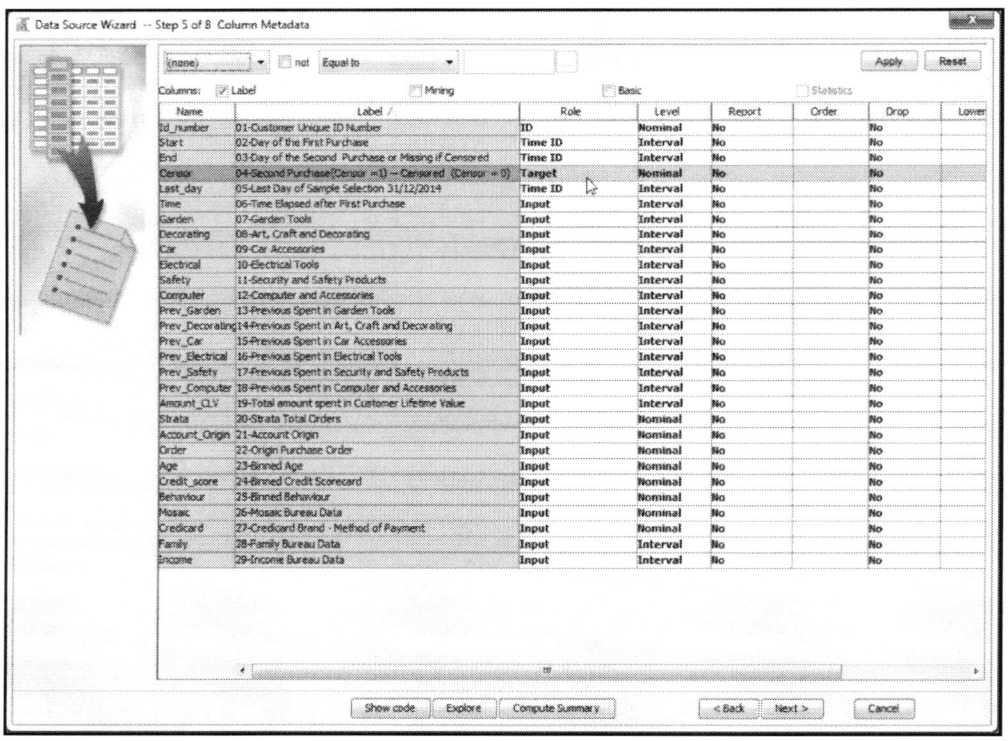

The Survival node in SAS Enterprise Miner requires the following variables:

- An ID variable to create the samples. This is represented by the first variable in the table (**Id_number**).

- At least two time ID variables represented by the following:
  - **Start**
  - **End**
- The target nominal variable represented by **Censor**.

5. Select both the **Last_day** and **Time** variables, and set their **Role** to **Rejected**. They are set to **Rejected** so that they are kept by SAS Enterprise Miner after the modeling process (but not entered into it). They are necessary later for the hazard analysis using PROC LIFETEST.

Figure 4.19: Assignment of Variable Roles

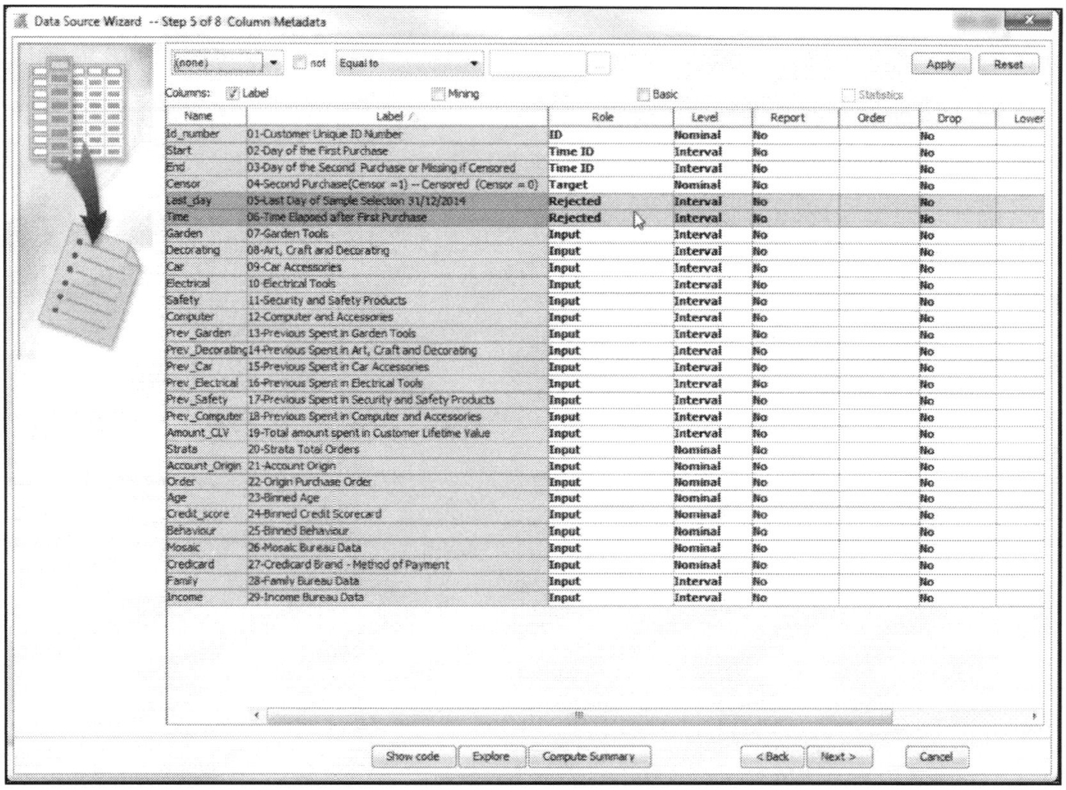

6. Click **Next**. The Data Source Wizard—Step 6 of 8 Create Sample window appears. Select **No**.

Figure 4.20: Nonselection of Sample Creation

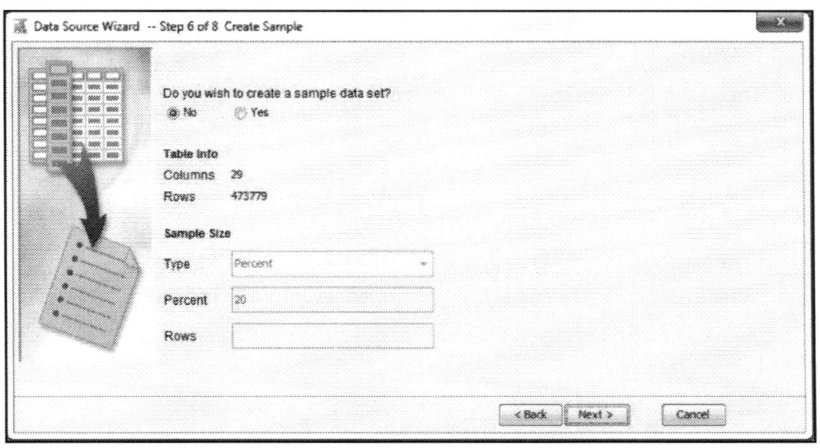

7. Click **Next**. Because training and validation data sets are still to be created from this data set, leave the role as **Raw**.

Figure 4.21: Data Source Attributes

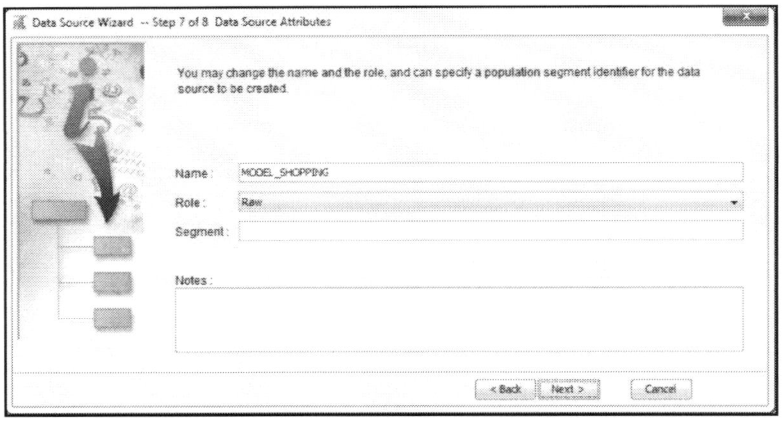

8. Click **Finish**. The Summary window shows the number of variables in each role.

Figure 4.22: Number of Variables per Role

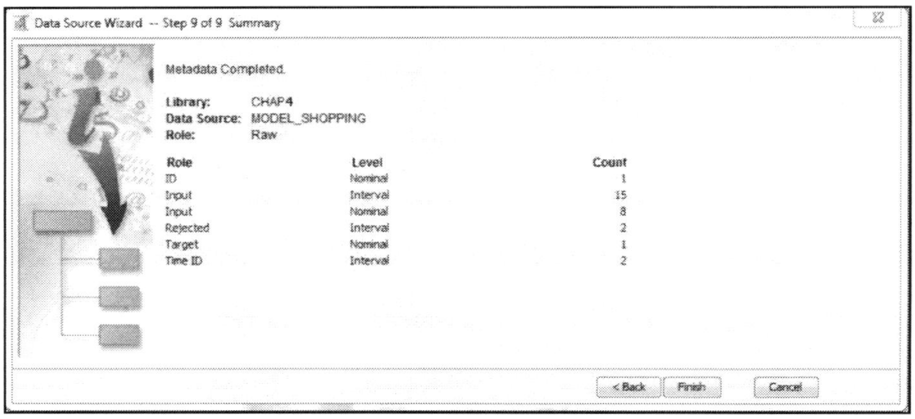

Step 5: Create a Process Flow Diagram

A process diagram workspace contains the steps to build your model.

1. To create a process diagram, you need only to specify its name. Right-click **Diagrams**, and click **Create Diagram**. Or, select **File ▶ New ▶ Diagram.**

Figure 4.23: Creation of a New Diagram

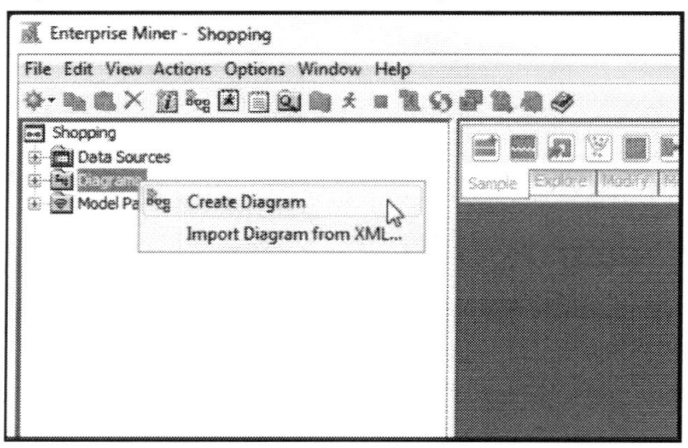

2. The Create New Diagram window appears. Name the diagram **1-Model 1 - Standard data set**. SAS creates a library named **EMWS1** within the workspace folder C:\TheBook\Chap4\Workspaces. (Early in the modeling process, it is worth keeping this library open. It provides visual guide to how SAS Enterprise Miner works and creates the tables.)

Figure 4.24: Diagram Name

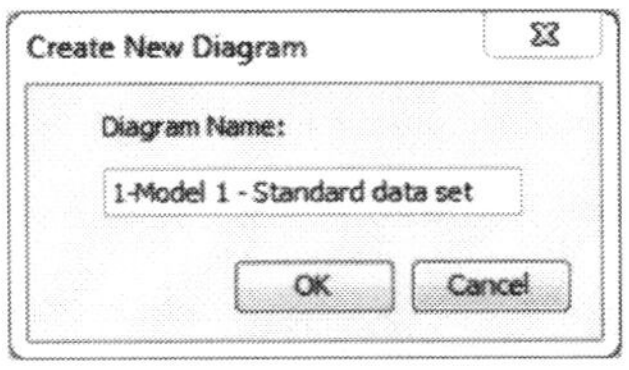

Figure 4.25: Open Library and Visibility of Processes

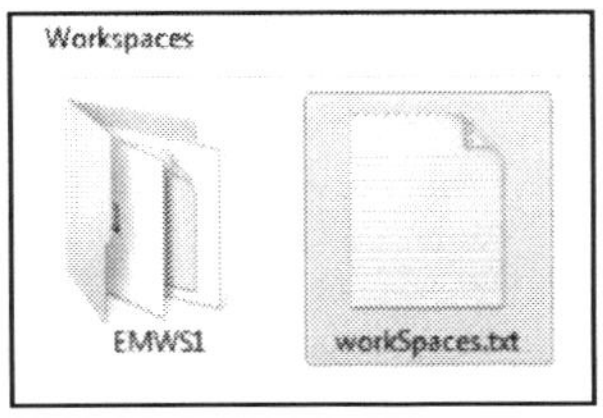

3. From **Data Sources** in the project panel, drag the data source **MODEL_SHOPPING** into the diagram **1-Model 1 - Standard data set**. The input data node as seen below is the first node in any diagram and represents the data source for the survival model. The input data node keeps the same variable as defined in the data source.

Figure 4.26: Data Source in the Process Diagram Panel

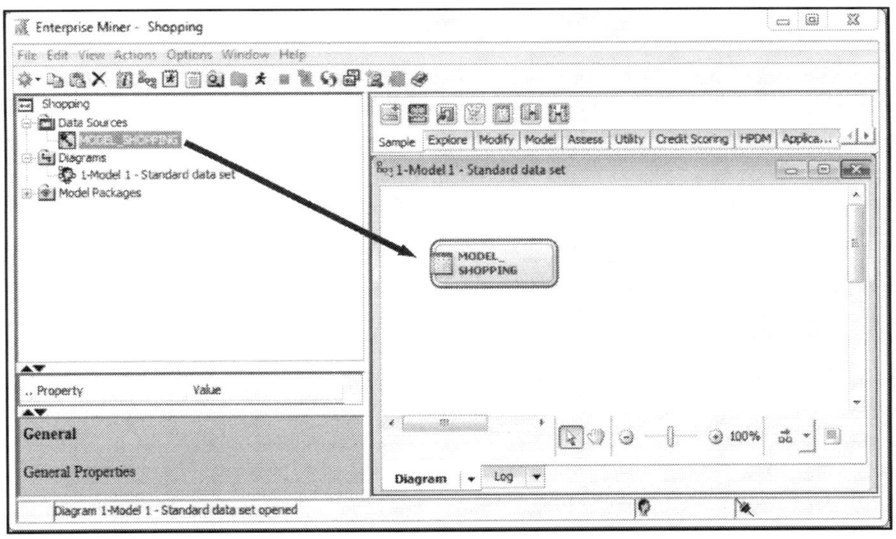

4. Select the input data node, and then change **Output Type** from **View** (default) to **Data**. This step is necessary to export the results as a SAS table. SAS Enterprise Miner generates a copy of the training data set and places it in the SAS Enterprise Miner project workspace folder EMWS1.

Figure 4.27: Input Data Node Train Properties

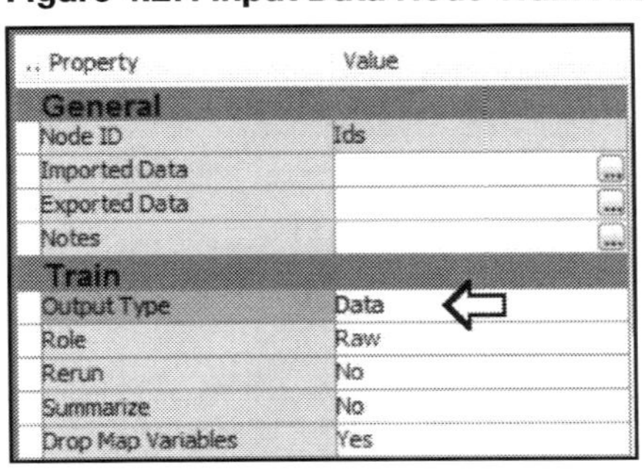

Step 6: Insert the Data Partition Node

The next step is to insert a Data Partition node. In developing survival models, you must partition the sample into a training data set (where the model is fit) and validation data set (where the model is evaluated).

A Data Partition node can statistically split the Model_Shopping data set into three data sets: one for training, one for validation, and one for scoring (or test) results. The latter data set is not used in building the model, but is used as a holdout sample. These data sets are carried along through the process flow and used during model assessment.

Insert and Connect Nodes

Complete the following steps:

1. Drag the **Data Partition** node from the **Sample** node group to the diagram.

Figure 4.28: Insertion of the Data Partition Node

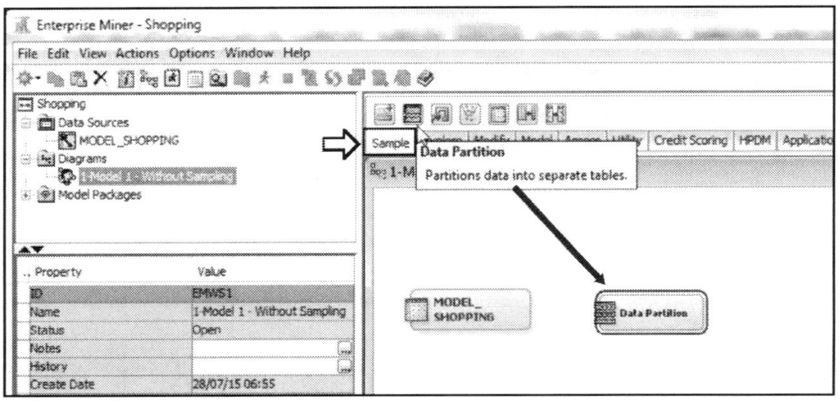

2. To connect the nodes, position the cursor on the right edge of the input data node (**MODEL_SHOPPING)** icon until a pencil appears.

Figure 4.29: Pencil Icon

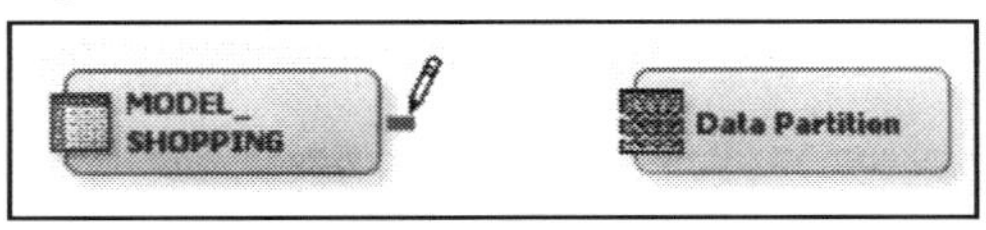

3. Using the mouse (appearing as a pencil), draw a line from the input data node (**MODEL_SHOPPING)** to the **Data Partition** node to connect the two nodes. Release the mouse, and the nodes are connected. This process is required because the Data Partition node must be preceded by a node that exports at least one data set.

Figure 4.30: Connection of Two Nodes

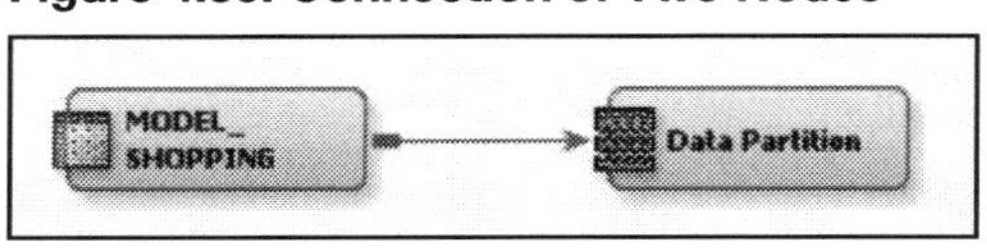

Run the Date Partition Node and Examine Results

Modify the default settings of the Data Partition node.

Figure 4.31: Data Partition Node Properties

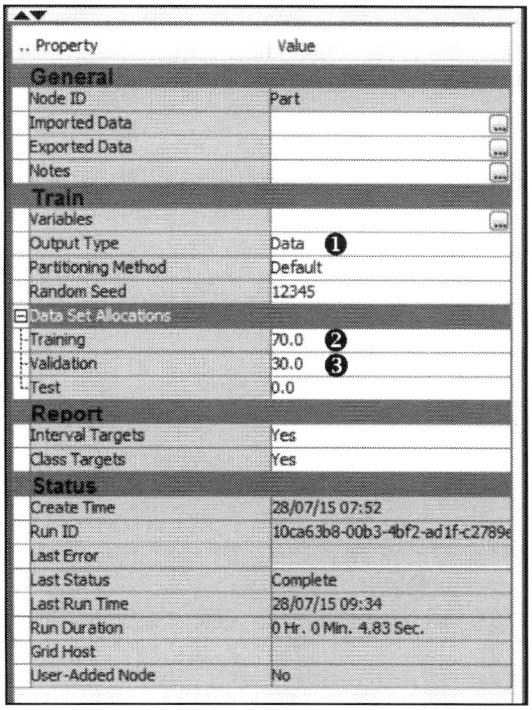

❶ The alternative option for **Output Type** is **View**. Because you need to work directly with the output from the Data Partition node in subsequent steps, specifying the **Output Type** as **Data** is preferable to avoid overhead associated with multiple passes to the **Model_Shopping** output data. The choice of View versus Data can be seen as a trade-off between disk space and execution time. For really large data, making multiple copies might use too much storage.

❷ **Training** should be **70%**.

❸ **Validation** should be **30%.** The Data Partition node splits the input data node output from Model_Shopping into three partitions—Training, Validation, and Test—based on the percentages input. The percentage that should be selected depends on the modeling performed and on convention. The default Training percentage is 40%, Validation percentage 30%, and Test percentage 30%. The Training data set is used for preliminary model fitting, the Validation data set to validate, and the Test data set for an independent assessment of the model. For the survival model, a scoring data set has been created for this purpose. Therefore, a Test partition is unnecessary, and the Training and Validation partitions should be split 70% and 30%. In other scenarios (for example, in certain applications of regression), a 50:30:20 or 60:30:10 split might be used.

Complete the following steps:

4. Right-click **Data Partition**, and select **Run**.

Figure 4.32: Selection of Run

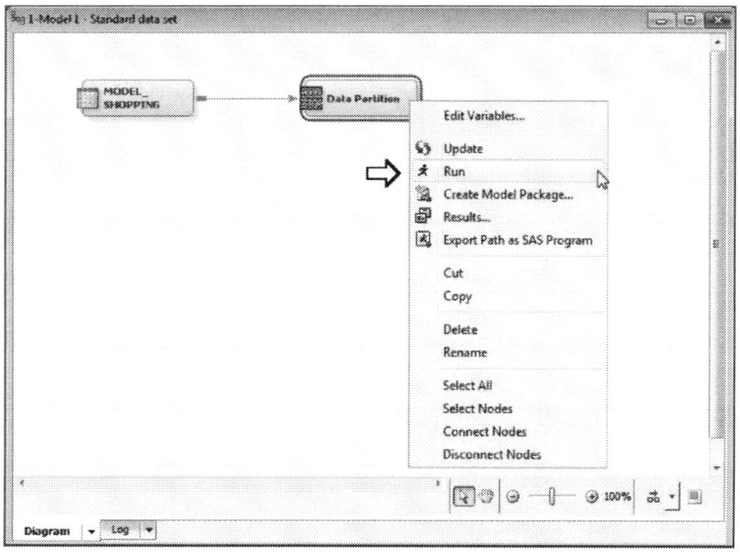

5. Once the run has completed and the green check is displayed, right-click **Data Partition**, and select **Results**.

Figure 4.33: Selection of Results

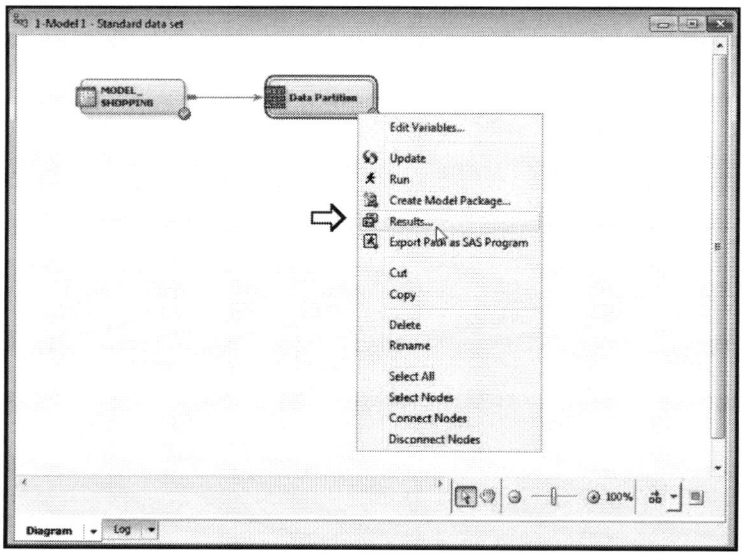

The Results window. The process flow for these results is shown in Figure 4.35.

Figure 4.34: Data Partition Node Results

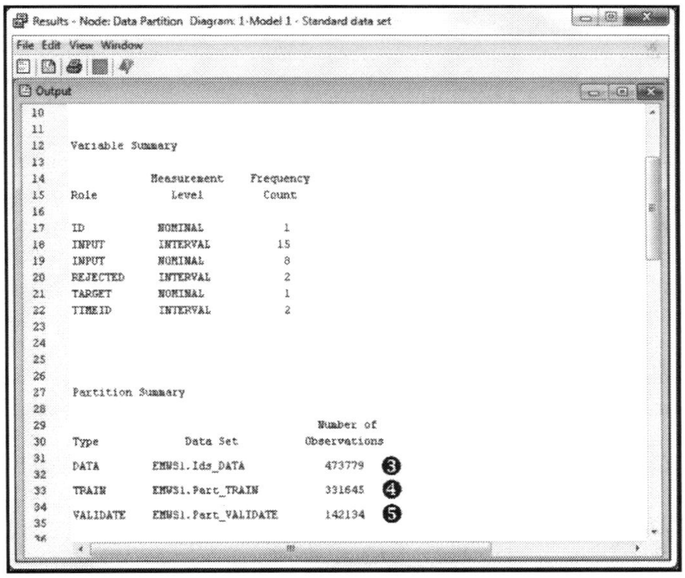

Figure 4.35: Process Flow for Data Partition Node Results

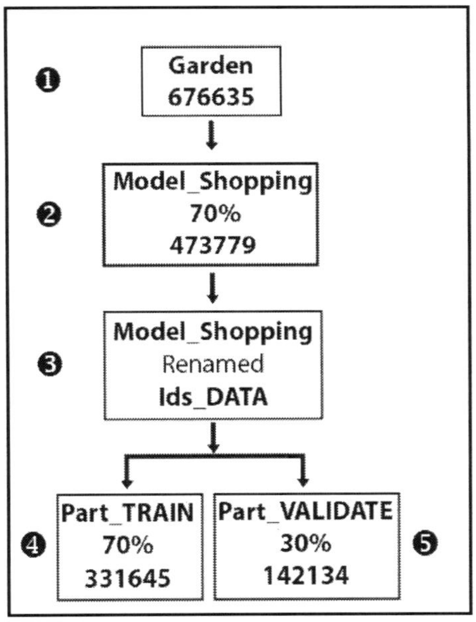

The process started by extracting a sample (70%, Model_Shopping) from the original Garden data set ❶. Then, the Model_Shopping ❷ data set is partitioned so that the training and validation elements are ready for input into the Survival node. The data set is not called Model_Shopping; instead, it is called Ids_DATA ❸ (Ids stands for Input Data Source). This is because each SAS Enterprise Miner node creates a new data set, and the Data Source node has renamed Model_Shopping as Ids_DATA. The resulting training portion is 70% ❹. The resulting validation portion is 30% ❺.

Examine Imported and Exported Data Sets

In SAS Enterprise Miner, each node imports, analyses, and creates a result. It then exports a modified version of the imported data set. It is of a crucial importance to see the actual results of the modeling process on the exported data. This enables you to validate the model at each stage of the analysis. Next, analyze the Imported and Exported data set created by the Data Partition node. To verify that the development (training) and validation data sets do exist, select the Data Partition node, and follow the steps below.

In Figure 4.36, the **Imported Data** property provides access to the imported data.

Figure 4.36: Access to Imported and Exported Data

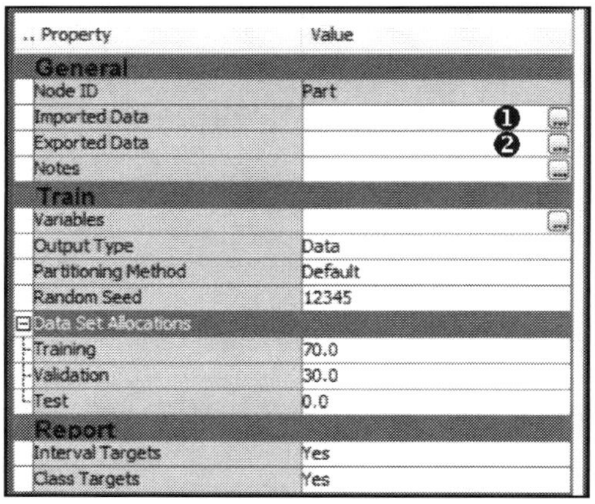

Complete the following steps:

1. To see the imported data set, click the ellipses to the right of **Imported Data** ❶ to show that Model_Shopping was renamed **EMWS1.Ids_DATA** by the Data Partition node.

Figure 4.37: Imported Data Set EMWS1.Ids_DATA

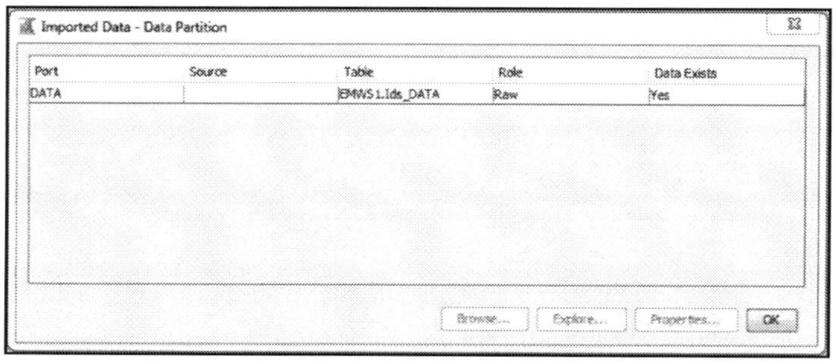

2. The Exported Data property ❷ provides access to the exported data. Click the ellipses to the right of Exported Data. A dialog box shows that the outputs **EMWS1.Part_TRAIN** and **EMWS1.Part_VALIDATE** from the Data Partition node applied to **EMWS1.Ids_DATA** are the exported data. **EMWS1.Part_TEST** appears in the dialog box, but is not exported as the data does not exist—that is, the percentage of data allocated to the test portion was zero.

Figure 4.38: Exported Data Set Part_TRAIN and Part_VALIDATE

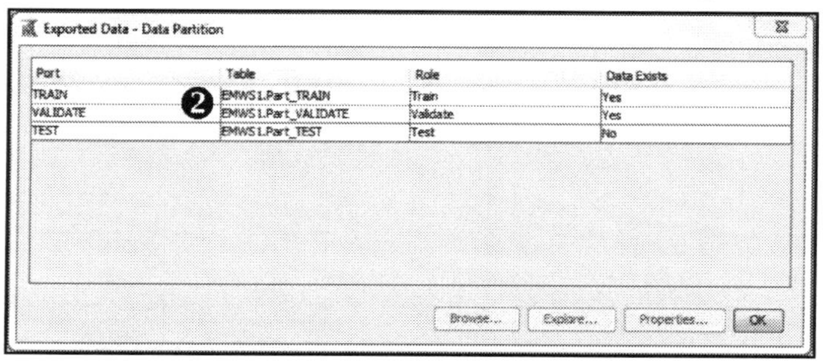

Step 7: Create the Survival Process Flow

A survival model process flow, as for any other process flow, starts with a data source, and sequentially applies SAS Enterprise Miner nodes connected by arrows to show the direction of the information flow to complete the analytic or modeling objective.

Complete the following steps:

1. To complete the survival process flow, insert the Survival node. Drag the Survival node from the **Applications** node group to the diagram.

Figure 4.39: Drag from the Applications Node Group

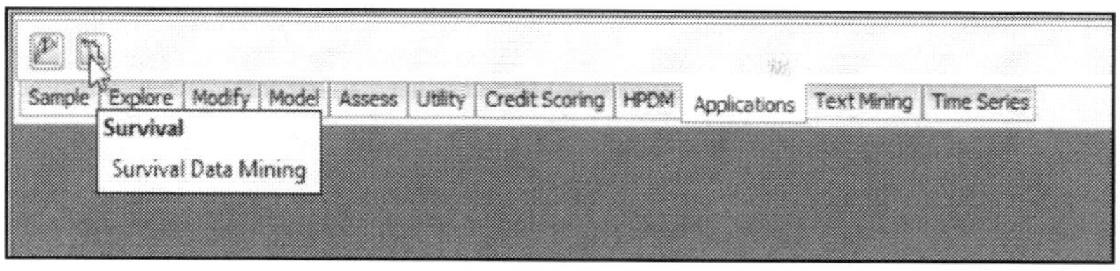

2. Connect the **Data Partition** node to the **Survival** node..

Figure 4.40: Diagram of Process Flow

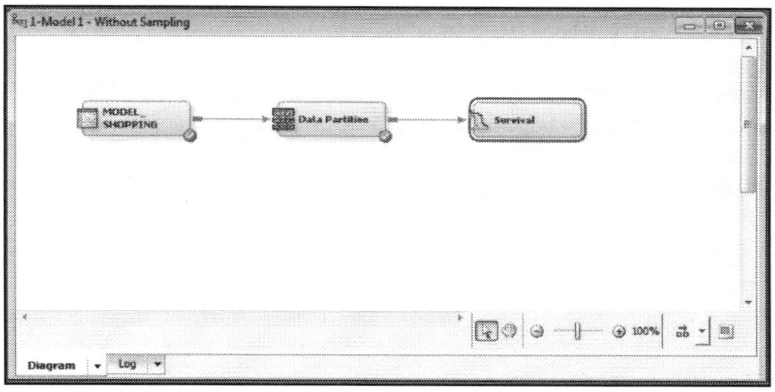

Running a Model and Examining Results

To introduce you to the Survival node, its most important options are presented in this chapter. In Chapters 5 and 6, all remaining options are discussed.

Survival Node Properties Panel

The Survival node properties panel presents all the options necessary to run a survival model.

Figure 4.41: Survival Node Properties Panel—Train

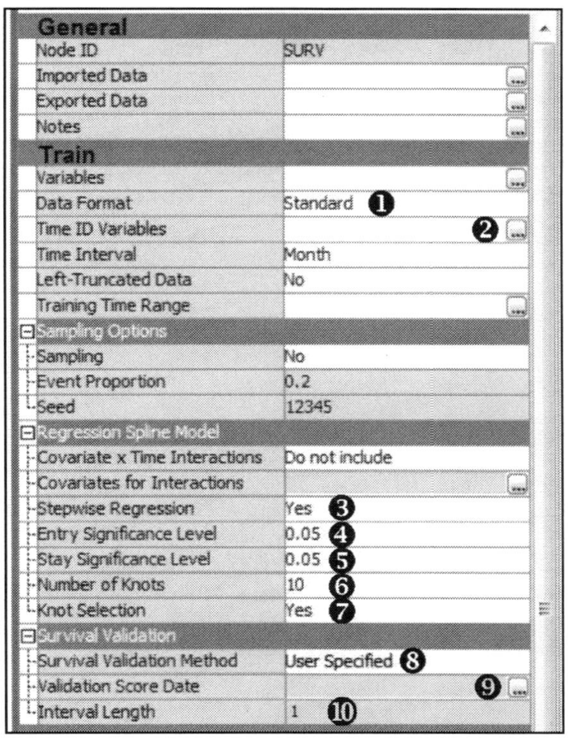

❶ Make sure that the data format is **Standard**. This means that the input data is cross-sectional (one row per customer). In other words, the data format is not Expanded.

❷ The **Time ID Variables** have already been identified during the data source stage. Click the ellipses to see the **Time ID Variables** property.

Figure 4.42: Time ID Variables Property

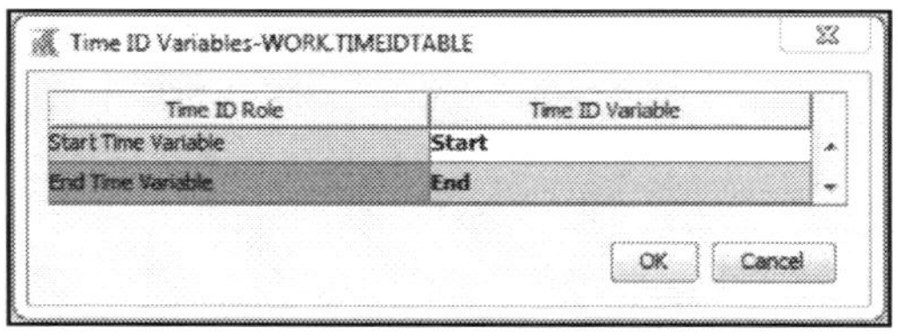

This is important information because SAS Enterprise Miner scans the input data and chooses the start date for modeling by finding the minimum date values across all observations for the variable specified as **Start Time Variable (Start)**. The censoring variable is created on the basis of the maximum date for the **End Time Variable (End)** and the time interval chosen (month in this model).

Regression Spline Model

Figure 4.43 shows the Regression Spline model properties.

Figure 4.43: Regression Spline Model Properties

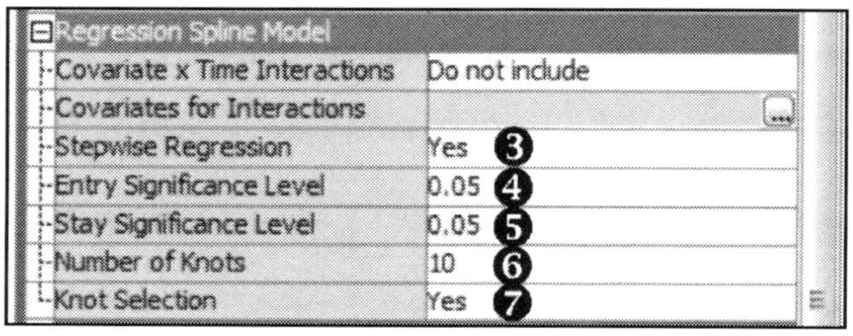

❸ Decide whether to use **Stepwise Regression**.

❹ Decide the significance level for a variable to enter into the model. The value 0.05 indicates 5% significance.

❺ Decide the significance level for a variable to stay in the model after another variable has been added.

❻ The Regression Spline Model creates variables, called *knots*. The default number is 5. The reason that we included 10 is explained later in Chapter 5. ❼ Specifies whether to use automatic knot selection when stepwise regression is being performed.

Survival Validation

Figure 4.44 shows the Survival Validation properties.

Figure 4.44: Survival Validation Properties

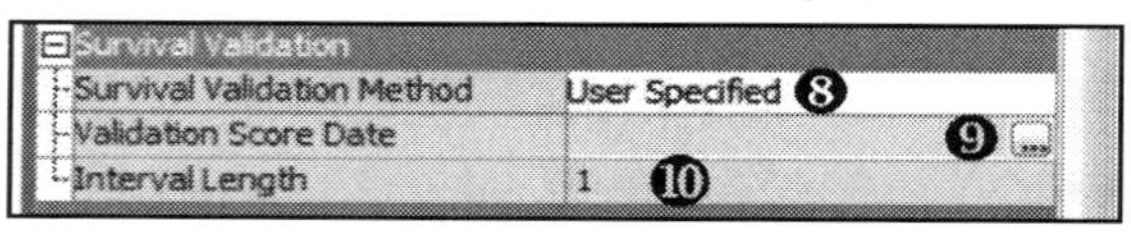

❽ **Survival Validation Method** specifies how the validation holdout sample is generated.

❾ **Validation Score Date** specifies the scoring date as **01Jan2014**, as shown in Figure 4.45.

❿ **Interval Length** specifies the length of time interval that is used to perform survival validation.

Figure 4.45: Validation Score Date Selection

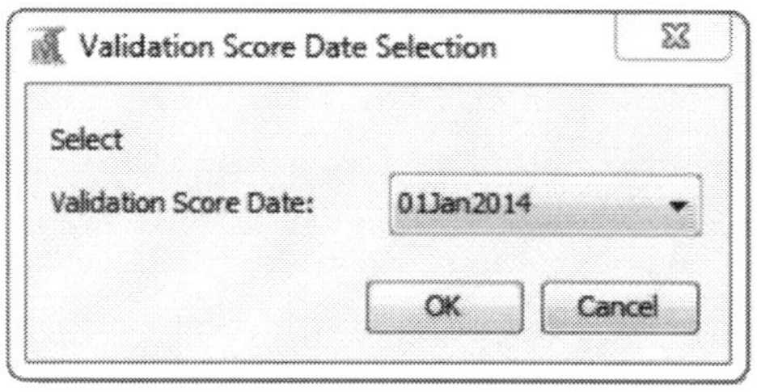

Score and Report

Complete the following steps:

1. Set all the score and report properties.

   Figure 4.46: Score and Report Properties

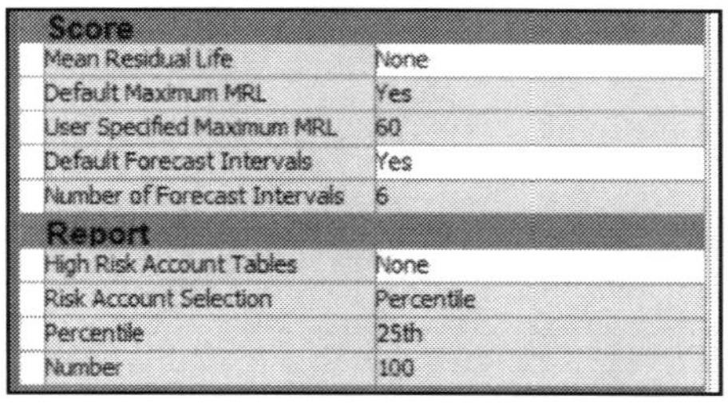

Score	
Mean Residual Life	None
Default Maximum MRL	Yes
User Specified Maximum MRL	60
Default Forecast Intervals	Yes
Number of Forecast Intervals	6
Report	
High Risk Account Tables	None
Risk Account Selection	Percentile
Percentile	25th
Number	100

2. In the diagram, right-click the **Survival** node, and select **Run**.

   Figure 4.47: Selection of Run for the Survival Node

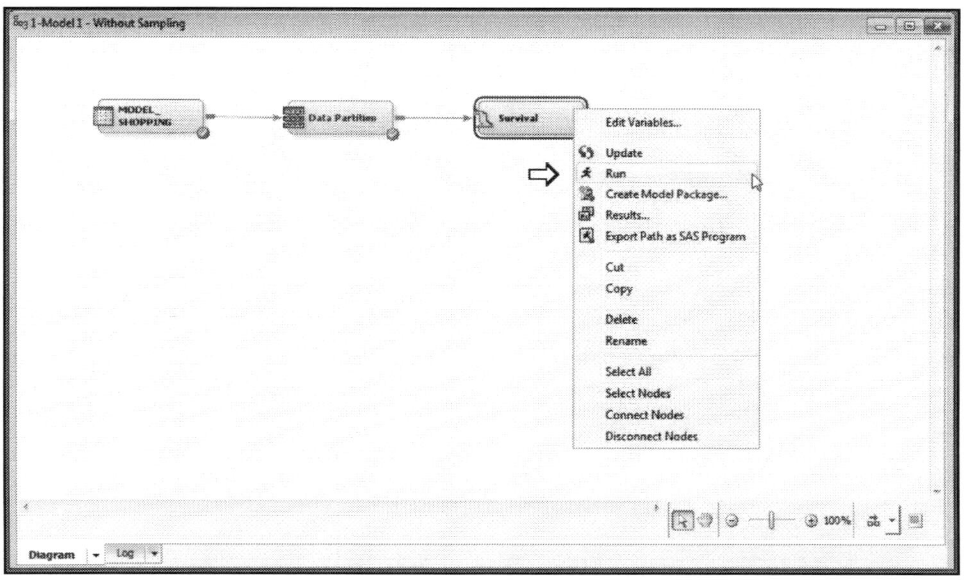

Results

After the run, click **Results** to examine the Survival node results.

Figure 4.48: Run Status

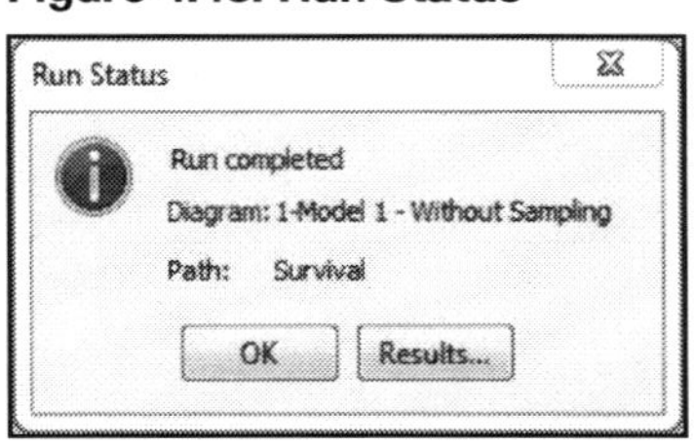

Output 4.1 shows the Survival node results, which include plots and tables.

Output 4.1: Survival Node Results

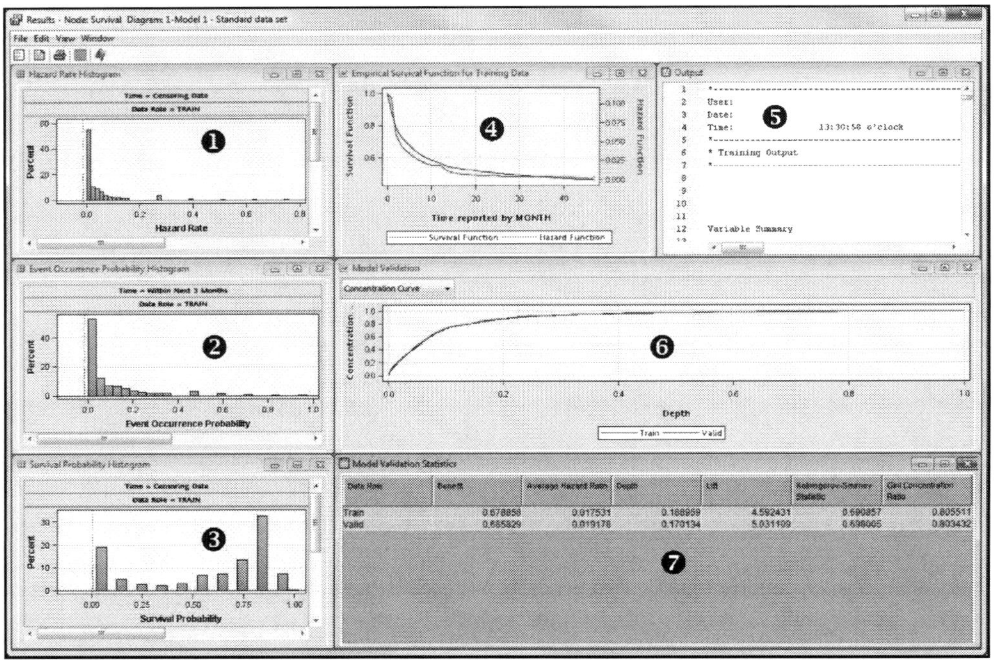

❶ The **Hazard Rate** histogram displays the distribution of the hazard rate for the month that contains the censoring date (31DEC2014) and for the next three months (by default) that follow the censoring date. Here are the default forecast intervals:

- Day = 30
- Week = 4
- Month = 3
- Quarter = 4
- Semi-Year = 2
- Year =1

❷ The **Event Occurrence Probability** histogram displays the distribution of the probabilities of having the event of interest (repurchase) within the next three forecast intervals (months).

❸ The **Survival Probability** histogram displays the distribution of the survival probabilities for the censoring date and for the next three months that follow the censoring date.

❹ This is the plot of the Hazard and Survival functions across the full-time period of 48 months.

❺ The SAS **Output** contains the SAS results from running the LIFETEST and DMREG procedures and provides complete information about the regression model.

❻ The **Model Validation** has three different plots:

- the concentration curve
- the lift
- the benefit

❼ The **Model Validation Statistics** display six statistics for the training and validation data sets:

- benefit
- average hazard ratio
- depth
- lift
- Kolmogorov-Smirnov Statistic
- Gini Concentration Ratio

Chapter 5: The Cubic Spline Regression and Model Interpretation

Introduction

Survival analysis models are inherently complex. They are more complicated than other modeling techniques adopted widely, such as linear and logistic regression in credit risk. For this reason, implementation of survival analysis models remains a relatively niche practice. This practice happens outside of sectors where there is established best practices and specialized training, such as for assessing mortality in clinical trials in the pharmaceutical industry. This is unfortunate because survival analysis has the potential to add significant value to analysis in other sectors.

This chapter breaks down the steps performed by the SAS Enterprise Miner Survival node with the Standard data format described in Chapter 4. It reviews the key statistical outputs produced by the node and explains them as simply as possible.

This chapter starts with cubic spline regression as a means to model the hazard as a function of time. Cubic spline regression is a technique to transform the variable of time to event into several time-dependent cubic spline basis (CSB) variables. These CSB variables are assessed by a model selection method in the same way as other input variables. This section explains the idea of cubic spline regression and shows how CSB variables are derived. The Survival node is run without any other input variables to explicitly show SAS Enterprise Miner creating CSB variables. This is possible because CSB variables are created based on a function of time. CSB variables are created first without applying stepwise model selection. Then, stepwise model selection is applied to highlight how interactions between the variables affect statistical performance within the model.

Modelers with little or no previous exposure to survival analysis are likely to have some familiarity with binary logistic regression. For this reason and because binary logistic regression is important to survival analysis, the key concepts and terminology of this technique are explained. This includes probability, odds, and logit. These are linked to the survival analysis Hazard function to define how the Hazard function is expressed as a function of the betas parameters estimated by the Survival node, both for the pre-existing input variables and the CSB variables.

The hazard, odds, and odds ratios are calculated for single independent variables: one numerical and one categorical. You learn how SAS Enterprise Miner handles these variables by looking at the output produced. Single variables have been chosen because they allow for an intuitive explanation of the relationship with the hazard, odds, and odds ratio. These explanations are put in a business context to show how the apparently obscure outputs of the model yield commercially relevant insight.

For an explanation of the SAS Enterprise Miner output for the Customer-Level data set, review terminology introduced in previous chapters. The potential for the SAS Enterprise Miner Interactive Binning node to mine dependencies from variables is touched upon. The hazard, odds, and odds ratio of a number of variables selected by the Customer-Level data set are manually derived, and possible business insight is explored.

This chapter explains the Survival and Hazard function graphs produced by SAS Enterprise Miner and shows how to access their source data. This is compared with the Life Table output from the LIFETEST procedure.

At the end of this chapter, you will have a greater understanding of how survival analysis differs from and is related to logistic regression, and how it can be performed very flexibly in SAS Enterprise Miner. The intention is to enable you to clearly see the potential commercial value of outputs produced. The time-to-next-purchase model is a good example of this.

SAS Enterprise Miner Strategy for Standard Data Format

SAS Enterprise Miner applies a series of steps in Figure 5.1.

Figure 5.1: SAS Enterprise Miner Model Process for Standard Data Format

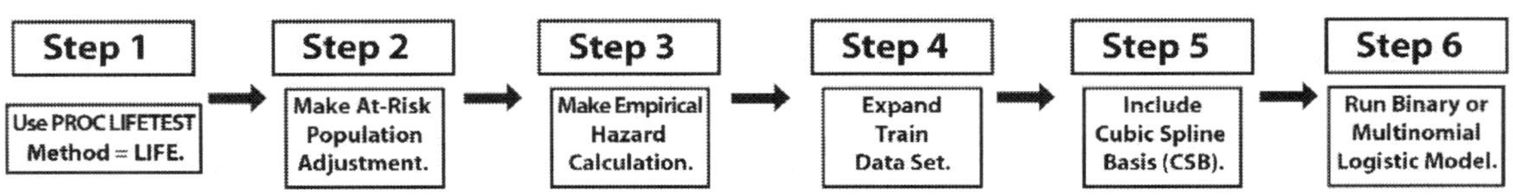

In this chapter, CSB variables are presented. The focus in the next few sections is on the interpretation of the coefficients and the CSB variables within the logistic survival model, as follows:

- Explanation of the key concepts in discrete logistic cubic spline regression.
- Demonstration of the fundamental hazard equation from logistic regression, using the numeric (Prev_Garden) variable to explain the logit, hazard, odds, and odds ratio.
- Explanation of the logit, hazard, odds, and odds ratio using just one categorical (Order) variable with generalized linear model (GLM) parameterization.
- Interpretation of the output created by the SAS Enterprise Miner Survival node for model 1 (using the Customer-Level data set and Standard data format with all variables), the model created in Chapter 4.
- Output of the Hazard function data set.

The purpose of the survival model is to calculate the probability of a customer to repurchase. Consider the following:

- Some books call the survival model the *hazard model* because the basis of the survival model is the Hazard function. In other words, the hazard (conditional probability) of a customer to repurchase in a specific time (month) after a first purchase is being modeled. You should be reminded that the hazard at time *t* is the conditional probability that an event occurs at time *t* given that it has not occurred prior to time *t*. Hazard is different from Prob ($T = t$), the unconditional probability of the event occurring at time *t*.

- Time is used in a discrete Hazard function because of the high number of tied customers repurchasing by month. The model is imprecisely called a *discrete survival model*, when it is more precisely a *discrete hazard model*.
- The discrete Time variable determines the shape of the Hazard function. This is of fundamental importance.

The Problem: The Nonlinearity of the Hazard Function

The importance of time to the model means that the model must include an appropriate parameterization of time. A way to model the impact of time on the probabilities (hazard) is needed. Isolating time as an input allows for simple calculation of future probabilities by increasing time. For example, the probability of a customer's repurchase in the next month or three years into the future can be calculated. This is important in econometric models to do things such as forecasting the probability of a customer to repurchase in two years, conditional on an increase of GDP by 2%.

Because the time relationship is so fundamental, various techniques take time into account to improve the model fit. Time and the Hazard function are plotted in Figure 5.2 to highlight what needs to be considered when you are modeling the hazard as a function of time.

Figure 5.2: Time and the Hazard Function

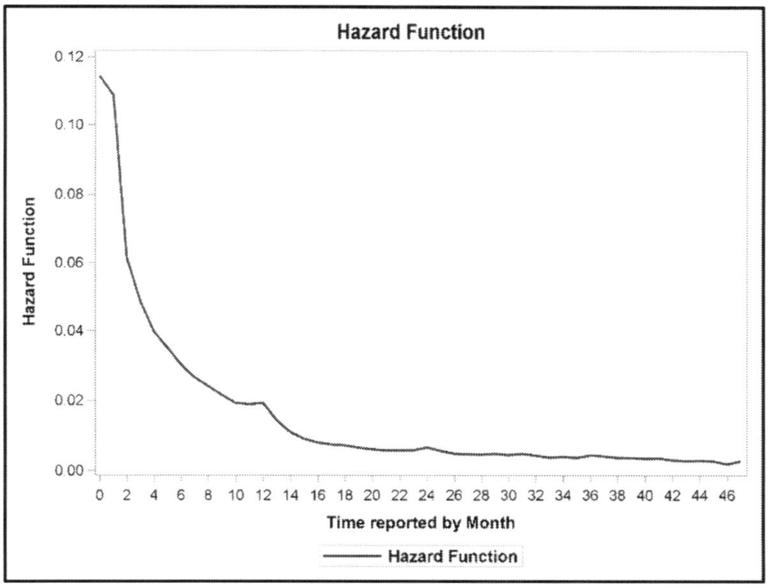

This Hazard function is nonlinear, which is the problem. Nonlinear relationships are more complicated to fit, and because they include only time as a linear parameter (as time = 1, 2, 3, 4…), they do not improve the model fit. A transformation is required to factor in the nonlinearity of the hazard, giving time the flexibility to adjust to the nonlinearity of the hazard.

The Solution: The Cubic Spline Basis Functions

CSB functions are segmented functions that consist of polynomials joined by knots. In Figure 5.3, you have a polynomial linear spline Hazard function in which the time (x axis) is divided into intervals separated by five knots. Polynomials have peaks and troughs that are undesirable and restrictive characteristics for modeling because they lead to biased estimation, particularly in the tail of the Hazard function.

Figure 5.3: A Polynomial Linear Spline Hazard Function with Five Knots

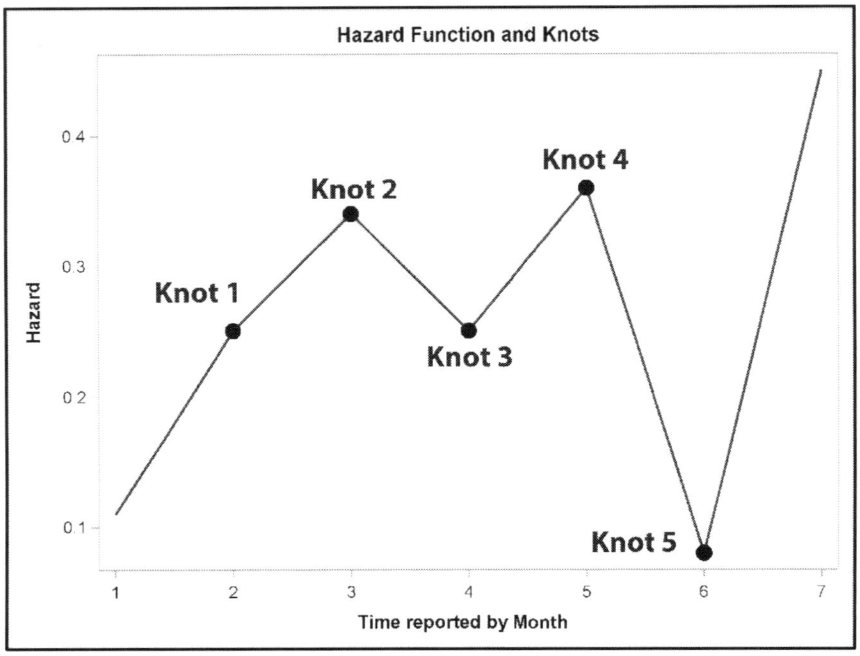

To overcome these undesirable and restrictive characteristics, SAS Enterprise Miner implements a smooth cubic spline Hazard function, giving more flexibility than a linear spline to the same data points, as shown in Figure 5.4. A smooth function is a function that has continuous derivatives.

Figure 5.4: A Smooth Cubic Spline Hazard Function with Five Knots

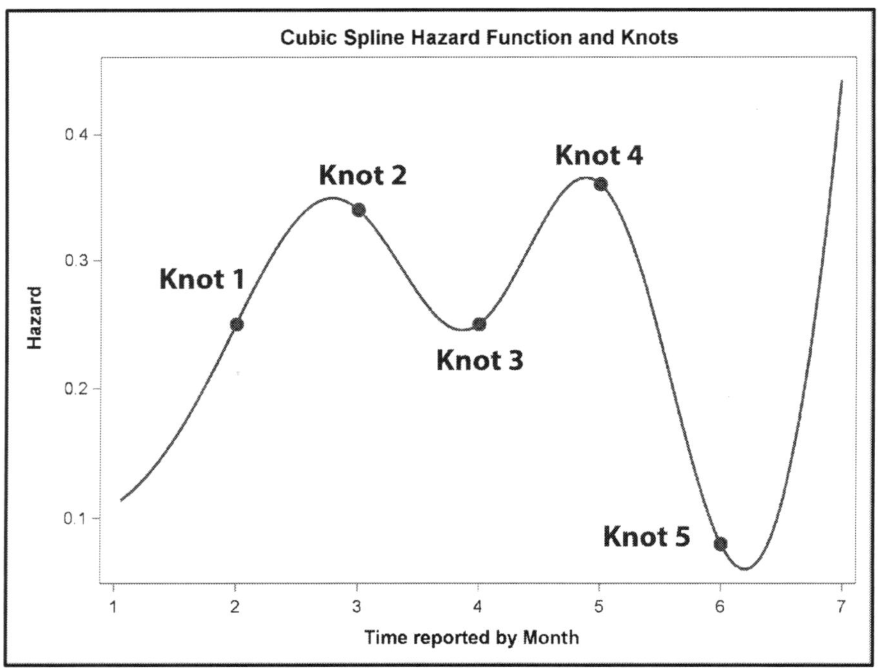

In a real-world data example, the choice of a correct function demonstrates how business knowledge is invaluable while you are going through the modeling process.

Figure 5.5 is a picture of Pão de Açúcar (Sugarloaf Mountain), which is located in Rio de Janeiro, Brazil. Besides being a tourist landmark, the shape of Sugarloaf Mountain is significant for those modeling the probability of a customer canceling their mobile phone contract in the next month. Brazilian mobile phone contracts are initially offered to customers as a two-year contract. Customers have the opportunity to renew the contract for a minimum of one additional year. These business considerations are key to explaining the resulting shape of the Hazard function for customers canceling in the next month. The shape of this Hazard function is different from the shape of the time-to-next-purchase model. The hazard event (cancellation) is presumably negative for the business rather than positive (repurchase).

Figure 5.5: Pão de Açúcar (Sugarloaf Mountain)

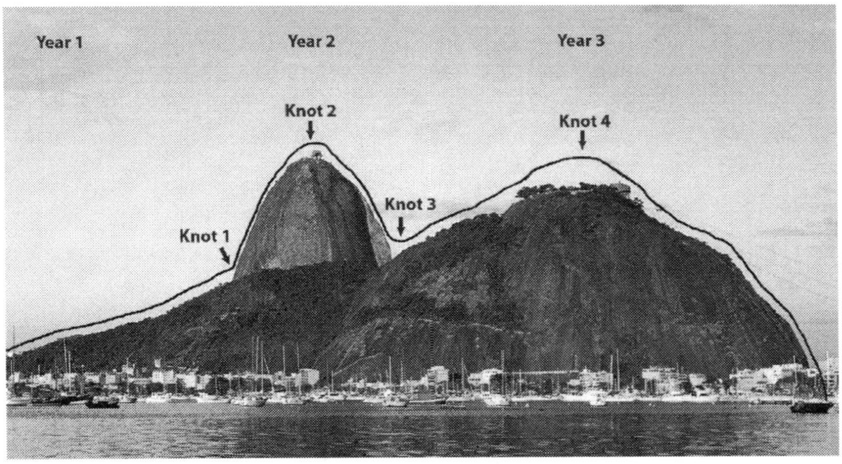

The knots in the Hazard function should be placed where customer behavior changes. At the end of the first year (**Knot 1**), some customers start to cancel their contracts. This is permitted by the contract if they lose their job or move to another city. After the contractual period of two years, when many customers have already canceled, hazard starts going down (**Knot 2**). The hazard then rises again up in year 3, as customers avoid signing a new one-year contract that takes them beyond three years. Finally, hazard declines after **Knot 4** because the remaining loyal customers are small in number and are presumably more price insensitive.

> **Key Tip:** Where the Hazard function shows abrupt changes, there should be a knot. The knots are points where the function makes a transformation. Business knowledge or empirical hazard plots can be used to identify candidate points.

For more information about knots, see Molinari (2001 and 2002), which offers an excellent discussion of how to interpret knot splines in the log Hazard function.

To be successful in creating a model using knots, two challenges must be overcome.

Two Challenges: Number of Knots to Choose and Placement of the Knots

The first challenge is to know how many knots to incorporate because every knot represents a cut to be effectuated in the function. In other words, how many cuts are there to effectuate in the Hazard function? Stone (1996) indicates that three to seven knots are needed for a cubic spline model to provide sufficient flexibility. These numbers serve as a framework for modeling nonlinearity between a Hazard function and a set of covariates. You verify the approach by trying models with different numbers of knots and comparing their performances.

Figure 5.6 shows that any number of knots can be attempted to improve the model fit, keeping in mind that correctly finding the optimal number of knots improves model performance.

Figure 5.6: How Many Knots?

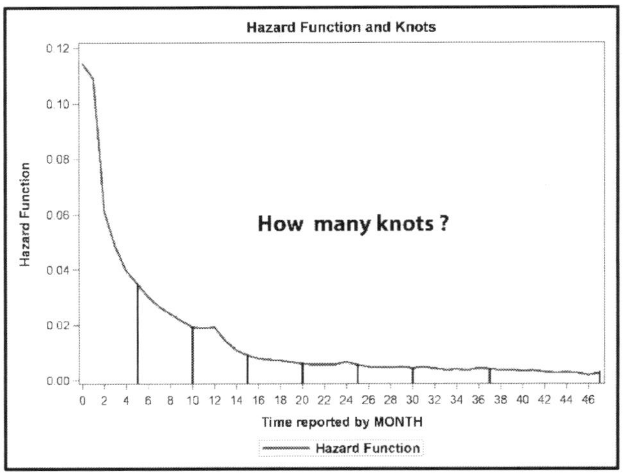

The second challenge is to know the value of each knot. Suppose the default option of five knots is selected. The values at which to place each knot (cut) must be found, as indicated in Figure 5.7.

Figure 5.7: Where to Place the Knots?

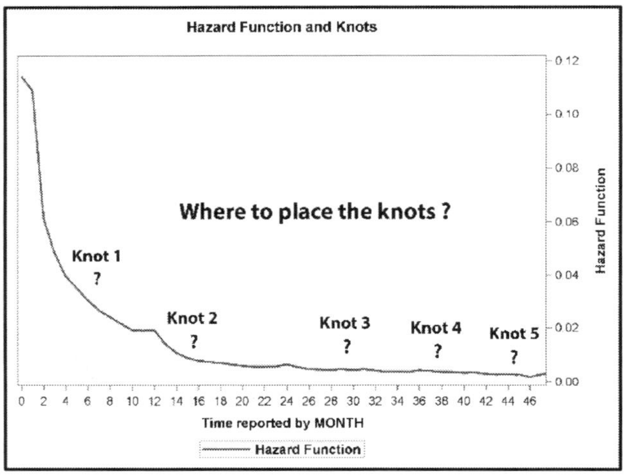

The Mathematical Definition of a Knot

To understand how the two challenges can be resolved, you must understand the mathematical definition of a knot.

There are many different definitions that could help you understand knots. The most elementary could be presented as $\text{CSB} = ax^0 + bx^1 + cx^2 + dx^3$, but the definition used by SAS Enterprise Miner is presented, which is one of the most suitable applications for survival models.

Remember that knots are the points where the function makes a transformation. What transformation? The principal transformation is implicit in the following formula applied by SAS Enterprise Miner:

$$\text{CSB}(t, k_j) = \begin{cases} -t^3 + 3k_j t^2 - 3k^2 t & \text{if } t \leq k_j \\ -k^3 & \text{if } t > k_j \end{cases} \tag{5.1}$$

The variables are as follows:

- t is the time effect. In the actual model, Time values are from 0 to 47. That is, the period of data collection has 48 months from 01/01/2011 to 31/12/2014. Thus, $t = 48$.

- *j* (1, 2, 3, 4, …) is the number of the actual knot being calculated ($k_j = k_1 = \text{Knot}_1$).
- *N* is the number of knots to be chosen by the modeler.
- *k* is the value of each knot implemented by SAS Enterprise Miner automatically. Each knot is calculated by dividing *t* by the number of knots *j* and considering only the integer part of the result, as demonstrated below.

The default number of knots computed by SAS Enterprise Miner is 5. Thus, for the actual example, **Knot 1** can be calculated as follows:

$$k_1 = \text{Knot}_1 = \frac{t}{N}$$

This means the following:

$$k_1 = \frac{48}{5} = 9.4$$

Thus, the first knot is $k_1 = 9$, retaining only the integer part. To compute the other knots— k_2 to k_5 —add the value of 9 to the first knot as indicated in Table 5.1, and repeat until reaching the maximum value of $t = 48$.

Table 5.1: Knot Calculation

Knot	Addition of the Value 9	Multiple Form	Resolved Form
1	$\text{Knot}_1 = 9$	$k_1 = 9*1 = 9$	$k_1 = 9$
2	$\text{Knot}_2 = 9+9 = 18$	$k_2 = 9*2 = 18$	$k_2 = 18$
3	$\text{Knot}_3 = 9+9+9 = 27$	$k_3 = 9*3 = 27$	$k_3 = 27$
4	$\text{Knot}_3 = 9+9+9+9 = 36$	$k_4 = 9*4 = 36$	$k_4 = 36$
5	$\text{Knot}_3 = 9+9+9+9+9 = 45$	$k_5 = 9*5 = 45$	$k_5 = 45$

By selecting a number of knots, SAS Enterprise Miner calculates the value of each knot as in Table 5.1 by replacing its value in the original formula. The necessary calculation for the first knot is as follows:

For knot 1, $k_1 = 9$, and

$$\text{CSB}(t, k_j) = \begin{cases} -t^3 + 3k_j t^2 - 3k^2 t \text{ if } t \le k_j \\ -k^3 \quad \text{if } t > k_j \end{cases}$$

Replacing $k_1 = 9$, the formula becomes the following:

$$\text{CSB}(t, k_1) = \begin{cases} -t^3 + 3*9*t^2 - 3*9^2*t & \text{if } t \le 9 \\ -9^3 & \text{if } t > 9 \end{cases}$$

$$\text{CSB}(t, k_1) = \begin{cases} -t^3 + 3*9*t^2 - 3*9^2*t & \text{if } t \le 9 \\ -729 & \text{if } t > 9 \end{cases}$$

The interpretation of the formula is straightforward. The values of knot 1 are calculated by the CSB formula, using the value of the Time (*t*) variable only if time is less than or equal to 9. Otherwise, the value is constant (−729). This is visualized in Figure 5.8.

Figure 5.8: Hazard Function and CSB Function for Knot 1

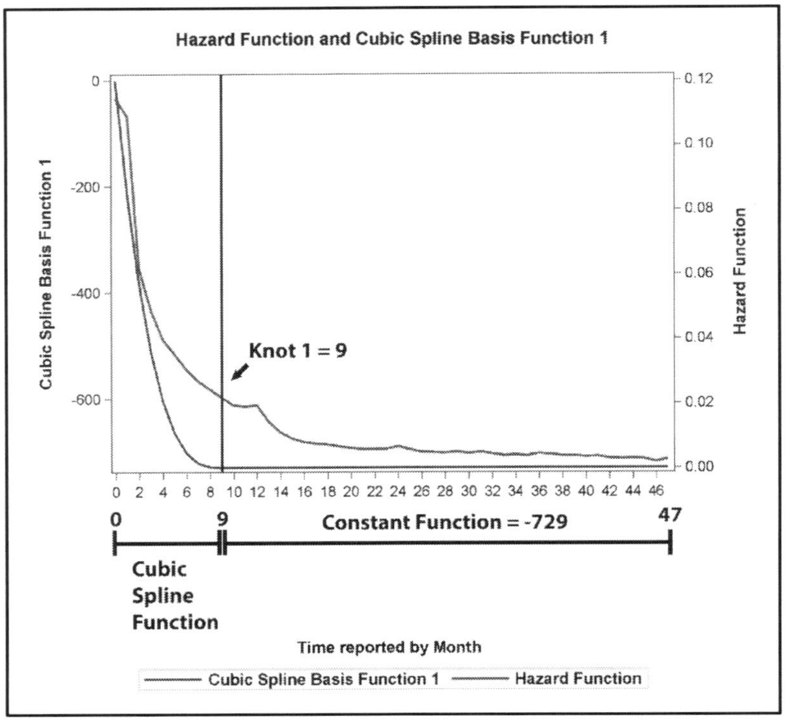

Overlaid with the Hazard function, the CSB function 1 attempts to improve the predictability of the Hazard function. Knot 1 is the point at which the CSB function changes from a cubic to a constant function. In econometric terms, the CSB function attempts to create a trend that follows the pattern of the Hazard function.

The Default Five-Knots Cubic Spline Basis Method without Stepwise Selection

The default number of knots is five, but the **Number of Knots** property in the **Regression Spline Model** section of the Survival node property panel can be changed to specify how many knots are needed. In this subsection, you run an example model using the default number. In the next subsection, you modify the default to have more flexibility and to measure the impact of having more knots.

Figure 5.9: Default Regression Spline Model Settings

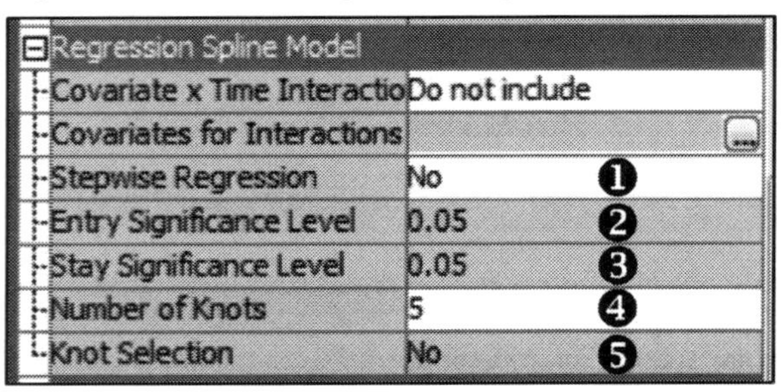

❶ From the drop-down menu, the **Stepwise Regression** method is set to **No**. Changing the stepwise regression to *No* causes SAS Enterprises Miner to automatically block the drop-down menu options indicated by ❷, ❸, and ❺. As a result, their rows are gray.

❹ By default, the number of knots included in the model is 5.

Using the selected options shown in Figure 5.9, SAS Enterprise Miner is set up to create a model with five knots and to retain all five knots whether they are sufficiently statistically significant to improve the model. This means that all the knots stay, regardless of their value to the model.

From the previous flowchart in Figure 5.1, **Step 5** includes the five knots in the Expanded data set.

Figure 5.10: Steps 4 and 5 from the Flowchart

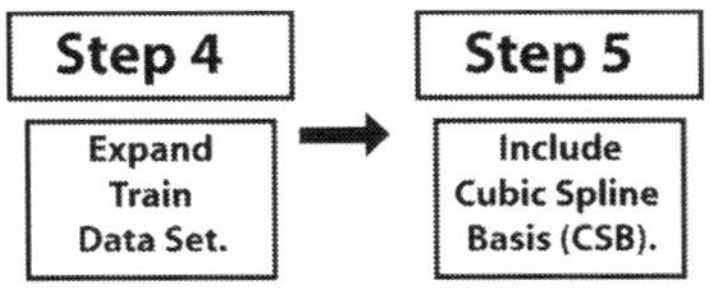

Step 5 is implemented using Base SAS in Program 5.1. This program is a straightforward application of Equation 5.1. It creates five cubic spline basis variables and adds labels to enhance the readability of the table.

Program 5.1: Including the Knots in the Expanded Data Set

```
data Expanded_Data_Set;
set  Expanded_Data_Set;
_csb1=(_t_ >  9)*(_t_- 9)**3 - _t_**3 +  3*9 *_t_**2 - 3 *9**2*_t_;
_csb2=(_t_ > 18)*(_t_-18)**3 - _t_**3 + 3*18 *_t_**2 - 3*18**2*_t_;
_csb3=(_t_ > 27)*(_t_-27)**3 - _t_**3 + 3*27 *_t_**2 - 3*27**2*_t_;
_csb4=(_t_ > 36)*(_t_-36)**3 - _t_**3 + 3*36 *_t_**2 - 3*36**2*_t_;
_csb5=(_t_ > 45)*(_t_-45)**3 - _t_**3 + 3*45 *_t_**2 - 3*45**2*_t_;
label _t_ = "Time reported by MONTH";
label _csb1 = "Cubic Spline Basis Function 1";
label _csb2 = "Cubic Spline Basis Function 2";
label _csb3 = "Cubic Spline Basis Function 3";
label _csb4 = "Cubic Spline Basis Function 4";
label _csb5 = "Cubic Spline Basis Function 5";
run;
```

Or, use IF/THEN statements:

```
data  Expanded_Data_Set;
set   Expanded_Data_Set;

/*----------Generate Cubic Spline Basis Functions-------------*/

if _T_ > 9   then _csb1 =(_T_-9)**3 - _T_**3 + 27*_T_**2 -    243*_T_;
else              _csb1= -_T_**3 + 27*_T_**2 - 243*_T_;

if _T_ > 18  then _csb2 =(_T_-18)**3 - _T_**3 + 54*_T_**2 -   972*_T_;
else              _csb2= -_T_**3 + 54*_T_**2 - 972*_T_;

if _T_ > 27  then _csb3 =(_T_-27)**3 - _T_**3 + 81*_T_**2 -  2187*_T_;
else              _csb3= -_T_**3 + 81*_T_**2 - 2187*_T_;

if _T_ > 36  then _csb4 =(_T_-36)**3 - _T_**3 + 108*_T_**2 - 3888*_T_;
else              _csb4= -_T_**3 + 108*_T_**2 - 3888*_T_;

if _T_ > 45  then _csb5 =(_T_-45)**3 - _T_**3 + 135*_T_**2 - 6075*_T_;
else              _csb5= -_T_**3 + 135*_T_**2 - 6075*_T_;
run;
```

Figure 5.11 shows the updated Hazard function with the knot values.

Figure 5.11: Hazard Function with Five Knots

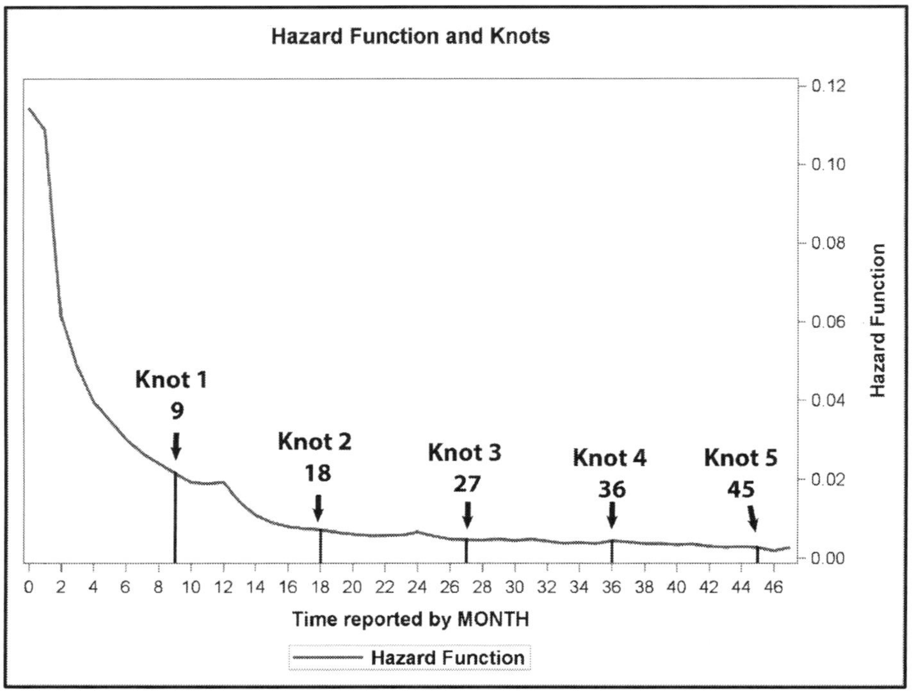

After running the regression spline model using SAS Enterprise Miner, the Survival node creates a number of knot variables named **_csb**+*number*, indicated in the **Effect** column in Output 5.1.

Output 5.1: Model with Five Knots and without Stepwise Regression Method

Type 3 Analysis of Effects

Effect	DF	Wald Chi-Square	Pr > ChiSq
_t_	1	14.0140	0.0002
_csb1	1	324.4101	<.0001
_csb2	1	44.1513	<.0001
_csb3	1	0.8045	0.3698
_csb4	1	2.3279	0.1271
_csb5	1	2.7021	0.1002

The output says the _csb3, _csb4, and _csb5 are not statistically significant at the 0.05 level and should not be included in the model. These _csb variables can be excluded as shown in the next section.

The Default Five-Knots Cubic Splines Basis Method Using the Stepwise Selection

Figure 5.12 shows the **Regression Spline Model** section of the Survival node property panel, with settings changed to use stepwise regression.

Figure 5.12: Regression Spline Model Using the Stepwise Selection

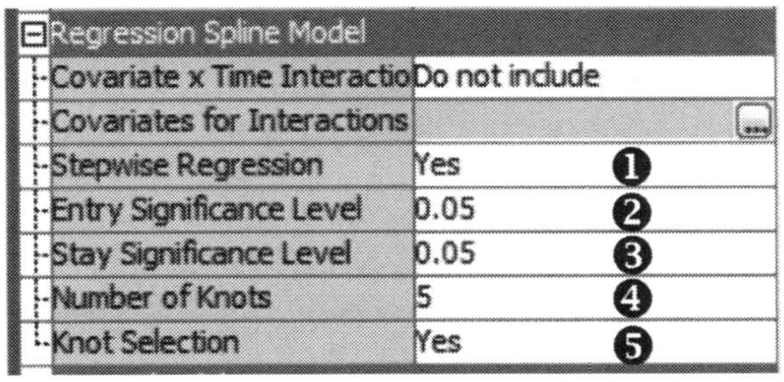

From the drop-down menu ❶, if **Stepwise Regression** is set to **Yes**, then the **Knot Selection** is also **Yes** ❺ and the **Entry Significance Level** and **Stay Significance Level** are kept at 0.05. The stepwise selection method will drop any knot whose level of significance is above 0.05 as indicated by ❷ and ❸. In the next section, the stepwise selection method, entry significance level, and stay significance level are explained in detail.

Output 5.2 shows the five input variables selected by the model. The _csb3 variable has been removed from the model because it did not have the level of statistical significance of 0.05, which is required to stay in the model. Although _csb3, _csb4, and _csb5 were all insignificant when no stepwise selection was performed, removal of _csb3 has revealed that without it, _csb4 and _csb5 are statistically significant at the 5% level. Even so, their place in the model is less secure than _csb1 and _csb2, for which the Wald Chi-Square values are much higher. The larger the Wald Chi-Square value, the greater the significance. For more information, refer to any fundamental statistics documentation.

Output 5.2: The Five Input Variables Selected by the Model

Type 3 Analysis of Effects

Effect	DF	Wald Chi-Square	Pr > ChiSq
_t_	1	33.9114	<.0001
_csb1	1	447.4500	<.0001
_csb2	1	144.0579	<.0001
_csb4	1	52.2483	<.0001
_csb5	1	23.0413	<.0001

Stone (2006) has demonstrated that the location of each knot is not crucial. He suggests placing the knots at fixed percentiles of the time, and that there is no need to have more than seven knots. Personal experience says to place 10 knots for data with more than four years (48 time points – months), and then to use the stepwise selection method to eliminate the knots that are not statistically significant. Each of the retained knots represents a predictor variable in the final model.

Even if the location of the knots is not known in advance, it is possible to know where they should be placed by following the pattern of the Hazard function and paying attention to the seasonality effect as seen in the Sugarloaf Mountain analysis.

The method of placing 10 knots allows the analysis to control the number of knots and to concentrate on what is relevant—the model interpretation of the input variables, which is the principal subject of this chapter.

In this section, look at each betas parameter estimated by the Survival node. You are interested in the interpretation and in the definition of the probability, odds, and the logit.

The Survival model looks at the odds for repurchasing, defined as follows:

$$\text{Odds} = \frac{\text{Prob (Repurchase)}}{1 - \text{Prob (Repurchase)}}$$

Prob (Repurchase) can be replaced by **Hazard(*x*)** for any value of a variable x as follows:

$$\text{Odds} = \frac{\text{Hazard}(x)}{1 - \text{Hazard}(x)}$$

Prob (Repurchase) is not equal to Hazard (Repurchase) for any time. However, the ratios are equal. This can be proven by defining Prob (Repurchase) in terms of hazard. The demonstration of this relationship is presented in Singer and Willett (2003).

By definition, the logit is the logarithm of the odds. The reversibility of the formulas from the logit to odds and vice versa is demonstrated.

Applying a logarithm (logit definition), you can write it as follows:

$$\log(\text{Odds}) = \log\left(\frac{\text{Hazard}(x)}{1 - \text{Hazard}(x)}\right)$$

A device to constrain the hazard to be between 0 and 1 can be calculated, equating the logit to the original function, expressed as follows:

$$\log(\text{Odds}) = \log\left(\frac{\text{Hazard}(x)}{1 - \text{Hazard}(x)}\right) = f(x)$$

Replacing $f(x)$ by $f(x)=\beta_0+\beta_1 x_1$ in the case of just one variable, x_1, you have the following:

$$\log\left(\frac{\text{Hazard}(x)}{1 - \text{Hazard}(x)}\right) = \beta_0 + \beta_1 x_1$$

Applying the exponential function (e = 2.71828) to both sides to eliminate the logarithm, the odds can be expressed as follows:

$$\text{Odds} = e^{\beta_0 + \beta_1 x_1}$$

Or, as follows:

$$\frac{\text{Hazard}(x)}{1 - \text{Hazard}(x)} = e^{\beta_0 + \beta_1 x_1}$$

With a small mathematical transformation, the formula can be expressed in an easier way:

$$\frac{\text{Hazard}(x)}{1-\text{Hazard}(x)} = e^{\beta_0+\beta_1 x_1}$$

$$\frac{\text{Hazard}(x)}{1-\text{Hazard}(x)}(1-\text{Hazard}(x)) = (1-\text{Hazard}(x)) * e^{\beta_0+\beta_1 x_1}$$

Isolate Hazard(x) by multiplying both sides by $(1-\text{Hazard}(x))$.

$$\text{Hazard}(x) = *e^{\beta_0+\beta_1 x_1} - \text{Hazard}(x) * e^{\beta_0+\beta_1 x_1}$$

Multiply out the brackets.

$$\text{Hazard}(x) + \text{Hazard}(x) * e^{\beta_0+\beta_1 x_1} = e^{\beta_0+\beta_1 x_1}$$

Move Hazard(x) from the right to the left side.

$$\text{Hazard}(x)(1+e^{\beta_0+\beta_1 x_1}) = e^{\beta_0+\beta_1 x_1}$$

Isolate Hazard(x) on the left side.

$$\text{Hazard}(x) = \frac{e^{\beta_0+\beta_1 x_1}}{1+e^{\beta_0+\beta_1 x_1}}$$

Another way of calculating hazard is as follows:

$$\text{Hazard}(x) = \frac{\dfrac{e^{\beta_0+\beta_1 x_1}}{e^{\beta_0+\beta_1 x_1}}}{\dfrac{1+e^{\beta_0+\beta_1 x_1}}{e^{\beta_0+\beta_1 x_1}}}$$

Divide both the numerator and denominator by $e^{\beta_0+\beta_1 x_1}$.

$$\text{Hazard}(x) = \frac{1}{\dfrac{1}{e^{\beta_0+\beta_1 x_1}} + \dfrac{e^{\beta_0+\beta_1 x_1}}{e^{\beta_0+\beta_1 x_1}}}$$

The top half is equal to 1. The bottom half can be expressed as two separate fractions with the same denominator.

$$\text{Hazard}(x) = \frac{1}{\dfrac{1}{e^{\beta_0+\beta_1 x_1}} + 1}$$

The term in the bottom half is equal to 1.

$$\text{Hazard}(x) = \frac{1}{e^{-(\beta_0+\beta_1 x_1)} + 1}$$

The inverse of e raised to a positive power can be expressed as e raised to a negative power.

$$\text{Hazard}(x) = \frac{1}{1+e^{-(\beta_0+\beta_1 x_1)}}$$

Books and papers express the Hazard function in two different ways:

$$\text{Hazard}(x) = \frac{e^{\beta_0+\beta_1 x_1}}{1+e^{\beta_0+\beta_1 x_1}}$$

Or, as follows:

$$\text{Hazard}(x) = \frac{1}{1+e^{-(\beta_0+\beta_1 x_1)}}$$

When you derive the Hazard function using SAS Enterprise Miner, the betas are estimated using PROC DMREG.

Example 1: Interpretation of Numeric Variables

In this section, a numeric variable (Prev_Garden) is used as the sole input for a pedagogical purpose. Only the necessary parts of the Analysis of Maximum Likelihood Estimates in the output within the SAS Enterprise Miner Survival node results are commented. This model is not intended to be fully general. The objective is to demonstrate how to interpret numeric variables. For this reason, wherever necessary, the model sacrifices realism in favor of expositional simplicity.

Understanding the Stepwise Regression Spline Model in SAS Enterprise Miner

Before you analyze the model betas coefficients, the stepwise spline selection method is explained to show how it affects the process followed by SAS Enterprise Miner.

Remember that you have specified the following parameters for the regression spline model.

Figure 5.13: Regression Spline Model

Regression Spline Model		
Covariate x Time Interactio	Do not include	
Covariates for Interactions		
Stepwise Regression	Yes	❶
Entry Significance Level	0.05	❷
Stay Significance Level	0.05	❸
Number of Knots	10	❹
Knot Selection	Yes	❺

Output 5.3 gives a summary of the stepwise selection method.

Output 5.3: Summary of the Stepwise Selection Method

Summary of Stepwise Selection ❶

Step	Effect Entered	Effect Removed	DF	Number In	Score Chi-Square	Wald Chi-Square	Pr > ChiSq
1	Prev_Garden ❷		1	2	84981.6499 ❷ ⇦		<.0001
2	_csb10		1	3	10970.1864		<.0001
3	_csb2		1	4	555.7506		<.0001
4	_csb1		1	5	196.9364		<.0001
5	_csb3		1	6	799.8975		<.0001
6	_csb9		1	7	50.0246		<.0001
7	_csb4		1	8	49.1776		<.0001
❹ 8		_csb3 ❸	1	7		0.9094	0.3403 ⇦ ❸
9	_csb6		1	8	31.7164		<.0001
10		_csb9	1	7		0.0029	0.9568 ⇦
11		_csb10	1	6		1.9063	0.1674 ⇦
12	_csb7		1	7	4.2599		0.0390
13	_csb3 ⇦		1	8	16.3546		<.0001
14	_csb8		1	9	3.9561		0.0467
15		_csb7	1	8		0.0000	1.0000

The selected model is the model trained in the last step (Step 15). It consists of the following effects:

Intercept _t_ _csb1 _csb2 _csb3 _csb4 _csb6 _csb8 Prev_Garden

The regression spline model creates a number of knot variables named _csb+*number* ❹ (from step 2 to step 15). Ten knots were included just to explain the stepwise selection method. Of greater interest is the interpretation of the numeric variable Prev_Garden ❷.

The stepwise regression method ❶ is selected. By default, this method begins with no candidate variables in the model. Then, step by step, variables that are significantly associated with the target (Censor = 1) are added. After a variable x_1 is added to the model, stepwise selection removes any other variable x_2 already in the model that is no longer significantly associated with the target.

In step 5, the variable _csb3 is added to the model. This is indicated by the first column (**Step**) of Output 5.3. However, in step 8 ❸, _csb3 is removed.

The first variable to enter the model is Prev_Garden because it has the highest Chi-Square value (**84981.6499**) ❷. This variable was added to the model in step 1 because **Pr > ChiSq** (last column) was below the entry significance level of 0.05.

You can see in the **Removed** column that the variable _csb3 was removed from the model because its **Pr > ChiSq** becomes **0.3403** and is above the stay significance level of 0.05. The same happens for the variables **_csb9** with **Pr > ChiSq** = **0.9568** and **_csb10** with **Pr > ChiSq** = **0.1674**, respectively, in steps 10 and 11.

In summary, a variable x_1 is removed because, with the entry of a new variable x_2 in the model, x_1 becomes no longer statistically significant at a stay significance level of 0.05. The stepwise selection process continues until either of the following conditions occurs:

- No more variables or knots meet the entry significance level of 0.05 (as occurs on the last row in Output 5.3), given that there is just one variable and 10 knots.
- A variable added in a step is the only variable deleted in the next step. In other words, no further variables are selected or retained.

SAS Enterprise Miner included 10 knots ❹. However, because variables can be added and removed in the stepwise selection method, the number of steps is 15.

The knots are entered because *Yes* was selected from the Knot Selection drop-down menu when the model was created.

Stepwise variable selection is performed based on the entry and stay significance levels. Once the variable selection terminates, the final model that optimizes the stepwise selection criterion is chosen and presented in the last row of Output 5.3.

Output 5.4 shows the summary of the variables included in the model.

Output 5.4: Type 3 Analysis of Effects

Type 3 Analysis of Effects

Effect	DF	Wald Chi-Square	Pr > ChiSq
_t_	1	112.2130	<.0001
_csb1	1	501.8462	<.0001
_csb2	1	120.7088	<.0001
_csb3 ❶	1	10.4139	0.0013
_csb4	1	89.0594	<.0001
_csb6	1	76.9639	<.0001
_csb8	1	9.9374	0.0016
Prev_Garden	1	53308.9301	<.0001

Even though the model has just one input variable, there are still the _t_ and CSB variables. All the variables created by SAS Enterprise Miner have an underscore ❶ added as prefix. Look at the Analysis of Maximum Likelihood Estimates in Output 5.5.

Output 5.5: The Analysis of Maximum Likelihood Estimates

Analysis of Maximum Likelihood Estimates

Parameter	_g_	DF	❶ Estimate		Standard Error	Wald Chi-Square	❹ Pr > ChiSq	Standardized Estimate	Exp(Est)
Intercept	1	1	-2.2761	β_0	0.00571	158947.6	<.0001		0.103
_t_	1	1	-0.0321	β_1	0.00303	112.21	<.0001	-0.1976	0.968
_csb1	1	1	-0.0201	β_2	0.000898	501.85	<.0001	-0.1869	0.980
_csb2	1	1	0.00696	β_3	0.000633	120.71	<.0001	0.5728	1.007
_csb3	1	1	0.00178	β_4	0.000553	10.41	0.0013	0.5303	1.002
_csb4	1	1	-0.00299	β_5	0.000317	89.06	<.0001	-2.1981	0.997
_csb6	1	1	0.000833	β_6	0.000095	76.96	<.0001	2.1534	1.001
_csb8	1	1	-0.00008	β_7	0.000024	9.94	0.0016	-0.4705	1.000
Prev_Garden	1	1	❷ 0.00432	β_8	0.000019	53308.93	<.0001	0.1405	1.004 ❸

The Analysis of Maximum Likelihood Estimates output has valuable information. There is the estimate of coefficients (betas) ❶. This value ❷ is of particular interest in relation to the numeric variable Prev_Garden. There is the **Exp (Est)** column, which indicates the odds ratio and is equal to *e* raised to the power of the Estimate value. The value of 1.004 ❸ for Prev_Garden is interpreted later. The **Pr > ChiSq** column ❹ shows that all variables have a *p*-value < 0.05 and are statistically significant at the 5% level.

Writing the Model

Before starting the interpretation, write the model equation using the following formula:

$$\text{Hazard}(x) = \frac{e^{\beta_0+\beta_1 x_1 \ldots \beta_n x_n}}{1+e^{\beta_0+\beta_1 x_1 \ldots \beta_n x_n}}$$

The model can be written as follows:

$$\text{Hazard}(x) = \frac{e^{\text{intercept}+\beta_1 * \_t\_ + \beta_2 * \_csb1 + \ldots.. + \beta_7 * \_csb8 + \beta_8 * \text{Prev\_Garden}}}{1+e^{\text{intercept}+\beta_1 * \_t\_ + \beta_2 * \_csb1 + \ldots.. + \beta_7 * \_csb8 + \beta_8 * \text{Prev\_Garden}}}$$

Replacing the estimate betas by their respective values, the equation becomes as follows:

$$\text{Hazard}(x) = \frac{e^{-2.2761-0.0321 * \_t\_ -0.0201 * \_csb1 + \ldots.. - 0.00008 * \_csb8 + 0.00432 * \text{Prev\_Garden}}}{1+e^{-2.2761-0.0321 * \_t\_ -0.0201 * \_csb1 + \ldots.. - 0.00008 * \_csb8 + 0.00432 * \text{Prev\_Garden}}}$$

Using the above formula, you are able to compute the hazard for any customer and score the probability of repurchase at any time for any value of a previous purchase in the Garden department.

Scoring new customers is one of the most important activities in predictive modeling. SAS Enterprise Miner is designed specifically to do almost all of this with its Score node. The validation process by month is implemented by Base SAS code in Chapter 7. This is necessary because each model needs a specific algorithm to calculate performance.

Understanding the Odds Ratio

The last column of Output 5.5 is the odds ratio estimate for each variable. These are really hazard ratios even though they are labeled odds ratios in Output 5.6. The only difference is that the **Odds Ratio Estimates** output does not display an odds ratio for the intercept.

Output 5.6: The Odds Ratio Estimates

Odds Ratio Estimates

Effect	_g_	Point Estimate
_t_	1	0.968
_csb1	1	0.980
_csb2	1	1.007
_csb3	1	1.002
_csb4	1	0.997
_csb6	1	1.001
_csb8	1	1.000
Prev_Garden	1	⇨ 1.004

Here is the calculation:

$$\text{Odds Ratio} = e^{\beta_{\text{Prev\_Garden}}}$$

$$\text{Odds Ratio} = e^{0.00432}$$

$$\text{Odds Ratio} = 1.004$$

Next, concentrate on the interpretation. Mathematically, the odds ratio is defined as the change in the odds of repurchasing when the value of the predictor variable (Prev_Garden) increases by one unit. Hence, you have the following:

$$\text{Odds Ratio} = \frac{\text{Odds}(x+1)}{\text{Odds}(x)}$$

As Nietzsche said, "There are no facts, only interpretations." The expression $\text{odds ratio} = 1.004$ requires interpretation.

Of interest is how a one-unit (dollar) increase in Prev_Garden (x to $x + 1$, or 100 to 101) will affect the odds for repurchasing. This is captured by the odds ratio:

$$\text{Odds Ratio} = \frac{\text{Odds}(100+1)}{\text{Odds}(100)}$$

The result ($\text{odds ratio} = 1.004$) is the corresponding odds hazard ratio for any one-unit increase in Prev_Garden. In business terms, this means that customers, who in previous purchases have spent one dollar more in the Garden department, have 1.004 times the odds for repurchasing. There is a positive relationship between the value of previous purchases in the Garden department and the odds for repurchasing.

To interpret continuous variables, you need to convert the odds ratio to a percentage increase or decrease in the odds. This conversion can be done as 100(odds ratio − 1).

This conversion of the odds ratio is known as Effect = 100(1.004 − 1) = 0.4%. It indicates a small (approximately 0.4%) but statistically significant increase in effect in the odds and, consequently, in the probability of repurchasing. This value is small because it corresponds to an increase of one dollar. Later, you see the effect of increasing by any value.

Scoring the Odds, Logit, and Hazard

In Program 5.2, you create four customers with all inputs (_t_, _csb1, _csb2, _csb3, _csb4, _csb6, and _csb8) having zero values. This dummy data set enables you to see the impact of changing only the variable of interest (Prev_Garden). This technique is called *sensitivity analysis*. The score code implementation is in SAS DATA steps for easy understanding. The variable Prev_Garden has four different values (1, 100, 101, and 200), and the impact on the probability for repurchasing for each value is worked out.

Program 5.2: Scoring Hazard and Odds

```
data Score;
input ID _t_ _csb1 _csb2 _csb3 _csb4 _csb6 _csb8 Prev_Garden;
datalines;
1 0 0 0 0 0 0 0   1
2 0 0 0 0 0 0 0 100
3 0 0 0 0 0 0 0 101
4 0 0 0 0 0 0 0 200
;
run;
```

In Output 5.7, you see in the last column the four values of Prev_Garden.

Output 5.7: Score

ID	_t_	_csb1	_csb2	_csb3	_csb4	_csb6	_csb8	Prev_Garden
1	0	0	0	0	0	0	0	1
2	0	0	0	0	0	0	0	100
3	0	0	0	0	0	0	0	101
4	0	0	0	0	0	0	0	200

In Program 5.3, the logit is calculated using all decimal cases of the betas coefficient in the Analysis of Maximum Likelihood Estimates. The logit is written as follows:

Logit = –2.2761 – 0.0321 * _t_ – 0.0201 * _csb1 + ... + 0.000833 * _csb8 + 0.00432 * Prev_Garden

Alternatively, as all other input variables are equal to 0, it could be written as follows:

Logit = –2.2761 + 0.00432 * Prev_Garden

Program 5.3: Hazard and Odds Calculation

```
Data   Score;
set    Score;
Logit  = -2.2760723528445    +
                -0.0320768458685    *   _t_    +
                -0.02011530664074   *  _csb1   +
                 0.00695692731619   *  _csb2   +
                 0.00178302023361   *  _csb3   +
                -0.00298710743741   *  _csb4   +
                 0.00083305375912   *  _csb6   +
                -0.00007655969899   *  _csb8   +
                 0.00431827742824 * Prev_Garden;
Hazard = exp(Logit) / (1+exp(Logit));
Odds = (Hazard) / (1-Hazard);
run;
```

The formulas in Table 5.2 score the different customers.

Table 5.2: Formulas for Scoring Customers

Logit	Hazard	Odds
$\text{Logit} = \beta_0 + \beta_1 x_1 \ldots \beta_n x_n$	$\text{Hazard}(x) = \frac{e^{\text{Logit}}}{1+e^{\text{Logit}}}$ or $\text{Hazard}(x) = \frac{e^{\beta_0+\beta_1 x_1 \ldots \beta_n x_n}}{1+e^{\beta_0+\beta_1 x_1 \ldots \beta_n x_n}}$	$\text{Odds} = \frac{\text{Hazard}}{1-\text{Hazard}}$

Output 5.8 shows the calculation of logit, hazard, and odds for each customer ID.

Output 5.8: Score with Logit, Hazard, and Odds

ID	_t_	_csb1	_csb2	_csb3	_csb4	_csb6	_csb8	Prev_Garden	Logit	Hazard	Odds
1	0	0	0	0	0	0	0	1	-2.27175	0.09349	0.10313
2	0	0	0	0	0	0	0	100	-1.84424	0.13655	0.15814
3	0	0	0	0	0	0	0	101	-1.83993	0.13706	0.15883
4	0	0	0	0	0	0	0	200	-1.41242	0.19585	0.24355

Calculating the Odds of Customers 2 and 3 with Prev_Garden = 100 and 101

We know the following:

$$\text{Odds} = \frac{\text{Hazard}}{1-\text{Hazard}}$$

Thus, you can calculate the Odds(100) and Odds(101), replacing Hazard(100) = 0.15814 and Hazard(101) = 0.15883 in the formula:

Table 5.3: Comparison of the Marginal Increase between Odds

Odds(100)	Odds(101)
$\text{Odds}(100) = \dfrac{\text{Hazard}(100)}{1-\text{Hazard}(100)}$	$\text{Odds}(101) = \dfrac{\text{Hazard}(101)}{1-\text{Hazard}(101)}$
$\text{Odds}(100) = \dfrac{0.13655}{1-0.13655}$	$\text{Odds}(101) = \dfrac{0.13706}{1-0.13706}$
$\text{Odds}(100) = 0.15814$	$\text{Odds}(101) = 0.15883$

Using this information, you can calculate the odds ratio. Interpretation of the odds ratio for customer 2 and customer 3 with Prev_Garden = 100 and 101, you know the following:

$$\text{Odds Ratio} = \frac{\text{Odds}(x+1)}{\text{Odds}(x)}$$

Substituting $x = 100$ in the equations gives the following:

$$\text{Odds Ratio} = \frac{\text{Odds}(100+1)}{\text{Odds}(100)} = \frac{\text{Odds}(101)}{\text{Odds}(100)}$$

Hence, you can calculate the odds ratio using the calculated Odds(100) and Odds(101):

$$\text{Odds Ratio} = \frac{\text{Odds}(101)}{\text{Odds}(100)}$$

$$\text{Odds Ratio} = \frac{0.15883}{0.15814}$$

$$\text{Odds Ratio} = 1.004$$

The result is the one-dollar increase from 100 to 101. The same calculation on any arbitrary one-unit increase produces the same result. Customer 3 spends only one dollar more than Customer 2 in previous Garden purchases, and this extra one dollar increases the odds for repurchasing in any month by 0.4%.

This is important from a business perspective because it would enable a Marketing department to rank customers based on their hazard conditional probability for repurchase, conditional on the total amount of previous Garden purchases.

Using the SAS DATA Step to Calculate the Odds Ratio for an Arbitrary Unit Increase

Sometimes, the increase of just one unit in the explicative variable makes it difficult to interpret the odds. Suppose that you want to know the odds for repurchasing given an increase in previous Garden purchases by a different amount, such as 200 dollars ($\Delta = 200$). For every 200-dollar increase in Prev_Garden, how much is the odds ratio affected?

Suppose that a Marketing department wants to know the odds ratio for a customer that has spent 200 dollars more in previous garden purchases than another customer. The answer is to replace Δ by 200 in the following expression:

$$\text{Odds Ratio} = \frac{\text{Odds}(x+\Delta)}{\text{Odds}(x)} = e^{\beta * \Delta}$$

If you follow the same approach that you did using Odds(100) and Odds(101), you can calculate the odds ratio for any arbitrary Δ-unit increase in the predictor variable (Prev_Garden) as follows:

$$\text{Odds Ratio} = \frac{\text{Odds}(x+1)}{\text{Odds}(x)} = e^{\beta}$$

Replacing 1 by any Δ unit gives you the following:

$$\text{Odds Ratio} = \frac{\text{Odds}(x+\Delta)}{\text{Odds}(x)} = e^{\beta * \Delta}$$

This relationship can be used to estimate the odds of repurchasing for a customer with any specified Prev_Garden value. In this example, it is 200. Replace Δ with 200:

$$\text{Odds Ratio} = \frac{\text{Odds}(x+200)}{\text{Odds}(x)} = e^{\beta * 200}$$

$$\text{Odds Ratio} = \frac{\text{Odds}(x+200)}{\text{Odds}(x)} = e^{0.00431827742824 * \mathbf{200}}$$

$$\text{Odds Ratio} = \frac{\text{Odds}(x+200)}{\text{Odds}(x)} = 2.3718$$

In Program 5.4, this calculation is demonstrated using DATA steps.

Program 5.4: Computing the Odds Ratio

```
Data Score;
set  Score;
Odds_ratio = exp (0.00431827742824 * Prev_Garden);
run;
```

Output 5.9 shows the calculated odds ratio values.

Output 5.9: Score with Logit, Hazard, Odds, and Odds Ratio

ID	_t_	_csb1	_csb2	_csb3	_csb4	_csb6	_csb8	Prev_Garden	Logit	Hazard	Odds	Odds_ratio
1	0	0	0	0	0	0	0	1	-2.27175	0.09349	0.10313	1.00433
2	0	0	0	0	0	0	0	100	-1.84424	0.13655	0.15814	1.54007
3	0	0	0	0	0	0	0	101	-1.83993	0.13706	0.15883	1.54673
4	0	0	0	0	0	0	0	200	-1.41242	0.19585	0.24355	2.37182

To interpret continuous variables, you need to convert the odds ratio to a percentage increase or decrease in the odds.

The odds ratio measures the effect of the input variable on the target adjusted for the effect of the other input variables. This can be calculated as 100(Odds Ratio − 1).

The odds ratio for a 200-dollar change in previous purchases is $100(2.37182-1)=137.182$. The odds for repurchasing increases 137.182% for every 200-dollar increase in previous Garden department spending, assuming that others variables do not change.

Note the extraordinary impact on the hazard probability, which increases from 9.349% in the first row for customer 1 compared to 19.585% for customer 4 in the last row. This is the key: customers with higher previous Garden department spending have a higher hazard probability of repurchasing.

To help make the impact of an increase in a variable (for example, Prev_Garden) on the odds ratio more intuitive, convert the odds ratio to a percentage change in the odds.

Using PROC LOGISTIC to Calculate the Odds Ratio for an Arbitrary Unit Increase

SAS Enterprise Miner does not currently have an option to compute the odds ratio for specific values. A possible solution is to use PROC LOGISTIC with the UNITS statement. The UNITS statement enables you to specify units of change for continuous exploratory variables for customized odds ratios.

Using the UNITS statement, you can obtain an odds ratio estimate for a 1, 100, 101, and 200-unit change in Prev_Garden. The data set Numeric was created by the Survival node in model development. The UNITS statement is an easy solution that can be incorporated using the SAS Code node in SAS Enterprise Miner.

Program 5.5: Computing the Odds Ratio Using PROC LOGISTIC

```
proc logistic data= Numeric;
model _g_ (event='1') = _t_ _csb1 _csb2 _csb3 _csb4 _csb6 _csb8 prev_garden;
units Prev_Garden = 1 100 101 200;
run;
```

The odds ratios are presented in Output 5.10.

Output 5.10: Odds Ratio for Selected Previous Values

Odds Ratios		
Effect	**Unit**	**Estimate**
Prev_Garden	1.0000	**1.004**
Prev_Garden	100.0	**1.541**
Prev_Garden	101.0	**1.547**
Prev_Garden	200.0	**2.373**

The results are absolutely the same, proving that you can replicate the results. Having the same results using different approaches and procedures is valuable in terms of quality control and validation.

Example 2: Interpretation of Categorical Variables

This section presents an example where the unique categorical variable Order is used as input. This is the last task in the chapter before interpreting the model results created by the Survival node. Numeric and categorical variables receive a different treatment in the SAS environment. SAS/STAT and SAS Enterprise Miner have a specific way to create class-level information.

Odds Calculation of Categorical Variables

SAS Enterprise Miner handles character variables using generalized linear model (GLM) parameterization by creating ordered values. By default, it does so on the basis of the alphanumeric order of the input variable.

In Output 5.11, the variable **Order** has three categories (**Internet**, **Post**, and **Telephone**) that have been ordered by the DMREG procedure. The reference level, by default, is the last level (in this case, Telephone). The parameter corresponding to the last level is constrained to be 0 with GLM coding. This coding is known as *dummy coding*. The dummy indicator for a variable is coded as 1 except for the last level, which is coded as 0. The parameter estimate for a given category is equal to the estimate of the category minus the estimate of the last category.

Output 5.11: The Analysis of Maximum Likelihood Estimates

Analysis of Maximum Likelihood Estimates

Parameter		_g_	DF	Estimate	Standard Error	Wald Chi-Square	Pr > ChiSq	Standardized Estimate	Exp(Est)
Intercept		1	1	-1.8226	0.00610	89256.64	<.0001		0.162
_t_		1	1	-0.0329	0.00262	157.93	<.0001	-0.2028	0.968
_csb1		1	1	-0.0204	0.000888	525.74	<.0001	-0.1891	0.980
_csb2		1	1	0.00707	0.000639	122.63	<.0001	0.5826	1.007
_csb3		1	1	0.00210	0.000579	13.20	0.0003	0.6255	1.002
_csb4		1	1	-0.00333	0.000355	87.87	<.0001	-2.4507	0.997
_csb6		1	1	0.00117	0.000162	52.23	<.0001	3.0292	1.001
_csb7		1	1	-0.00028	0.000073	15.03	0.0001	-1.1597	1.000
Order	Internet	1	1	-0.2169	0.00573	1432.22	<.0001		0.805
Order	Post	1	1	-0.6107	0.00809	5692.71	<.0001		0.543
Order	Telephone	1	0	0	.	.	.	.	.

Output 5.12 shows the odds ratio estimates.

Output 5.12: The Odds Ratio Estimates

Odds Ratio Estimates

Effect	_g_	Point Estimate
_t_	1	0.968
_csb1	1	0.980
_csb2	1	1.007
_csb3	1	1.002
_csb4	1	0.997
_csb6	1	1.001
_csb7	1	1.000
Order Internet vs Telephone	1	0.805
Order Post vs Telephone	1	0.543

The summary of the categories is presented in Output 5.13. It shows you how the called GLM matrix was constructed.

Output 5.13: Class Level Using GLM Parameterization

Class Level Information

Class	Value	Design Variables		
Order	Internet	1	0	0
	Post	0	1	0
	Telephone	0	0	1

Start by creating three customers, one for each category, with all inputs (_t_, _csb1, _csb2, _csb3, _csb4, _csb6, and _csb7) having 0 values. This gives you the impact of changing only the variable of interest (Order). Program 5.6 shows this program.

Program 5.6: Scoring Hazard and Odds

```
data Score;
input ID _t_ _csb1 _csb2 _csb3 _csb4 _csb6 _csb7 Order $9.;
datalines;
1 0 0 0 0 0 0 0 Internet
2 0 0 0 0 0 0 0 Post
3 0 0 0 0 0 0 0 Telephone
;
run;
```

Using GLM parameterization, considering that all values for the other variables are 0, the model equation can be written as follows:

Logit (Order = **'Internet')** = –1.8226 – 0.2169
Logit (Order = **'Post')** = –1.8226 – 0.6107
Logit (Order = **'Telephone')** = –1.8226 + 0

The SAS DATA step in Program 5.7 implements the model scoring code. The process of scoring and parameterization using GLM is very important to data mining. Being able to replicate SAS output results using SAS code shows a detailed understanding of the mechanics of how the SAS procedure is working.

Program 5.7: Model Scoring

```
Data   Score;
set    Score;
Logit =   -1.82260568952988                 +
        ( -0.03292007993739 ) *   _t_      +
        ( -0.02035468098936 ) *  _csb1     +
        (  0.00707491586773 ) *  _csb2     +
        (  0.00210285918955 ) *  _csb3     +
        ( -0.00333030196019 ) *  _csb4     +
        (  0.00117186976447 ) *  _csb6     +
        ( -0.00028111903118 ) *  _csb7     ;
     if (Order ='Internet')  then  Logit = Logit +( -0.21688313523966);
else if (Order ='Post')      then  Logit = Logit +( -0.61070997901126);
else if (Order ='Telephone') then  Logit = Logit +                 0);
Hazard = exp(Logit) / (1+exp(Logit));
Odds   = (Hazard) / (1-Hazard);
run;
```

Interpretations

Program 5.7 generates Output 5.14.

Output 5.14: Score with Logit, Hazard, and Odds

ID	_t_	_csb1	_csb2	_csb3	_csb4	_csb6	_csb7	Order	Logit	Hazard	Odds
1	0	0	0	0	0	0	0	Internet	-2.03949	0.11512	0.13010
2	0	0	0	0	0	0	0	Post	-2.43332	0.08067	0.08775
3	0	0	0	0	0	0	0	Telephone	-1.82261	0.13912	0.16160

Tables 5.4 through 5.6 give the calculations of the logit, hazard, and odds for each category in the example.

Table 5.4: Interpretation of the Statistics for Customer 1 Order = Internet

Logit (Order = 'Internet')	Hazard (Order = 'Internet')	Odds (Order = 'Internet')
$\text{Logit} = \beta_0 + \beta_1 x_1 .. \beta_n x_n$	$\text{Hazard}(x) = \frac{e^{\text{Logit}}}{1+e^{\text{Logit}}}$	$\text{Odds} = \frac{\text{Hazard}}{1-\text{Hazard}}$
$\text{Logit} = -1.8226 - 0.2169$	$\text{Hazard}(x) = \frac{e^{-2.03949}}{1+e^{-2.03949}}$	$\text{Odds} = \frac{0.11512}{1-0.11512}$
$\text{Logit} = -2.03949$	$\text{Hazard}(x) = 0.11512$	$\text{Odds} = 0.13010$

Table 5.5: Interpretation of the Statistics for Customer 2 Order = Post

Logit (Order = 'Post')	Hazard (Order = 'Post')	Odds (Order = 'Post')
$\text{Logit} = -1.8226 - 0.6107$	$\text{Hazard}(x) = \frac{e^{-2.43332}}{1+e^{-2.43332}}$	$\text{Odds} = \frac{0.08067}{1-0.08067}$
$\text{Logit} = -2.43332$	$\text{Hazard}(x) = 0.08067$	$\text{Odds} = 0.08775$

Table 5.6: Interpretation of the Statistics for Customer 3 Order = Telephone

Logit (Order = 'Telephone')	Hazard (Order = 'Telephone')	Odds (Order = 'Telephone')
$\text{Logit} = -1.8226 + 0$	$\text{Hazard}(x) = \frac{e^{-1.8226}}{1+e^{-1.8226}}$	$\text{Odds} = \frac{0.13912}{1-0.13912}$
$\text{Logit} = -1.8226$	$\text{Hazard}(x) = 0.13912$	$\text{Odds} = 0.16160$

By going through the calculation steps in these tables, you learn the hazard for each category of Order. You can tell that customers buying by telephone ($\text{Hazard}(x) = 0.13912$) have a higher probability of repurchase than customers buying by post ($\text{Hazard}(x) = 0.08067$) or by Internet ($\text{Hazard}(x) = 0.11512$). Not only could you use this information to rank the customers using Order, but it quantifies the relationship across the full database.

The last output to interpret is the odds ratio for each category.

Odds Ratio Internet * Telephone

For odds ratio Internet * telephone, the calculation is as follows:

$$\text{Odds Ratio (Internet * Telephone)} = \frac{\text{Odds Ratio Internet}}{\text{Odds Ratio Telephone}}$$

$$\text{Odds Ratio (Internet * Telephone)} = \frac{0.13010}{0.16160}$$

$$\text{Odds Ratio (Internet * Telephone)} = 0.805$$

The odds ratio for comparing customers buying by Internet with customers buying by telephone is 0.805. Customers who purchase by telephone have 1/0.805 = 1.24 times higher odds of repurchasing than those who purchase by Internet.

Odds Ratio Post * Telephone

For odds ratio post * telephone, the calculation is as follows:

$$\text{Odds Ratio (Post * Telephone)} = \frac{\text{Odds Ratio Post}}{\text{Odds Ratio Telephone}}$$

$$\text{Odds Ratio (Post * Telephone)} = \frac{0.08775}{0.16160}$$

$$\text{Odds Ratio (Post * Telephone)} = 0.543$$

The odds ratio for comparing customers buying by post with customers buying by telephone is 0.543. Customers who purchase by telephone have 1/0.543 = 1.84 times higher odds of repurchasing than those who purchase by post.

Use of PROC LOGISTIC to Generate an Odds Ratio Plot

These interpretations can be improved and validated using PROC LOGISTIC odds ratio comparison plots.

Program 5.8: Computing the Odds Ratio Plots Using PROC LOGISTIC

```
proc logistic data=Categorical
plots(only)=(effect(clband yrange=(0,0.03) ❶
x=(Order))oddsratio(type=horizontalstat))  ❷;
class Order;
model _g_ (event='1') =  _t_  _csb1 _csb2 _csb3 _csb4 _csb6 _csb8 Order
/coding = glm cloods = pl ❸;
oddsratio "Comparison of Order Purchase" Order /diff=all cl=pl ❹;
run;
```

The required plot is created ❶. The default plots generated by specifying the ONLY option are suppressed. CLBAND displays the confidence limits on the plots. YRANGE restricts the y axis range from 0 to 0.03. The TYPE = HORIZONTALSTAT option ❷ displays the values of the odds ratios and their confidence limits on the right side of the plots. CLOODS = PL ❸ requests confidence intervals for the odds ratio. The ODDSRATIO statement ❹, using DIFF = ALL, specifies that the computed odds ratio for a classification variable be compared against all pairs of categories of the variable. CL = PL specifies the profile-likelihood confidence intervals.

The odds ratio estimates are presented in Output 5.15.

Output 5.15: Odds Ratio Estimates

Odds Ratio Estimates and Profile-Likelihood Confidence Intervals				
Label	**Odds Ratio**	**Estimate**	**95% Confidence Limits**	
Comparison of Order Purchase	**Order Internet vs Post**	1.482	1.459	1.506
Comparison of Order Purchase 2	**Order Internet vs Telephone**	0.804	0.795	0.813
Comparison of Order Purchase 3	**Order Post vs Telephone**	0.543	0.534	0.551

An odds ratio close to 1 would indicate that one category versus another has little impact on the odds for repurchasing and that the separate categories would not have power in the survival model. As shown in Figure 5.14, all the results are far from the middle line of 1, indicated by the odds ratio.

Figure 5.14: Odds Ratio with 95% Profile-Likelihood Confidence Limits

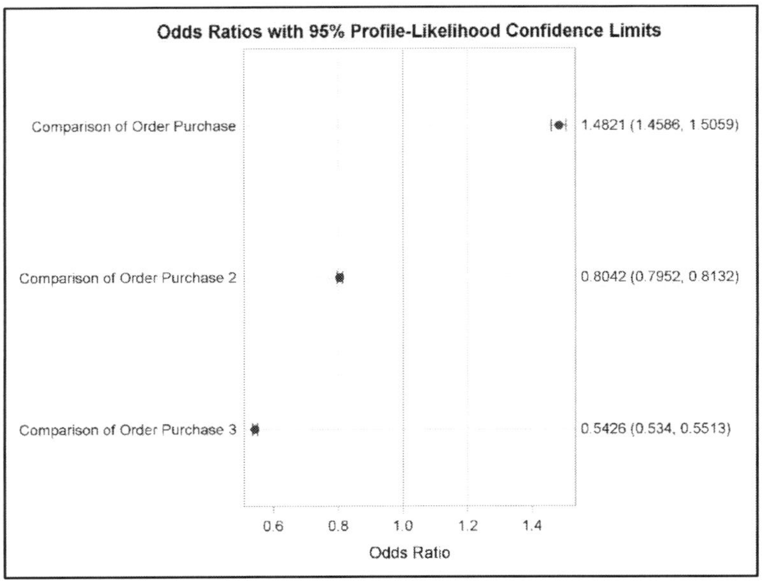

From this figure, you can interpret another relationship not presented by the SAS Enterprise Miner Survival node: the comparison between Internet and post.

The interpretation of the odds ratio Internet * post is as follows:

$$\text{Odds Ratio (Internet * Post)} = \frac{\text{Odds Ratio Internet}}{\text{Odds Ratio Post}}$$

$$\text{Odds Ratio (Internet * Post)} = \frac{0.13010}{0.08775}$$

$$\text{Odds Ratio (Internet * Post)} = 1.482$$

The odds ratio for comparing customers buying by Internet with customers buying by post is 1.482. Customers who purchase by Internet have 1.482 times higher odds of repurchasing than those who purchase by post.

The last figure is the predicted probability for the target by each category, which shows that customers buying by telephone have the highest probabilities of repurchasing.

Figure 5.15: Predicted Probabilities for Repurchase by Order

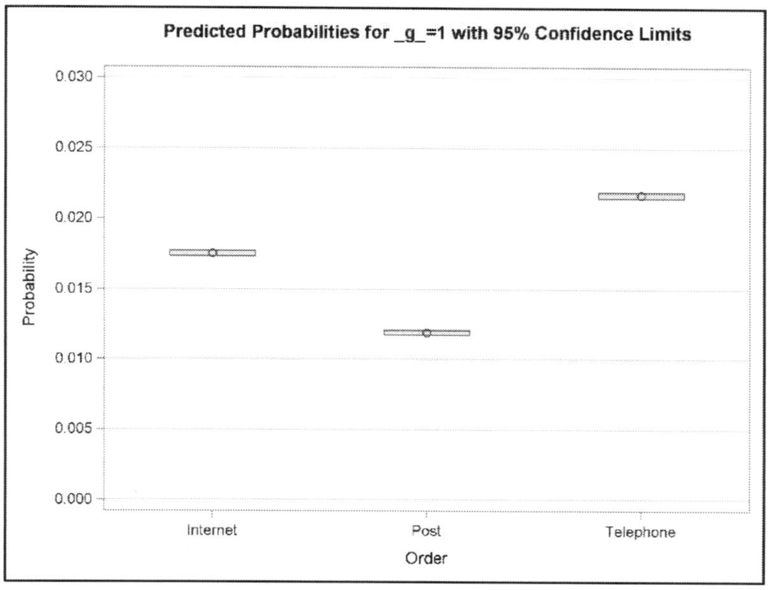

This section has presented all of the necessary tools—the logistic model (PROC LOGISTIC), logit, hazard, and odds—to enable you to interpret the survival model created by SAS Enterprise Miner in Chapter 4. A method to score new customers using SAS DATA steps and PROC LOGISTIC was presented, and the odds ratio for categorical and numeric variables was interpreted.

Next up, more complex analysis.

Model Output

A very important part of the results created by the Survival node is model output. Model output provides complete information about the regression model. In what follows, every output result created by the DMREG procedure is commented on in detail.

Model Information

Output 5.16 shows the model information.

Output 5.16: Model Information

```
The DMREG Procedure
                    Model Information

Training Data Set                ❶ WORK.DMDB_TRAIN.DATA
DMDB Catalog                       WORK.CAT_TRAIN

Target Variable                  ❷ _g_
Target Measurement Level           Nominal
Number of Target Categories        2
Error                              MBernoulli
Link Function                    ❸ Logit

Number of Model Parameters       ❹ 81

Number of Observations           ❺ 4880100
                Target Profile

 Ordered                           Total
   Value             _g_       Frequency

       1               1          152965
       2               0         4727135
```

The model information output presents the most important information about the model in a condensed table.

The training data set ❶ is the Expanded data set created by the Survival node that contains _t_ and the _csb variables. The number of observations (4,880,100) ❺ is explained by the preparation that expands the data from one record per customer to one record per month per customer.

The **Number of Model Parameters** ❹ is the most eye-catching information in this output. Although the training data set has less than 30 variables, the number of parameters is 81. The explanation is that some of the input variables are categorical. Encoding a categorical variable using GLM parameterization requires the creation of dummy variables for each categorical variable.

More surprising than the number of parameters and number of observations is the reported Target variable name ❷. The Survival node renamed the binary (1 or 0) Target variable from Censor to _g_. In the next chapter, the Target variable is discussed in detail. The most important information about the logistic regression ❸ is provided by the Link function, which shows that you are modeling the hazard with a binary target using a Logit function.

In Output 5.17, the class-level information presents all of the input categorical variables entering in the stepwise selection method, even if the variable was not retained in the final model.

Output 5.17: Class-Level Information

Class Level Information

Class	Value	Design Variables															
Account_Origin	Branch	1	0	0	0												
	Internet	0	1	0	0												
	Post	0	0	1	0												
	Telephone	0	0	0	1												
Age	18 - 31	1	0	0	0	0	0	0									
	32 - 43	0	1	0	0	0	0	0									
	44 - 56	0	0	1	0	0	0	0									
	57 - 68	0	0	0	1	0	0	0									
	69 - 81	0	0	0	0	1	0	0									
	82 - high	0	0	0	0	0	1	0									
	Missing	0	0	0	0	0	0	1									
Behaviour	1-AAA	1	0	0	0	0	0	0									
	2-AA	0	1	0	0	0	0	0									
	3-A	0	0	1	0	0	0	0									
	4-BBB	0	0	0	1	0	0	0									
	5-BB	0	0	0	0	1	0	0									
	6-B	0	0	0	0	0	1	0									
	Unknown	0	0	0	0	0	0	1									
Credicard	A	1	0	0	0	0	0										
	B	0	1	0	0	0	0										
	C	0	0	1	0	0	0										
	D	0	0	0	1	0	0										
	E	0	0	0	0	1	0										
	F	0	0	0	0	0	1										
Credit_score	0 - 400	1	0	0	0	0											
	400 - 600	0	1	0	0	0											
	600 - 800	0	0	1	0	0											
	800 - 1000	0	0	0	1	0											
	Missing	0	0	0	0	1											
Mosaic	01	1	0	0	0	0	0	0	0	0	0	0	0	0	0	0	0
	02	0	1	0	0	0	0	0	0	0	0	0	0	0	0	0	0
	03	0	0	1	0	0	0	0	0	0	0	0	0	0	0	0	0
	04	0	0	0	1	0	0	0	0	0	0	0	0	0	0	0	0
	05	0	0	0	0	1	0	0	0	0	0	0	0	0	0	0	0
	06	0	0	0	0	0	1	0	0	0	0	0	0	0	0	0	0
	07	0	0	0	0	0	0	1	0	0	0	0	0	0	0	0	0
	08	0	0	0	0	0	0	0	1	0	0	0	0	0	0	0	0
	09	0	0	0	0	0	0	0	0	1	0	0	0	0	0	0	0
	10	0	0	0	0	0	0	0	0	0	1	0	0	0	0	0	0
	11	0	0	0	0	0	0	0	0	0	0	1	0	0	0	0	0
	12	0	0	0	0	0	0	0	0	0	0	0	1	0	0	0	0
	13	0	0	0	0	0	0	0	0	0	0	0	0	1	0	0	0
	14	0	0	0	0	0	0	0	0	0	0	0	0	0	1	0	0
	15	0	0	0	0	0	0	0	0	0	0	0	0	0	0	1	0
	99	0	0	0	0	0	0	0	0	0	0	0	0	0	0	0	1
Order	Internet	1	0	0													
	Post	0	1	0													
	Telephone	0	0	1													
Strata	01-02-(2011-2013)	1	0	0	0	0	0										
	01-02-(2014)	0	1	0	0	0	0										
	03-04	0	0	1	0	0	0										
	05-10	0	0	0	1	0	0										
	11-20	0	0	0	0	1	0										
	21-High ⇦	0	0	0	0	0	1										

For the Strata categorical variable, GLM parameterization generates six columns for its main effect in the model design matrix. Each column is a dummy indicator variable for a category level. The columns are ordered by the alphanumeric order of the category values.

The reason that **21-High** is indicated in the class-level information table is that the model parameter estimate for **Strata** = **01-02-(2011-2013)** measures the difference in effect between the 01-02-(2011-2013) category and 21-High, the last category. In the subsection "Strata Analysis," you provide the calculation and interpretation using every category of the Strata variable.

In Output 5.18, the most important information from the Summary of Stepwise Selection table is the Wald Chi-Square statistic. You see that **Strata** has the highest value (**235604.728**), indicating that the variable will be the first included in the model by the stepwise selection method.

Output 5.18: Summary of Stepwise Selection

Summary of Stepwise Selection

Step	Effect Entered	Removed	DF	Number In	Score Chi-Square	Wald Chi-Square	Pr > ChiSq
1	Strata		5	2	235604.728		<.0001
2	Behaviour		6	3	23181.9597		<.0001
3	_csb10		1	4	5541.2570		<.0001
4	Prev_Garden		1	5	2009.5813		<.0001
5	Order		2	6	1141.2056		<.0001
6	Account_Origin		3	7	1248.2470		<.0001
7	_csb2		1	8	763.6357		<.0001
8	Garden		1	9	489.5650		<.0001
9	Prev_Decorating		1	10	454.0739		<.0001
10	Decorating		1	11	557.5197		<.0001
11	Credicard		5	12	391.5670		<.0001
12	Prev_Safety		1	13	501.3682		<.0001
13	_csb1		1	14	220.8554		<.0001
14	_csb3		1	15	805.2194		<.0001
15	Prev_Car		1	16	193.4198		<.0001
16	Car		1	17	288.2916		<.0001
17	Credit_score		4	18	128.6984		<.0001
18	Prev_Electrical		1	19	103.2323		<.0001
19	Mosaic		15	20	89.7150		<.0001
20	Prev_Computer		1	21	42.2871		<.0001
21	_csb9		1	22	32.5655		<.0001
22	_csb4		1	23	73.6746		<.0001
23		_csb3	1	22		0.4489	0.5028
24	Amount_CLV		1	23	22.8587		<.0001
25	_csb6		1	24	18.6444		<.0001
26		_csb9	1	23		0.6029	0.4375
27	_csb3		1	24	24.3088		<.0001
28	Age		6	25	19.4086		0.0035
29	_csb7		1	26	4.5946		0.0321
30		_csb10	1	25		0.1006	0.7512

Age (step 28) has the lowest Wald Chi-Square value (**19.4086**), indicating that it is the last variable to include in the model. The variable _t_ is included by default in the model, but is not part of the stepwise selection method.

SAS Enterprise Miner produces Output 5.19, which shows the variables statistically significant at the STAY = 0.05 level, controlling for other input variables in the model. The variables in ❶ and ❷ are numeric. The variables in ❸ are categorical.

Output 5.19: Type 3 Analysis of Effects

Type 3 Analysis of Effects

Effect	DF	Wald Chi-Square	Pr > ChiSq
_t_	1	53.0311	<.0001
_csb1	1	459.1650	<.0001
_csb2	1	82.2395	<.0001
_csb3 ❶	1	27.6098	<.0001
_csb4	1	109.5351	<.0001
_csb6	1	62.9468	<.0001
_csb7	1	26.6587	<.0001
Account_Origin	3	1090.4614	<.0001
⇨ Age	6	⇨ 18.8630	⇨ 0.0044
Behaviour	6	15532.4664	<.0001
Credicard	5	660.3675	<.0001
Credit_score ❸	4	128.9094	<.0001
Mosaic	15	87.7625	<.0001
Order	2	2079.8240	<.0001
Strata	5	54418.8780	<.0001
Amount_CLV	1	19.6603	<.0001
Car	1	283.6591	<.0001
Decorating	1	521.3278	<.0001
Garden	1	578.6375	<.0001
Prev_Car ❷	1	406.7606	<.0001
Prev_Computer	1	66.1819	<.0001
Prev_Decorating	1	885.5248	<.0001
Prev_Electrical	1	127.3495	<.0001
Prev_Garden	1	1146.6425	<.0001
Prev_Safety	1	291.3021	<.0001

The Wald Chi-Square test for effects of variables having DF = 1 (degrees of freedom) is the same as for parameter estimates in Output 5.20. To determine the number of degrees of freedom for the effects of categorical variables in a logistic model with a binary outcome (such as Censor (1 or 0)), apply the formula DF = L - 1, where L is the number of categories.

For example, the variable Order has three categories (Internet, Post, and Telephone). Therefore, L = 3, and their DF = 3 − 1 = 2. All numeric variables have DF = 1.

Age has the lowest Wald Chi-Square value and consequently has the lowest **Pr > ChiSq** = **0.0044**. This is a good indication that you can improve model performance by modifying the binning process of the variable. The modification of the numeric continuous variable Age using a different bin can be tested running another model by changing just the variable and comparing the results.

In Figure 5.16, include the Interactive Binning node before the Survival node, and run the model again by modifying the variable of interest.

Figure 5.16: Interactive Binning Node

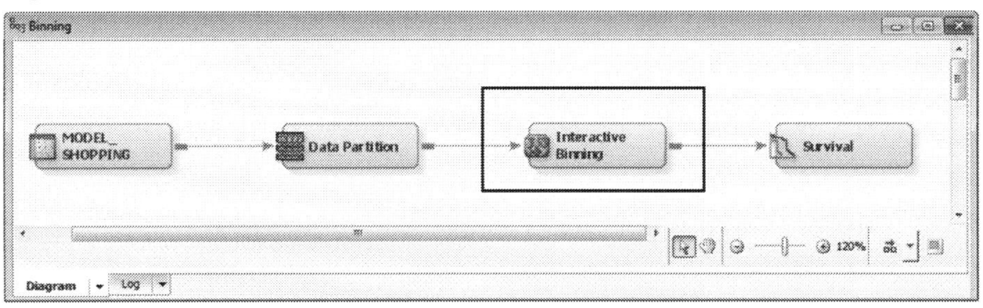

The Interactive Binning node belongs to the Modify category. The Interactive Binning node is a grouping tool that improves models by computing initial bins by quantiles. Then, you can interactively split and combine the initial bins, creating classes in order to reduce the number of unique levels and to attempt to improve the predictive power of each input having continuous distributions.

In Output 5.19, the variable Strata has the highest Wald Chi-Square. In Output 5.20, the coefficients, hazard, and odds for each category are analyzed using just one variable.

Output 5.20: Analysis of Maximum Likelihood Estimates

Analysis of Maximum Likelihood Estimates

Parameter		_g_	DF	Estimate	Standard Error	Wald Chi-Square	Pr > ChiSq	Standardized Estimate	Exp(Est)
Intercept		1	1	-1.3082	0.0497	693.52	<.0001		0.270
_t_		1	1	-0.0190	0.00261	53.03	<.0001	-0.1170	0.981
_csb1		1	1	-0.0200	0.000936	459.16	<.0001	-0.1862	0.980
_csb2		1	1	0.00600	0.000662	82.24	<.0001	0.4940	1.006
_csb3		1	1	0.00311	0.000593	27.61	<.0001	0.9262	1.003
_csb4		1	1	-0.00378	0.000361	109.54	<.0001	-2.7810	0.996
_csb6		1	1	0.00130	0.000164	62.95	<.0001	3.3545	1.001
_csb7		1	1	-0.00038	0.000073	26.66	<.0001	-1.5547	1.000
Account_Origin	Branch	1	1	-0.00123	0.0128	0.01	0.9231		0.999
Account_Origin	Internet	1	1	0.3395	0.0111	939.40	<.0001		1.404
Account_Origin	Post	1	1	0.0782	0.0111	49.67	<.0001		1.081
Account_Origin	Telephone	1	0	0	.	.	.	.	.
Age	18 - 31	1	1	-0.0477	0.0181	6.91	0.0086		0.953
Age	32 - 43	1	1	-0.0385	0.0168	5.27	0.0217		0.962
Age	44 - 56	1	1	-0.0536	0.0149	12.93	0.0003		0.948
Age	57 - 68	1	1	-0.0345	0.0137	6.37	0.0116		0.966
Age	69 - 81	1	1	-0.0184	0.0133	1.91	0.1674		0.982
Age	82 - high	1	1	-0.0101	0.0158	0.41	0.5203		0.990
Age	Missing	1	0	0	.	.	.	.	.
Behaviour	1-AAA	1	1	0.4696	0.0392	143.86	<.0001		1.599
Behaviour	2-AA	1	1	0.6341	0.0350	327.44	<.0001		1.885
Behaviour	3-A	1	1	-0.5934	0.0370	257.61	<.0001		0.552
Behaviour	4-BBB	1	1	-0.2852	0.0349	66.88	<.0001		0.752
Behaviour	5-BB	1	1	0.9447	0.0358	696.70	<.0001		2.572
Behaviour	6-B	1	1	1.0548	0.0377	782.81	<.0001		2.872
Behaviour	Unknown	1	0	0	.	.	.	.	.
Credicard	A	1	1	-0.7744	0.0528	215.37	<.0001		0.461
Credicard	B	1	1	-0.6523	0.0536	148.14	<.0001		0.521
Credicard	C	1	1	-0.4357	0.0455	91.55	<.0001		0.647
Credicard	D	1	1	-0.6065	0.0458	175.10	<.0001		0.545
Credicard	E	1	1	-0.6043	0.0640	89.22	<.0001		0.546
Credicard	F	1	0	0	.	.	.	.	.
Credit_score	0 - 400	1	1	-0.3296	0.0318	107.70	<.0001		0.719
Credit_score	400 - 600	1	1	-0.0291	0.0147	3.93	0.0474		0.971
Credit_score	600 - 800	1	1	-0.0116	0.0107	1.18	0.2774		0.988
Credit_score	800 - 1000	1	1	-0.0435	0.00869	25.03	<.0001		0.957
Credit_score	Missing	1	0	0	.	.	.	.	.
Mosaic	01	1	1	-0.0686	0.0345	3.96	0.0465		0.934
Mosaic	02	1	1	-0.0562	0.0305	3.40	0.0653		0.945
Mosaic	03	1	1	-0.0534	0.0315	2.88	0.0896		0.948
Mosaic	04	1	1	-0.0247	0.0301	0.67	0.4115		0.976
Mosaic	05	1	1	-0.0478	0.0309	2.40	0.1214		0.953
Mosaic	06	1	1	-0.0424	0.0301	1.99	0.1582		0.958
Mosaic	07	1	1	-0.0390	0.0323	1.46	0.2272		0.962
Mosaic	08	1	1	-0.0163	0.0331	0.24	0.6224		0.984
Mosaic	09	1	1	0.00804	0.0299	0.07	0.7880		1.008
Mosaic	10	1	1	0.0185	0.0308	0.36	0.5487		1.019
Mosaic	11	1	1	-0.0518	0.0324	2.56	0.1098		0.950
Mosaic	12	1	1	0.00277	0.0306	0.01	0.9278		1.003
Mosaic	13	1	1	-0.0142	0.0303	0.22	0.6386		0.986
Mosaic	14	1	1	-0.0576	0.0311	3.42	0.0643		0.944
Mosaic	15	1	1	-0.0721	0.0323	4.99	0.0255		0.930
Mosaic	99	1	0	0	.	.	.	.	.
Order	Internet	1	1	-0.4268	0.00990	1856.43	<.0001		0.653
Order	Post	1	1	-0.2255	0.0104	471.24	<.0001		0.798
Order	Telephone	1	0	0	.	.	.	.	.
Strata	01-02-(2011-2013)	1	1	-1.6319	0.0224	5328.16	<.0001		0.196
Strata	01-02-(2014)	1	1	-1.1327	0.0239	2253.84	<.0001		0.322
Strata	03-04	1	1	0.3942	0.0214	339.25	<.0001		1.483
Strata	05-10	1	1	0.3180	0.0216	216.81	<.0001		1.374
Strata	11-20	1	1	0.1964	0.0173	129.28	<.0001		1.217
Strata	21-High	1	0	0	.	.	.	.	.
Amount_CLV		1	1	-0.00005	0.000011	19.66	<.0001	-0.00875	1.000
Car		1	1	-0.00219	0.000130	283.66	<.0001	-0.0461	0.998
Decorating		1	1	-0.00364	0.000159	521.33	<.0001	-0.0834	0.996
Garden		1	1	-0.00223	0.000093	578.64	<.0001	-0.0870	0.998
Prev_Car		1	1	0.00351	0.000174	406.76	<.0001	0.0538	1.004
Prev_Computer		1	1	0.000183	0.000022	66.18	<.0001	0.0102	1.000
Prev_Decorating		1	1	0.00551	0.000185	885.52	<.0001	0.0955	1.006
Prev_Electrical		1	1	0.00105	0.000093	127.35	<.0001	0.0108	1.001
Prev_Garden		1	1	0.00347	0.000102	1146.64	<.0001	0.1128	1.003
Prev_Safety		1	1	0.00122	0.000071	291.30	<.0001	0.0161	1.001

Two other important variables that should be analyzed are Garden and Prev_Garden.

Strata Analysis

Extract only the necessary information required from Output 5.20 to create Output 5.21.

Output 5.21: Strata Coefficients and Odds

Parameter		Estimate	Exp(Est)
Strata	01-02-(2011-2013)	-1.6319	0.196
Strata	01-02-(2014)	-1.1327	0.322
Strata	03-04	0.3942	1.483
Strata	05-10	0.3180	1.374
Strata	11-20	0.1964	1.217
Strata	21-High	0	.

In Program 5.9, start by creating six customer IDs, one for each category of Strata, with all inputs having zero values. This gives you the impact of changing only the variable of interest.

Program 5.9: Scoring Hazard and Odds for Strata

```
Data  Score;
input ID Strata $17.;
datalines;
1 01-02-(2011-2013)
2 01-02-(2014)
3 03-05
4 06-10
5 11-20
6 21-High
;
run;
```

Using the GLM parameterization with the betas coefficients and simplifying all values for other variables to 0, the model equation can be written as follows in Program 5.10:

Program 5.10: Hazard and Odds Code for Categorical Variables

```
Data  Score;
set   Score;
     if (strata = "01-02-(2011-2013)") then Logit = -1.3082 +( -1.6319 );
else if (strata = "01-02-(2014)")      then Logit = -1.3082 +( -1.1327 );
else if (strata = "03-05")             then Logit = -1.3082 +(  0.3942 );
else if (strata = "06-10")             then Logit = -1.3082 +(  0.3180 );
else if (strata = "11-20")             then Logit = -1.3082 +(  0.1964 );
else if (strata = "21-High")           then Logit = -1.3082 +(       0 );
Hazard = exp(Logit) / (1+exp(Logit));
Odds   = (Hazard) / (1-Hazard);
run;
```

Output 5.22 shows the variables created after running Program 5.10.

Output 5.22: Score with Logit, Hazard, and Odds

ID	strata	Logit	Hazard	Odds
1	01-02-(2011-2013)	-2.9401	**0.05021**	0.05286
2	01-02-(2014)	-2.4409	**0.08011**	0.08708
3	03-05	-0.9140	**0.28618**	0.40092
4	06-10	-0.9902	**0.27087**	0.37150
5	11-20	-1.1118	**0.24754**	0.32897
6	21-High	-1.3082	**0.21279**	0.27031

The focus of this analysis is the variable of interest—the Hazard probability. These results are very conclusive.

- Customers in the **Strata** = **01-02-(2011-2013)** and **Strata** = **01-02-(2014)**, IDs **1** and **2** respectively, have the lowest odds for repurchasing. The difference in the **Hazard (0.05021** to **0.08011**) is due to the fact that new customers who bought only in 2014 (01-02-(2014)) have a higher propensity to buy again than customers who have more than one year since their first purchase (Strata = 01-02-(2011-2013)). This might be partly explained by the memory effect, where some customers forget or do not care how they originally made their purchase and never return to buy again. Customers in both strata 01-02-(2011-2013) and 01-02-(2014) have lower hazard probabilities to repurchase than customers who are in other strata.
- The hazard probabilities of the customers of **Strata** = **03-05** to **Strata** = **21-High** decrease linearly as a function of the number of purchases realized in the past. For six or more previous Garden purchases, the number of Garden purchases previously made decreases the chance of repurchase. One explanation for this is that customer demand might have been exhausted. Garden equipment is usually durable and is bought for a functional purpose, so customers who have made a significant number of previous purchases might have their demand satisfied. They have a garden table, hedge trimmer, manicured lawn, and everything else being sold, so they do not need to repurchase. Another explanation is that these customers might have a greater inclination to shop around and choose other suppliers (for example, trade discount providers). The many purchases made are actually infrequent convenience purchases. These customers usually buy through specialist channels at discounted prices.

Output 5.23 shows the estimates of the variables Garden and Prev_Garden.

Output 5.23: Garden and Prev_Garden Analysis

Parameter		Estimate	Pr > ChiSq	Exp(Est)
Car		-0.00219	<.0001	0.998
Decorating		-0.00364	<.0001	0.996
Garden	⇦	-0.00223	<.0001	0.998
Prev_Car		0.00351	<.0001	1.004
Prev_Computer		0.000183	<.0001	1.000
Prev_Decorating		0.00551	<.0001	1.006
Prev_Electrical		0.00105	<.0001	1.001
Prev_Garden	⇦	0.00347	<.0001	1.003
Prev_Safety		0.00122	<.0001	1.001

Table 5.7 shows the calculation and the interpretation of the variables.

Table 5.7: Odds Ratio Calculation and Interpretation of Variables

Variable and Calculation	Interpretation
Garden Odds Ratio = $e^{\beta_{Garden}}$ Odds Ratio = $e^{-0.00223}$ Odds Ratio = 0.998 ⇩	This small EFFECT = 100(0.998–1) = –0.2 % indicates a decrease in the odds and consequently in the probability of repurchasing. Note that **Garden** is the value of the first purchase. You have the same interpretation for the other variables **Car (0.998)** and **Decorating (0.996)**. If the amount spent in the first purchase is high, customers are less likely to repurchase. For every one-dollar increase in Garden, the odds ratio decreases by 0.2%. The relationship is negative.
Prev_Garden Odds Ratio = $e^{\beta_{Prev\_Garden}}$ Odds Ratio = $e^{0.00347}$ Odds Ratio = 1.003 ⇧	Note that **Prev_Garden** is the value of all purchases realized before the first purchase indicated by variable Garden. It is a sum of all purchases made previously by the customer. For every one-dollar increase in Prev_Garden, the odds for repurchase increase by 1.003. The relationship is positive. Customers who have spent more in the past are more likely to spend again.

The odds ratio estimates in Output 5.24 show the point estimate for every variable included in the model.

Output 5.24: Odds Ratio Estimates

Odds Ratio Estimates

Effect		_g_	Point Estimate
_t_		1	0.981
_csb1		1	0.980
_csb2		1	1.006
_csb3		1	1.003
_csb4		1	0.996
_csb6		1	1.001
_csb7		1	1.000
Account_Origin	Branch vs Telephone	1	0.999
Account_Origin	Internet vs Telephone	1	1.404
Account_Origin	Post vs Telephone	1	1.081
Age	18 - 31 vs Missing	1	0.953
Age	32 - 43 vs Missing	1	0.962
Age	44 - 56 vs Missing	1	0.948
Age	57 - 68 vs Missing	1	0.966
Age	69 - 81 vs Missing	1	0.982
Age	82 - high vs Missing	1	0.990
Behaviour	1-AAA vs Unknown	1	1.599
Behaviour	2-AA vs Unknown	1	1.885
Behaviour	3-A vs Unknown	1	0.552
Behaviour	4-BBB vs Unknown	1	0.752
Behaviour	5-BB vs Unknown	1	2.572
Behaviour	6-B vs Unknown	1	2.872
Credicard	A vs F	1	0.461
Credicard	B vs F	1	0.521
Credicard	C vs F	1	0.647
Credicard	D vs F	1	0.545
Credicard	E vs F	1	0.546
Credit_score	0 - 400 vs Missing	1	0.719
Credit_score	400 - 600 vs Missing	1	0.971
Credit_score	600 - 800 vs Missing	1	0.988
Credit_score	800 - 1000 vs Missing	1	0.957
Mosaic	01 vs 99	1	0.934
Mosaic	02 vs 99	1	0.945
Mosaic	03 vs 99	1	0.948
Mosaic	04 vs 99	1	0.976
Mosaic	05 vs 99	1	0.953
Mosaic	06 vs 99	1	0.958
Mosaic	07 vs 99	1	0.962
Mosaic	08 vs 99	1	0.984
Mosaic	09 vs 99	1	1.008
Mosaic	10 vs 99	1	1.019
Mosaic	11 vs 99	1	0.950
Mosaic	12 vs 99	1	1.003
Mosaic	13 vs 99	1	0.986
Mosaic	14 vs 99	1	0.944
Mosaic	15 vs 99	1	0.930
Order	Internet vs Telephone	1	0.653
Order	Post vs Telephone	1	0.798
Strata	01-02-(2011-2013) vs 21-Hig	1	0.196
Strata	01-02-(2014) vs 21-High	1	0.322
Strata	03-04 vs 21-High	1	1.483
Strata	05-10 vs 21-High	1	1.374
Strata	11-20 vs 21-High	1	1.217
Amount_CLV		1	1.000
Car		1	0.998
Decorating		1	0.996
Garden		1	0.998
Prev_Car		1	1.004
Prev_Computer		1	1.000
Prev_Decorating		1	1.006
Prev_Electrical		1	1.001
Prev_Garden		1	1.003
Prev_Safety		1	1.001

The odds ratio estimates in Output 5.24 show that between the numeric variables, a one-dollar increase in **Prev_Decorating (1.006)** produces the largest change in the repurchase odds. This is a strategic advantage for this department. A customer who bought decorations from the company is more likely to repurchase than a customer who bought electrical tools (**Prev_Electrical** = **1.001**).

The Hazard and Survival functions have been thoroughly explained. SAS Enterprise Miner presents both functions overlaid on two axes. The left vertical axis represents the Survival function, and the right vertical axis represents the Hazard function. The horizontal axis is the Time unit in months. Note that the graph displays both functions as if the data is continuous, even though a discrete survival model has been applied.

This graph is useful for validation of model robustness. To check that the model created from 70% of data is accurate for all data (Model_Shopping data set), this graphic can be compared with the equivalent Survival and Hazard functions graphic generated for all data. The pattern and proportion of the curves should be the same in the Survival and Hazard functions graphic, as is true in this case.

Output 5.25: Survival and Hazard Functions

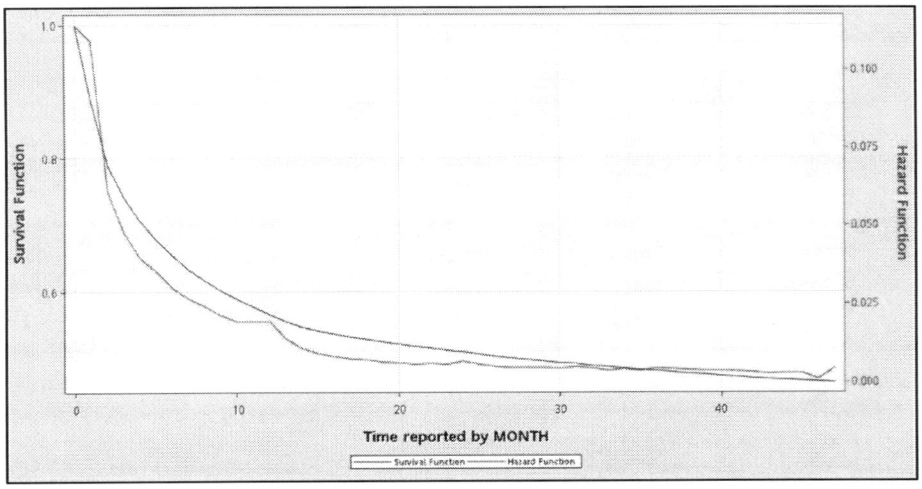

You can see the data set used to create this graph by clicking on the figure, and then selecting the Table icon as seen in Figure 5.17. You will see the data set in SAS Enterprise Miner.

Figure 5.17: Table Icone

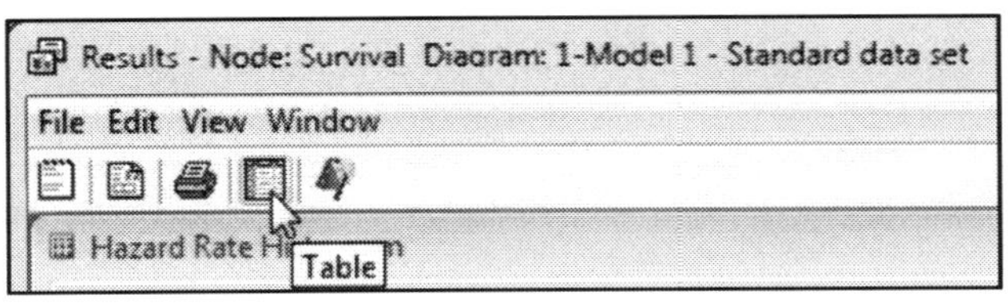

Scroll down the window to view the Empirical Survival function for the Training data set as presented in Output 5.26. To see the data set used to create Output 5.26, click on the figure, and then select the Table icon.

Output 5.26: Empirical Survival Function for Training Data

Results - Node: Survival Diagram: 1-Model 1 - Standard data set

File Edit View Window

Table: Empirical Survival Function for Training Data

Time reported by MONTH	Subject Number at Risk	Hazard Function	Survival Function
0	331645	0.114396	1
1	289795	0.109308	0.885604
2	251515	0.061106	0.7888
3	230562	0.047922	0.7406
4	215241	0.039491	0.705109
5	202490	0.035231	0.677263
6	191294	0.02998	0.653402
7	180370	0.026967	0.633813
8	171531	0.024305	0.616722
9	163387	0.021415	0.601732
10	155035	0.019383	0.588846
11	148589	0.019355	0.577433
12	142715	0.018234	0.566256
13	137454	0.013968	0.555365
14	130254	0.010932	0.547607
15	123977	0.009115	0.54162
16	119042	0.008039	0.536684
17	114699	0.007341	0.532369
18	110702	0.007055	0.528461
19	105974	0.006407	0.524733
20	100965	0.006032	0.521371
21	96022	0.005582	0.518226
22	91312	0.005782	0.515333
23	87806	0.005729	0.512353
24	84231	0.006684	0.509418
25	81158	0.00568	0.506013
26	75905	0.004901	0.503139
27	70606	0.00466	0.500673
28	66827	0.004549	0.49834
29	63504	0.00474	0.496073
30	60337	0.004442	0.493722
31	56356	0.004862	0.491529
32	52330	0.004433	0.489139
33	48707	0.003675	0.486971
34	44534	0.004177	0.485181
35	40941	0.003639	0.483155
36	37977	0.004476	0.481396
37	35462	0.00423	0.479241
38	31875	0.003827	0.477214
39	27784	0.003671	0.475388
40	24234	0.003507	0.473643
41	21278	0.003384	0.471981
42	18650	0.00311	0.470384
43	15893	0.00258	0.468921
44	12325	0.002921	0.467712
45	9217	0.002929	0.466345
46	5260	.0007605	0.464979
47	2333	0.004286	0.464626

The Empirical Survival function for the Training Data was created using the SAS Enterprise Miner strategy in Figure 5.18.

Figure 5.18: SAS Enterprise Miner Adjustment Flowchart

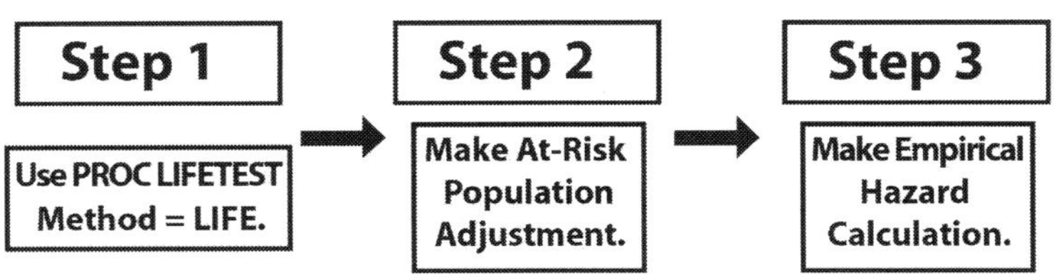

Output 5.26 was created in step 3. Data was adjusted in step 2. You can see in the second column the adjusted **Subject Number at Risk**, followed by the **Hazard Function** and **Survival Function**.

Output 5.27 shows the life table survival estimates. These results were created using the midpoint interval. If you compare its values with values in Output 2.12 from Chapter 2, you will realize that they are not the same because they are adjusted.

Output 5.27: Life Table Survival Estimates Output

The LIFETEST Procedure

Life Table Survival Estimates

Interval [Lower,	Upper)	Number Failed	Number Censored	Effective Sample Size	Conditional Probability of Failure	Conditional Probability Standard Error	Survival	Failure
0	1	37939	3911	329689.5	0.1151	0.000556	1.0000	0
1	2	31677	6603	286493.5	0.1106	0.000586	0.8849	0.1151
2	3	15369	5584	248723.0	0.0618	0.000483	0.7871	0.2129
3	4	11049	4272	228426.0	0.0484	0.000449	0.7384	0.2616
4	5	8500	4251	213115.5	0.0399	0.000424	0.7027	0.2973
5	6	7134	4062	200459.0	0.0356	0.000414	0.6747	0.3253
6	7	5735	5189	188699.5	0.0304	0.000395	0.6507	0.3493
7	8	4864	3975	178382.5	0.0273	0.000386	0.6309	0.3691
8	9	4169	3975	169543.5	0.0246	0.000376	0.6137	0.3863
9	10	3499	4853	160960.5	0.0217	0.000363	0.5986	0.4014
10	11	3005	3441	153314.5	0.0196	0.000354	0.5856	0.4144
11	12	2876	2998	147090.0	0.0196	0.000361	0.5741	0.4259
12	13	2745	2516	141457.0	0.0194	0.000367	0.5629	0.4371
.	.	.	.	.	.	.	.	.
.	.	.	.	.	.	.	.	.
36	37	170	2345	36804.5	0.00462	0.000353	0.4769	0.5231
37	38	150	3437	33743.5	0.00445	0.000362	0.4747	0.5253
38	39	122	3969	29890.5	0.00408	0.000369	0.4726	0.5274
39	40	102	3448	26060.0	0.00391	0.000387	0.4707	0.5293
40	41	85	2871	22798.5	0.00373	0.000404	0.4688	0.5312
41	42	72	2556	20000.0	0.00360	0.000423	0.4671	0.5329
42	43	58	2699	17300.5	0.00335	0.000439	0.4654	0.5346
43	44	41	3527	14129.5	0.00290	0.000453	0.4638	0.5362
44	45	36	3072	10789.0	0.00334	0.000555	0.4625	0.5375
45	46	27	3930	7252.0	0.00372	0.000715	0.4609	0.5391
46	47	4	2923	3798.5	0.00105	0.000526	0.4592	0.5408
47	.	10	2323	1171.5	0.00854	0.00269	0.4587	0.5413

Survival and Hazard Functions Saved in a Data Set

The automatic graphs created by SAS Enterprise Miner use precompiled templates to presents results for analytical purposes. Sometimes graphics for presentation purposes are required for display to stakeholders and for model documentation. To generate these graphics, save the required data in a SAS data set, and then use the SGPLOT procedure. This tool is more suitable because it creates graphs in conjunction with the SAS ODS Graphics Editor.

The ability to save the Hazard and Survival function values in a SAS data set is useful for Audit and Validation teams who want to replicate the models for validation purposes.

To save the data set used to create the Hazard and Survival functions, complete the following steps:

1. Click the Survival graph. Select the Table icon. SAS Enterprise Miner shows the data set as shown in Output 5.28.
2. Select **File ► Save As**, and choose a folder in which to save your data set, as seen in Output 5.28.

Output 5.28: Hazard and Survival Function Data

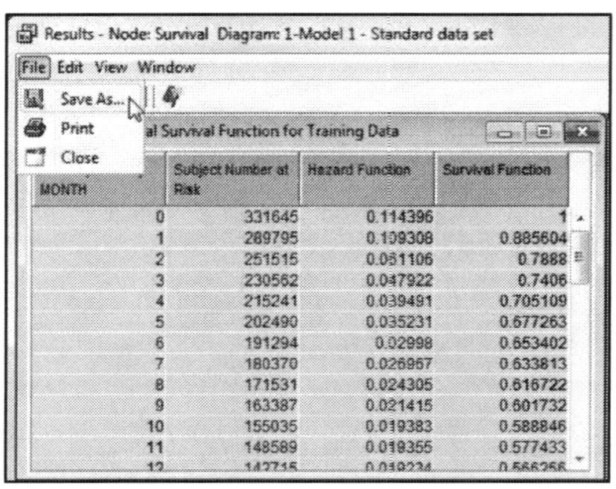

It is not in the scope of this book to teach graphic development. Output 5.29 shows the graphic produced from the SGPLOT procedure. The code to produce this figure is available from the author page as explained in "About This Book."

Output 5.29: Survival and Hazard Function Graphic Created by SGPLOT Procedure

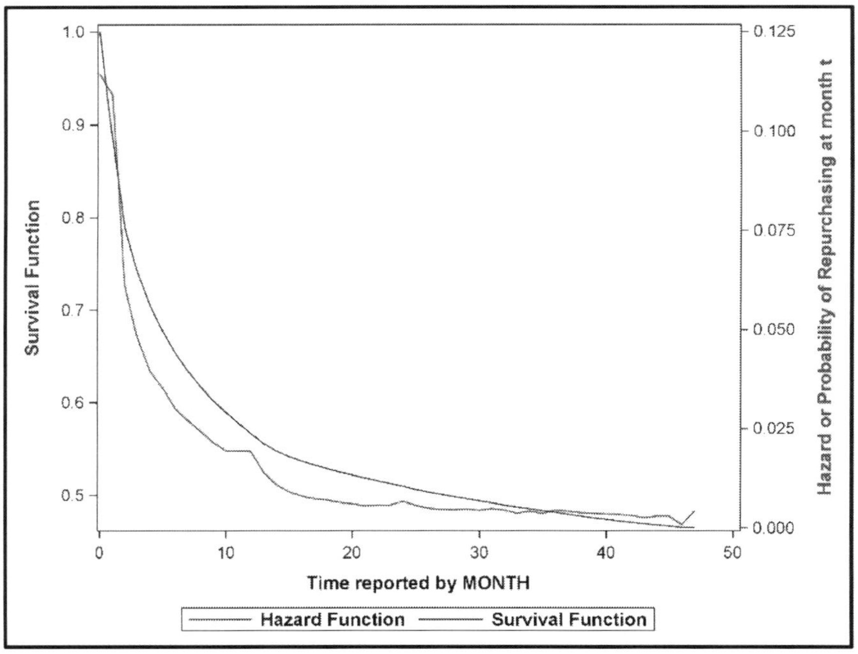

Chapter 6: The Fully Expanded Data Set Model

Introduction

Chapter 5 showed how the Customer-Level data set is expanded during the modeling process by the SAS Enterprise Miner Survival node. In this chapter, the same model is implemented with a data set that has been pre-expanded. If the data preparation and manipulation are correct, then the models produce the same results, as is demonstrated.

Preparing an Expanded data set is a fundamental skill needed to create advanced models using time-dependent covariates such as stress tests, competing risk, and IFRS 9 models. The data preparation and interpretation are the same, but what makes these models more complicated is including economic variables, such as GDP or unemployment.

The SAS Enterprise Miner model process consists of six steps as shown in Figure 6.1. The difference in the model process covered in this chapter is that when you enter an Expanded data set format rather than a Standard data set format, SAS Enterprise Miner does not need to expand the data set format. This means that step 4 is no longer required. Therefore, in Figure 6.1, it is crossed out.

Figure 6.1: SAS Enterprise Miner Model Process

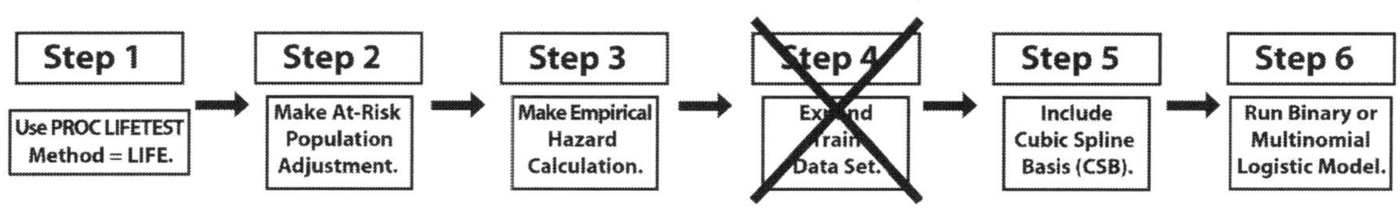

Saving the Expanded Data Set

To extend the capabilities of SAS Enterprise Miner, the SAS Enterprise Miner SAS Code node adds functionality for developing SAS programs.

Include a SAS Code Node

To include a SAS Code node, complete the following steps:

1. Drag a SAS Code node onto the diagram. The SAS Code node is found in the Utility node group.

Figure 6.2: Including the SAS Code Node

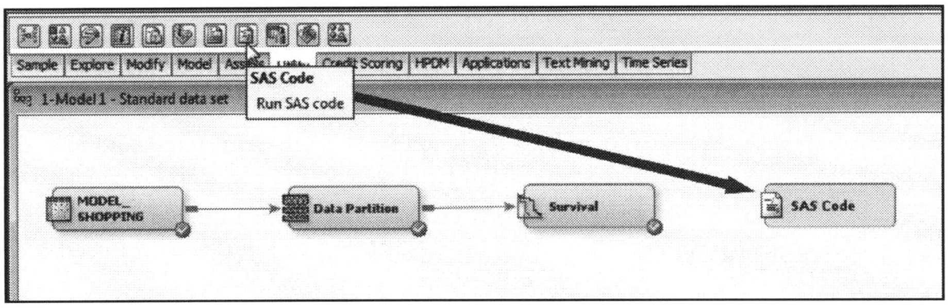

2. Connect the Survival node to the SAS Code node.

Figure 6.3: Connecting the Node

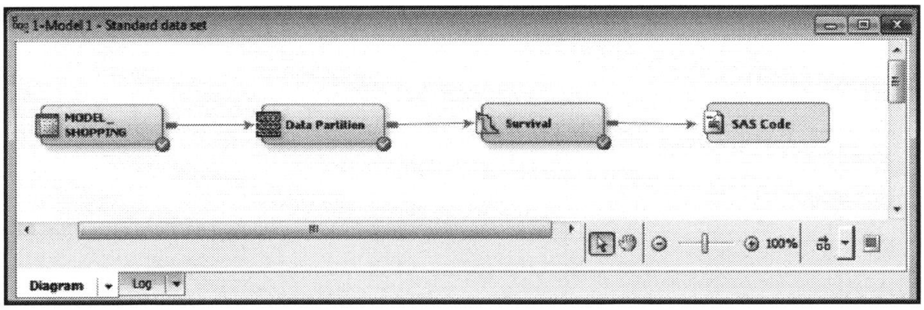

Rename the SAS Code Node

Rename the SAS Code node by completing the following steps:

1. Right-click the SAS Code node named **SAS Code**.
2. Click **Rename**.

Figure 6.4: Selecting Rename

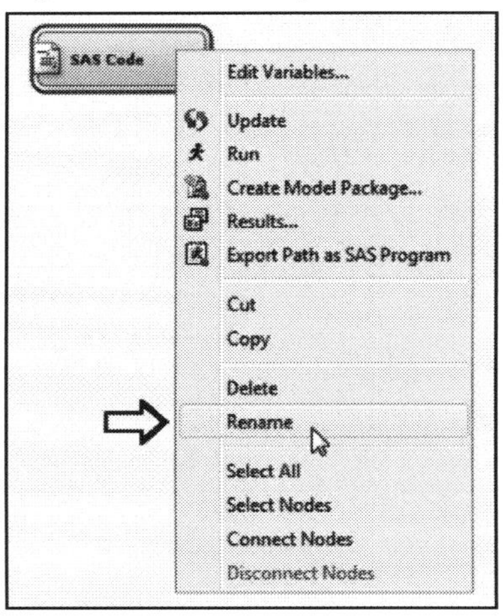

3. Enter **SAS Code - EXPANDED** as the name of the diagram.

Figure 6.5: Entering the Node Name

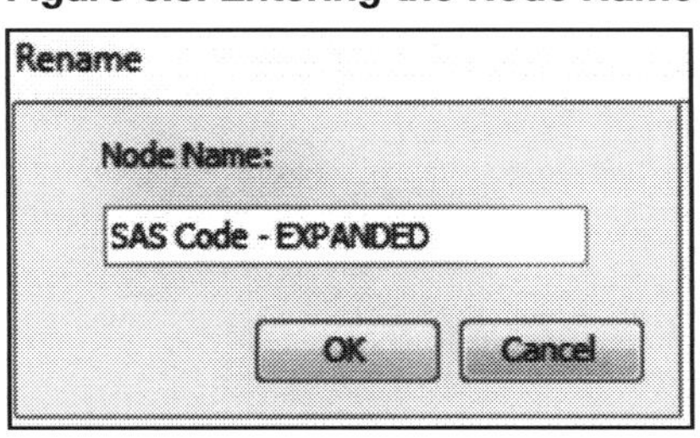

4. Click **OK**.

   The updated diagram should look like Figure 6.6.

   Figure 6.6: Completed Process Flow Including SAS Code Node

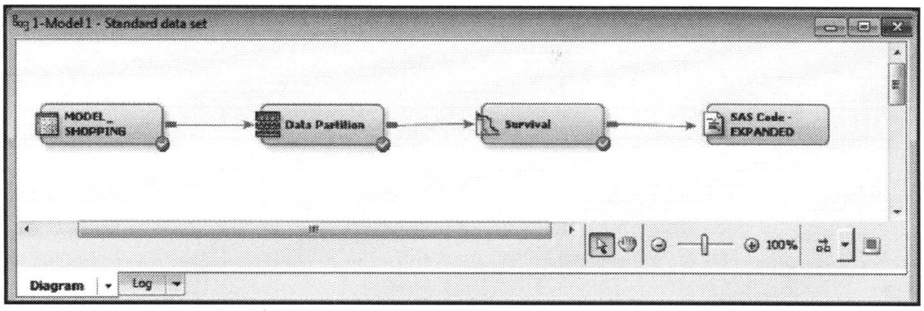

Create a Permanent Library

A permanent library is required to allow SAS Enterprise Miner to save the Expanded data set. To create a permanent library:

1. Click the SAS Code node to access the properties panel.
2. Click the ellipses for the **Code Editor** row, located on the properties panel **(Train)** of the SAS Code node shown in Figure 6.7.

   Figure 6.7: Properties Panel (Train)

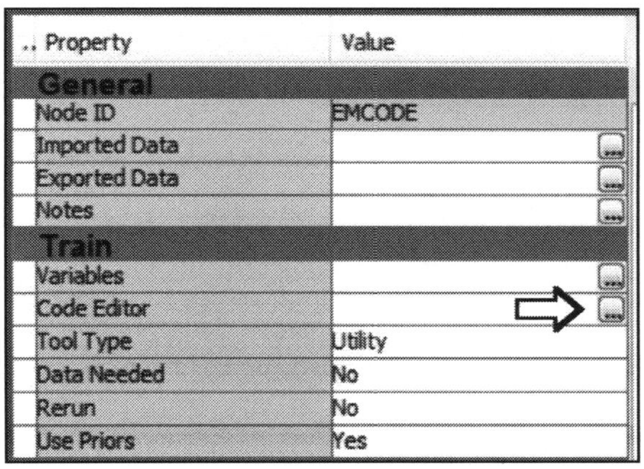

   The **Training Code—Code Node** opens as shown in Figure 6.8.

Figure 6.8: Training Code—Code Node

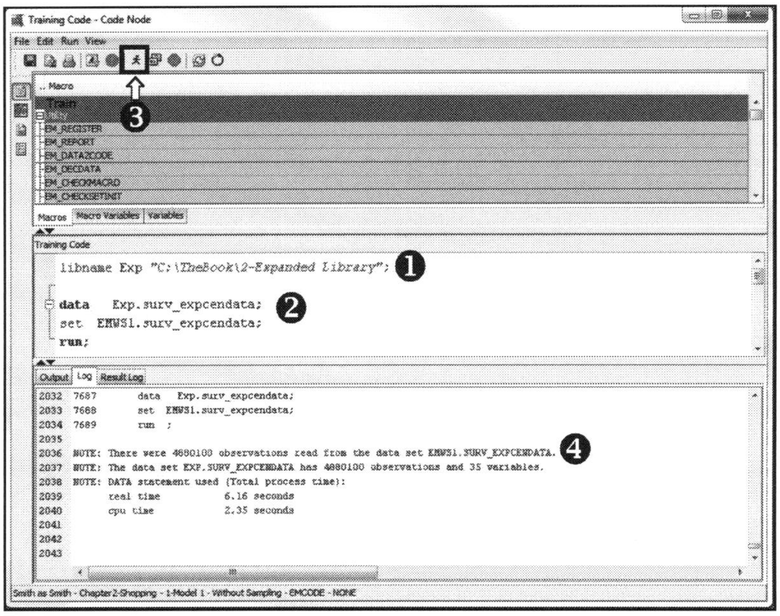

3. Create a new folder (**2-Expanded Library**) within the **C:\TheBook** directory ❶ to save the Expanded data set.
4. Create a permanent library named **Exp** ❶ by entering `libname Exp "C:\TheBook\2-Expanded Library`. Instead of entering the code, you can open a SAS source file in Notepad or in the SAS windowing environment, and then copy and paste the code as needed.
5. Using a SAS DATA step, the **SURV_EXPCENDATA** data set ❷ is copied from the workspace **EMWS1** to the **Exp** library.
6. Run the program by clicking the running man icon ❸. After running the SAS code, you can verify that the **SURV_EXPCENDATA** ❹ data set has **4880100** observations by selecting **Log**.

Explore the SURV_EXPCENDATA Data Set

To explore the data set:

1. Click **View**, and then **Explorer**.

Figure 6.9: Click View and Explorer

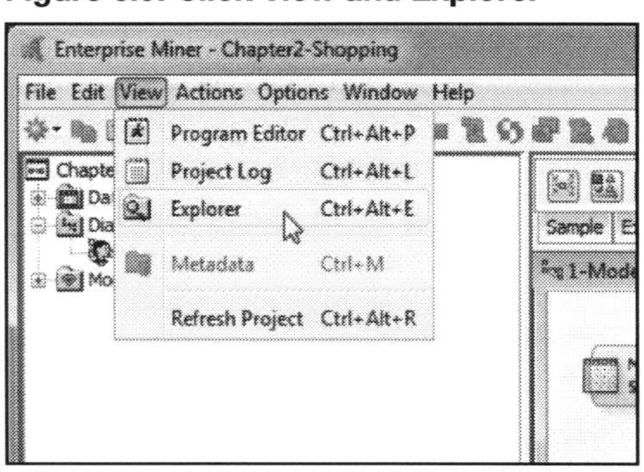

2. Click **SAS Libraries**, and then the library **Exp**.

Figure 6.10: Clicking the SAS Library Exp

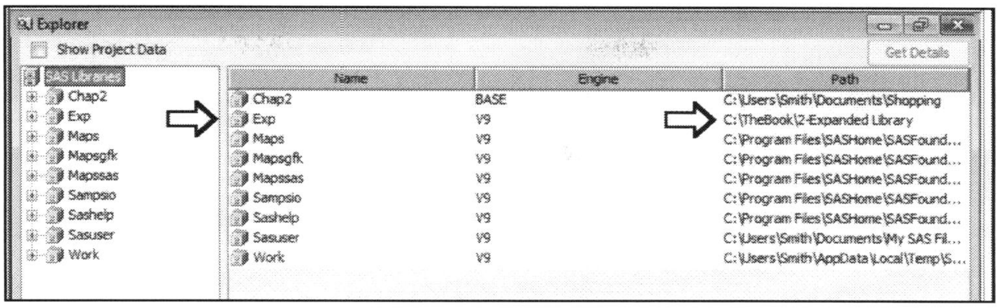

3. Double-click the **Surv_expcendata** data set.

Figure 6.11: Double-Click the Surv_expcendata Data Set

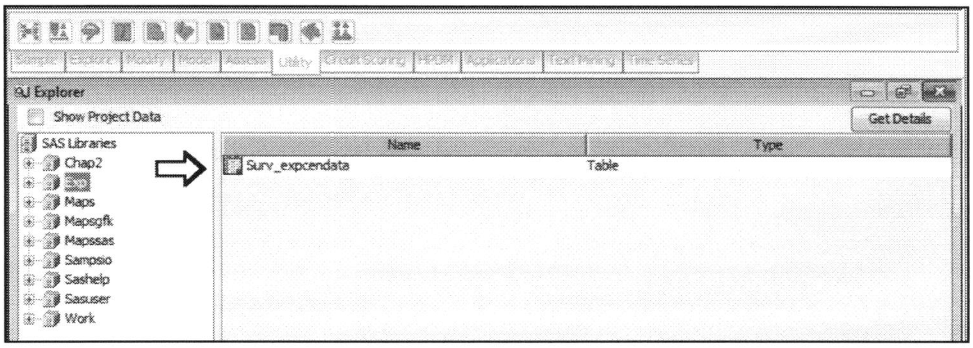

The SURV_EXPCENDATA data set opens as shown in Figure 6.12.

Figure 6.12: Expanded Data Set

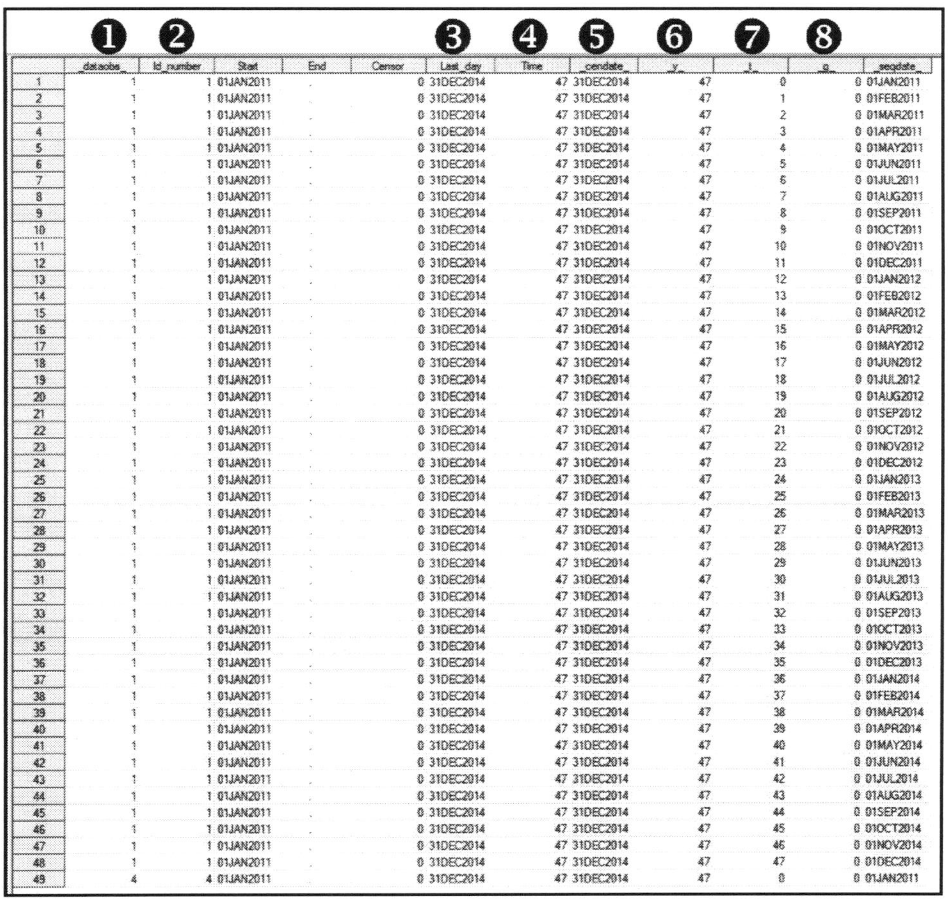

	❶ _dataobs_	❷ Id_number	Start	End	Censor	❸ Last_day	❹ Time	❺ _cendate_	❻ _y_	❼ _t_	❽ _g_	_seqdate_
1	1	1	01JAN2011	.	0	31DEC2014	47	31DEC2014	47	0	0	01JAN2011
2	1	1	01JAN2011	.	0	31DEC2014	47	31DEC2014	47	1	0	01FEB2011
3	1	1	01JAN2011	.	0	31DEC2014	47	31DEC2014	47	2	0	01MAR2011
4	1	1	01JAN2011	.	0	31DEC2014	47	31DEC2014	47	3	0	01APR2011
5	1	1	01JAN2011	.	0	31DEC2014	47	31DEC2014	47	4	0	01MAY2011
6	1	1	01JAN2011	.	0	31DEC2014	47	31DEC2014	47	5	0	01JUN2011
7	1	1	01JAN2011	.	0	31DEC2014	47	31DEC2014	47	6	0	01JUL2011
8	1	1	01JAN2011	.	0	31DEC2014	47	31DEC2014	47	7	0	01AUG2011
9	1	1	01JAN2011	.	0	31DEC2014	47	31DEC2014	47	8	0	01SEP2011
10	1	1	01JAN2011	.	0	31DEC2014	47	31DEC2014	47	9	0	01OCT2011
11	1	1	01JAN2011	.	0	31DEC2014	47	31DEC2014	47	10	0	01NOV2011
12	1	1	01JAN2011	.	0	31DEC2014	47	31DEC2014	47	11	0	01DEC2011
13	1	1	01JAN2011	.	0	31DEC2014	47	31DEC2014	47	12	0	01JAN2012
14	1	1	01JAN2011	.	0	31DEC2014	47	31DEC2014	47	13	0	01FEB2012
15	1	1	01JAN2011	.	0	31DEC2014	47	31DEC2014	47	14	0	01MAR2012
16	1	1	01JAN2011	.	0	31DEC2014	47	31DEC2014	47	15	0	01APR2012
17	1	1	01JAN2011	.	0	31DEC2014	47	31DEC2014	47	16	0	01MAY2012
18	1	1	01JAN2011	.	0	31DEC2014	47	31DEC2014	47	17	0	01JUN2012
19	1	1	01JAN2011	.	0	31DEC2014	47	31DEC2014	47	18	0	01JUL2012
20	1	1	01JAN2011	.	0	31DEC2014	47	31DEC2014	47	19	0	01AUG2012
21	1	1	01JAN2011	.	0	31DEC2014	47	31DEC2014	47	20	0	01SEP2012
22	1	1	01JAN2011	.	0	31DEC2014	47	31DEC2014	47	21	0	01OCT2012
23	1	1	01JAN2011	.	0	31DEC2014	47	31DEC2014	47	22	0	01NOV2012
24	1	1	01JAN2011	.	0	31DEC2014	47	31DEC2014	47	23	0	01DEC2012
25	1	1	01JAN2011	.	0	31DEC2014	47	31DEC2014	47	24	0	01JAN2013
26	1	1	01JAN2011	.	0	31DEC2014	47	31DEC2014	47	25	0	01FEB2013
27	1	1	01JAN2011	.	0	31DEC2014	47	31DEC2014	47	26	0	01MAR2013
28	1	1	01JAN2011	.	0	31DEC2014	47	31DEC2014	47	27	0	01APR2013
29	1	1	01JAN2011	.	0	31DEC2014	47	31DEC2014	47	28	0	01MAY2013
30	1	1	01JAN2011	.	0	31DEC2014	47	31DEC2014	47	29	0	01JUN2013
31	1	1	01JAN2011	.	0	31DEC2014	47	31DEC2014	47	30	0	01JUL2013
32	1	1	01JAN2011	.	0	31DEC2014	47	31DEC2014	47	31	0	01AUG2013
33	1	1	01JAN2011	.	0	31DEC2014	47	31DEC2014	47	32	0	01SEP2013
34	1	1	01JAN2011	.	0	31DEC2014	47	31DEC2014	47	33	0	01OCT2013
35	1	1	01JAN2011	.	0	31DEC2014	47	31DEC2014	47	34	0	01NOV2013
36	1	1	01JAN2011	.	0	31DEC2014	47	31DEC2014	47	35	0	01DEC2013
37	1	1	01JAN2011	.	0	31DEC2014	47	31DEC2014	47	36	0	01JAN2014
38	1	1	01JAN2011	.	0	31DEC2014	47	31DEC2014	47	37	0	01FEB2014
39	1	1	01JAN2011	.	0	31DEC2014	47	31DEC2014	47	38	0	01MAR2014
40	1	1	01JAN2011	.	0	31DEC2014	47	31DEC2014	47	39	0	01APR2014
41	1	1	01JAN2011	.	0	31DEC2014	47	31DEC2014	47	40	0	01MAY2014
42	1	1	01JAN2011	.	0	31DEC2014	47	31DEC2014	47	41	0	01JUN2014
43	1	1	01JAN2011	.	0	31DEC2014	47	31DEC2014	47	42	0	01JUL2014
44	1	1	01JAN2011	.	0	31DEC2014	47	31DEC2014	47	43	0	01AUG2014
45	1	1	01JAN2011	.	0	31DEC2014	47	31DEC2014	47	44	0	01SEP2014
46	1	1	01JAN2011	.	0	31DEC2014	47	31DEC2014	47	45	0	01OCT2014
47	1	1	01JAN2011	.	0	31DEC2014	47	31DEC2014	47	46	0	01NOV2014
48	1	1	01JAN2011	.	0	31DEC2014	47	31DEC2014	47	47	0	01DEC2014
49	4	4	01JAN2011	.	0	31DEC2014	47	31DEC2014	47	0	0	01JAN2011

SURV_EXPCENDATA is one of the most important data sets in this book. It shows multiple observations per customer in an Expanded longitudinal format.

All variables created by SAS Enterprise Miner have an underscore prefix. Many of the variables previously discussed mirror these variables. Here are the explanations for each variable:

- Columns ❶ and ❷ have the same information, which is the customer ID number.
- Columns ❸ and ❹ have the same information, which is the last day of data collection.
- Columns ❹ and ❻ have the same information. The variable Time was calculated in Chapter 2, Program 2.1.
- Column ❼ _t_ tracks the time in a longitudinal format from 0 to a maximum of 47 rows. It is required to score new customers and is discussed in detail in Chapter 8.
- Column ❽ is the Target variable in a longitudinal format where the following is true:

$$\_g\_ = \text{Target} = \begin{cases} 1 = \text{if the Censor} = 1 \text{ (Outcome is \textbf{Repurchase} in the month of study.)} \\ 0 = \text{if the Censor} = 0 \text{ (Outcome is \textbf{No Repurchase} in the month of study.)} \end{cases}$$

Running the Expanded Model

Now you are ready to run the fully expanded model.

Drop Unnecessary Variables

First, you need to drop unnecessary variables. The only required variable is _t_, which is an input variable representing each month's activity. To drop the unnecessary variables, you can choose one of two options:

- Run Program 6.1 outside SAS Enterprise Miner using Base SAS.
- Modify the SAS Code node by including the DROP statement found in Program 6.1.

Program 6.1: Dropping Unnecessary Variables

```
data EXP.SURV_EXPCENDATA;
set  EXP.SURV_EXPCENDATA;
drop Last_day Time _cendate_ _y_ _g_ _seqdate_;
run;
```

Create a Second Diagram and Assign Variable Roles

Next, create a second diagram in the process flow panel and assign roles:

1. Create a second diagram as shown in Figure 6.13. But, this time, do not include the Data Partition node. Connect the **SURV_EXPCENDATA** data set to the **Survival** node.

Figure 6.13: Model 2—Fully Expanded Data Set

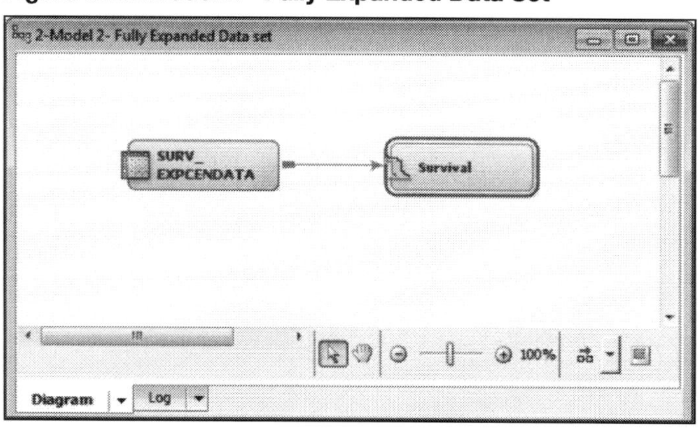

2. Select the role of each variable.

Figure 6.14: Selection of the Role of Each Variable

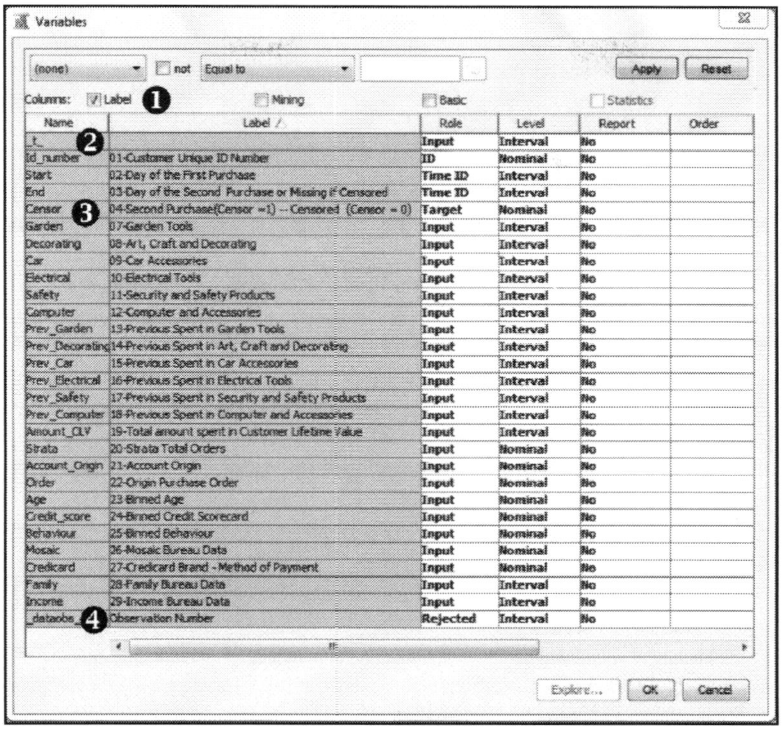

❶ Select **Label** to be able to visualize and sort the variable names using the column labels.
❷ The **_t_** variable is at the top of the list of columns. Its **Role** is **Input**.
❸ The variables **Last_day** and **Time** are missing because they were dropped.
❹ The **_dataobs_** variable is set to **Rejected** for **Role**.

The CSB variables are not part of this data set because they are created by the Survival node in the modeling process.

Set the Properties and Run

Complete the final steps:

1. Keep all parameters of the Survival node properties panel the same as they are for model 1 in Chapter 5.
2. Click the Survival node. Change the **Data Format** option in the properties panel to **Fully Expanded**.

Figure 6.15: Selection of Fully Expanded in the Properties Panel

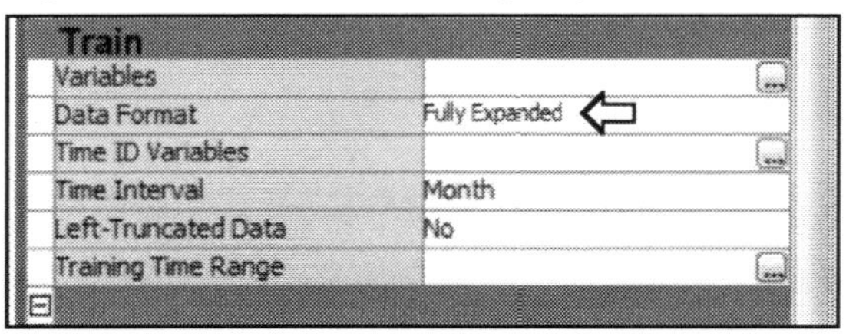

3. Run the model.

Comparing the Results

After running the model, you can verify that all results in the SAS output are identical. Most important is to compare the Type 3 Analysis of Effects as shown in Output 6.1.

Output 6.1: Type 3 Analysis of Effects—Expanded Model

Type 3 Analysis of Effects

Effect	DF	Wald Chi-Square	Pr > ChiSq
_t_	1	53.0311	<.0001
_csb1	1	459.1650	<.0001
_csb2	1	82.2395	<.0001
_csb3	1	27.6098	<.0001
_csb4	1	109.5351	<.0001
_csb6	1	62.9468	<.0001
_csb7	1	26.6587	<.0001
Account_Origin	3	1090.4614	<.0001
Age	6	18.8630	0.0044
Behaviour	6	15532.4664	<.0001
Credicard	5	660.3675	<.0001
Credit_score	4	128.9094	<.0001
Mosaic	15	87.7625	<.0001
Order	2	2079.8240	<.0001
Strata	5	54418.8780	<.0001
Amount_CLV	1	19.6603	<.0001
Car	1	283.6591	<.0001
Decorating	1	521.3278	<.0001
Garden	1	578.6375	<.0001
Prev_Car	1	406.7606	<.0001
Prev_Computer	1	66.1819	<.0001
Prev_Decorating	1	885.5248	<.0001
Prev_Electrical	1	127.3495	<.0001
Prev_Garden	1	1146.6425	<.0001
Prev_Safety	1	291.3021	<.0001

Chapter 7: Statistics for Performance and Validation

Introduction

One of the most important and difficult steps in survival analysis is to assess the performance and validation of the model. This chapter presents a pragmatic approach that explains the statistical definitions and SAS codes to validate survival analysis models. A well-working and constructed survival model should have model and validation data sets with statistics that indicate similar performance.

Given the lack of validation in professional environments demonstrated by the 2008 to 2010 crisis, can a model be implemented to do what it is designed to do without a methodological approach? Unfortunately, from experience, high-quality analysts who deliver model validation are the exception, rather than the norm, and most models are implemented without an internal independent validation.

The problem is that validation requires advanced knowledge of probabilities, SAS programming, and model building experience using censored variables. This is one of most challenging components of the validation process with companies facing difficulties in implementing IFRS 9 models.

In this chapter, all the necessary steps to validate a model are demonstrated. The performance measures need to be applied to the training and validation data sets. The techniques are general and provide a framework for more advanced models such as competing risk, stress tests, and IFRS 9 models. Graphical interpretation in a validation context is one of the least advanced areas of validation. For this reason, a summary in the last section of this chapter is included as a template.

Twofold Focus

Despite the importance of validation, there is no book (at the time of this writing) that demonstrates how to interpret validation in terms of following a set structure and established process and that goes beyond the statistical results. This chapter addresses this lack by being strongly oriented toward real practice. The focus is twofold:

1. First, each validation statistic created by SAS Enterprise Miner is presented. SAS Enterprise Miner and the LOGISTIC procedure can be used to score a validation data set used for assessment. Statistics that measure the predictive accuracy of the model include sensitivity and positive predicted value. Graphics such as the ROC curve, the lift chart, and Kolmogorov-Smirnov statistic are easily created to assess the performance of the model.
2. Second, a framework is provided using SAS code and graphical analysis that shows how to validate models by comparison with a reference graphic model template.

SAS Enterprise Miner for Practical Solutions

The underlying principle in any validation model is that the results should be demonstrated and replicated. The practical question is how to demonstrate each statistic for the model and validation data sets with a minimum level of statistical programming skills. A good starting point is to understand all the statistics and graphics presented by SAS Enterprise Miner:

- depth
- concentration curve
- lift
- benefit
- Gini Concentration Ratio
- Kolmogorov-Smirnov Statistic

The numbers in Figure 7.1 correspond to the SAS Enterprise Miner Survival node results in Chapter 5. By the end of this chapter, you should be able to create and understand all statistics automatically developed by SAS Enterprise Miner. And, you should have learned how to compare different models.

Figure 7.1: Survival Model Validation Statistics

Model Validation Statistics

Data Role	Benefit	Average Hazard Ratio	Depth	Lift	Kolmogorov-Smirnov Statistic	Gini Concentration Ratio
Train	0.678858	0.017531	0.188969	4.592431	0.690857	0.805511
Valid	0.685829	0.019178	0.170134	5.031109	0.698005	0.803432

To assess the predictive performance of the SAS Enterprise Miner survival model output, all the necessary statistical tools (the above statistics) for performance and validation are organized in a series of steps presented in Figure 7.2. An assessment is made of whether the model is fit to be implemented. And, a demonstration is given on how to obtain the above statistics and how to use them in the performance and validation process using a comprehensive step-by-step approach. Steps 1 to 14 are presented in this chapter, and step 15 is presented in Chapter 8.

Figure 7.2: Steps for Performance and Validation Statistics

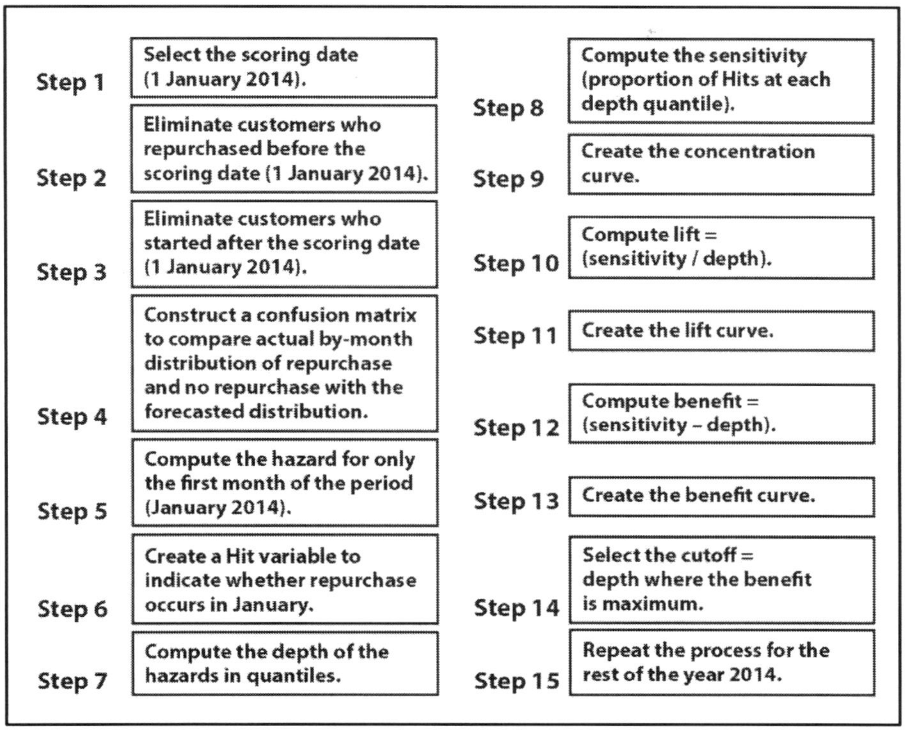

Comparison of Model Validation Approaches

The focus of this subsection is to explain the traditional approaches to model validation for logistic regression and survival regression. Model validation is based on a sample process. For this reason, the sample processes for logistic regression and survival regression are explained.

Validation: An Explanation

Validation is the control technique used to verify the reproducibility of a statistical model. It is a method to test the use of a model or to assess its ability to forecast by comparing actuals against forecast output. The main reason that validation is one of the most important steps in the modeling process is that the validity of any model created is based on the model performance while using another data set or a subset of the data. Other considerations when validating a model include the following:

- Assessment of the assumptions, theory, and the data used by the models, including data accuracy, consistency, and integrity checks. (Model theory and scoring code should be periodically reviewed by an independent validation department.)
- Process, output data sets, and reporting.
- Financial implications for the operational risk of using the model because a complex model is at risk of error.

In May 2005, the Basel Committee published a document that became a key reference point for validation of models in financial services. "Working Paper No. 14. Studies on the Validation of Internal Rating Systems" is a guideline about validation, but it does not discuss how to validate survival models (Basel 2005). This is not surprising because the validation of survival models is an open field of empirical research.

This chapter demonstrates the principal tools used by SAS Enterprise Miner to compare the performance of the training and validation data sets to validate the ability of the model to forecast the total number of customers repurchasing by month.

The time series graphic in Figure 7.3 provides a dynamic display of model behavior because the model is used to forecast each month. Any sudden changes in this graphic indicates a possible lack of performance and should be investigated. The graphic shows that the model performs very well as the Actual x Calibrated Forecast follows the monthly seasonality. This proves that the model is a reasonable representation of the actual business demand. The graphic shows that the model is invariant, and this ensures confidence in the model because it provides for its validity and stability over time.

Figure 7.3: Validation and Performance of Survival Analysis Models

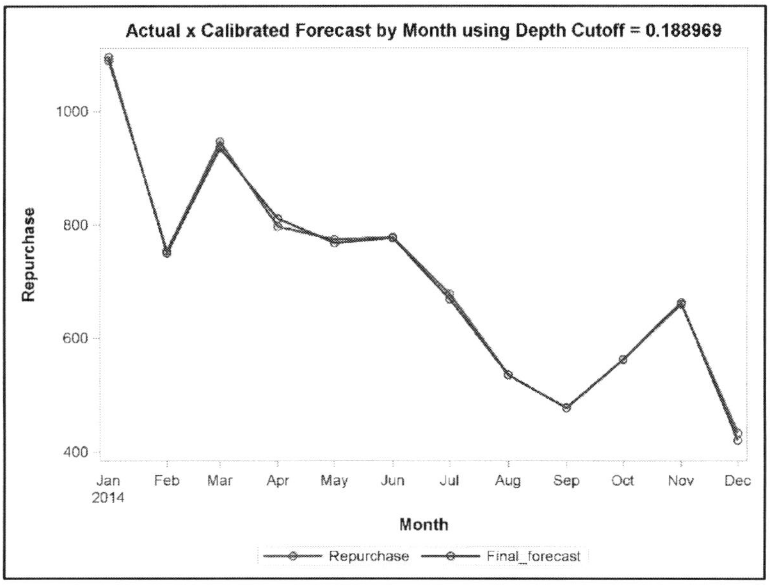

By the end of Chapter 7, you will be able to create this graph.

Traditional Logistic Regression

In its purest form, the assessment of a logistic regression model is performed under the assumption that the data used to fit the model is not also used in the validation of the model. This implies that the validation of the model should be broken down into two components: the evaluation of performance in the **Validation** data set and an assessment of the model in the **Out of Time** data set.

The process is illustrated in Figure 7.4 using a mortgage database to predict default.

Figure 7.4: Logistic Validation Project Flowchart

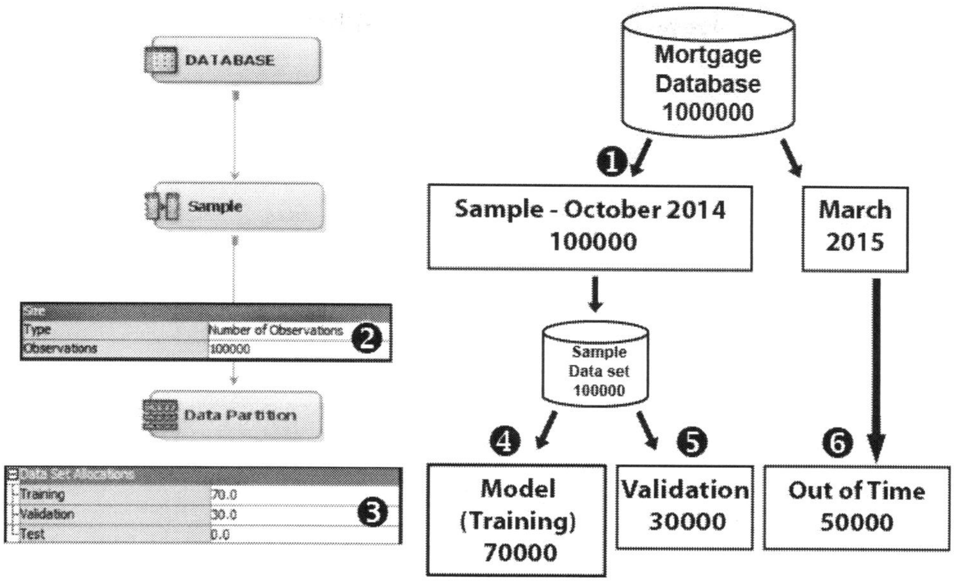

The first step is to extract a Sample ❶ from the Mortgage Database. This is achieved in SAS Enterprise Miner using the Sample node and by choosing the number of observations as **100000** in the properties panel ❷.

This Sample data is split into **Model (Training)** ❹ and **Validation** ❺ data sets by using data set allocation as shown in ❸. The model is fit (trained in Data Mining jargon) using the Model data set and then assessed in the Validation data set.

The discriminatory power of the default logistic model denotes its ability to discriminate between defaulting and non-defaulting borrowers in a data set. This ability is tested in an independent data set, Out of Time, to verify if the model is able to generalize, or in other words, to accurately predict the behavior of new customers. Otherwise, the model might be overfitted to the development data set. In a logistic regression model, the key to identifying over-fitting is to verify if there is a large difference between the Model and Validation data sets in terms of the appropriate statistical performance. The closer this performance is, the better. The same is valid for Survival Analysis as will be demonstrated later.

A model, which has been built on a training data set, is likely to be much better fitted to that data than to a Validation data set. In reality, the model might be overfitted for both training and validation and might not fit nearly so well for the rest of the database. The industry standard practice is that once the model has been built using the training data set and tested using the validation data set, it should be assessed by doing the following:

- Using a second independent testing sample from the database extracted from a different month or year called the Out of Time or Out of Sample database.
- Using a scoring sample to predict the target.
- Comparing the predicted target to the actual target in the Out of Time or Out of Sample data set.

The most important point to take away from the logistic flowchart is that the Out of Time data set is created using a sample collected from a different period of time than the model and validation data sets. In Figure 7.4, the model is built and validation is performed on data from October 2014. Testing is performed on data from March 2015 from the Out of Time database.

Survival Regression (Steps 1 through 4)

The validation process for survival models is compared with the validation process for logistic regression models. Although many model validation techniques apply regardless of the model, Figure 7.5 focuses specifically on the validation technique for survival models.

Figure 7.5: Survival Validation Project Flowchart

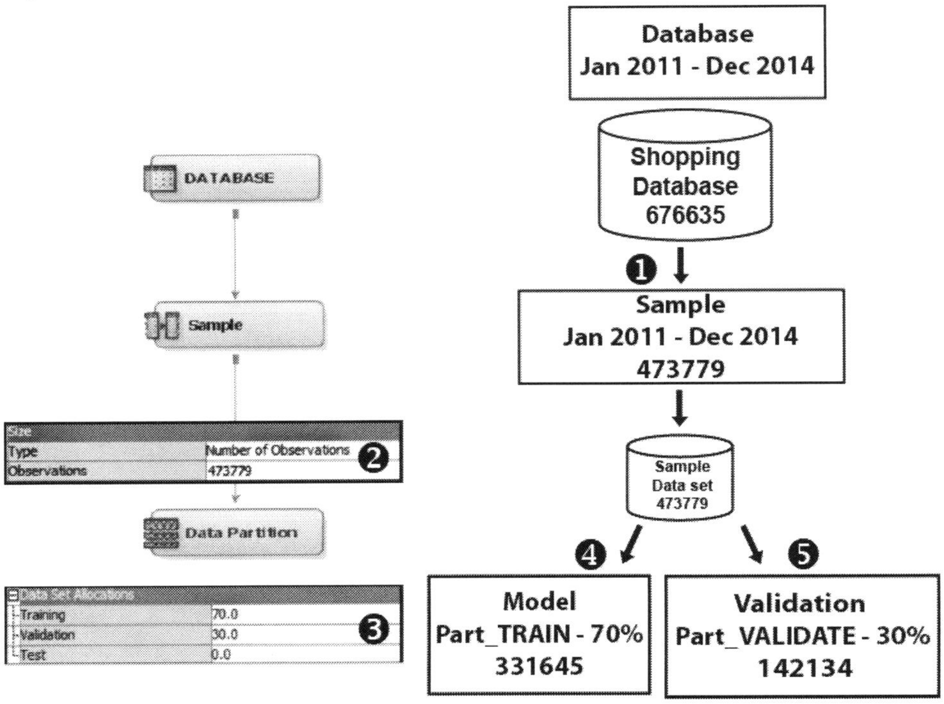

Step 1: Select the Scoring Date

Despite its apparent simplicity, the approach in Figure 7.5 presents some extremely difficult validation challenges for regulators and managers. To validate the accuracy of the survival model, managers must first choose a period to be validated (between January 2011 and December 2014 in the time-to-next-purchase model that was developed in Chapter 4). They must validate the accuracy of the model within this period. Validating survival models requires that managers develop a detailed understanding of the scoring process by time (months in the actual model). This is covered in detail in Chapter 8.

Figure 7.6: Survival Validation Step 1

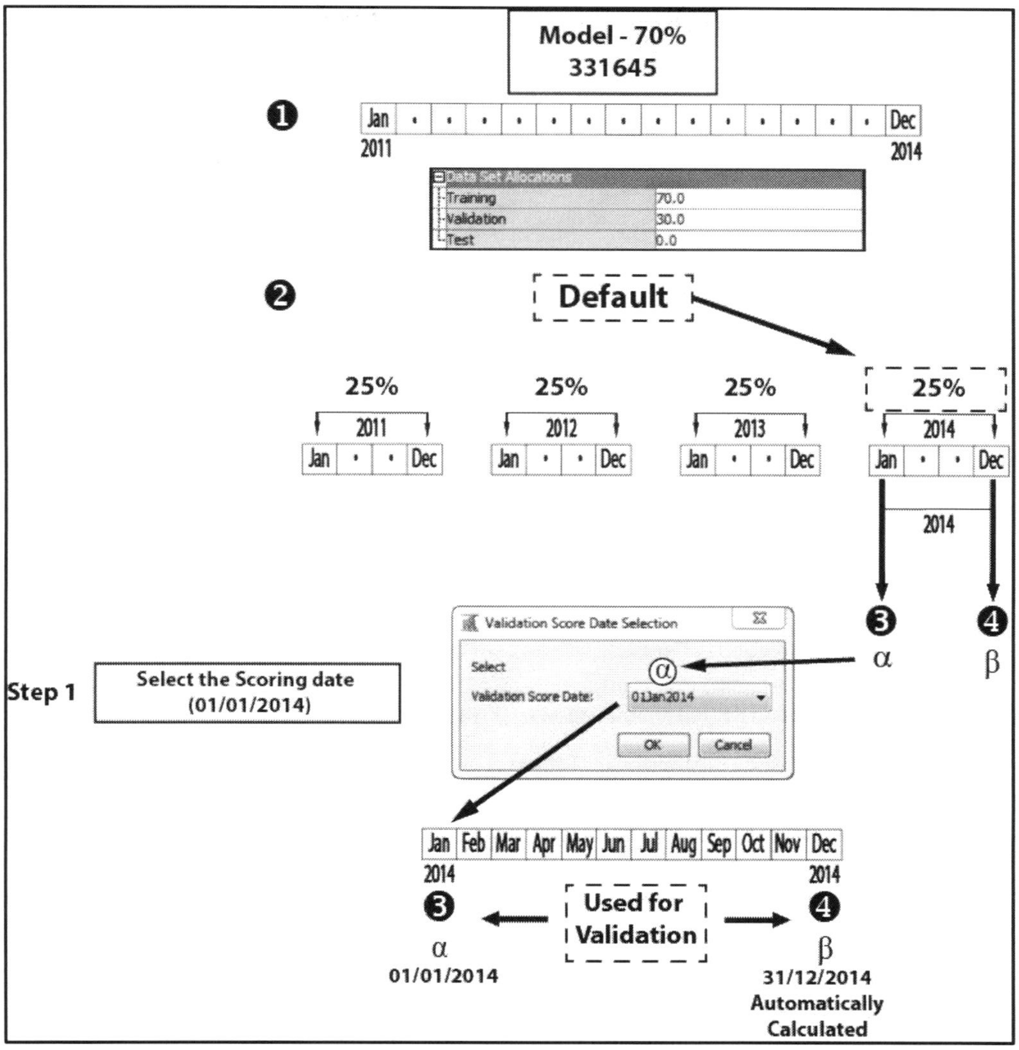

The process starts when the model is fitted using the **Model** (Part_TRAIN) data set with **331645** observations within the full period from 01/01/2011 to 31/12/2014 ❶.

The Survival Validation Method property has two settings: Default and User Specified. If the method specified is **Default** ❷, then the time interval is divided into four equal parts (quarters) using 25% of the available data to validate the model. The hypothetical scoring date α corresponds to the date closest to the beginning of the last quarter. The choice of α is not trivial. It has a huge impact on how the model is validated.

In the actual model, α = 01Jan2014 ❸. The end of the last quarter β is automatically calculated by SAS Enterprise Miner ❹ as β = 31Dec2014 in the flowchart. This is the last day of data collection.

If the method in the **Survival Validation Method** property is set to **User Specified**, as shown in Figure 7.7, then the analyst can use the **Validation Score Date** property to open the **Score Date Selection**.

Figure 7.7: Survival Validation Method—User Specified

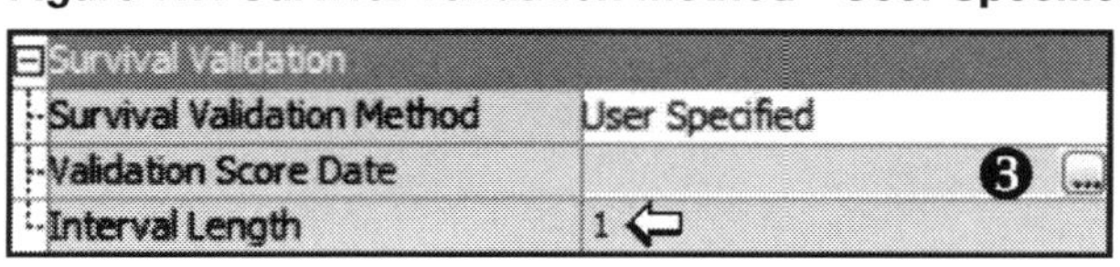

By clicking the ellipses ❸ for the **Validation Score Date** row, you open the **Validation Score Date Selection** window.

Figure 7.8: Validation Score Date Selection

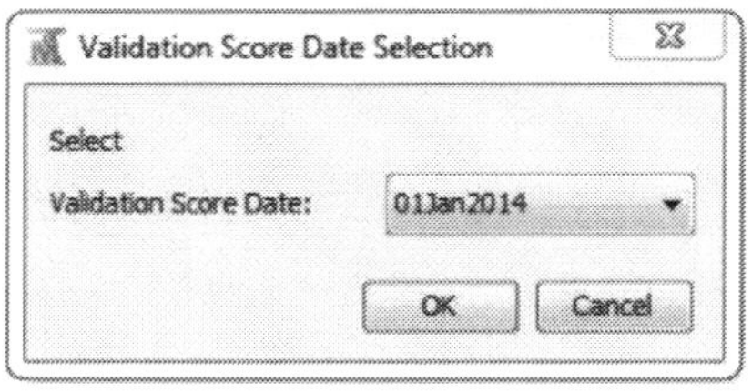

The drop-down box allows a hypothetical date to be specified. The **Interval Length** is set to **1** (as indicated by the white arrow in Figure 7.7) because of the need to validate by one month for every month of 2014.

Figure 7.9: Validation Date Data

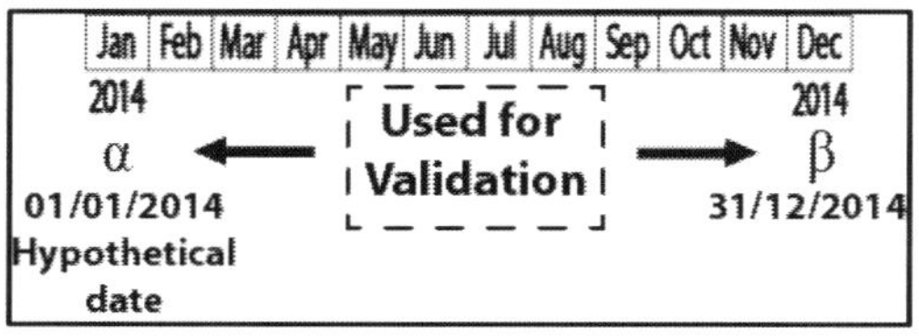

To check that the model describes the data well, you should determine whether the model performs adequately in each month. This involves verifying whether the model can forecast the number of customers that will repurchase each month from January 2014 to December 2014 as closely as possible, taking into account the seasonality of each month. If this is not true, the model cannot be validated.

The selection of the interval length as 1 ensures that the model is assessed by customers repurchasing by month. An interval length of 3 would look at customers repurchasing by quarter, and an interval length of 12 would look at customers repurchasing by year. The ability to change the interval length provides required flexibility to the validation.

Step 2: Eliminate Customers Who Repurchased before the Scoring Date

After the period is selected, SAS Enterprise Miner eliminates all customers repurchasing before the hypothetical validation score date (01Jan2014). It also eliminates customers making first purchases after the hypothetical validation score date. Of interest are customers who are eligible to be validated, who were in the database before 01/01/2014, and who can realize a second purchase from this date to the end of the period, as seen in Figure 7.10.

Figure 7.10: Keeping Eligible Customers

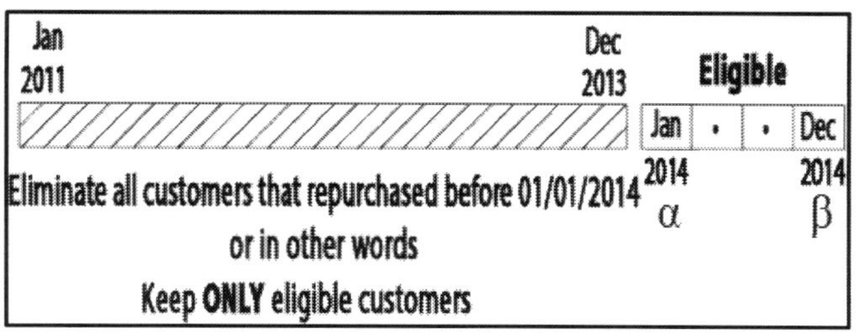

There is a requirement to validate the customers who were in the database before the hypothetical censoring date α. Those customers are eligible to repurchase in the period of interest between α = 01Jan2014 and β = 31Dec2014.

The equivalent Base SAS code is presented in Program 7.1, where customers who repurchased before the scoring date are excluded.

Program 7.1: Eliminating Customers Who Repurchased before the Scoring Date

```
data train;
set  part_train;
if (End < "01JAN2014"D and End ^=. ) then delete;
run;
```

Step 3: Eliminate Customers Who Started after the Scoring Date

Program 7.2 excludes all customers starting after 01JAN2014.

Program 7.2: Eliminating Customers Who Started after the Scoring Date

```
DATA train;
set  train;
if Start >= "01JAN2014"D then delete;
run;
```

You could include a WHERE statement to exclude customers in both periods, as shown below:

```
where Start < "01jan2014"d  and ("01jan2014"d <= End <= "31dec2014"d);
```

The first condition **Start < "01jan2014"d** excludes all customers who made a first purchase in 2014. The second condition **"01jan2014"d <= End <= "31dec2014"d** keeps only customers that made a repurchase in 2014. In summary, the focus is on customers that made their first purchase before 2014 and are eligible to make a repurchase in 2014.

Step 4: Access the Accuracy of the Model with a Confusion Matrix

In this step, a detailed strategy analyzes customers that made a repurchase between 01/01/2011 and 31/12/2013. This must be done before starting the validation process to know how many customers are eligible to be validated in each month. This is critical information. Program 7.3 computes all necessary information to create the confusion matrix.

Program 7.3: Repurchase by Month in 2014 for Old Customers

```
proc freq data = train;
tables end * censor / nocol nopercent norow missing;
format end monyy7.;
run;
```

The results of Program 7.3 appear in Output 7.1.

Output 7.1: Repurchases for Eligible Customers in Each Month of 2014

Month of the Repurchase	Censor = 0 No Repurchase	Censor = 1 Repurchase	Total
.	❶ 125600	0	125600
JAN2014	0	❷ 2527	2527
FEB2014	0	1733	1733
MAR2014	0	2335	2335
APR2014	0	1799	1799
MAY2014	0	1876	1876
JUN2014	0	1765	1765
JUL2014	0	1627	1627
AUG2014	0	1249	1249
SEP2014	0	1145	1145
OCT2014	0	1293	1293
NOV2014	0	1505	1505
DEC2014	0	1046	1046
Total	125600	19900	❸ 145500

❶ **125600** represents the number of customers who will not repurchase until the end of the study period (12/31/2014).

❷ The number **2527** represents the total number of customers who repurchased in January. This is the actual number to be compared to the forecast number. This is the key number to be obtained from this table.

❸ **145500** represents the total number of eligible customers.

What constitutes a good model is subjective. But, from a performance and modeling point of view, the principal method for judging the accuracy of the model is based on how accurately the forecast that is extracted from the model corresponds to the actual measures in Output 7.1, which were obtained from the empirical data.

One of the preferred methods of computing the accuracy rate in financial services is to construct a confusion matrix to compare the actual (empirical or observed) distribution of repurchase and no repurchase by month with the forecasted (predicted) distribution.

The task of creating a confusion matrix can be accomplished in easy steps because the confusion matrix is a cross-tabulation of the actual and predicted repurchases. The output of interest is when the forecast actually occurs in the month of interest (January 2014). This output is called *hits*.

In practice, the event of interest in the model is repurchase, which can either occur or not occur. For this reason, in the confusion matrix, repurchase is represented in the second column of Figure 7.11 as predicted = 1 (repurchase) and is called a positive event.

In the process of building a confusion matrix for survival models, a rule that corresponds to a threshold value (cutoff) of the average Hazard function is required. Statistics such as sensitivity and lift depend on the choice of cutoff value for the average Hazard function.

For example, customers with an average Hazard function greater than 0.04 might be more likely to repurchase in a particular month. Each cutoff value produces a different result, performance, and confusion matrix. The key idea in this chapter is to calculate the optimal cutoff and how to use it.

Figure 7.11: Confusion Matrix

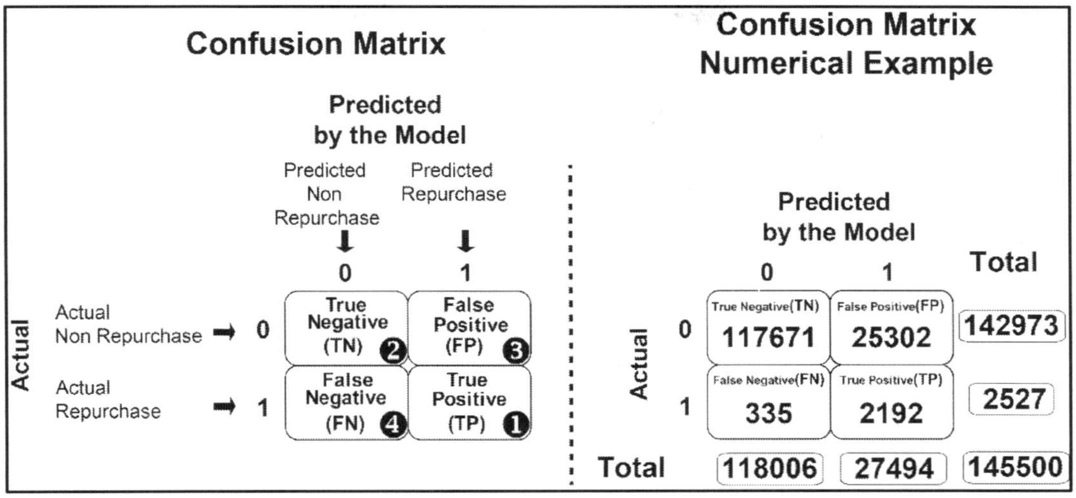

The definition of each cell of the confusion matrix is provided. Later, the numerical example is presented in greater detail.

❶ True Positive (TP)—The model predicts Repurchase in the month, and the actual result is Repurchase. It is the event of interest. For this reason, is often called positive.

❷ True Negative (TN)—The model predicts Non Repurchase in the month, and the actual result is Non Repurchase.

❸ False Positive (FP)—The model predicts Repurchase in the month, and the actual result is Non Repurchase.

❹ False Negative (FN)—The model predicts Non Repurchase in the month, and the actual result is Repurchase.

After the 2008 crisis, it has become more difficult to target new customers. Choosing the correct number of customers to target is the principal information to be extracted from a confusion matrix. The goal is to predict how many customers will be responsive to an offer for a new product.

Statistics for Performance and Validation

Regardless of the technique, success at data mining requires that the model offers a representation of reality that provides value to the business beyond the cost of commissioning the work. The criteria for judging the goodness of models are based on how closely the statistical measures extracted from the training (or model) data set compare to the same measures extracted from the validation data set. There is a general rule: if the statistics presented in Figure 7.1 are too different (more than 10% is suspicious), the model will not perform well. The model validation statistics of the time-to-next-purchase model are all very close.

In this section, unnecessary detail is avoided, and the focus is on each statistic from the model validation statistics output, which is important to model performance. If the model behaves correctly, the measures extracted from the model and validation data sets should be within reasonable cutoffs that are accepted by the appropriate research authorities. Data mining does not always obey scientific laws. Business knowledge and expert intuition sometimes offer valuable insight not provided by statistics.

Step 5: Compute the Hazard for Only the First Month of the Period

This chapter assumes that the average Hazard function has already been calculated and used to score the data. The process of scoring is presented in detail in Chapter 8.

In the following subsections, each statistic created by SAS Enterprise Miner in Figure 7.1 is examined in detail. A framework is provided for how to use these statistics for validation of the training and validation data sets. The approach is to define each variable, and then to calculate using Base SAS or SAS/STAT, taking into account the business context.

Step 6: Create a Hit Variable Indicating Whether Repurchase Occurs in January

Before presenting each statistic of Figure 7.1, the *Hit* variable must be defined. It is a fundamental variable created by SAS Enterprise Miner and is required for the calculation of each statistic.

Hit is a binary variable that indicates whether the event of interest occurred in the time of interest. It is otherwise known as a flag because it indicates exactly the subject of interest.

Program 7.4 creates the Hit variable.

Program 7.4 Create the Hit Variable

```
data train;
set  train;
_ystar_ ❹ =_y_ ❶ - _t0_ ❷ ;
_hit_ ❺ = (_ystar_ < 1 and Censor^=0 and Censor ne .);
run;
```

❶ **_y_** How many months after the first purchase. In other words, this is how many months the customer is in the database or their repurchase time in months.
❷ **_t0_** How many months from the first purchase to the month being validated (January 2014).
❸ **Ahf** Average Hazard function, automatically calculated (scored) by the Survival node. It is explained in detail in Chapter 8.
❹ The calculated **_ystar_** is the difference between **_y_** and **_t0_** in months.
❺ **_hit_** is a binary variable that indicates whether repurchase occurred in the month of interest (January 2014):

$$\_hit\_ = \begin{cases} \mathbf{1} \text{ if Repurchase occurs in January 2014} \\ \mathbf{0} \text{ if Repurchase does not occur in January 2014} \end{cases}$$

For pedagogical purposes, three groups of customers are presented in Outputs 7.2 to 7.4, and the first customer of each group is analyzed.

Output 7.2: Group 1

	Id_number	Start	End	Censor	❶ _y_	❷ _t0_	❸ ahf	❹ _ystar_	❺ _hit_
❻	**1**	**01JAN2011**	.	**0**	**47**	**36**	**0.00161**	**11**	**0**
	9611	01FEB2011	.	0	46	35	0.00200	11	0

❻ Customer **1** had not repurchased by the end of the period (December 2014), so **Censor** = **0**.

- **_t0_** = **36**. The customer is present for 36 months of the study period (Jan 2011 to Jan 2014).
- **_ystar_** = **11** (47 − 36).
- **_hit_** = **0** as **_ystar_** > 0.

From a validation and performance point of view, both customers 1 and 9611 are of no interest because they did not repurchase until the end of study. **Censor** and **_hit_** are set to **0**.

Output 7.3: Group 2

	Id_number	Start	End	Censor	❶ _y_	❷ _t0_	❸ ahf	❹ _ystar_	❺ _hit_
❼	**385**	**03JAN2011**	**18APR2014**	**1**	**39**	**36**	**0.02085**	**3**	**0**
	387	03JAN2011	02SEP2014	1	44	36	0.02466	8	0
	630	04JAN2011	14MAR2014	1	38	36	0.01493	2	0
	632	04JAN2011	02JUL2014	1	42	36	0.00245	6	0
	872	05JAN2011	18OCT2014	1	45	36	0.00229	9	0
	1135	06JAN2011	29JUN2014	1	41	36	0.02227	5	0

❼ Customer **385** repurchased in April 2014. **Censor** = **1**.

- **_t0_ = 36**. The customer is present for 36 months of the study period (Jan 2011 to Jan 2014). The customer is dropped after the period (month) of repurchase (April 2014). This customer is important in the validation process only in April 2014. **Censor = 1**, but the customer did not repurchase in the month of interest (Jan 2014). Therefore, **_hit_** is set to **0**.
- **_ystar_** = **3** (39 - 36).
- **_hit_** = **0** as **_ystar_** > 0.

Output 7.4: Group 3

	Id_number	Start	End	Censor	_y_ ❶	_t0_ ❷	ahf ❸	_ystar_ ❹	_hit_ ❺
	11308	04FEB2011	13JAN2014	1	35	35	0.00486	0	1
❽	26997	14MAR2011	19JAN2014	1	34	34	0.01529	0	1
❽	50618	06MAY2011	13JAN2014	1	32	32	0.03035	0	1
❽	75584	10JUL2011	06JAN2014	1	30	30	0.00494	0	1
❽	97197	09SEP2011	05JAN2014	1	28	28	0.00230	0	1
❽	107980	03OCT2011	15JAN2014	1	27	27	0.02755	0	1

❽ Customer **11308** repurchased in January 2014. **Censor** = **1**.

- **_t0_** = **35**. The customer is present for 35 months of the study period (Feb 2011 to Jan 2014).
- **_ystar_** = **0** (35 – 35).
- **_hit_** = **1** as **_ystar_** = **0**.

From a validation and performance point of view, group 3 ❽ is the center of attention because they repurchased in January 2014 and _hit_ = 1.

Step 7: Compute the Depth of the Hazard in Quantiles

To give a consistent definition of depth, the Train data set needs to be sorted in descending order by the average Hazard function. The data set opens as presented in Output 7.5.

```
proc sort data=TRAIN;
by descending ahf;
run;
```

The sort has been performed to introduce the concept of depth. The sort is not required for the RANK procedure, which is used to create the Depth variable. This is because PROC RANK includes a sort implicitly.

Output 7.5: Partial Output of Train Data Set Sorted by Average Hazard Function

Id_number	Censor	Ahf	ROW
483157	1	0.68159	1
483183	1	0.66421	2
.	.	.	.
.	.	.	.
.	.	.	.
97619	0	0.00073	145499
37577	0	0.00072	145500

After you open the Train data set, you see that the highest average Hazard ratio value of **0.68159** is in the first row, and the lowest value of **0.00072** is in the last row. In business terms, this means that the customer **Id_number** = **483157** has the highest probability of repurchase in January, and that the customer **Id_number** = **37577** has the lowest probability of repurchase.

Depth is a transformation of the average Hazard function into deciles (fractions), going from 0 to 1 in value. By reversing the order of the average Hazard function, the value of **0.68159** is transformed into 0.0001, and **0.00072** is transformed into 1.0. See the Depth column ❺ in Output 7.6.

The depth transformation is implemented in Program 7.5.

Program 7.5: Create the Depth Variable

```
proc rank data=TRAIN Descending ❶ fraction ❷ out=Depth ❸ (where=(_hit_=1));
var ahf ❹;          /* ahf - Average Hazard function */
ranks Depth ❺;
run;
```

❶ **Descending** reverses the order of the rankings so that the highest value of **ahf** (average Hazard function) receives the rank of 1. The next highest value receives the rank of 2, and so on.

❷ **Fraction** computes fractional ranks by dividing each rank by the number of observations having no missing values in the ranking variable (**ahf**). In Program 7.5, this number is 145,500, the number of customers in the Train data set.

❸ Creates an output data set named **Depth**, selecting only the rows where **_hit_** = **1**. This shows the importance of the _hit_ variable acting as a flag to identify the customers in the calculation of the depth statistics. The data set output has 2,527 rows. The values of depth in each observation no longer increase by an equal fraction because the _hit_ = 0 observations have been excluded.

❹ The **VAR** statement specifies the variable (**ahf**) to rank.

❺ The **RANKS** statement creates a new variable **Depth** that contains the rank of the variable (**ahf**). By default, this variable has values going from 1 to the number of observations that have no missing values in the ranking variable (**ahf**). (In this case, it is 145,500. Specifying the **Fraction** option means that **Depth** has fractional values obtained by dividing the rank numbers by 145,500.

Run Program 7.5 and open the Depth data set. The table in Output 7.6 shows what the Depth data set and variable of interest **Depth** ❺ look like without subsetting by _hit_ = 1.

Output 7.6: Depth Table (Partial Output)

	Id_number	Censor	_y_	_t_	_t0_	ahf ❹	_ystar_	_hit_	Depth ❺	ROW ❻
	483157	1	1	1	1	**0.68159**	0	1	**0.00001**	1
	483183	1	1	1	1	**0.66421**	0	1	**0.00001**	2
	482819	1	1	1	1	**0.66334**	0	1	**0.00002**	3
	480484	1	9	1	1	**0.65366**	8	0	**0.00003**	4
	479378	1	3	1	1	**0.64674**	2	0	**0.00003**	5
❼	483690	1	0	0	0	**0.64627**	0	1	**0.00004**	6
	483540	1	1	1	1	**0.64236**	0	1	**0.00005**	7
	481514	1	4	1	1	**0.63461**	3	0	**0.00005**	8
	468309	1	2	2	2	**0.61620**	0	1	**0.00006**	9
	467184	1	2	2	2	**0.60887**	0	1	**0.00007**	10
	.	.	.	.	.	.	.	.	.	.
	.	.	.	.	.	.	.	.	.	.
	.	.	.	.	.	.	.	.	.	.
	124742	0	37	26	26	**0.00095**	11	0	**0.99993**	145490
	98108	0	39	28	28	**0.00091**	11	0	**0.99994**	145491
	110384	0	38	27	27	**0.00089**	11	0	**0.99995**	145492
	243340	0	28	17	17	**0.00089**	11	0	**0.99995**	145493
	54154	0	43	32	32	**0.00087**	11	0	**0.99996**	145494
❽	1725	0	47	36	36	**0.00087**	11	0	**0.99997**	145495
	138	0	47	36	36	**0.00081**	11	0	**0.99997**	145496
	206459	0	31	20	20	**0.00078**	11	0	**0.99998**	145497
	222322	0	30	19	19	**0.00077**	11	0	**0.99999**	145498
	97619	0	39	28	28	**0.00073**	11	0	**0.99999**	145499
	37577	0	44	33	33	**0.00072**	11	0	**1.00000**	145500

The partial output of the Depth data set has some fundamental variables of interest:

- Looking at **ahf** ❹ verifies that the column has higher hazard values in the top and receives lower ranks as indicated by **Depth** ❺. The variable **ROW** ❻ at the end of the table indicates that there are 145,500 rows. Only the first 10 and the last 10 rows are presented. The final data set Depth created by PROC RANK has only 2,527 rows because the WHERE statement in Program 7.5 shows only those customers with _hit_ = 1. The reason is to enable the calculation of the Sensitivity variable in the next section. The main difference between Depth and Sensitivity is that Depth is calculated with reference to all observations (_hit_ equals 0 or 1, as in Output 7.6), whereas Sensitivity is derived from observations where _hit_ = 1.
- The created variable Depth ❺ has its values ordered from close to 0.0001 to 1. These values are used as the X axis in the concentration curve. See Figure 7.13.
- Note that the higher the ❹ **ahf**, the lower the ❺ **Depth** in the same row. This means that the customers with a higher probability of repurchase are at the start ❼ of the ordered depth in the concentration curve. The customers at the bottom ❽ with high **Depth** have low probabilities and are at the end of the concentration curve.

Step 8: Compute the Sensitivity

Depth forms the X axis of the concentration curve that is created by SAS Enterprise Miner. See the model validation display in Figure 7.13. In this section, we explain how to create the Y axis of the same figure, known as the sensitivity.

Definition

The sensitivity at a given depth and cutoff is defined as true positives (TP) divided by the total of repurchases in population (FN + TP), which are both used to create the confusion matrix. The main purpose of the matrix is to measure the proportion of repurchases that are correctly identified by the model in the actual month (Time).

Figure 7.12: Confusion Matrix with Sensitivity

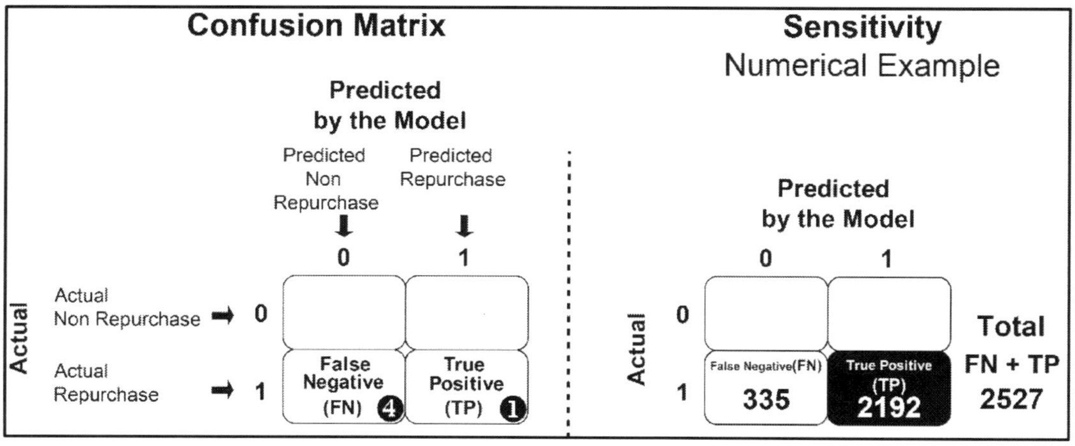

$$\text{Sensitivity} = \frac{TP}{FN + TP}$$

$$\text{Sensitivity} = \frac{\text{Number of True Positives}}{\text{Number of False Negatives} + \text{Number of True Positives}}$$

$$\text{Sensitivity} = \frac{\text{Number of True Positives}}{\text{Total number of Repurchases in Population}}$$

Calculation Used in the Model Created in Chapter 4

Here is the calculation used in the model created in Chapter 4:

$$\text{Sensitivity} = \frac{TP}{FN+TP} = \frac{2192}{335 + 2192}$$

$$\text{Sensitivity} = \frac{2192}{2527}$$

$$\text{Sensitivity} = 0.867432$$

The number is the proportion of correctly predicted customers that repurchased in January 2014 divided by the total number of repurchases in the population in the same month. In other words, the sensitivity reflects how good the model is at finding customers who actually repurchase in January 2014.

The sensitivity is also the proportion of hits in each decile (**Depth**). It is created by running a similar PROC RANK step as was used to create the Depth variable. The only difference is that there is no need to reverse the order of the input variable Depth. The calculation is implemented in Program 7.6.

Program 7.6: Creating the Sensitivity Variable

```
proc rank data=Depth ❶ out=Sensitivity ❷ fraction;
var Depth ❸;
ranks Sensitivity ❹;
run;
```

❶ **Depth** is the input data set created in the last section. It contains all eligible customers making a repurchase in January 2014. It has 2,527 observations.

❷ The output data set is named **Sensitivity**. It, too, contains 2,527 observations because there is no subsetting where the condition has been applied.

❸ The variable **Depth** to rank is specified.

❹ The **RANKS** statement creates a new variable, **Sensitivity**, that contains the rank of the variable (**Depth**). It is important to understand the difference between how the **RANKS** statement is used to create **Sensitivity** and how the **RANKS** statement is used to create the **Depth**:

- The DESCENDING option has been omitted. This is because sensitivity increases as depth increases, but depth increases as the average Hazard function decreases.
- For depth, the RANKS statement is applied to all observations in the Train data set (_hit_ = 0 or 1). But, for sensitivity, the RANKS statement is applied to only observations where _hit_ = 1. The relationship between the values of Depth and Sensitivity is explained by the concentration curve.

The definition of sensitivity ❹ used by the concentration curve is based purely on the actuals (_hit_ = 1). This allows for a graphical comparison with the modeled average Hazard function via the Depth variable. Maximizing sensitivity minus depth in the concentration curve is analogous to maximizing the sum of sensitivity and specificity in the confusion matrix.

The definition of sensitivity for the concentration curve and sensitivity for the confusion matrix are defined identically. Sensitivity for the concentration curve is based only on the actual hits because FN+TP always equals the total number of actual hits for any cutoff.

Step 9: Create the Concentration Curve

Figure 7.13 is the concentration curve that is generated by SAS Enterprise Miner. The X axis is the Depth variable and the Y axis is the Sensitivity variable created in Program 7.6.

Figure 7.13: Concentration Curve

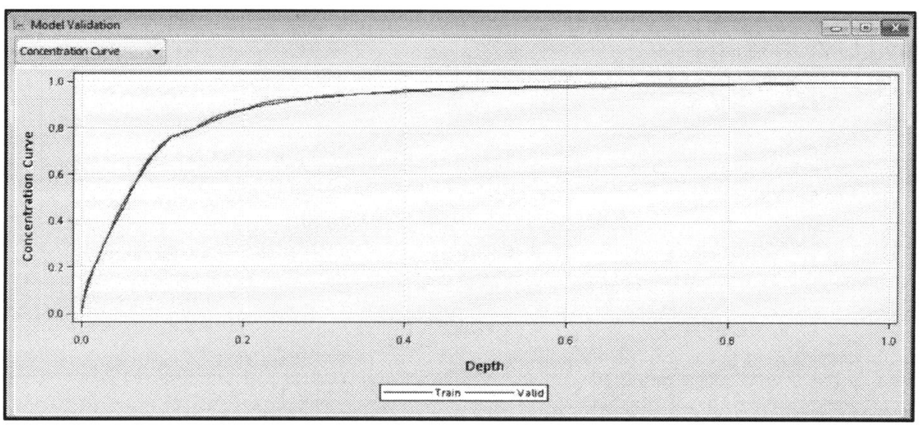

In Figure 7.13, the training and validation concentration curves have similar performance. This shows that the model passes visual control. Later, a statistical control about the concentration curve is explained. Figure 7.14 is an additional graph created by the SGPLOT procedure to explain the features of the concentration curve.

Figure 7.14: Concentration Curve—PROC SGPLOT

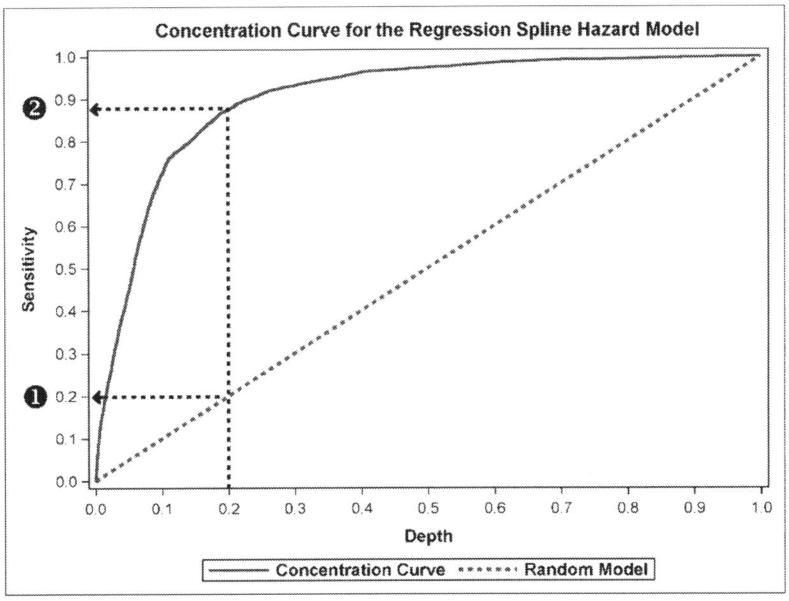

The question is, "How should you analyze this graph?" In general, models need to be compared to choose the best one. The concentration curve created by the SGPLOT procedure is similar to the ones created by SAS Enterprise Miner, with added references lines and a better display to improve the analysis. This graphic is similar, but it is not identical. SAS Enterprise Miner shows Train and Valid, and this one shows only the concentration curve versus a random model.

The area under the concentration curve (AUCC) is one of the best indicators of the accuracy of a model because it measures the proportion of hits on the Y axis and the depth of the average Hazard function on the X axis. The AUCC is directly proportional to the distance between the concentration curve and reference line, which is another useful graphical guideline. The reference line indicates using a 45° angle and represents a model that cannot predict the association of the hits using the average Hazard function. The closer the concentration curve is to the reference line, the poorer the model.

Figure 7.14 shows that the top two deciles (Depth = 0.2) capture more than 85% ❷ of the customers that repurchased in January. This is compared to a random model where the same deciles capture only 20% ❶ of those repurchasing. From now on, Depth = 0.2 is referred to as a "guess" because this value gives us a point of reference to move to more sophisticated analysis later. Below are two key things to remember:

- A perfectly baseline (random) model, where the average Hazard function is assigned to the customers arbitrarily and has no discriminatory power, would give a 45° angle to the X axis and would intersect the origin through (0,0) and (1,1).
- As the concentration curve bows above the perfectly baseline (random) diagonal, the predictive discriminatory power increases. A perfect model would reach the (0,1) point where sensitivity equals 1. This perfect foresight (omniscient) model would assign all repurchasing customers an average Hazard function value of 1 and non-repurchasing customers 0.

In Figure 7.15, four graphs show the distance between the concentration curve and reference line from model ❶ to model ❹. The general rule is this: the larger the area and the bigger the distance between the random model represented by the reference line and the concentration curve, the better the model. Model ❹ is better than model ❶ because it has a much larger area under its curve and a much bigger distance from the reference line. The larger the area between the concentration curve and the random reference line, the more the model is able to concentrate on customers who repurchase in the top deciles.

Figure 7.15: Comparing Different Models Using the Concentration Curve

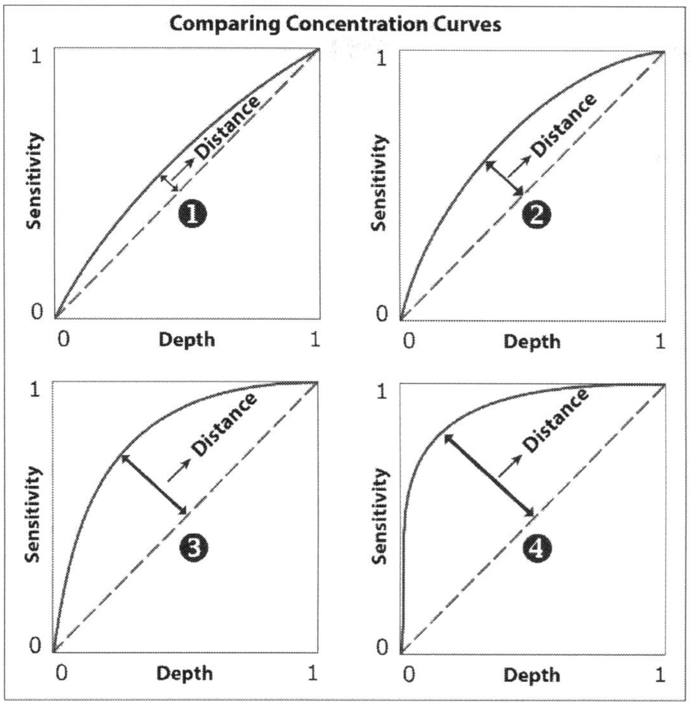

SAS Enterprise Miner presents two important statistical measures related to the concentration curve: the Gini Concentration Ratio and the Kolmogorov-Smirnov statistic. The later sections "Gini Concentration Ratio" and "Kolmogorov-Smirnov" demonstrate the formulas and purposes of these statistics.

Step 10: Compute Lift

In step 7, the data set is sorted in descending order by the average Hazard function. A successful model should have a high concentration of _hits_ at the top of this sorted data set. This performance can be measured in terms of lift. The lift measures the accuracy of only the top part of the model—10%, 20%, and so on—on the basis that if the model is good, this portion will contain a large proportion of the _hits_.

The goal is not to predict whether everybody in the data set repurchases, but to find the best depth (in the X axis) that maximizes lift. To succeed in this task, you must define lift.

Lift ❶ is calculated as the ratio of the sensitivity of the top quantile of the ranked observations to the depth. This calculation is implemented in Program 7.7.

Program 7.7: Create the Lift Variable

```
data Lift;
set Sensitivity;
Lift=Sensitivity/Depth; ❶
run;
```

Step 11: Create the Lift Curve

Using the data set Lift, SAS Enterprise Miner creates the lift curve presented in Figure 7.16.

Figure 7.16: Lift Curve—SAS Enterprise Miner Output

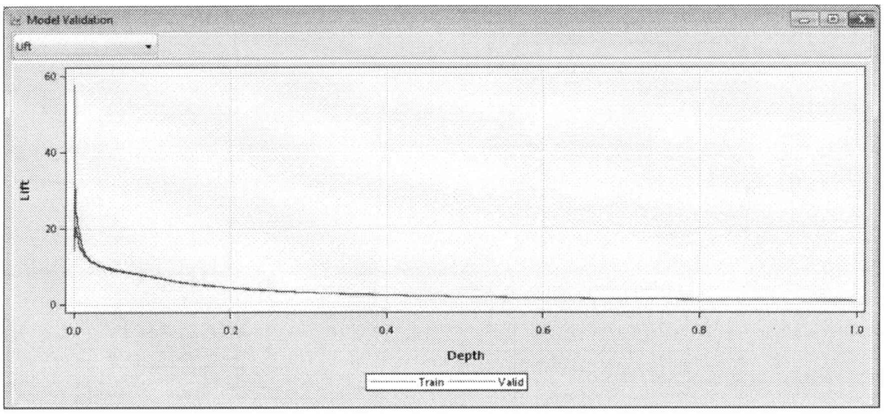

The default lift curve created by SAS Enterprise Miner gives a first snapshot of the performance. Using advanced options of PROC SGPLOT to create reference lines gives us powerful insights.

Figure 7.17: Lift Curve—SGPLOT Procedure

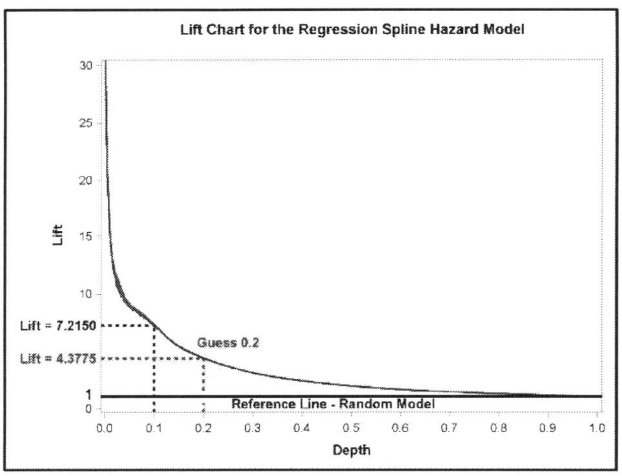

The lift is calculated for a given depth and is widely used in database-based marketing campaigns to decide how many customers in a database to send promotional letters to. Figure 7.17 illustrates that the customers in the top 20% decile are **4.3775** times more likely to repurchase than is expected by a random model. For the top 10% of the sorted data set, customers are **7.2150** times more likely to repurchase. The value 0.2 (20%) is indicated as an example. However, the solution is to find the depth value that maximizes this lift function. In summary, the lift graph shows how more likely customers are to repurchase using the modeled average Hazard function than if they were selected using a random model (as presented by the reference line (equal to value 1 on the Y axis)).

Lift curves are typically monotonically decreasing, although a poor model or sampling variance might yield lift curves that are not monotonic. Typically, the maximum is the first point plotted. The magnitude of the lift at the first point depends on how you construct the curve. This is performed by using the Survival node definition or by binning as is done in most other SAS Enterprise Miner modeling nodes.

As depth increases from 0 to 1, the lift decreases by 0.1.

Figure 7.17, in conjunction with Figure 7.14, show that the top two deciles capture about 85% of the customers that repurchased in January 2014.

Figure 7.18: Lift Curve Using Needle Graph—The SGPLOT Procedure

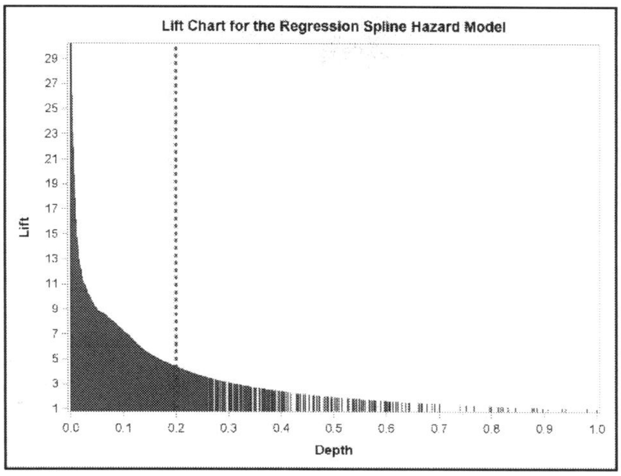

In Figure 7.18, the lift curve has been generated using a needle graph and the SGPLOT procedure. When you observe the density of customers who repurchased, it appears that most of the customers are concentrated in the area below a depth of 0.2. This is an indication that the model is performing well. A flat lift line with a low density curve is an indication of a poor model.

A lift curve shows the same information as a ROC or concentration curve, but it focuses on the ordering at the beginning of the data set. The Y axis shows the ratio of how that portion of the population repurchased compared to the rate of the population as a whole.

In Figure 7.19, four graphs show the lift for different models.

Figure 7.19: Comparing Lift Curves

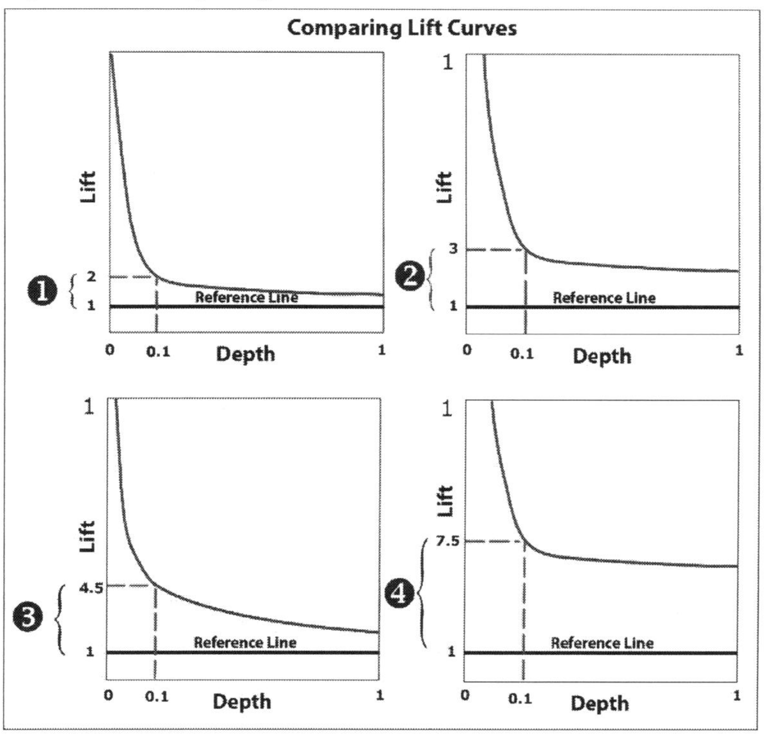

The value 0.1 (10%) for the depth (X axis) is chosen to compare the performance of several models. The general rule is this: the bigger the distance between the reference line and the lift curve, the better the model. From model ❶ to model ❹, you can see that as the distance increases, the model discriminatory power increases. Model ❹ is the best because customers are 7.5 times more likely to repurchase in the top 10% decile than by a random model represented by the reference line (equal to lift = 1 on the Y axis).

Step 12: Compute Benefit

The *benefit* is defined as the difference between the sensitivity and the depth. For validation purposes, the maximum benefit needs to be determined because its value is related to the required depth cutoff.

In Figure 7.20, supposing that the depth is increased from 0.2 to 0.6, the benefit is not at the maximum point. To find the maximum point of benefit, depth must be subtracted from the concentration curve (sensitivity).

Figure 7.20: Maximum Benefit

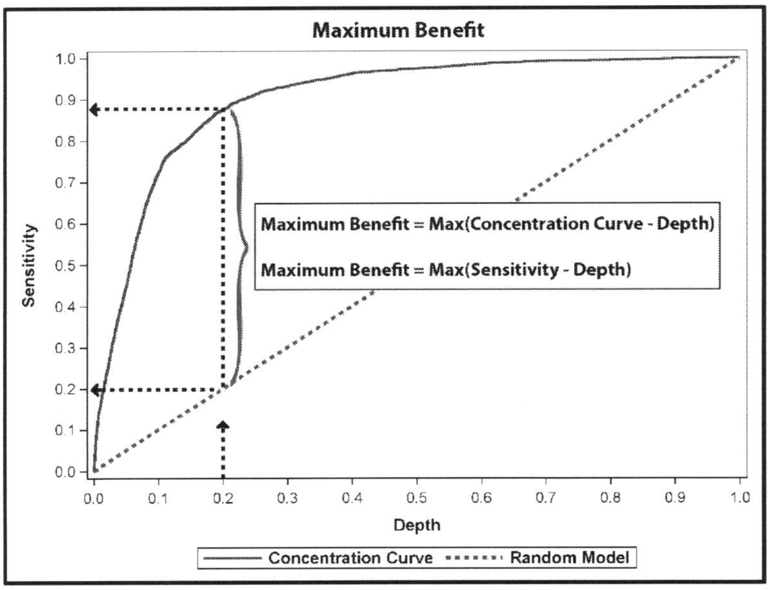

Program 7.8 calculates **Benefit** ❶ by subtracting **Depth** from the **Sensitivity**.

Program 7.8: The Benefit Variable

```
Data Benefit;
set Lift;
Benefit=Sensitivity-Depth; ❶
run;
```

Step 13: Create the Benefit Curve

After benefit has been calculated, SAS Enterprise Miner creates the benefit curve, which has **Depth** on the X axis and **Benefit** on the Y axis.

Figure 7.21: Benefit Curve

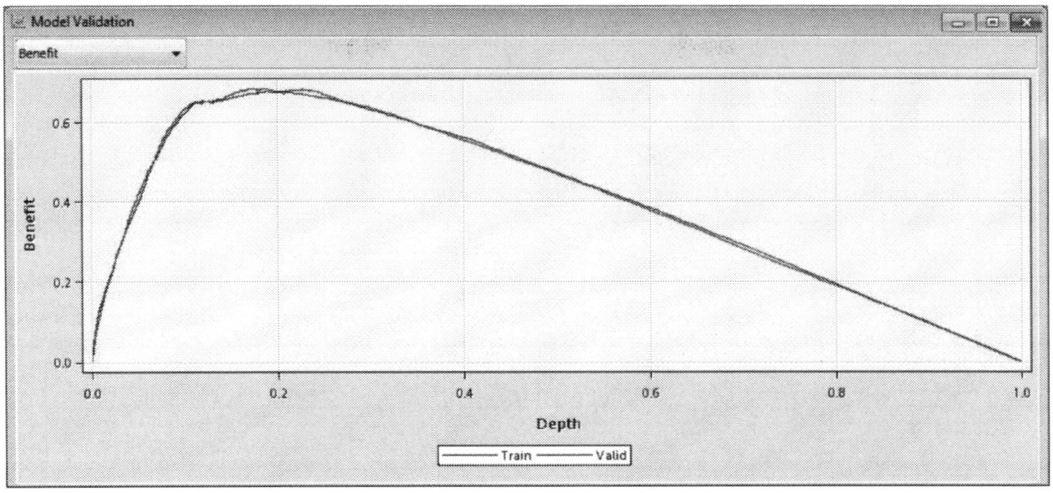

Step 14: Select the Cutoff=Depth Where the Benefit Is Maximum

The interpretation of the benefit curve is straightforward. Until now, the approach to determine an optimal cutoff has been to guess at an approximate value (in these steps, 0.2 (20%) has been used). An example of where this might be used is to target 20% of customers for a marketing campaign.

By carefully analyzing the graphics and using the SGPLOT procedure, you can see that the guess estimate of 20% as the cutoff is fairly close. To find the precise cutoff value, you must calculate the maximum benefit on the Y axis and find the corresponding value of depth.

The graphs in Figure 7.22 were created using PROC SGPLOT (replicating SAS Enterprise Miner graphs, including the needle graph). In this needle graph, there is a high concentration of customers below the depth value of 0.25. As depth increases, the concentration of customers repurchasing gradually decreases.

Figure 7.22: Benefit Curve—PROC SGPLOT

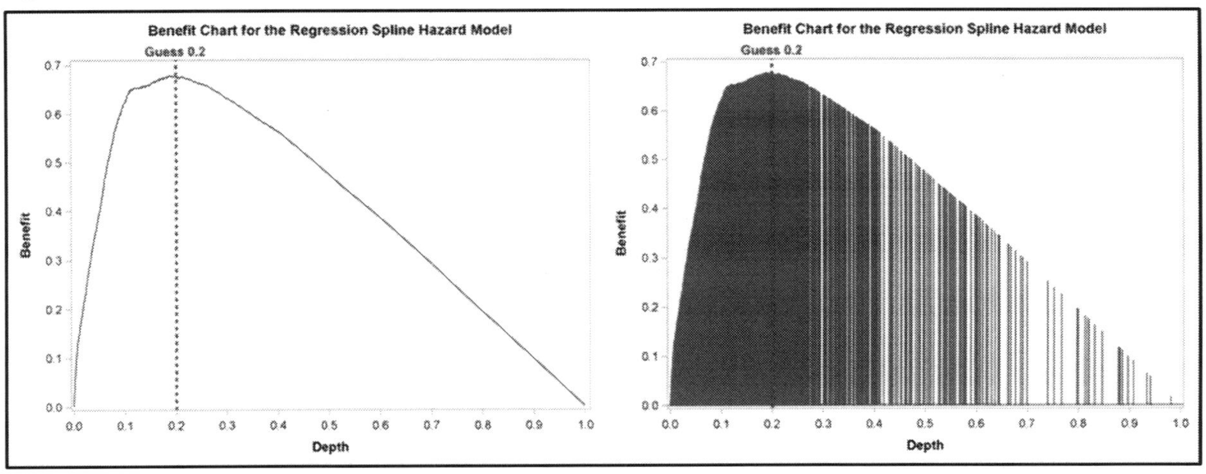

Computing the Maximum Benefit—Method 1

There are two methods for computing maximum benefit. Program 7.9 is the first of these.

Program 7.9: Computing the Maximum Benefit—Method 1

```
proc sort data=Benefit ❶;
by benefit;
run;

data Cutoff_depth_1;
set Benefit End ❷ = End_of_file;
if End_of_file then output;
keep Benefit ❸ Ahf ❹ Depth ❺;
run;
```

The first method uses the sorted **Benefit** ❶ data set to create the **Cutoff_depth_1** data set. The value of benefit in the last observation represents the largest value of benefit because the data set is sorted.

To extract the maximum benefit from the data set **Cutoff_depth_1** in Program 7.9, the END= option ❷ creates the last observation in the data set. The END= option creates a temporary variable **End_of_file** whose value is 1 when the DATA step is processing the last observation. For all other observations, the value of End_of_file is 0. Although the DATA step uses the temporary variable **End_of_file** in END=End_of_file, SAS does not add it to the resulting data set.

When the DATA step begins processing the last observation, the value of End_of_year changes from 0 to 1. Only the final observation containing the variables of interest (**Benefit** ❸ , **Ahf** ❹, and **Depth** ❺), which are indicated by the **KEEP** statement, is written to the output data set **Cutoff_depth_1**.

Output 7.7 shows the output data set Cutoff_depth_1, which contains the required information: The value of **Depth=0.188969207216494** ❺ is very close to the guess value of 0.2 (20%) in Figure 7.22. The statistics in Output 7.7 match the SAS Enterprise Miner statistics in Figure 7.1. To generate the same statistics for the validation data set, you can run the same code on it as used for the Train data set.

Output 7.7: Depth and Average Hazard Ratio at the Maximum Benefit

Data Role	Benefit	Average Hazard Ratio	Depth
Train	❸ 0.67885839123038	❹ 0.01753084132298	❺ 0.18896907216494

Figure 7.23 is annotated with the maximum benefit value of **0.67889** and the corresponding depth value of **0.18896**. When the maximum benefit is 0.67889, the optimal cutoff value of the depth is 0.1889. This optimal depth value is of fundamental importance as is demonstrated.

Figure 7.23: Depth Cutoff at Maximum Benefit

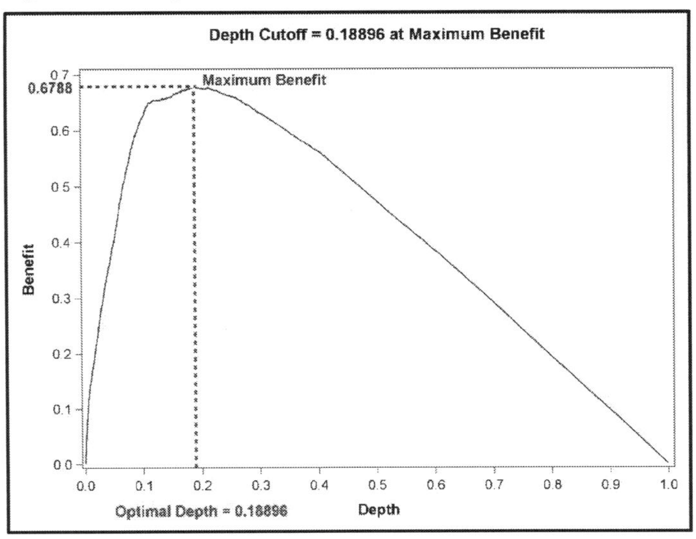

How to use and interpret the optimal depth value is covered in the next section. For the moment, the focus is on showing a more efficient way to compute the depth at the maximum benefit, which is the one implemented by SAS Enterprise Miner.

Computing the Maximum Benefit—Method 2

The basic difference between Program 7.9 and Program 7.10 is that there is no need to sort the data set. This is because the WHERE statement ❻ selects the *single* observation where the benefit is at the maximum. In this sense, PROC SQL is more efficient code to achieve the same result.

Program 7.10: Computing the Maximum Benefit—Method 2

```
proc sql;
create table Cutoff_Depth_2 as select Benefit ❸, Ahf ❹, Depth ❺
from Benefit
where Benefit =(select max(benefit) from Benefit) ❻;
quit;
```

The Depth Measure and the Hazard Measure: Which to Choose

Calculating the depth and average Hazard function provides two highly insightful statistics. A framework is required for their deployment. Figure 7.24 shows how to answer two key questions asked by businesses in sectors such as Marketing ❶, Credit Risk ❷, and Telecommunications ❸.

Figure 7.24: A Comparison of Cutoff Calculation Methods

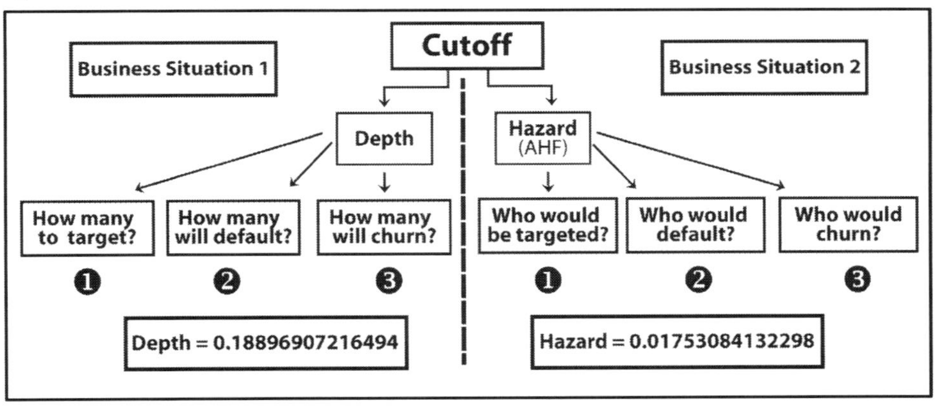

Two Business Situations

Before the answers are explored, you should understand the differences between the two business situations.

Situation 1

A manager wants to start a marketing campaign and needs to know how many customers to target within the budget allocated to the Marketing department.

The answer to this question can be found using **Depth = 0.18896907216494** as cutoff in four steps, which the SAS code implements.

1. Create the average Hazard function or Survival function statistic by scoring the data set. The scoring process is demonstrated in Chapter 8.
2. Sort the data in descending order by the computed Hazard or Survival function to place the customers with the highest hazard at the top of the table.
3. Create a variable to identify the number of customers.

4. Multiply the total number of customers in the data set by the depth cutoff to find the total number of customers in the data set that should be targeted. These customers are at the top of the data set as seen in Figure 7.25 and are indicated by a dummy variable whose value is 1.

Figure 7.25: The Number of Customers to Be Targeted

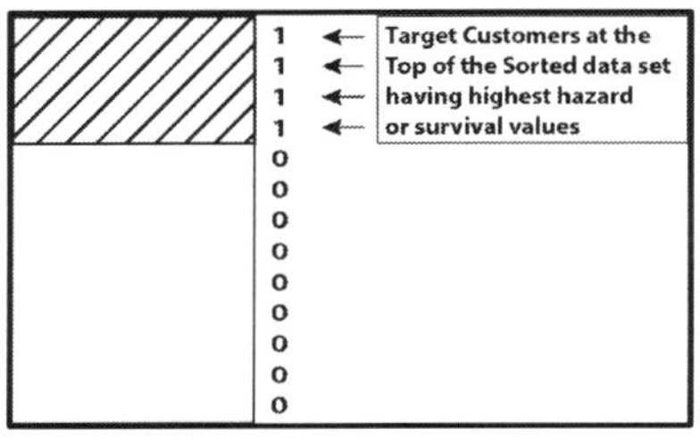

Situation 2

A manager wants to start a marketing campaign and needs to know which customers to target. The answer to this question is different because the average **Hazard** function cutoff value of **0.01753084132298** needs to be used in two steps that the SAS code implements:

1. Score the data set by calculating the average Hazard function statistic.
2. Select customers having an average Hazard function > 0. 01753084132298 to find those that should be targeted. There is no need to sort the data set because these customers can be anywhere in the table or external database. They are indicated by a dummy variable whose value is 1 in Figure 7.26.

Figure 7.26: Which Customers to Target

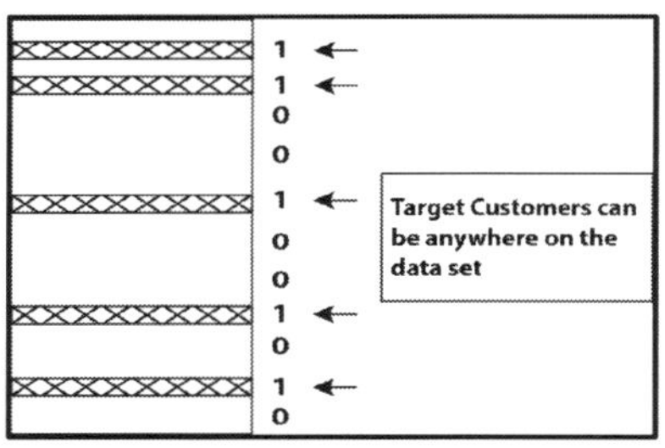

Business Situation 1: Use of Depth as Cutoff

This section shows how to use the depth cutoff value to find the optimum number of customers to target in terms of model performance and the resulting confusion matrix.

The depth value of 0.18896907216494, which is calculated using Program 7.9 or Program 7.10, is used in Program 7.11 to create the variable **predicted_depth** ❺. That variable has the value of 1 for the customers who should be targeted, and 0 for those who should not.

Program 7.11: Using the Depth Value as Cutoff

```
proc sort data = train; ❷
    by descending ahf ❶;
run;

data train;
set  train;
    Row_cutoff = _n_; ❸
run ;
    data train_depth_cutoff;
set train;
        if Row_cuttoff <= floor(145500* 0.18896907216494)❹ then predicted_depth =1 ❺;
    else if Row_cuttoff >  floor(145500* 0.18896907216494)❹ then predicted_depth =0 ❺;
    run;
```

❶ The variable **ahf** (average Hazard function) was already created by SAS Enterprise Miner using the model to score the **Train** data set. Chapter 8 demonstrates how to score new customers.

❷ Sort the data set by descending **ahf.**

❸ Create the variable **Row_cutoff** to identify the observation (row) number.

❹ Compute the total number of customers to be targeted. The calculation shows that the total number of customers to be targeted is 27,494. **Row_cuttoff** = **145500 * 0.18896907216494**, which is **27494**.

❺ Create a flag variable **predicted_depth** to indicate the customers to target. Any customer having a row_cuttoff lower than 27494 is flagged to be targeted by the variable **predicted_depth = 1**. Customers targeted as **predicted_depth = 0** should be ignored because they have a low average Hazard function value. The resulting table is shown in Figure 7.27.

Figure 7.27: Results of Using the Depth Value as Cutoff

Id_number	❶ Ahf (Hazard)	❸ Row_cuttoff	❺ Predicted_DEPTH
483157	0.68158639170700	1	1
483183	0.66420890433612	2	1
482819	0.66334158440855	3	1
480484	0.65365613893848	4	1
479378	0.64673901307520	5	1
.	.	.	.
.	.	.	.
481708	0.01753333301719	27490	1
478630	0.01753286389080	27491	1
447738	0.01753248034025	27492	1
86539	0.01753238869851	27493	1
436993	0.01753196959219	27494	1
.	.	.	.
.	.	.	.
431989	0.01753084132298	27495	0
304230	0.01753003607363	27496	0
387348	0.01752994871434	27497	0
455782	0.01752967380167	27498	0
479056	0.01752907309957	27499	0
.	.	.	.
.	.	.	.
138	0.00081019858918	145496	0
206459	0.00078202941535	145497	0
222322	0.00077441554142	145498	0
97619	0.00072976480044	145499	0
37577	0.00072024689030	145500	0

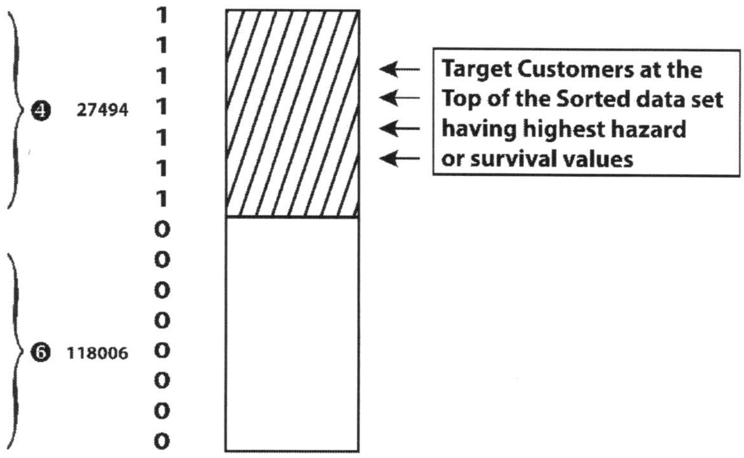

A confusion matrix can be developed using the created variables **predicted_depth** and **_hit_**, as presented in Program 7.12.

Program 7.12: Computing a Confusion Matrix

```
proc freq data = train_depth_cutoff;
tables _hit_ * predicted_depth /nocol nopercent norow;
run;
```

Output 7.8 shows the results of Program 7.12.

Output 7.8: Depth Value Cutoff and Confusion Matrix

Confusion Matrix			
	Predict Repurchase Using (Predicted_depth)		
(Actual Repurchase) _Hit_	0	1	Total
0	117671	25302	142973
1	**335**	**2192**	2527
Total	❻118006	❹ **27494**	145500

In Figure 7.28, sensitivity shows that using the optimal depth cutoff, the model has succeeded in correctly identifying **0.8674** percent of the actual repurchases in January. In other words, **2192** from **2527** customers who repurchased in January are identified as part of the **27494** ❹ customers with the highest average Hazard function. The figure of **118006** ❻ represents the number of customers that should be ignored because they have a lower probability of repurchase in January 2014.

The information extracted from the confusion matrix is rich and summarized in Figure 7.28.

Figure 7.28: Summary of Information from the Confusion Matrix

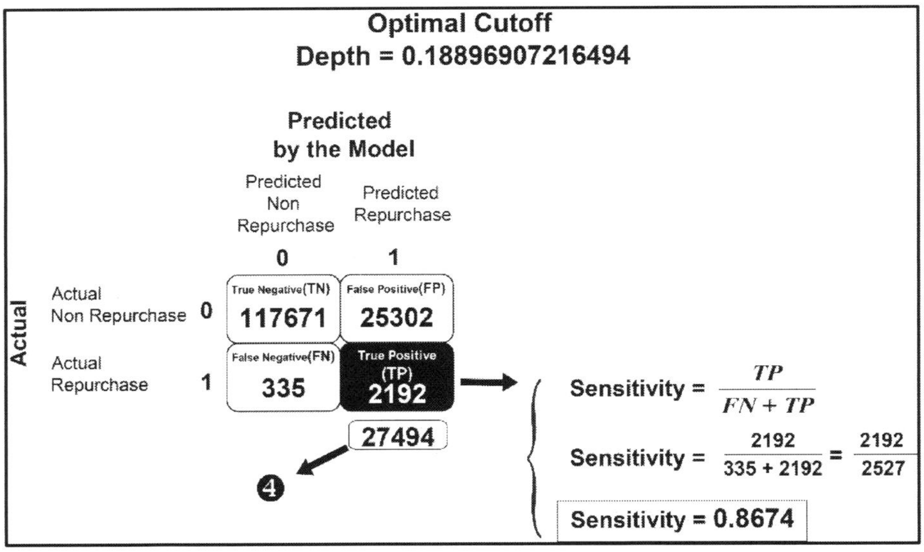

The confusion matrix gives you an efficient way to analyze the performance of the model in January 2014. However, before you select the 27,494 customers to be targeted, it is important to have a good understanding of the customer base and the numbers presented. The number 27,494 is the optimal number of customers to be targeted. Later in this chapter, the section "Specificity and Suboptimal Cutoffs" demonstrates that this number is optimal.

Business Situation 2: Use of Average Hazard Function Value as Cutoff

This section shows how to use the average Hazard function value to find the optimum number of customers to target in terms of model performance and the confusion matrix.

First, the **predicted_ahf** variable is created with Program 7.13.

Program 7.13: Creating the predicted_ahf Variable

```
data train_cutoff_ahf;
set  train;
     if ahf ❶  > 0.01753084132298 then predicted_ahf = 1; ❷
else if ahf ❶ <= 0.01753084132298 then predicted_ahf = 0; ❷
run;
```

The **ahf** ❶ value, which is calculated using Program 7.9 or Program 7.10, is used in Program 7.13 to create the variable **predicted_ahf** ❷. **predicted_ahf** has the value of 1 for customers with an average Hazard function greater than 0.01753084132298, or 0, otherwise.

The customers who should be targeted (predicted_ahf = 1) ❸ as seen in Figure 7.29 can be anywhere in the table.

Figure 7.29: Results of Using the Average Hazard Function as Cutoff

Id_number	❶ Ahf (Hazard)	❷ Predicted_ahf
385	**0.02085481880998**	1
400	0.00415367051968	0
3116	0.00199485603436	0
4603	**0.03698071182118**	1
4617	0.00187246669971	0
7866	**0.03306959856691**	1
7869	0.0021647315077	0
8917	**0.04255318261159**	1
8932	0.00225168656452	0
9165	**0.02160950132265**	1
21493	**0.02420699319889**	1
21500	0.00306014155553	0
28128	**0.02227700205572**	1
43780	**0.04939989527324**	1
43781	**0.04642981098685**	1
68881	**0.06433130602275**	1
68896	0.00466143610295	0

❸

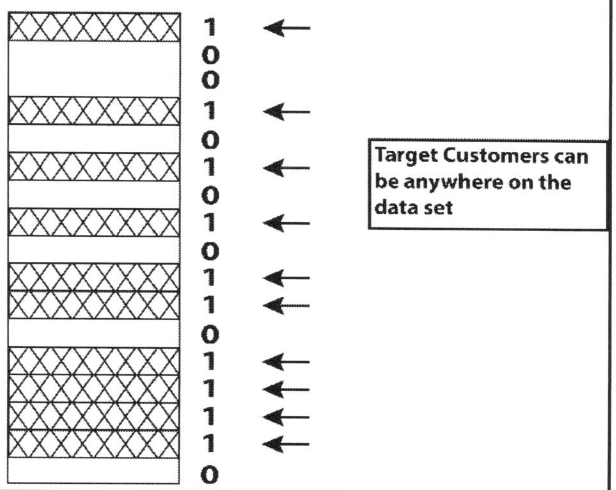

A confusion matrix is created using PROC FREQ. It results in the same values found in Output 7.8.

```
proc freq data = train_cutoff_ahf;
tables _hit_ * predicted_ahf ❷ / nocol nopercent norow;
run;
```

The results appear in Output 7.9.

Output 7.9: predicted_ahf-Cutoff Confusion Matrix

Table of (Actual Repurchase) by Predicted_ahf			
	Predicted_ahf		
(Actual Repurchase)	0	1	Total
0	117671	25302	142973
1	335	2192	2527
Total	118006	27494	145500

Specificity and Suboptimal Cutoffs

Specificity, which is also called the true negative rate, measures the proportion of non-repurchases that are correctly identified by the model.

The sensitivity at a given depth cutoff is defined as the true positives (TP) divided by the total positives (FN + TP). This value was used to create the previous confusion matrix. Sensitivity measures the proportion of repurchases that are correctly identified by the model. In contrast, specificity is defined as the true negatives (TN) divided by the total negatives (TN + FP) from the confusion matrix. It measures the proportion of non-repurchases that are correctly identified by the model.

Figure 7.30 shows the calculated specificity.

Figure 7.30: Specificity Confusion Matrix

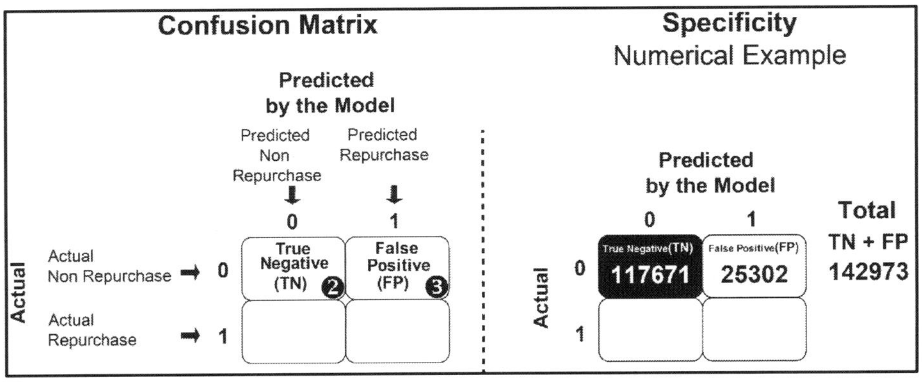

$$\text{Specificity} = \frac{\text{TN}}{\text{TN} + \text{FP}}$$

$$\text{Specificity} = \frac{\text{Number of True Negatives}}{\text{Number of True Negatives} + \text{Number of False Positives}}$$

$$\text{Specificity} = \frac{\text{Number of True Negatives}}{\text{Total Number of Non-repurchases in Population}}$$

$$\text{Specificity} = \frac{\text{TN}}{\text{TN} + \text{FP}} = \frac{117671}{117671 + 25302}$$

$$\text{Specificity} = \frac{117671}{142973}$$

$$\text{Specificity} = 0.8230$$

Using the information extracted from the PROC FREQ output, a confusion matrix can be created for the hazard at optimal cutoff using depth or hazard, as shown in Figure 7.31.

Figure 7.31: Confusion Matrix Using Optimal Cutoff (Depth or Hazard)

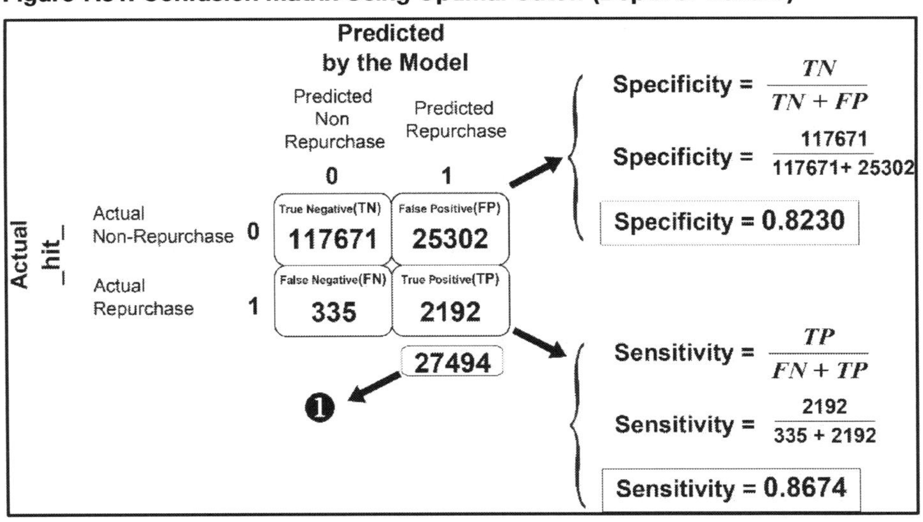

The relevant value is 0.017531. This number maximizes the depth and the average Hazard function for both cutoffs at the same time. Output 7.10 show what happens when this number is changed by altering the hazard cutoff value.

Output 7.10: Optimal Cutoff Changed by Alteration of the Hazard Cutoff Value

	Cut-off
	0.015
	0.016
Optimal	**0.017531**
	0.018
	0.019
	0.020

Calculations for sensitivity and specificity for different average Hazard function values that are cut off between 0.015 and 0.02 demonstrate the implication of choosing a suboptimal cutoff. A macro can perform the calculation. (The code is available at https://support.sas.com/authors.)

Each output is placed in a confusion matrix in Figure 7.32.

Figure 7.32: Summary of Hazard Cutoff and Confusion Matrix (Partial Output 1)

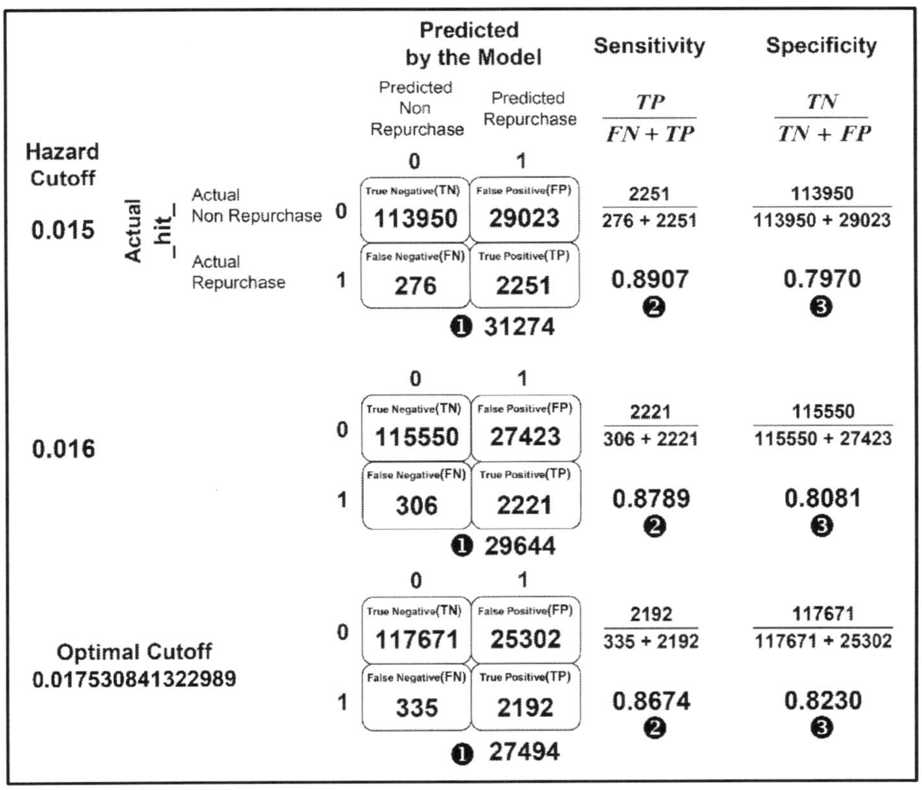

Figure 7.33: Summary of Hazard Cutoff and Confusion Matrix (Partial Output 2)

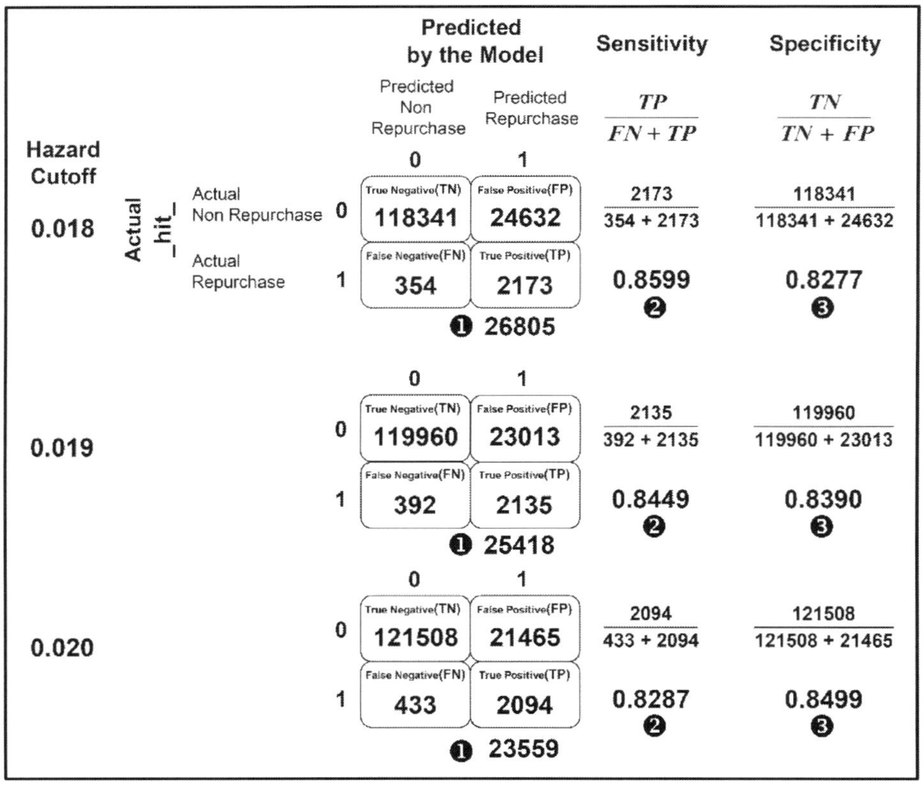

The number 27494 ❶ in Figure 7.32, relative to the optimal cutoff, represents the number of customers to target given the need to maximize the Sum ❹ of sensitivity and specificity as shown in Output 7.11. This assumes that sensitivity and specificity are of equal importance, which is reasonable in most cases. To apply this, suppose that the business wants to identify customers most likely to repurchase in January 2014 for a promotional campaign by letter (mail), which costs the business for each letter sent.

If more than 27,494 letters are sent (hazard cutoff < optimal), more repurchasing customers are reached (TP and sensitivity ❷ higher). However, this comes at a greater cost of mailing customers who do not repurchase (TN and specificity ❸ lower).

If fewer than 27,494 letters are sent (hazard cut off > optimal), then fewer repurchasing customers are reached (TP and sensitivity lower). But, this will more than offset the reduced number of wasted mailings to customers who do not repurchase (TN and specificity higher).

The assumption that sensitivity and specificity are of equal importance is reasonable in this case because the benefit of the customer responding to the promotion and the cost of sending the letter are not quantified. A more complex approach would involve looking at the expected value of customers receiving the promotion versus the cost of doing the mailing.

Output 7.11 summarizes this by using depth at maximum benefit. The optimal cutoff point is obtained by maximizing the sum of sensitivity and specificity.

Output 7.11: Optimal Cutoff

Cut-off	TN (True Negative)	FP (False Positive)	FN (False Negative)	TP (True Positive)	Total	Sensitivity ❷	Specificity ❸	Sum
0.015000	113950	29023	276	2251	145500	0.89078	0.79700	1.68778
0.016000	115550	27423	306	2221	145500	0.87891	0.80819	1.68710
⇨ **0.017531**	**117671**	**25302**	**335**	**2192**	**145500**	**0.86743**	**0.82303**	❹ **1.69046**
0.018000	118341	24632	354	2173	145500	0.85991	0.82772	1.68763
0.019000	119960	23013	392	2135	145500	0.84488	0.83904	1.68391
0.020000	121508	21465	433	2094	145500	0.82865	0.84987	1.67852

Figure 7.34 shows the relationship between optimal cutoff and the sum of sensitivity and specificity.

Figure 7.34: Optimal Cutoff and the Sum of Sensitivity and Specificity

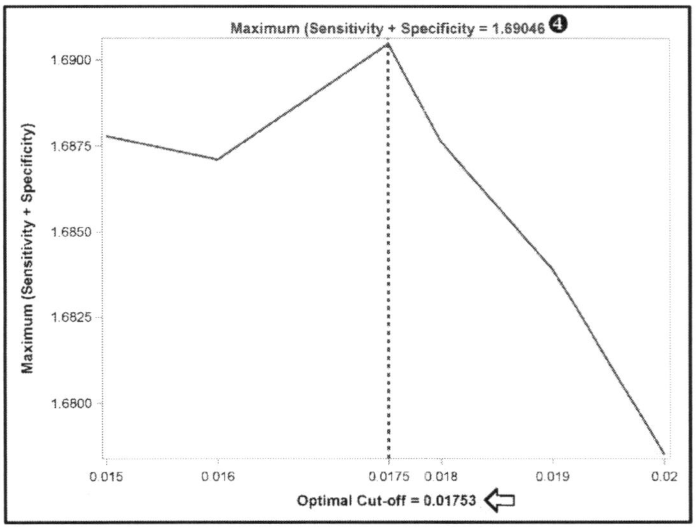

Gini Concentration Ratio

In this section, we describe and illustrate the SAS Enterprise Miner approach for computing the AUC and the Gini Concentration Ratio. The Gini Concentration Ratio is a measure of the discriminatory performance of the model. Or, in other words, how well the fitted hazard model distinguishes between observed customers who repurchase (Repurchase = 1) and customers who do not (Repurchase = 0).

The Gini Concentration Ratio is related to the AUCC and the reference line for a random model.

The Gini Concentration Ratio can be calculated as follows: Gini concentration ratio = 2 (AUCC − ½) or as a function of the sensitivity and depth, which is the formula implemented by SAS Enterprise Miner, as follows:

$$\text{Gini Concentration Ratio} = 2*(\text{Sumarea} + (1 - \text{Depth})) - 1$$

The AUCC of the actual model is in Figure 7.35.

Figure 7.35: Area Under Concentration Curve (AUCC)

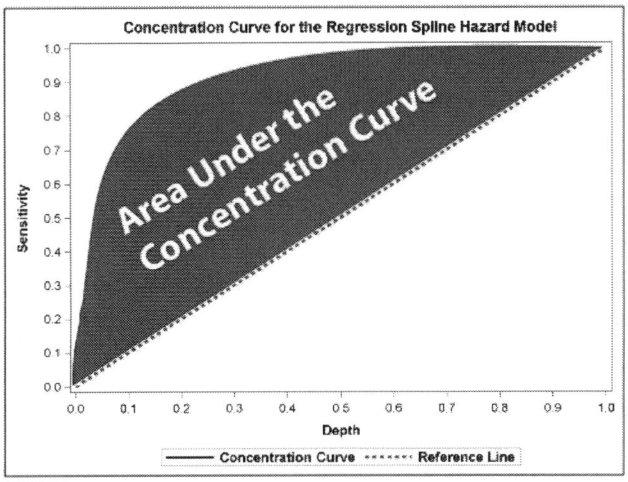

The calculation is performed in three steps in Program 7.14, using the **Benefit** data set that was created in the last section.

Program 7.14: The Gini Concentration Ratio

```
data Gini_Concentration_Ratio;
set Benefit end = eof;
area = lag(Sensitivity) * (Depth - lag(depth)); ❶
sumarea + area; ❷
if eof then do;     /* eof = end of file */
  GC_Ratio = 2 * (sumarea + (1 - Depth)) - 1; ❸
end;
run;
```

❶ Calculate the area for each cutoff value of depth (0.1, 0.2, 0.3, and so on).

❷ Obtain the cumulative sum of the area for all values of depth using a SUM statement.

❸ Apply the formula in ❸.

Output 7.12 contains the last eight observations of the Gini_Concentration_Ratio data set and the key variables. The **GC_Ratio** ❸ value in the last row is exactly the same as in Figure 7.1 relative to the Train data set.

Output 7.12: Gini_Concentration_Ratio Data Set (Partial Output)

Observation	Area ❶	Sumarea ❷	GC_Ratio
2520	0.000644	0.783661	.
2521	0.004750	0.788410	.
2522	0.010854	0.799264	.
2523	0.010172	0.809437	.
2524	0.026700	0.836137	.
2525	0.006302	0.842438	.
2526	0.041912	0.884350	.
2527	0.017471	0.901821	❸ **0.805511**

The Gini Concentration Ratio is related to the AUCC. One way of interpreting it is by comparing the AUCC of different models. The bigger the AUCC, the better the model, and the higher the Gini Concentration Ratio. Model ❹ (**AUCC** = **0.86**) has better performance than model ❶ (**AUCC** = **0.62**) as seen in Figure 7.36.

Figure 7.36: Comparing Area Under Concentration Curves

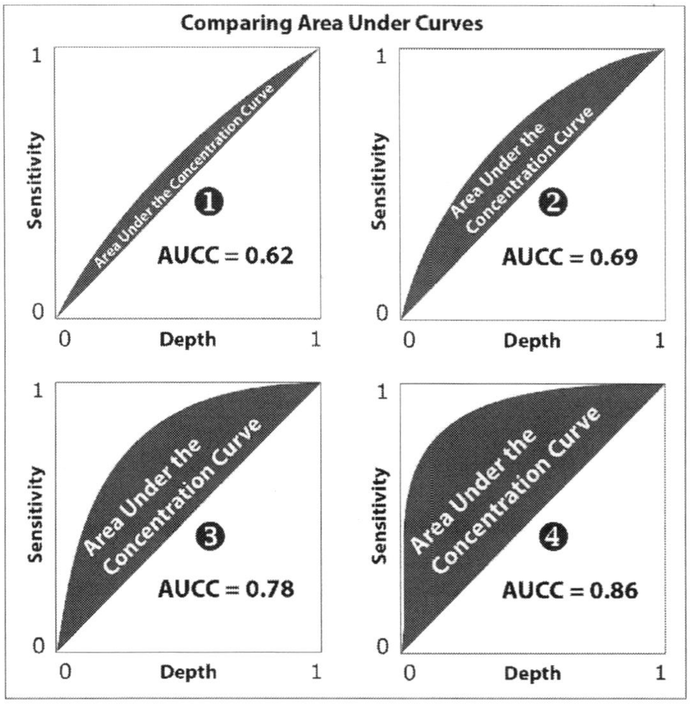

Kolmogorov-Smirnov

The Kolmogorov-Smirnov statistic is the maximum vertical distance (represented by D) between two cumulative distributions. This statistic helps assess how well a model discriminates between customers that repurchase and those who do not repurchase. The statistics are based on the distance between the empirical distribution functions. In the survival model, these populations are identified by the following:

- _hit_
- non _hit_

Figure 7.37 shows the Kolmogorov-Smirnov distance calculation using the following formula:

$$\text{Distance}_{KS} = \text{Max}\left[(\text{EDF})^{\text{Hit}=0} - (\text{EDF})^{\text{Hit}=1}\right]$$

The Kolmogorov-Smirnov distance can also be calculated as follows:

$$\text{Distance}_{KS} = \text{Max}\left[\frac{\text{Benefit}}{1 - \text{Mean(hit)}}\right]$$

This is the maximum benefit divided by the proportion of non-hits in the data set.

Figure 7.37: The Kolmogorov-Smirnov Distance—PROC SGPLOT

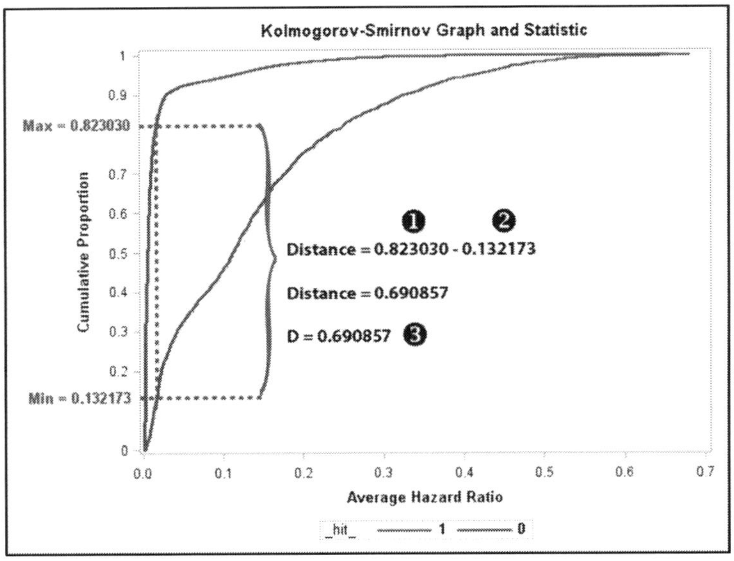

The graph shows the cumulative proportion of hits (repurchase) and non-hits (non-repurchase), which is the difference between the two populations. The better the ability of the model to separate the repurchase customers from the non-repurchase customers, the greater the distance between the two populations. The graph shows the point that most effectively separates the repurchases from non-repurchases in the population.

In the plotted graph, the Kolmogorov-Smirnov statistic value shows that the model does a good job of separating the two populations. These values are computed using PROC NPAR1WAY and later using PROC SQL.

The Kolmogorov-Smirnov statistic also determines the best cutoff in survival models. The best cutoff maximizes the distance (D) between customers that repurchase in January (_hit_ = 1) from non-repurchase (_hit_ = 0).

Graphics can be used to compare Kolmogorov-Smirnov distances as shown in Figure 7.38.

Figure 7.38: Comparing the Kolmogorov-Smirnov Distance and Gini Concentration Ratio

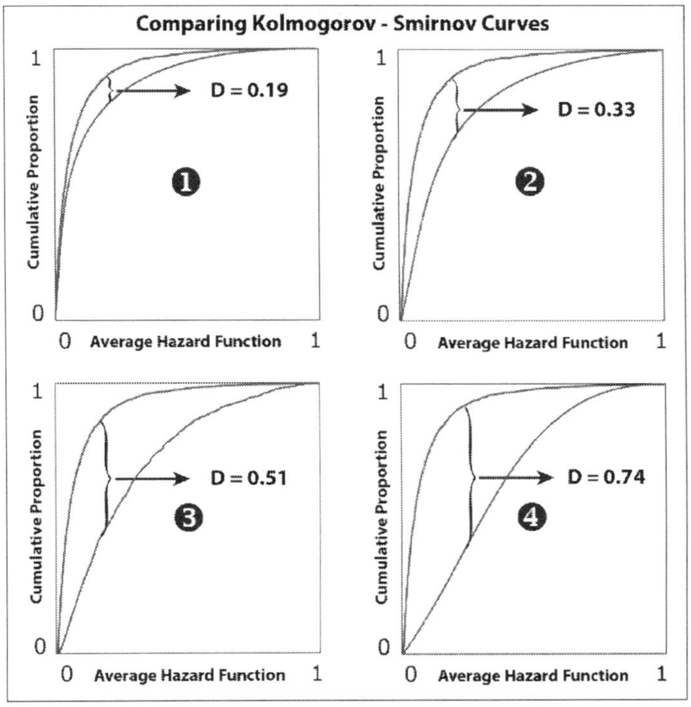

The value for the Kolmogorov-Smirnov statistic can range from 0 to 1. A 1 indicates that the model does a perfect job of predicting all customers that repurchased in the period of interest and in separating the two populations of those repurchasing and those not repurchasing. In comparing different models, the general rule is the better the model, the higher the distance D value. Model ❹ (**D = 0.74**) has a better performance than model ❶ (**D = 0.19**).

Method 1—PROC NPAR1WAY

The Kolmogorov-Smirnov statistic can be calculated using the NPAR1WAY procedure in Program 7.15.

The following statements request empirical distribution function (EDF) statistics. These statistics test whether the distribution of a variable is the same across different groups. The **EDF** ❶ option requests the EDF analysis. The variable **_hit_** ❸ is the **CLASS** variable (having values 1 or 0), and the variable **ahf** ❹ specified in the **VAR** statement is the average Hazard function variable.

The **PLOTS** = ❷ option requests an EDF plot for average Hazard function, classified by _hit_. SAS ODS Graphics must be enabled before producing plots.

Program 7.15: The Kolmogorov-Smirnov Statistic Using PROC NPAR1WAY

```
proc npar1way data=train edf ❶ plots = edfplot ❷;
class _hit_ ❸;
var     ahf ❹;
run;
```

Results appear in Outputs 7.13 and 7.14.

Output 7.13: The Kolmogorov-Smirnov Statistic

Kolmogorov-Smirnov Test for Variable ahf Classified by Variable _hit_			
hit	N	EDF at Maximum	Deviation from Mean at Maximum
1	2527	❶ **0.132173**	-34.125719
0	142973	❷ **0.823030**	4.536881
Total	145500	0.811031	
Maximum Deviation Occurred at Observation 86501			
Value of ahf at Maximum = 0.017530			

Output 7.14: The Kolmogorov-Smirnov Distance

Kolmogorov-Smirnov Two-Sample Test (Asymptotic)			
KS	0.090252	D	❸ **0.690857**
KSa	34.425978	Pr > KSa	<.0001

❶ This represents **_hit_ = 1**, the EDF value at the average Hazard function value, which maximizes the distance between the _hit_ = 1 and _hit_ = 0 EDF functions.

❷ This represents **_hit_ = 0**, the EDF value at the average Hazard function value, which maximizes the distance between the _hit_ = 1 and _hit_ = 0 EDF functions.

❸ This is the **D** (Distance) value, which has been maximized. It is equal to ❷ – ❶.

Distance = **0.823030** ❷ – **0.132173** ❶

Distance = **0.690857** ❸

Values ❶, ❷, and ❸ were used to demonstrate the calculation in Program 7.15.

Method 2—PROC SQL

SAS Enterprise Miner uses an adjusted formula to calculate the Kolmogorov-Smirnov statistic. The Kolmogorov-Smirnov statistic is the maximum benefit divided by the proportion of non-hits in the population included in the Train data set.

In Program 7.16, PROC SQL is used to calculate the Kolmogorov-Smirnov statistic and replicate Figure 7.1 by creating all statistical variables.

Program 7.16: The Kolmogorov-Smirnov Statistic

```
proc sql noprint;
create table Kolmogorov_Smirnov ❶ as select
Benefit,
Ahf,
Depth,
Lift,
Benefit/(select 1-mean(_hit_) ❷ from Train ❸) as KS ❹
from Gini_Concentration_Ratio ❺
where benefit=(select max(benefit) ❻ from Gini_Concentration_Ratio);
quit;
```

❶ Creates a new table named **Kolmogorov_Smirnov** with the output results and variables **Benefit**, **Ahf**, **Depth**, **Lift**, and **KS**.

❷ Computes the Kolmogorov-Smirnov statistic by dividing the benefit by the average of the _hit_ calculated from the original Train ❸ data set. It saves the result as **KS** ❹. KS is calculated using the data set created in the last section, **Gini_Concentration_Ratio** ❺.

The **WHERE** statement ❻ keeps only the observations where the benefit is at the maximum.

Output 7.15 replicates Figure 7.1 by including all the statistical variables for the Train and validation data sets. To achieve the valid results in Output 7.16, run the same SAS steps using the validation data set.

Output 7.15: The Kolmogorov-Smirnov Statistic and Other Statistics

Survival Fit Statistic Table						
Data Role	Benefit	Average Hazard Ratio	Depth	Lift	Kolmogorov-Smirnov Statistic	Gini Concentration Ratio
Train	0.678858	0.017531	0.188969	4.592431	0.690857	0.805511
Valid	0.685829	0.019178	0.170134	5.031109	0.698005	0.803432

Output 7.16: Survival Model Validation Statistics

Model Validation Statistics

Data Role	Benefit	Average Hazard Ratio	Depth	Lift	Kolmogorov-Smirnov Statistic	Gini Concentration Ratio
Train	0.678858	0.017531	0.188969	4.592431	0.690857	0.805511
Valid	0.685829	0.019178	0.170134	5.031109	0.698005	0.803432

Output 7.16 shows the following:

- The **Benefit** column contains the maximum benefit defined as sensitivity minus depth. It is a measure of how well the model identifies positive hits (repurchasing customers in January 2014) versus a random model, and it ranges between 0 and 1. The higher the value, the better.
- The **Average Hazard Ratio** column is the hazard value for January 2014 at the point where the benefit is at the maximum.
- The **Depth** column contains the depth at which the maximum benefit occurs. In the Train data set, the best value occurs at depth = 0.188669 (about 19% of the data). This is key information, and it is used when model performance by month is evaluated.
- The **Lift** column is the sensitivity divided by the depth and lift value. It contains the value of lift at maximum benefit. There are 4.59 times more repurchases identified by the model than by random chance. The higher the value, the better.
- The **Kolmogorov-Smirnov Statistic** column shows the maximum distance in terms of the cumulative proportion between customers repurchasing and not repurchasing based on the Hazard function. A value above 0.69 indicates a very good model because the average Hazard function discriminates well between the two populations (repurchasing and non-repurchasing).

The Gini Concentration Ratio measures how well the average Hazard function (depth) explains sensitivity by measuring the AUCC. With the fitted model applied to the training data, set the ratio to 0.805511. When applied to the validation data set, the Gini Concentration Ratio is 0.803432. Both values are extremely high. A very good model generates a ratio between 0.6 and 0.75. The results indicate that the fitted model is better than the uninformative random model when applied to the training data.

Density Analysis and PROC KDE

In this section, the probability density function (PDF) from the observed average Hazard function is compared for customers who repurchased in January 2014 with those who did not repurchase. This is shown in the same graph.

Figure 7.37 compares four models. In model ❶, there is a very small difference between both densities. In other words, the model cannot differentiate between customers who repurchase and those that do not. The bigger the distance, the better the model discriminates. In this sense, model ❹ is better than model ❶.

Figure 7.39: Comparing Densities

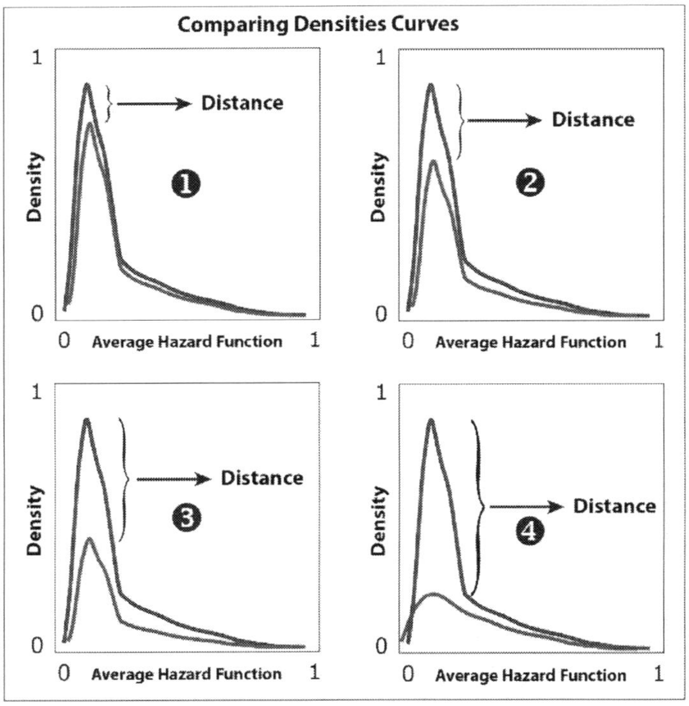

PROC KDE approximates the hypothesized probability density function (PDF) from the observed average Hazard function by averaging across the data points to create a smooth approximation known as *kernel*. PROC KDE automatically creates the kernel density in the same graph, which is explained below in detail.

By default, PROC KDE produces a histogram with an overlaid kernel density estimate. But, for comparison purposes, the analysis is performed by creating two data sets and merging them before applying a PROC SGPLOT.

Program 7.17: Using PROC KDE to Compare Densities

```
proc kde data=train (where=(_hit_ = 0 ❷)) ;
univar ahf/out=non_repurchase ❶ (rename=(density=non_repurchase value=ahf))
noprint;
run;

proc kde data=train (where=(_hit_ = 1 ❹)) ;
univar ahf/out=repurchase ❸ (rename=(density=repurchase value=ahf))noprint;
run;

data densities; ❺
merge non_repurchase repurchase;
by ahf;
run;

proc sgplot data=densities; ❻
series y=repurchase     x=ahf;
series y=non_repurchase x=ahf;
run;
```

❶ **OUT= non_repurchase** creates the data that contains the kernel density by using the **WHERE** ❷ statement to select the customers who did not repurchase in January 2014.

❸ **OUT= repurchase** creates an output data set.

❹ Use the **WHERE** statement to select the customers who repurchased in January 2014.

❺ Merge both data sets. In ❻, create the density graph using PROC SGPLOT.

Figure 7.40: Comparing Densities

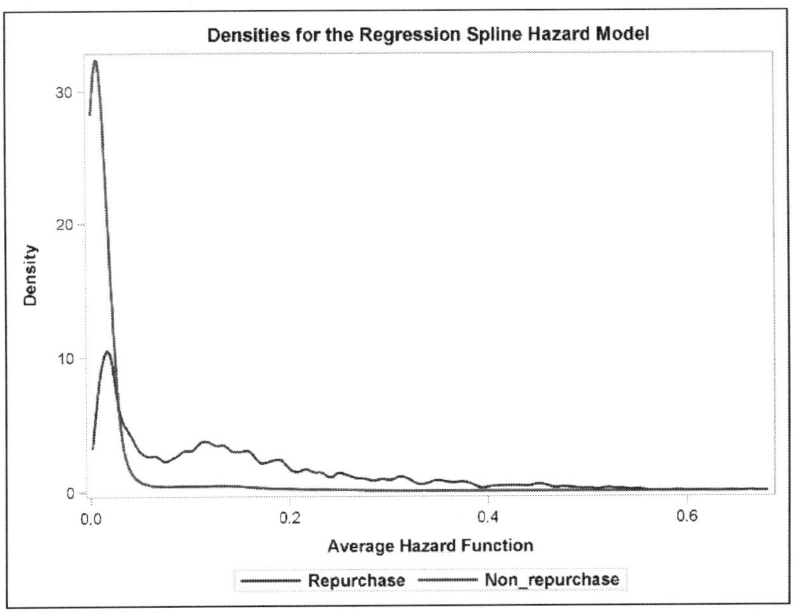

The more the PDF and density overlap, the weaker the model because it cannot discriminate between customers who repurchase from those who do not repurchase. The actual model performs well to discriminate between both populations.

A Comprehensive Validation Approach

A detailed and comprehensive validation approach is presented in dashboard format in Figure 7.41.

Figure 7.41: A Comprehensive Validation Approach Visually Summarized

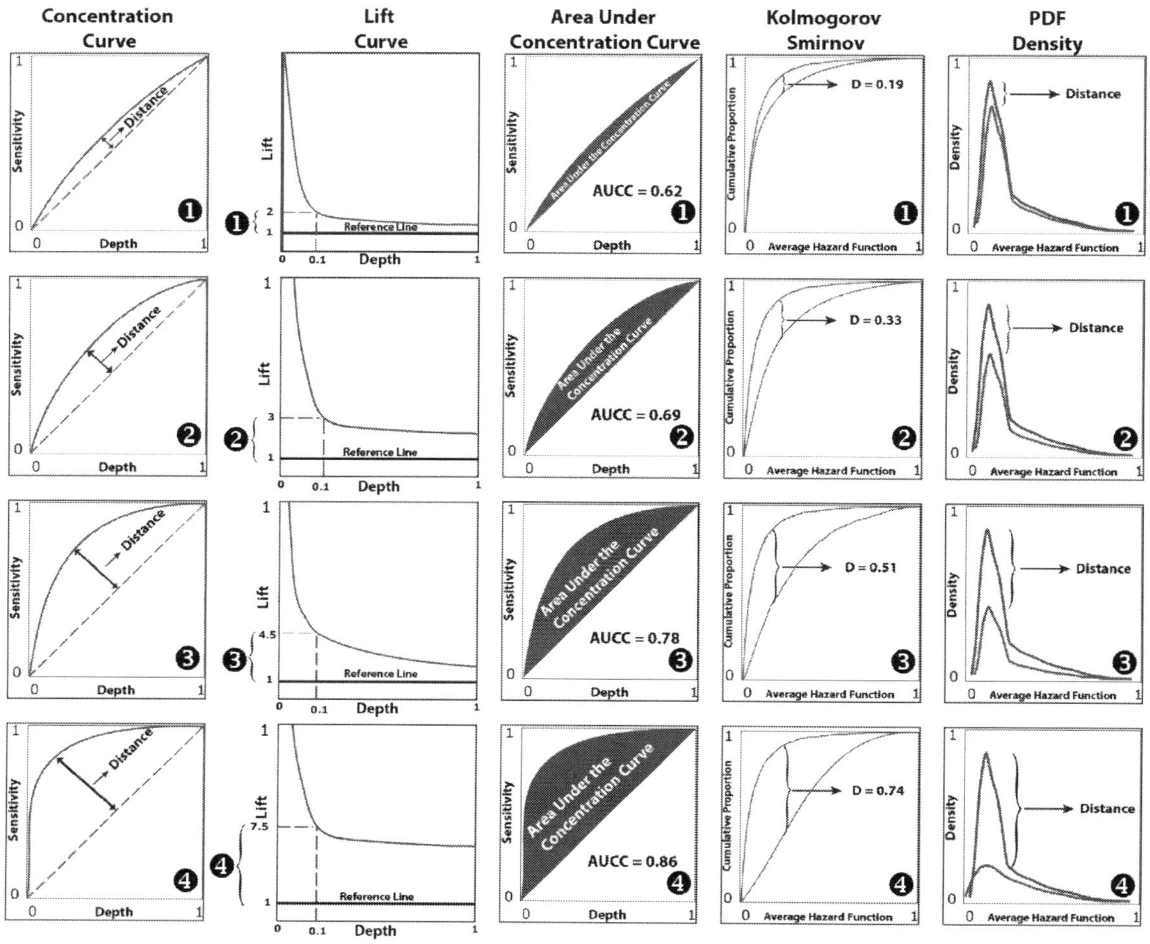

The graphs show how better models have a concentration curve with a greater maximum distance from a random model. They have a large AUCC. Better models identify higher numbers of repurchasing customers than a random model as seen in lift. Better models discriminate between repurchasing and non-repurchasing customers more effectively as reflected in the Kolmogorov-Smirnov statistic and the density plot.

Several important conclusions from this chapter are generalizable about a time-to-next-purchase model. They can be applied to different areas of research, such as the following:

- Macroeconometric Stress Test
- Mortgage Prepayment and Default Analysis
- Employee Turnover
- Mobile Cancellation (Churn)
- IFRS 9 Lifetime Probability of Default

Chapter 8: Scoring New and Old Customers

Introduction

"If you fail to understand the score code, you have failed everything in predictive modeling or data mining in general."

—Jimmy Hosang, expert SAS consultant

In this book, the goal of the modeler is to build an analytical framework to score new or old customers' probabilities of repurchase. This is the main outcome of survival models. Once the model has been built and the parameters have been estimated and validated, the model must be implemented by scoring new customers for a marketing campaign. The purpose of survival data mining, or any predictive modeling for that matter, is to score customers. This chapter demonstrates how to do just that.

For budget- and demand-planning forecasting, a survival model requires that you develop efficient score code to forecast the total number of customers who are going to default in the next quarter or repurchase in the next month. The model must do this without pursuing a zero-error forecast. Score code to calibrate the results is implemented in the last part of this chapter.

In the sections "Scoring Using SAS Enterprise Miner" and "Scoring Using SAS DATA Steps," you learn how to score using SAS Enterprise Miner and SAS DATA steps, respectively. The simplified framework for scoring should focus on four operational elements:

- The data preparation (the _T_ variable is a required element to be explicitly calculated in the data preparation stage)
- The data set process
- The score code
- The process to select the customers who have the highest hazard

To introduce the scoring process, recall that the model created in Chapter 4 was developed using four years of data, from January 2011 to December 2014, as seen in Figure 8.1. From January 2015, you can score or calculate the hazard or probability of repurchase of any customer in a data set having the same input (or map) variables as the original survival model.

Figure 8.1: Model Timeline and Forecast Period

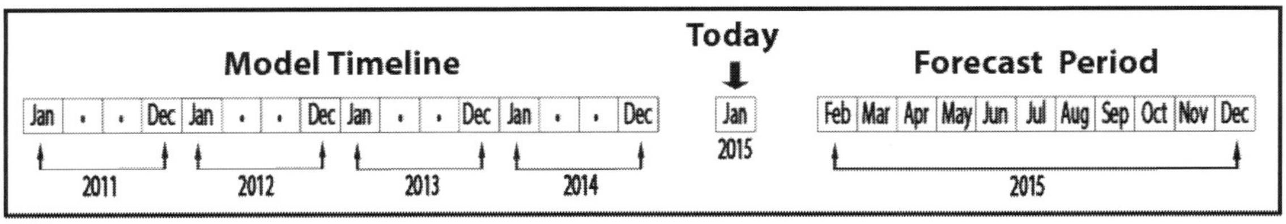

Once a survival analysis model has been created by SAS Enterprise Miner, the next and final step is to implement the model-making predictions on new data (customers) or on a holdout sample for validation purposes. In survival analysis, the score code is created based on the final model (Part_TRAIN). It is called the score code file. The score code file contains the betas coefficients and all of the information necessary to score the model.

The implementation process using the score code is referred to as *scoring the data*. One of the most important business and practical considerations in data mining is scorability (or how the model is implemented in either old or new customers).

A scoring data set is considered new data because these customers were not used in the modeling process as seen in Figure 8.2. In Chapter 3, you split the Garden data set into two parts. The first part was Model_Shopping ❶, which was used in Chapter 4 to build (Part_TRAIN) and validate (Part_VALIDATE) the model. The second part, Score_Shopping ❷, which has 202,856 customers, is used in this chapter to score the model.

Figure 8.2: Sample Flowchart

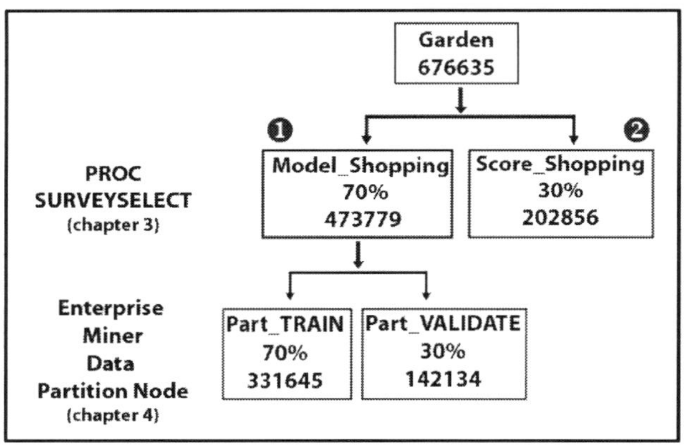

SAS Enterprise Miner offers two options for scoring the Score_Shopping data set.

Figure 8.3: Two Options for Scoring Score_Shopping

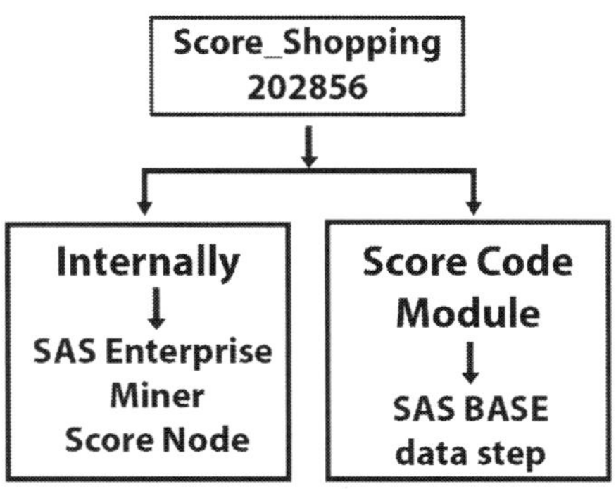

- Scoring internally, using the SAS Enterprise Miner Score node, produces perhaps the most advanced and accurate way of scoring a data set. It deploys complex analytical models that are designed to pass any operational control risk and validation process. When using internally scored data sets, you need to integrate the Score node into the model diagram before saving a copy of the scored data set to a SAS library external to SAS Enterprise Miner.

- A score code module scores the data set outside of SAS Enterprise Miner using Base SAS or SAS Enterprise Guide.

Business Situation 1: Scoring Customers

Imagine it is January of 2015 and you need to create and implement a model to deliver a loyalty promotion or a catalog campaign by targeting customers who have the highest hazard probabilities of repurchase in a specific forecast period, which can be three months (the default used by SAS Enterprise Miner) or any other period. This business situation is developed in detail later, but can be seen in Figure 8.4.

Figure 8.4: Scoring in January 2015

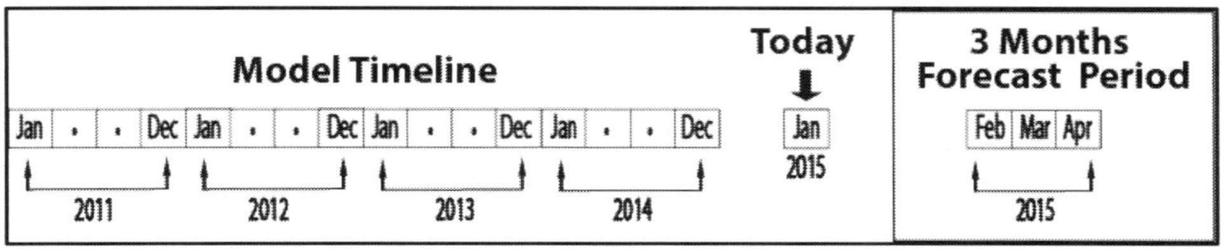

Special cases of models that include a stress test for Basel regulation and IFRS 9 models require that the forecast period be more than 20 years, such as with mortgages. There are no differences in terms of modeling, but the score code and implementation of these models can be complex.

Preparing the Scoring Data Set

In this chapter, you use a scoring data set called Score_Shopping. The customers in this data set are scored using score code. The model is scored (or applied) to new data for which the variables are known, but the event (repurchase) has not yet occurred. (That is, the END variable that indicates the event or outcome of interest is not known.)

By applying the score code, you create a new variable that indicates the hazard of probability of repurchase in a specific time (month) for every customer in the data set. For the Marketing department to choose who to target, the hazard must be sorted from highest to lowest. This scoring process is preceded by the preparation of the data on which the model is going to be applied. You cannot just import the data into the SAS Enterprise Miner flowchart. First, you need to create the required time variable (_t_).

The principal reason to prepare the data set for scoring in careful steps is that if you fail in creating the required _t_ variable, SAS Enterprise Miner does not score the data set. Data preparation is presented in Figure 8.5.

Figure 8.5: Scoring Flowchart

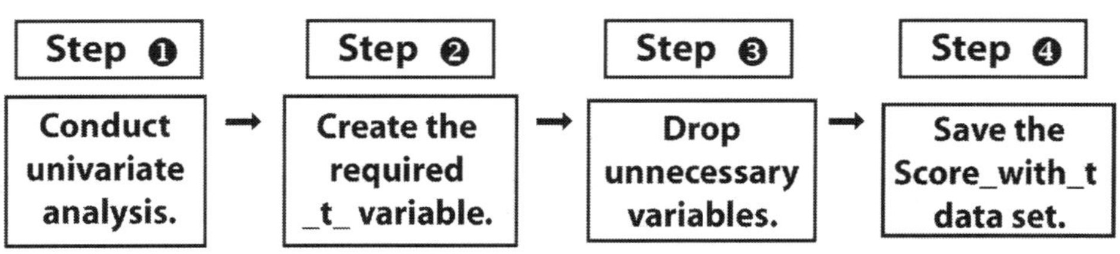

Most of the time, the scoring process is performed weeks after the sample development was processed because scoring is the final stage of modeling. One reason for this is to produce a univariate analysis at the start of the scoring process. Another reason is that some information needs to be obtained and summarized from the table that must be scored to validate the process later using either SAS Enterprise Miner or SAS DATA steps. It is always important to verify the data sets to avoid unnecessary mistakes. Furthermore, this information can be reported in model documentation for further implementation or audit.

Step 1: Conduct Univariate Analysis

The required information can be extracted from the table using Program 8.1. The data set that needs to be scored, Score_Shopping, was created in Chapter 3.

The **Censor** variable extracts the necessary information and indicates the situation of each customer at a specific point in time. A simple **PROC FREQ** gives you the necessary summarized information.

Program 8.1: Using PROC FREQ in Univariate Analysis

```
proc freq data = Score_Shopping;
tables Censor;
run;
```

Output 8.1: Score_Shopping Data Set (January 2010 to December 2014)

The FREQ Procedure

Censor	Frequency	Percent	Cumulative Frequency	Cumulative Percent
0	❶ 109368	53.91	109368	53.91
1	❷ 93488	46.09	❸ 202856	100.00

After you run the program, the result of primary interest is **109368** ❶ because it signifies the number of customers who did not repurchase in the period (Censor = 0). By the end of the scoring process, this is the number of customers you will have to rank using the hazard or probability of repurchase to start a marketing campaign.

You do not target all 109,368 customers. Rather, you target the customers having the highest hazard. (This number is based on a cutoff that you chose using the depth of the Train data set in the validation process in Chapter 7. The number **93488** ❷ represents customers who already repurchased before the scoring date (January 2015) and who must be excluded from the scoring table. The total number of customers in the sample is **202856** ❸, and it is relevant only for validation purposes.

Step 2: Create the Required _t_ Variable

The purpose of Program 8.2 is to create the _t_ variable, which the Survival node needs. The program is an easier version of the code to create the Time variable in Chapter 1. The difference is basically that this code is not using the END variable in the calculations. Another important variable not in Chapter 1 is **Currentdate** ❺, which is replacing the Last_day variable. Variables ❶, ❷, and ❸ were already in the data set.

Program 8.2: Creating the Variable _t_

```
Data Score_with_t_;
Set  Score_Shopping;
Currentdate = "01JAN2015"D; ❹
format Currentdate DATE9.;
_T_ = intck("MONTH", Start, Currentdate); ❺
run;
```

Output 8.2 shows selected Id_numbers.

Output 8.2: Selected Customers for SCORE_WITH_T_ Data Set

	Id_number	Start	End	Censor ❶	Last_day ❷	Time ❸	Currentdate ❹	_T_ ❺
	4	01JAN2011	.	0	31DEC2014	47	01JAN2015	48
❻	**43**	**01JAN2011**	**04JAN2011**	**1**	**31DEC2014**	**0**	**01JAN2015**	**48**
❻	**340**	**03JAN2011**	**01APR2011**	**1**	**31DEC2014**	**3**	**01JAN2015**	**48**
❻	**873**	**05JAN2011**	**30NOV2014**	**1**	**31DEC2014**	**46**	**01JAN2015**	**48**
	9613	01FEB2011	.	0	31DEC2014	46	01JAN2015	47
	61528	01JUN2011	.	0	31DEC2014	42	01JAN2015	43
	94107	01SEP2011	.	0	31DEC2014	39	01JAN2015	40
	235406	01AUG2012	.	0	31DEC2014	28	01JAN2015	29
	593615	01AUG2014	.	0	31DEC2014	4	01JAN2015	5

The **Censor** variable ❶ identifies the customers (Censor=1) to be deleted later because they already repurchased by the date indicated by the END variable. This group of customers is represented by ❻.

The **Last_day** ❷ variable indicates the last day of data collection. It is the end of the study period.

Time ❸ is the period, counted by months, during which the customer spends without repurchasing until the Last_day. **Currentdate** ❹ is the day that you want to score the data set. It is an input to be used in the **_T_** calculation implemented in ❺.

The Intck function (explained in Chapter 1) computes the number of months between the **Start** and **Currentdate**. It is used to create the **_T_** ❺ variable using the monthly interval MONTH. In the first row, the variable **Time** has its computed value of **47**, but the **_T_** variable has its value of **48** because **Currentdate 01JAN2015** is one month after the end of the study period (December 2014). In other words, the time on book of the customer was increased by 1.

Step 3: Drop Unnecessary Variables

In Program 8.3, all customers who were identified as having repurchased before the censoring date are deleted ❶, thus satisfying one of the conditions (**Censor =1** or **End^=.**).

Sometimes, it is necessary to reduce the size of the data set by excluding unnecessary variables. In the case of survival models, the candidate variables are entered in the **DROP** statement ❷. At the same time, you could drop the variables that were not retained in the final model.

Program 8.3: Dropping Variables

```
Data Score_with_t_;
Set  Score_with_t_;
If Censor =1 or End^=. then delete; ❶
Drop Time Censor End Last_day; ❷
run;
```

After running Program 8.2, the data set SCORE_WITH_T_ is ready to be imported into SAS Enterprise Miner and scored.

Step 4: Save the SCORE_WITH_T_ Data Set

You need to save a copy of the SCORE_WITH_T_ data set in the same library where you created the model in Chapter 4. This library is named Chap4, but you could create a new library following the steps in Chapter 4.

The library path is C:\TheBook\Chap4.

Scoring Using SAS Enterprise Miner

In this section, the scoring process using the SAS Enterprise Miner Survival node is presented. Later, in the section "Analyzing the Optimized Score Code," you look in detail at the SAS score code.

Overview of the Score Code Node

Users of the SAS Enterprise Miner Survival node develop models that use measured attributes to either characterize or predict the time of an event. These models are developed on historical data where an event has been measured or inferred. The models are then applied to new data for which the attributes are known, but the event has not yet occurred.

For example, a model can be created based on a credit institution's records of mortgage payments that customers made and missed last year (for example, a Building Society). The model can be used to predict which customers will miss payments this year or to predict the lifetime probability of default using an IFRS 9 model.

The scoring process developed by SAS Enterprise Miner is implemented using the Score node shown in Figure 8.6.

Figure 8.6: Score Node

The Score Code Export node exports SAS score code created by SAS Enterprise Miner to a format that can be used by Base SAS or SAS Enterprise Guide to score new data. Modelers run this code in production systems to make business decisions for each record of new data. This process is sometimes called *deployment*.

The purpose of a scoring task within the Score node is to run the score code of the survival model and produce scoring results that you can use for delivering the marketing campaign.

The Score node has some important functions:

- Manage the score code that was generated from the modeling node and all predecessor nodes in the entire process flow diagram. In this book, the modeling node is the Survival node.
- Save the score code generated from the modeling node to a folder in the SAS Enterprise Miner workspace.
- Execute the score code to score a data set by generating a predicted value as hazard or survival probability, but the data source *must* have the same inputs used in the final model.
- Create scoring modules for use outside of SAS Enterprise Miner.

To create the production scoring data set to be delivered to a marketing campaign, the following tasks must be performed using SAS Enterprise Miner:

- Define the score data source.
- Integrate (import) the score data source to the model diagram.
- Integrate (import) the Score node to the model diagram.
- Save the score data set to a folder or library.

A good practice is to select the final model before beginning all scoring tasks. Later, when you are satisfied with the model's results, performance, and validation, you are ready to put the model into production.

The SAS DATA step implements the robustness of SAS Enterprise Miner optimized score code directly to the SCORE_WITH_T data set.

To use the Score Code node, you need a process flow diagram with nodes that produce score code and that flow to a Score node. The Score node aggregates the score code for the entire analysis path of the diagram. The Survival node must precede the Score Code node in the process flow diagram.

Step 1: Create a Score Data Source

The first task is to create a score data source, which is similar to creating a new data source as you did in Chapter 4.

1. From the main menu, select **File ▶ New ▶ Data Source**, or right-click **Data Source** in the project panel. Select **Create Data Source** to launch the Data Source Wizard. The Data Source Wizard appears.
2. In Step 2 of the Data Source Wizard, select the **Score_with_t** data set from the **Chap4** library. Click **OK**.

Figure 8.7: Selecting a SAS Table

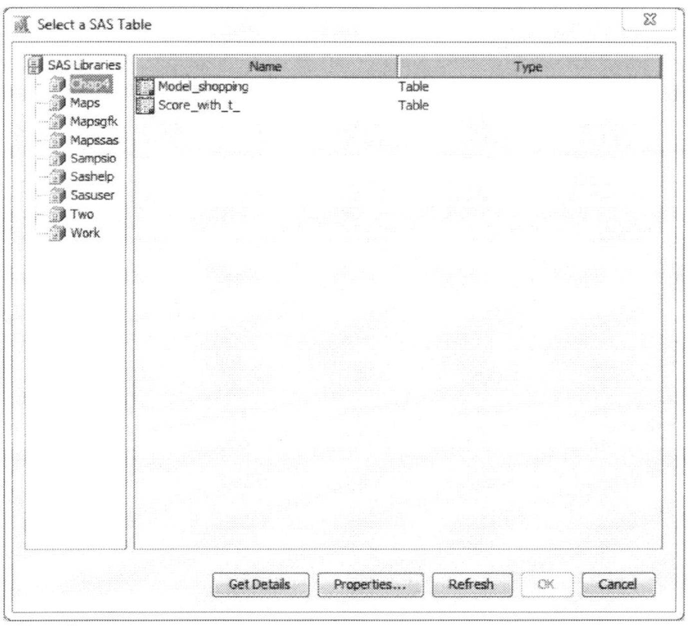

3. Click **Next** until you reach the **Data Source Wizard—Step 5 of 8 Column Metadata** page. Notice that the _T_ variable in the second row has a required **Input** role in the **Role** column. It is not necessary to modify the variables because the role and level of each variable is built into the score code by the Survival node.

Figure 8.8: Selecting the _T_ Variable

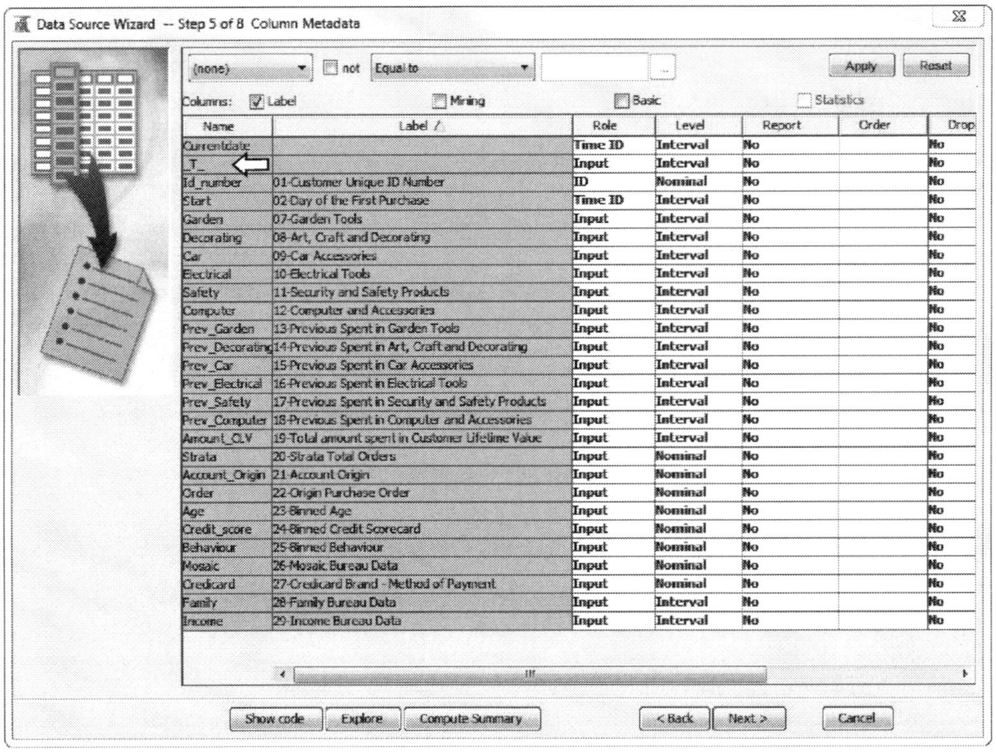

4. Click **Next** until you reach the **Data Source Wizard—Step 7 of 8 Data Source Attributes** page. Change the **Role** to **Score**. Click **Next**, and accept the default settings in Step 8. Click **Finish**.

Figure 8.9: Changing the Role to Score

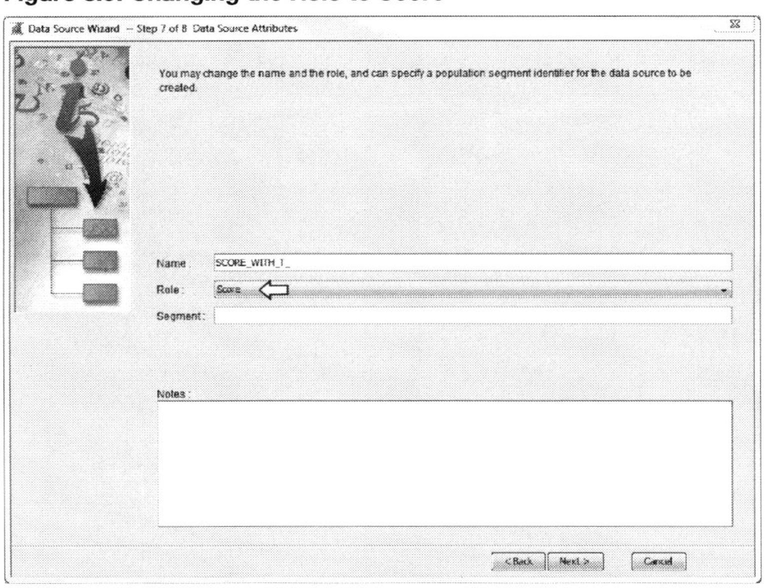

The data source **SCORE_WITH_T** is ready for scoring.

Step 2: Create a New Diagram

In this section, you create a new diagram by copying parts of other nodes or models.

1. Open the diagram **1-Model 1 - Standard data set**.
2. Select all three nodes as in Figure 8.10, right-click, and select **Copy**.

Figure 8.10: Selecting All Three Nodes

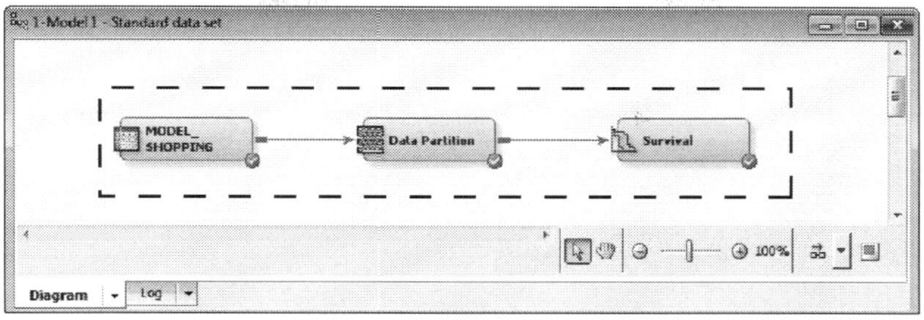

3. Select **File ▶ New ▶ Diagram**. The **Create New Diagram** window appears and requests a diagram name. Name the diagram as seen in Figure 8.11. Click **OK**.

Figure 8.11: Naming the Diagram

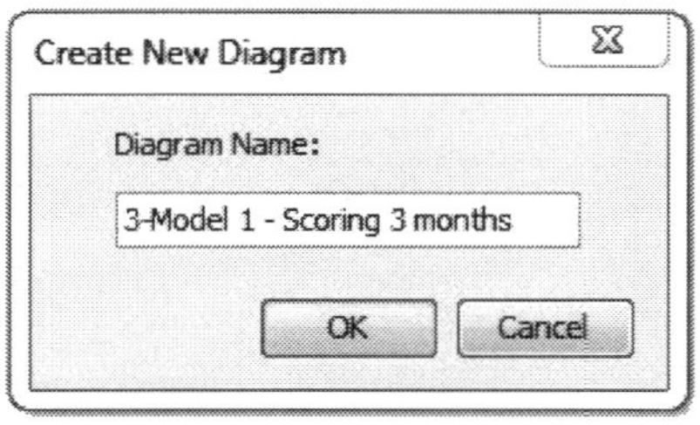

Step 3: Drag the Score_with_t Data Set

1. Open the diagram named **3-Model 1 - Scoring 3 months,** and paste the nodes that you copied during Step 2.
2. From **Data Sources** in the project panel, drag the data source **SCORE_WITH_T** to the **3-Model 1 - Scoring 3 months** diagram as seen in Figure 8.12.

Figure 8.12: Dragging the Data Source to the Diagram

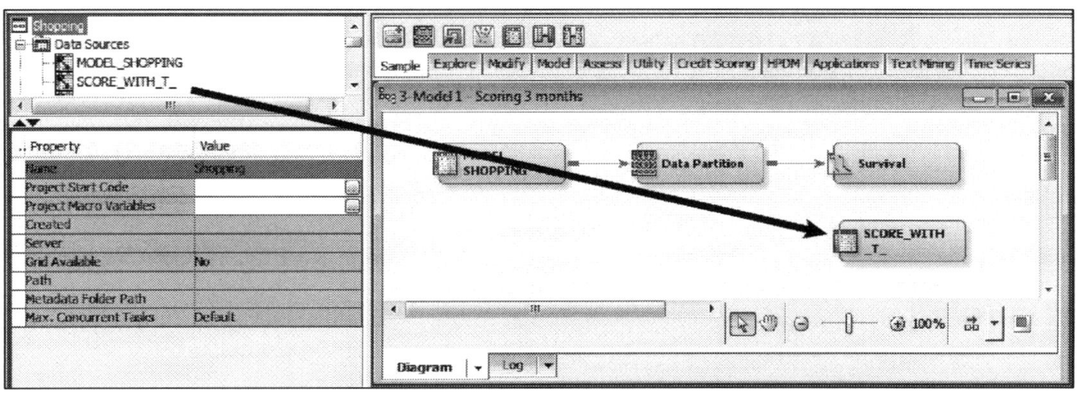

The next step is to include the Score node in the diagram.

Step 4: Include the Score Node

The principal reason to include the Score node is to attach the model's parameters from the Survival node to be applied to the score data source (**SCORE_WITH_T**).

Drag the **Score** node from the **Assess** tab to the **3-Model 1 - Scoring 3 months** diagram workspace and to the right of the Survival node as shown in Figure 8.13.

Figure 8.13: Dragging the Score Node to the Diagram Workspace

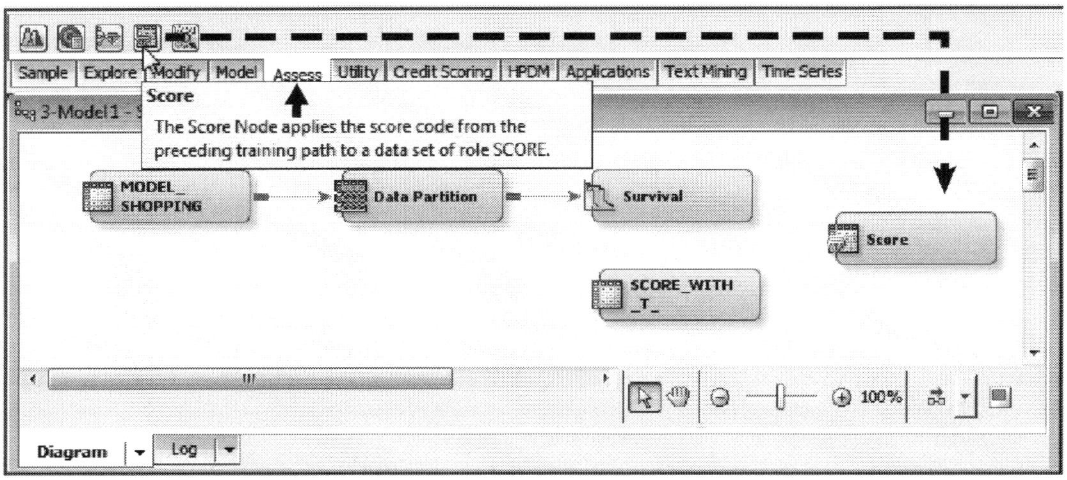

Step 5: Connect the Score Node

The next step is to connect the Score node to the process flow diagram.

Connect the **SCORE_WITH_T** data source node and the **Survival** node to the **Score** node as shown in Figure 8.14.

Figure 8.14: Connecting Data Source Node and Survival Node to Score Node

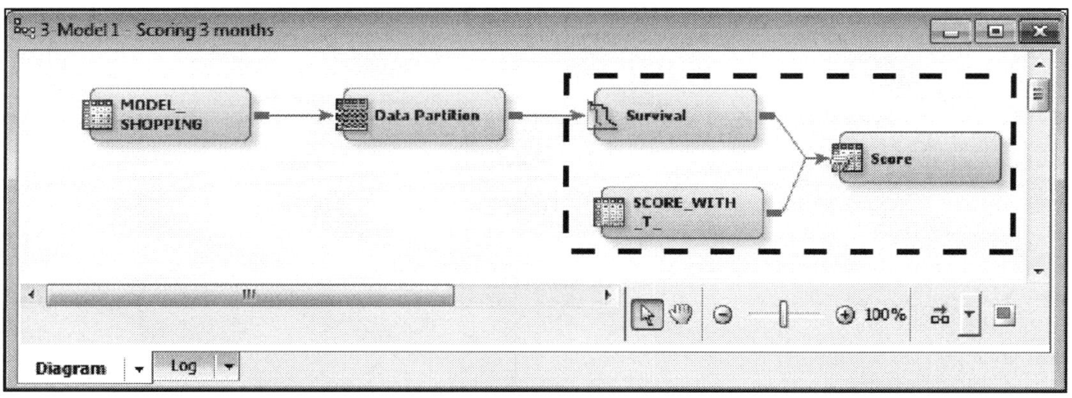

The next step is to modify some options of the Score node and Survival node.

Step 6: Forecast Three Months

You can use the properties panel of the Survival node to modify the forecast intervals. One important property of the Score node to exploit is that if you modify the settings in the Survival node and run the process flow, the score code is updated automatically.

1. Click the Survival node.
2. In the properties panel in Figure 8.15, change the **Default Forecast Intervals** ❶ from **Yes** to **No**. If you leave it as **Yes**, the default forecast interval for models using month as time period is three months.

Figure 8.15: Changing the Default Forecast Intervals Setting

Score		
Mean Residual Life	None	
Default Maximum MRL	Yes	
User Specified Maximum MRL	60	
Default Forecast Intervals	No	❶
Number of Forecast Interval	3	❷

The Default Forecast Intervals property specifies the number of time units in the future that you want the score code to generate for the Survival and Hazard functions. If Default Forecast Intervals is set to Yes, the following time unit values are used in the interval function that the model was created: Day = 30, Week = 4, Month = 3, Quarter = 4, Semi-Year = 2, and Year = 1. The Number of Forecast Interval property specifies the number of time intervals into the future to use as the basis for the Survival and Hazard calculations.

3. Change the **Number of Forecast Interval** ❷ to **3**. The implication of this modification can be seen in the following score code:

```
Label T_FCST = "Number of Time Units in Future";

T_FCST =_T_+ 3;
```

The variable **T_FCST** is automatically created by SAS Enterprise Miner. It represents the number of time units in the future. The variable is the sum of **_T_** and **3**, which represents the number of time units in the future. In this case, the Survival node scores the data by forecasting from February to April 2015 as shown in Figure 8.16.

Figure 8.16: Survival Node Scoring of Data by Forecasting Three Months

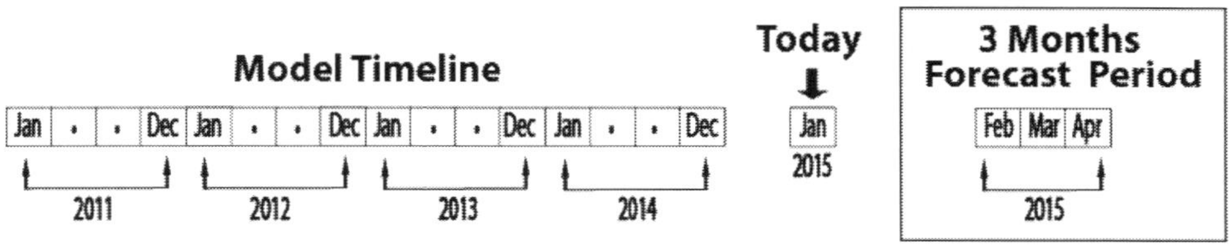

If you select 6 ❷ as the **Number of Forecast Interval** as shown in Figure 8.17, the SAS Enterprise Miner Survival node would have forecasted the months from February to July 2015, as shown in Figure 8.18.

Figure 8.17: Choosing the Number of Forecast Interval

Score		
Mean Residual Life	None	
Default Maximum MRL	Yes	
User Specified Maximum MRL	60	
Default Forecast Intervals	No	❶
Number of Forecast Interval	6	❷

Figure 8.18: Survival Node Scoring of Data by Forecasting Six Months

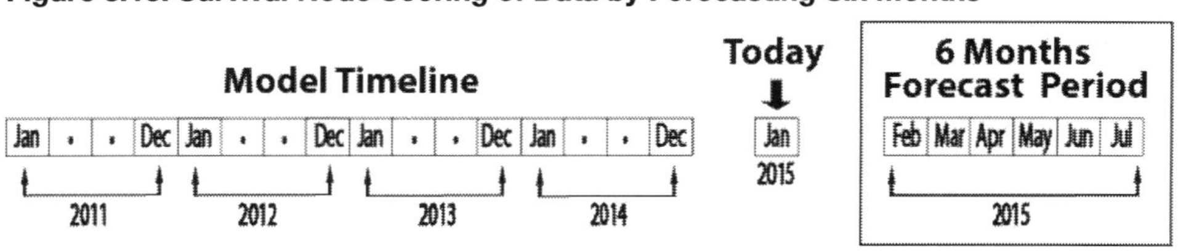

The score code would have been the following:

```
Label T_FCST = "Number of Time Units in Future";

T_FCST =_T_+6;
```

4. Click the **Score** node, and change **Train** in the properties panel as shown in Figure 8.19.

Figure 8.19: Changing Settings for Type of Scored Data and Whether to Hide Variables

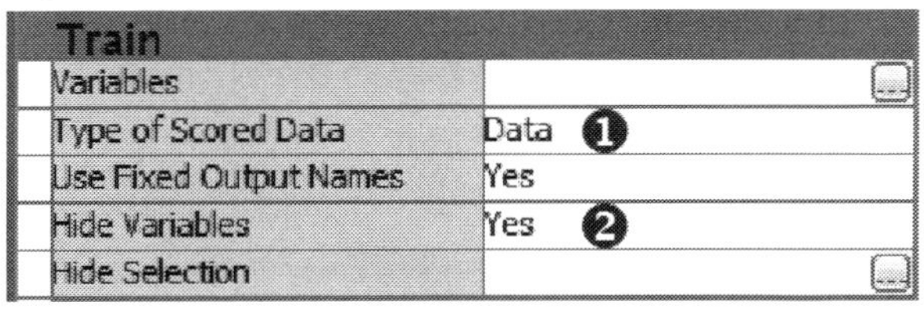

5. Change the **Type of Scored Data** ❶ from **View** to **Data**. You need to export the final result as a data set, not as a view. The default setting for **Hide Variables** is **No**. Set **Hide Variables** to **Yes** ❷ to prevent the original variables from appearing in the exported metadata when the data set is scored. When set to **Yes**, the original variables are removed from the exported metadata, but not removed from the exported data sets and data views.
6. Next, change the default output setting as shown in Figure 8.20.

Figure 8.20: Changing the Default Output

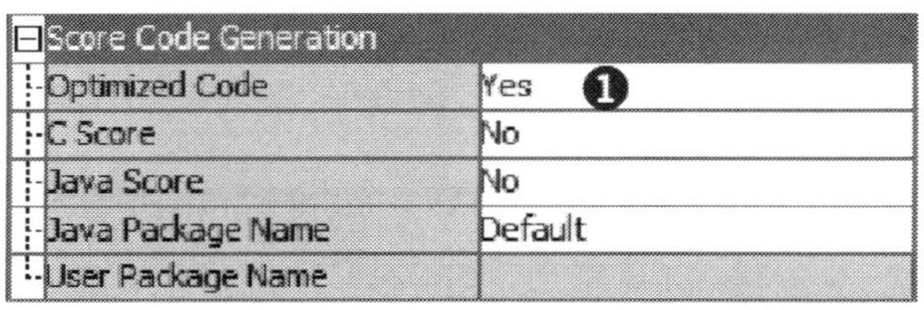

❶ The default setting for the **Optimized Code** property is **Yes**. A good strategy is to set the property to **Yes** and compare the score code and the optimized code. In this way, you can see each code's performance in terms of time if you work in a server environment or if you are using SAS Enterprise Guide to implement the model.

Because the optimized code excludes unnecessary code that is present in the unoptimized score code, the optimized score code should never take more time to execute. For simple code and small data, the execution time saved might be inconsequential.

7. Run the Score node and inspect the results. The **Results—Node: Score** window opens as shown in Figure 8.21.

Figure 8.21: Examining the Results

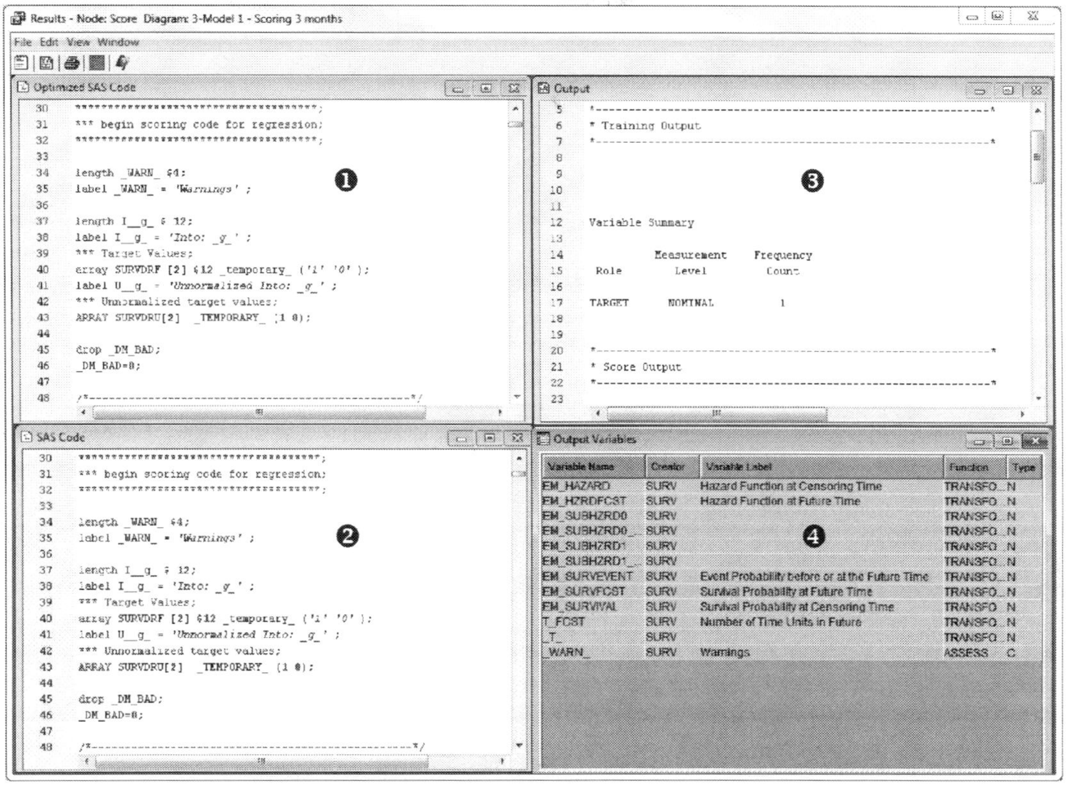

The score code re-creates the analytical model developed in the Survival process flow diagram and is shown in the left two panes. ❶ and ❷ are, respectively, the optimized score code and the score code that were executed.

The score code produced by SAS Enterprise Miner creates both intermediate variables (such as imputed values of missing values, transformations, and encodings) and output variables (such as predicted value and probability). Any of these created variables can be used in a scoring process.

The number of input parameters in a scoring function has a direct impact on performance. The more parameters there are, the more time it takes to score a row. A recommended best practice is to make sure that only variables that are involved in a model score evaluation are exported from SAS Enterprise Miner. That is the primary reason that SAS Enterprise Miner creates the optimized score code. The second reason is that the optimized SAS code is more efficient because it does not include all the calculations to impute all the input variables.

The score code and the optimized score code are named PATHPUBLISHSCORECODE.sas and OPTIMIZEDCODE.sas, respectively. You can find both of these in the project file's Workspace folder. For example, on your computer, the code might be saved by the Score node in the folder C:\TheBook\Workspace\EMWS4\Score\.

Output ❸ presents the variables used as input in the score code. Results are shown in Output 8.3.

Output 8.3: Variables Used as Input in the Score Code

Score Input Variables

Variable Name	Role	Creator	Comment	Label	Variable Hidden	Used in Score Code
Account_Origin	INPUT			21-Account Origin	N	Y
Age	INPUT			23-Binned Age	N	Y
Amount_CLV	INPUT			19-Total amount spent in Customer Lifetime Value	N	Y
Behaviour	INPUT			25-Binned Behaviour	N	Y
Car	INPUT			09-Car Accessories	N	Y
Credicard	INPUT			27-Credicard Brand - Method of Payment	N	Y
Credit_score	INPUT			24-Binned Credit Scorecard	N	Y
Decorating	INPUT			08-Art, Craft and Decorating	N	Y
Garden	INPUT			07-Garden Tools	N	Y
Mosaic	INPUT			26-Mosaic Bureau Data	N	Y
Order	INPUT			22-Origin Purchase Order	N	Y
Prev_Car	INPUT			15-Previous Spent in Car Accessories	N	Y
Prev_Computer	INPUT			18-Previous Spent in Computer and Accessories	N	Y
Prev_Decorating	INPUT			14-Previous Spent in Art, Craft and Decorating	N	Y
Prev_Electrical	INPUT			16-Previous Spent in Electrical Tools	N	Y
Prev_Garden	INPUT			13-Previous Spent in Garden Tools	N	Y
Prev_Safety	INPUT			17-Previous Spent in Security and Safety Products	N	Y
Strata	INPUT			20-Strata Total Orders	N	Y

After you execute the Score node, you should verify the new scoring variables created in the Output Variables ❹ table. The Output Variables table shows all the variables created by the score code. Of major interest are the Survival and Hazard functions.

Step 7: Export the Optimized Score Code

To score another data set in a SAS environment such as SAS Enterprise Guide or Base SAS, you need to export the optimized score code by saving it as a SAS file. To do this, perform the following steps:

1. Open the Score node results.
2. In the Results window, click or maximize the Optimized SAS Code ❶ window, and select **File ▶ Save As** as seen in Figure 8.22.

Figure 8.22: Selecting File and Save As

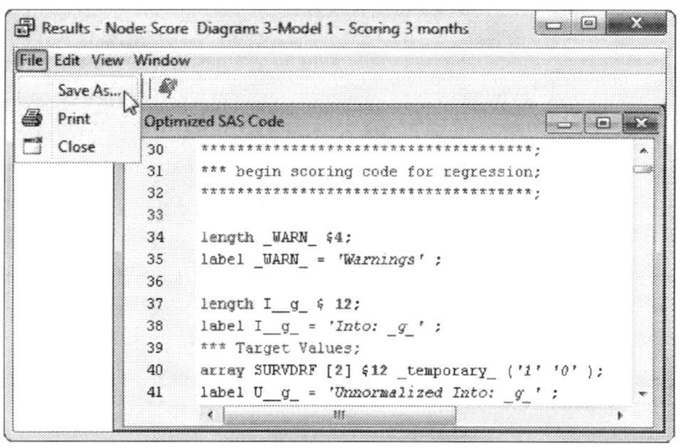

3. Save the file as **Exported Optimized SAS Score Code**. In the Save window, navigate to an appropriate location to save the score code, and enter any name in the **Filename** field. Close the Score node Results window. This enables you to make changes to a model without losing the score code for an accurate model.

Step 8: Export the Scored Table

A scoring output table named Score_SCORE is the SAS data set created by SAS Enterprise Miner. This table contains the data from executing the optimized scoring code by the Score node. The table Score_SCORE is in the current project's Workspace directory.

To deliver the model probabilities to the Marketing team, you need to make a copy of this table in another location (folder or server). Before you do that, you need to verify that the table exists and locate where it is.

1. Click the ellipses for the **Exported Data** row in the Score node properties panel.

Figure 8.23: Selecting Exported Data

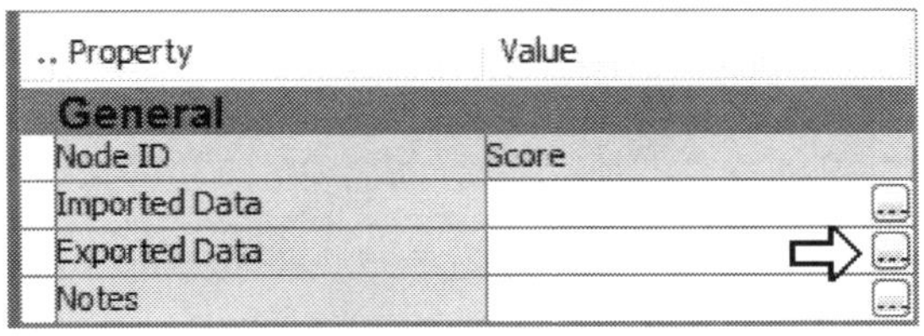

2. Select the **Score_SCORE** table from the **Exported Dat—Score** dialog box as shown in Figure 8.24.

Figure 8.24: Selecting the Score_SCORE Table

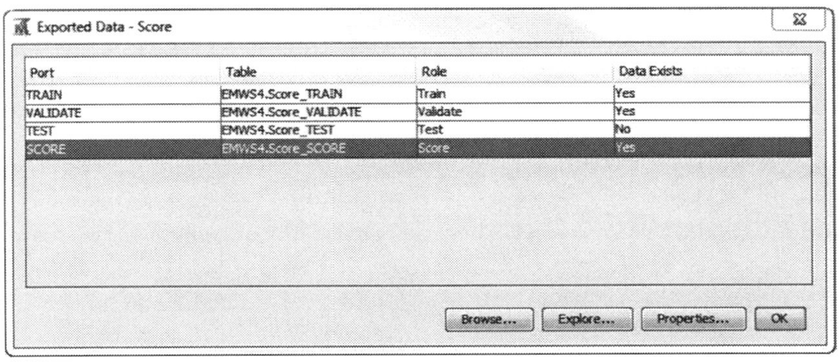

3. Click **Browse**. The **Score_SCORE** table, which contains the values of the scored survival, hazard, and other variables opens, as shown in Figure 8.25.

Figure 8.25: Opening the Score_SCORE Table

EMWS4.Score_SCORE

	Hazard Function at Censoring Time	Hazard Function at Future Time	T_FCST
1	.002134104093466587	0.0020161683942701105	51.0
2	.0018685851700563014	0.001765296723995768	51.0
3	.0015202646192561948	0.0014362023349535449	51.0
4	.00215999034521955	0.0020406270352384946	51.0
5	.005269184810032433	0.004978861490906749	51.0
6	.005863827531236937	0.005540922890677033	51.0
7	.0018934676498485515	0.0017888062576979702	51.0
8	.0019242277512396063	0.0018178691917288836	51.0
9	.002146629812452341	0.002028003318838772	51.0
10	.002065666523600954	0.0019515054518639678	51.0
11	.002037468967429673	0.001924863255240679	51.0
12	.0032231667872817103	0.003045230544217419	51.0
13	.0033378483778951223	0.0031536011207830956	51.0
14	.007420032487776732	0.007012036424098797	51.0
15	.0016002289928862907	0.0015117518124035025	51.0
16	.0022926304407285708	0.0021659532117352083	51.0
17	.00558549346797144	0.005277834537657704	51.0
18	.0015122354923908404	0.0014286165394849124	51.0
19	.002326737276025633	0.002198179656665446	51.0
20	.007677478445455149	0.007255429996915328	51.0
21	.003322246077475807	0.0031388573457668944	51.0
22	.0015765445749057146	0.0014893749600904274	51.0
23	.002154775972412969	0.00203570022622902	51.0
24	.00225655514828733	0.0021318669678366308	51.0
25	.0021933290472137966	0.002072127231741395	51.0
26	.005966372009886808	0.005637852554489323	51.0
27	.0019129920920199516	0.0018072534407721534	51.0
28	.0018181175433591254	0.0017176139596716676	51.0
29	.006698730343061501	0.006330142681225568	51.0
30	.0020201306414701424	0.0019084813417998671	51.0
31	.004444036266246695	0.004198985344247424	51.0

Of particular interest are the variables **Hazard Function at Censoring Time** and **Hazard Function at Future Time**. They represent the model's prediction probabilities of repurchase in January 2015 and April 2015. The next step is to copy this table to another folder. To accomplish this step, use the SAS Code node.

The SAS Code node is probably the most powerful node in SAS Enterprise Miner because it incorporates SAS analysis and procedures into the process flow diagrams. One important limitation is that any score code generated by the SAS Code node is not included in the optimized score code, which might have an impact on deployment.

4. Drag the **SAS Code** node from the **Utility** tab to the right of the **Score** node in the **3-Model 1 - Scoring 3 months** diagram workspace as seen in Figure 8.26. Connect the **Score** node to the **SAS Code** node. Another possibility is to use the Save Data node.

Figure 8.26: Dragging the SAS Code Node to the Diagram

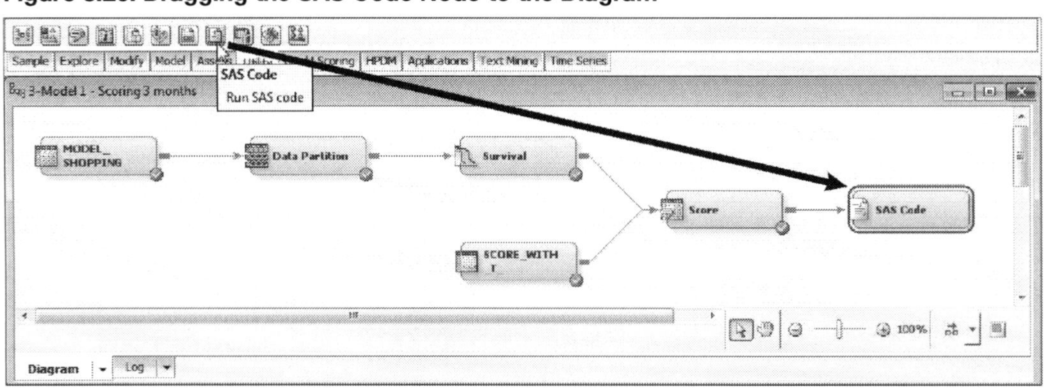

5. Select the **SAS Code** node, and then click the ellipses for the **Code Editor** row in the properties panel, as shown in Figure 8.27.

Figure 8.27: Selecting the Code Editor

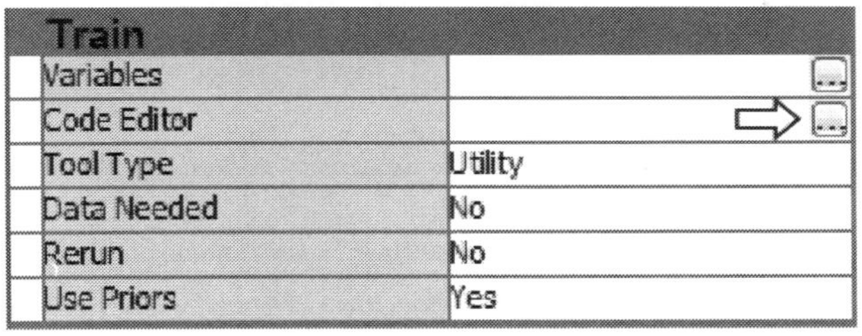

The **Training Code—Code Node** windows appears. **Training Code ❶** is the most important area because it enables you to write SAS code.

Figure 8.28: Opening the Training Code - Code Node Window

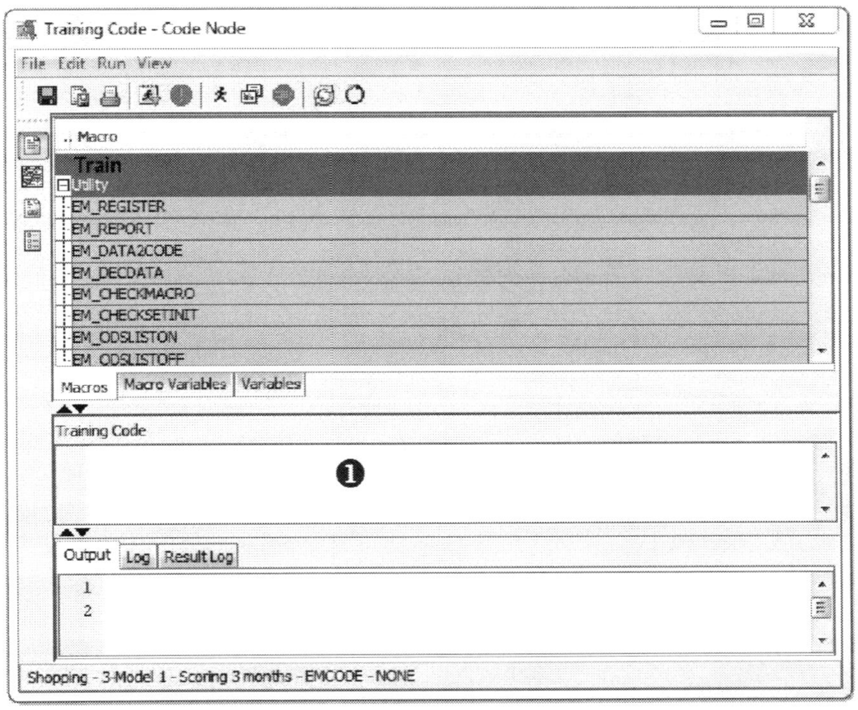

Enter the program shown in Figure 8.29 into the Training Code area.

Figure 8.29: Entering the Program into the Training Code—Code Node Window

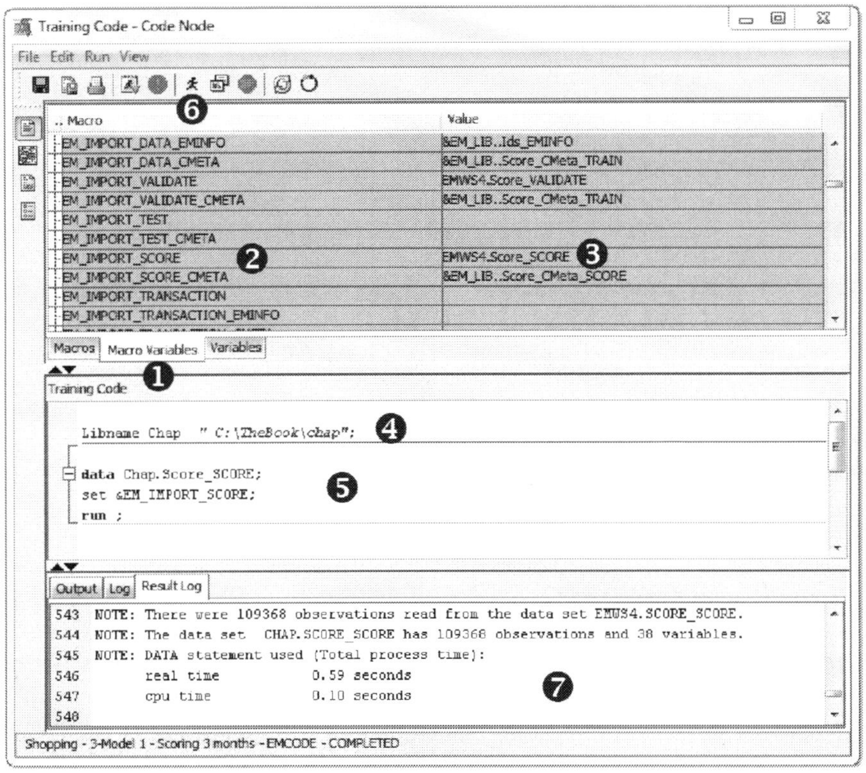

The Code Editor has three tabs: **Macros**, **Macro Variables,** and **Variables**. The **Macros** and **Macro Variables** tabs contain the system-defined macro variables and their values if they are already assigned by SAS.

6. Select the **Macro Variables** ❶ tab. The tab has a list of SAS variable macros that you can reference in your SAS code.
7. Examine the **Imports** section of the **Macro Variable Column** list. A macro variable named **EM_IMPORT_SCORE** ❷ appears in this section. You can use the **EM_IMPORT_SCORE** macro variable to reference the score code that you imported into the SAS Code node. In ❸, you find the respective macro value (**EMWS4.Score_SCORE**).
8. Create a permanent library named **Chap** ❹.
9. Using a SAS DATA step, copy the **Score_SCORE** data set from the workspace **EMWS4** to the **Chap** library ❺.
10. Run the program by clicking the running man icon ❻. After running the SAS code, you can verify that **Score_SCORE** has **109368** observations by selecting the **Result Log** ❼.
11. To save the changes, select **File ▶ Save** or click the **Save All** icon. To close the Training Code windows, select **File ▶ Exit**.

Analyzing the Optimized Score Code

This section describes the process and methods that SAS Enterprise Miner used to create the optimized score code. It discusses some key pieces of the code including missing data, the probabilities, and labels linked to the variables.

The optimized score code is developed using advanced SAS programming. Because this book is an introduction to survival models, each fundamental part of the SAS code is explained in detail by splitting the optimized score code into parts.

Another reason to split the score code into parts is the complexity of SAS programming. By the end of the section, it should be clear to you that SAS Enterprise Miner achieves accuracy and efficiency. But, to understand each concept, look in detail at the key features of different parts of the code to avoid unnecessary mistakes in the scoring process.

The fundamental reason to analyze the optimized score code is to perform modifications to the original optimized score code, which, in turn, creates some of the most fundamental variables such as the hazard or probability of repurchase, average hazard, or average survival.

In the case of survival models, the score code generates the formulas in the form of a single DATA step that can be used in most SAS environments without SAS Enterprise Miner.

Program 8.4 is the necessary score code generated by SAS Enterprise Miner. It can be used as a template to implement more complex models.

Part 1: Warn Variable

WARN is the first variable created in the score code in Program 8.4.

Program 8.4: Scoring Customers

```
length _WARN_ $4; ❶
label _WARN_ = 'Warnings';
```

When predicted values cannot be computed using the model (for example, when required inputs are missing), a variable named **_WARN_** ❶ in the scored data set indicates why the model could not be applied. This variable tells you the type of problem in computing predicted values. If you have lots of missing inputs, you should use the Impute node to impute missing values before using the Score node. The Impute node should also be used before the modeling nodes. If it is used, then the score code should have the imputation rules based on the training data included. The character variable_WARN_ is either blank (indicating that there were no problems) or it contains one or more of the following character codes:

Code	Meaning
M	Missing inputs, one or more variables in the model have a missing value.
P	Invalid posterior probability (for example, <0 or >1).
U	Unrecognized input category. Problem with a categorical variable (for example, a missing or undefined category).

If you have a class variable with more than 16 characters, then the scored observation will have a value of U in the _WARN_ column of your scored data set. This warning indicates an unrecognized input category. The warning appears because the class-level name was truncated when scoring occurred. As a result, SAS Enterprise Miner does not recognize the level of the categorical variable as a valid value. Regardless of whether the value is recognized, predicted values are computed for all cases for assessment purposes.

An example of problems with warnings can be found in "Problem Note *10170*: Incorrect length of score variables in score code causes warning and wrong values" at http://support.sas.com/kb/10/170.html. Here is an excerpt from the problem note:

> For an interval target, the P_ variable is the unconditional mean of the target variable.
>
> For categorical targets, the P_ variables are set to the prior probabilities.
>
> To circumvent the problem, change the length of the variable in the score code. For example, to change the length of a variable from 16 to 32, change the first line of score code from:

```
%macro DMNORLEN; 16 %mend DMNORLEN;
```

to this:

```
%macro DMNORLEN;32 %mend DMNORLEN;
```

Part 2: Survival Score Code Labels and the Future Time Variable

In the process of analytical scoring, the Survival node automatically adds labels to the more important variables. You will look at each of these variables in detail later. For the moment, the labels and the forecasting period are explained.

```
/*------------------------*/
/*   Survival Score Code  */
/*------------------------*/
label EM_SURVIVAL  = "Survival Probability at Censoring Time"; ❶
label EM_SURVFCST  = "Survival Probability at Future Time";❷
label EM_SURVEVENT = "Event Probability before or at the Future Time";
label EM_HAZARD    = "Hazard Function at Censoring Time";
label EM_HZRDFCST  = "Hazard Function at Future Time";
label T_FCST       = "Number of Time Units in Future";

BadObs = 0;
if _T_ ❸ ne . and BadObs=0 then do;

T_FCST  ❹ =_T_+ 3;
```

The **Censoring Time** ❶ is the month that you are scoring. In this example, it is January 2015, and the value of the **_T_** ❸ variable is 48. The code statement **if _T_ ne . and BadObs=0 then do** indicates that if the _t_ variable is not present in the score data, then the score values for subhazards, survival functions, and so on, are not computed.

The **Future Time** ❷ is three months after the censoring time. In this example, it is April 2015, and the value of the **T_FCST** ❹ variable is 51 (48 + 3) as seen in Figure 8.30.

Figure 8.30: Three-Month Forecast Period

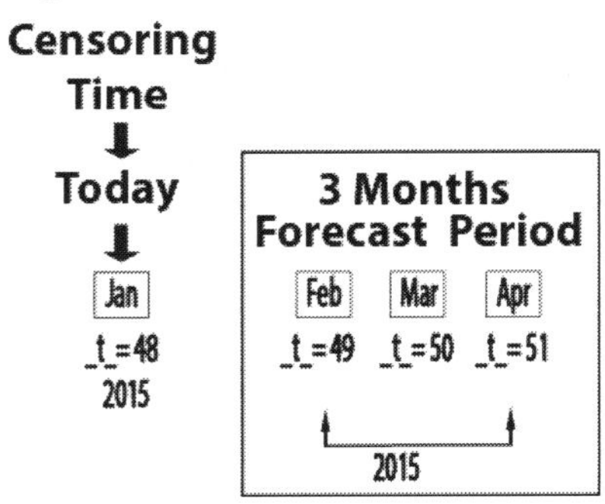

The information about the variables and labels is presented in Figure 8.31—the **Output Variables** table—which was extracted from the Score node results (see Figure 8.21). These variables were created by the Survival node as indicated in the second column (**Creator**). In the last row, you find the variable **_WARN_**.

Figure 8.31: Viewing the Output Variables from Results—Score Node

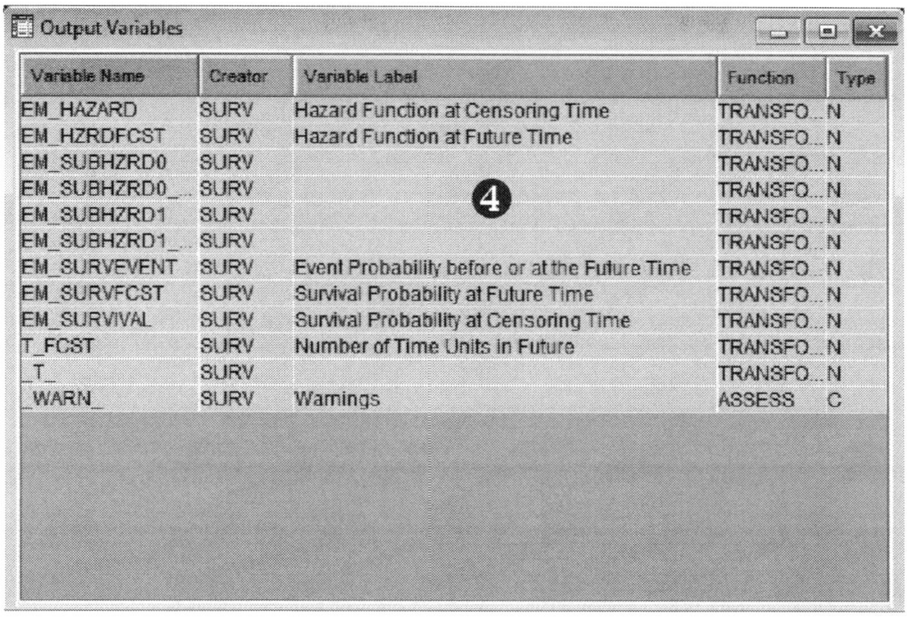
Output Variables

Variable Name	Creator	Variable Label	Function	Type
EM_HAZARD	SURV	Hazard Function at Censoring Time	TRANSFO...	N
EM_HZRDFCST	SURV	Hazard Function at Future Time	TRANSFO...	N
EM_SUBHZRD0	SURV		TRANSFO...	N
EM_SUBHZRD0_...	SURV		TRANSFO...	N
EM_SUBHZRD1	SURV		TRANSFO...	N
EM_SUBHZRD1_...	SURV		TRANSFO...	N
EM_SURVEVENT	SURV	Event Probability before or at the Future Time	TRANSFO...	N
EM_SURVFCST	SURV	Survival Probability at Future Time	TRANSFO...	N
EM_SURVIVAL	SURV	Survival Probability at Censoring Time	TRANSFO...	N
T_FCST	SURV	Number of Time Units in Future	TRANSFO...	N
_T_	SURV		TRANSFO...	N
WARN	SURV	Warnings	ASSESS	C

Part 3: Cubic Spline Basis Functions

This part of the score code generates the CSB functions by omitting any CSB variables not retained or used to calculate the final survival or hazard probabilities. The modeling process included 10 CSB variables, but only the numbers 1, 2, 3, 4, 6, and 7 were retained by the stepwise selection algorithm for the final model (and therefore included in the score code).

```
/*------------------------------------------*/
/*   Generate Cubic Spline Basis Functions  */
/*------------------------------------------*/
If _T_ > 4  then _csb1 =(_T_-4)**3 - _T_**3 + 12*_T_**2 - 48*_T_;
Else _csb1=-_T_**3 + 12*_T_**2 - 48*_T_;
.
.
if _T_ > 28 then _csb7 =(_T_-28)**3 - _T_**3 + 84*_T_**2 - 2352*_T_;
else _csb7=-_T_**3 + 84*_T_**2 - 2352*_T_;
```

Part 4: Missing Values Numerical Variables

Part 4 of the score code controls missing values for *all* numeric variables. However, only Amount_CLV is explained in this section.

```
*** Check Amount_CLV for missing values;
if missing( Amount_CLV ) then do;
   substr(_warn_,1,1) = 'M'; ❶
   _DM_BAD = 1; ❷
end;
```

❶ If the Amount_CLV variable is identified as missing by the MISSING function, then the DO-END included in the code executes. It has two basic objectives:

- First, the score code is using the SUBSTR function on the left side of the assignment statement. It replaces the value of variable **_WARN_** with the expression on the right side by **M**, which indicates that this variable is missing. Remember that the SUBSTR function replaces length characters starting at the character position that you specify. In this case, the position is 1.
- Second, the dummy variable _DM_BAD ❷ is set to 1, working as a flag to indicate that the variable has a missing value.

Part 5: Missing Values and Categorical Variables

Part 5 repeats the same strategy in Part 4 for missing values. But, it takes into account only the categorical variables. The Account_Origin variable is presented.

```
if missing( Account_Origin ) then do;
   _1_0 = .;
   _1_1 = .;
   _1_2 = .;
   _1_3 = .;
   substr(_warn_,1,1) = 'M'; ❶
   _DM_BAD = 1;
      if _dm9   = 'INTERNET'  then do;
      _1_1 = 1;
   end;
   else if _dm9 = 'TELEPHONE' then do;
      _1_3 = 1;
   end;
   else if _dm9 = 'POST' then do;
      _1_2 = 1;
   end;
   else if _dm9 = 'BRANCH' then do;
      _1_0 = 1;
   end;
   else do;
      _1_0 = .;
      _1_1 = .;
      _1_2 = .;
      _1_3 = .;
      substr(_warn_,2,1) = 'U'; ❷
      _DM_BAD = 1; ❸
   end;
end;
```

If **Account_Origin** is missing, the program flags **_WARN_** as **M** ❶ for missing. But, if the level of the categorical variable is different from those included in the modeling process as **INTERNET**, **TELEPHONE**, **POST**, or **BRANCH**, the **_WARN_** variable is flagged as **U** ❷, unrecognized input category. The variable _DM_BAD is set to 1 ❸, which identifies the bad data.

Part 6: Replacement of Missing Inputs by Average Values

_DM_BAD ❶ will be greater than zero if you have a variable flagged as missing in Part 4 or 5. In this case, the **_P0** and **_P1** are not calculated for the specific customer. They are replaced by the average value indicated by ❷ and ❸.

The **GOTO** statement ❹ is a control point. If the condition is true (that is, _DM_BAD > 0), then the GOTO statement instructs SAS to jump to a label. The label identifies the GOTO destination called **SURVDR1**, and execution continues from there.

```
*** If missing inputs, use averages;
if _DM_BAD > 0 then do; ❶
   _P0 = 0.0313446446;  ❷
   _P1 = 0.9686553554; ❸
   goto SURVDR1; ❹
end;
```

You should verify the _WARN_ variable after you run the optimized score code. And, you should replace any missing values if you are not satisfied with the average probabilities ❷ and ❸, which are replaced by default.

Using average probabilities can be a poor strategy that can have a huge impact on the number of people to be targeted if the data set contains a lot of missing data. There is no easy solution or magic trick to fix missing data. Various options must be considered (for example, multiple imputation) before you apply the score code.

The main purpose of multiple imputations is to reflect some measure of uncertainty about parameter estimates due to missing data. For predictive modeling, the best strategy is to develop reasonable imputation rules on the training data and apply them to the validation or test data to evaluate the whole modeling process's performance. Decisions made in predictive modeling are based more on the law of large numbers than on statistical significance.

Part 7: Computation of the Linear Predictor

Once all missing variables are flagged, the program creates the linear predictor by including each input variable, called **Effect**.

```
***  Effect: _t_ ; ❶
_TEMP = _t_ ;
_LP0 = _LP0 + ( -0.01898874519179 * _TEMP);
.
.
***  Effect: _csb1 ; ❷
_TEMP = _csb1 ;
_LP0 = _LP0 + ( -0.02004902864914 * _TEMP);
.
.
***  Effect: Account_Origin ; ❸
_TEMP = 1;
_LP0 = _LP0 + ( -0.00123480400156) * _TEMP * _1_0;
_LP0 = _LP0 + (  0.33948928699627) * _TEMP * _1_1;
_LP0 = _LP0 + (  0.07819239436532) * _TEMP * _1_2;
_LP0 = _LP0 + (                 0) * _TEMP * _1_3;
.
.
***  Effect: Amount_CLV ; ❹
_TEMP = Amount_CLV ;
_LP0 = _LP0 + (    -0.00005036962493 * _TEMP);
.
.
_LP0 =                 -1.30824778337146 + _LP0; ❺
```

Every variable has its betas coefficient and level if they are categorical.

❶ The **_t_** variable.

❷ The **_csb1** variable.

❸ Categorical variable.

❹ Numerical variable.

❺ The final linear predictor is updated by adding the intercept.

The linear predictor is a fundamental part of the calculation because it enters the Hazard function in the numerator and in the denominator:

$$\text{Hazard}(x) = \frac{e^{\text{Linear}}}{1 + e^{\text{Linear}}}$$

or

$$\text{Hazard}(x) = \frac{1}{1 + e^{\text{-Linear}}}$$

Part 8: Computation of Posterior Probabilities and Predicted Level

In Part 8, by using the linear predictor as input, the program implements the Hazard function in Part 7:

- The probability of repurchase, labeled **Predicted: _g_=1**.
- The probability of non-repurchase, labeled **Predicted: _g_=0**.

Remember that scoring a data set in a survival analysis context means applying a previously fitted model to a new data set. This is done to compute the posterior probabilities (survival and hazard), given the values of the explanatory (input) variables in each customer. Posterior probabilities are probabilities that are proportional to the frequencies of the response category (Censor or Target) in the training data (the data used to fit the model). Posterior probabilities is perhaps the most important concept in this optimized score code.

```
_LPMAX=0;
_LP0 = exp(_LP0 - _LPMAX);
_LPMAX = exp(-_LPMAX);
_P1 = 1 / (_LPMAX + _LP0);
_P0 = _LP0 * _P1;
_P1 = _LPMAX * _P1;

*** Posterior Probabilities and Predicted Level;
label P__g_1 = 'Predicted: _g_=1';
label P__g_0 = 'Predicted: _g_=0';

*************************************;
***** end scoring code for regression;
*************************************;
```

Part 9: Computation of Survival, Hazard, and Subhazard

Once the logit transformation has been applied and the posterior probabilities are calculated, the score code moves to its last section, Part 9, to compute the variables whose labels were presented in Part 1.

```
label EM_SURVFCST = "Survival Probability at Future Time";❶
label EM_SURVIVAL = "Survival Probability at Censoring Time";❷
label EM_SURVEVENT = "Event Probability before or at the Future Time";❸
```

These three variables are described in detail later. The code continues as follows:

```
EM_SUBHZRD1_SURV = P__g_1;
EM_SUBHZRD0_SURV = 1-(EM_SUBHZRD1_SURV);
EM_HZRDFCST = EM_SUBHZRD1_SURV;
EM_SURVFCST ❶ = EM_SURVFCST*(1-EM_HZRDFCST);
if _T_=_T0_ then EM_SURVIVAL ❷ = EM_SURVFCST;
if EM_SURVIVAL >0 then do;
if _T_=t0_fcst then EM_SURVEVENT ❸ =(EM_SURVIVAL-
EM_SURVFCST)/EM_SURVIVAL;
 end;
 else do;
  if _T_=t0_fcst then EM_SURVEVENT =(EM_SURVIVAL-EM_SURVFCST)/0.00001;
 end;
 _t_+1;
 end;
 _T_ = _T0_;
end;
run;
```

Scoring Using SAS DATA Steps

In this section, you learn how to use the optimized score code using DATA steps. Later, the scoring results for customer Id_number = 4 are presented.

The alternative to scoring new data using SAS Enterprise Miner is to use the optimized score code that you saved to score a data set using Base SAS or SAS Enterprise Guide. The score code created by SAS Enterprise Miner can be used directly in a SAS program.

Step 1: Run Macros DMNORLEN and DMNORMCP

If you are working without SAS Enterprise Miner, then you need to run the macros DMNORLEN and DMNORMCP before running the following score code because these macros are invoked in the score code.

Program 8.5: Running the DMNORLEN and DMNORMCP Macros

```
/*--------------------------------------------------------------
 * name: dmnorlen.sas
 * purpose: maximum length of normalized category levels for EM
 * scoring code
 --------------------------------------------------------------*/

%macro DMNORLEN;
32
%mend DMNORLEN;

/*-----------------------------------------------------------
 * name: dmnormcp.sas
 * purpose: normalize category levels for EM scoring code
 -----------------------------------------------------------*/

%macro DMNORMCP(in,out);
  &out=dmnorm(&in,%dmnorlen);
%mend DMNORMCP;
```

Step 2: Score the Score_with_t Data Set

Program 8.6 is just a modification of the optimized score code. The program requires only Base SAS to run. Therefore, you can run the program on any of the systems in which you have installed Base SAS, regardless of whether SAS Enterprise Miner is installed. Remember that the SCORE_WITH_T data set contains all the same customer input variables, but it also contains the _t_ input variable. This enables you to compare the predicted hazard probabilities created by SAS Enterprise Miner with the predicted hazard probabilities created by SAS using Program 8.6. If you did not make any mistakes, the results will be the same.

To score the data set using Base SAS, open the optimized score code. At the beginning of the code, enter the following lines:

Program 8.6: Including a DATA Statement

```
data Scored_with_SAS_BASE;
set  SCORE_WITH_T;
```

Program 8.7 creates the Scored_with_SAS_BASE data set and uses SCORE_WITH_T as an input data set to be scored.

Program 8.7: Scoring Using Base SAS

```
DATA Scored_with_SAS_BASE;
SET  SCORE_WITH_T_;

************************************;
*** begin scoring code for regression;
************************************;
length _WARN_ $4;
label _WARN_ = 'Warnings';
.
. . . Other lines of code not shown here . . .
.
*------------------------------------*;
* TOOL: Score Node;
* TYPE: ASSESS;
* NODE: Score;
*-------------------------------------*;
run;
```

The same program can be written using the %INCLUDE statement, which includes and executes SAS statements and data lines by importing a SAS programming statement, data lines, or both, into a current SAS program.

When you execute a program that contains the **%INCLUDE** statement, SAS executes the code, including any statements or data lines that are in the program. In this case, SAS can read an external file saved in a folder:

Program 8.8: Scoring Using a %INCLUDE Statement

```
DATA Scored_with_SAS_BASE;
SET  SCORE_WITH_T_;
%include "Optimized Score Code.sas";
run;
```

Sorting the observations by **DESCENDING** values of **EM_HZRDFCST** necessarily arranges the most likely customers to repurchase at the top of the printed results:

```
PROC SORT DATA = Scored_with_SAS_BASE;
BY DESCENDING EM_HZRDFCST;
run;

Title "The First 10 Observations";
PROC PRINT DATA = Scored_with_SAS_BASE (obs=10);
VAR Id_number EM_HZRDFCST;
run;
```

This code prints the value of the **Id_number** as well as **EM_HZRDFCST**. EM_HZRDFCST is the predicted probability of repurchase or **Hazard Function at Future Time**. In Output 8.4, the 10 observations with the greatest values of **EM_HZRDFCST** are printed in descending order.

Output 8.4: The First 10 Observations Sorted by Hazard Function

The First 10 Observations

Obs	01-Customer Unique ID Number	Hazard Function at Future Time
1	642611	0.074633
2	566815	0.073584
3	608621	0.071662
4	643809	0.070913
5	616369	0.070732
6	593677	0.069999
7	658948	0.068934
8	669825	0.068384
9	664656	0.067584
10	597586	0.067134

Analyzing Customer ID = 4

In this section, you scrutinize the scoring data set and variables created by the optimized score code. For simplicity, the calculations use only the customer Id_number = 4.

Modifying the Original Scoring Program

In Program 8.9, you create a new **ID_NUMBER_4** data set from **SCORE_WITH_T_**.

Program 8.9: Modifying the Original Scoring Program to Create a New ID_NUMBER_4 Data Set

```
data   id_number_4;
set    score_with_t_;
where  id_number = 4;
run;
```

The result of running Program 8.9 is shown in Output 8.5.

Output 8.5: Viewing the Row for the New ID_NUMBER_4 Data Set

Id_number	Start ❶	Garden ❷	....	....	....	Income ❸	Currentdate ❹	_T_ ❺
4	01JAN2011	0	....	....	....	9	01JAN2015	48

To clarify the explanation of the ID_NUMBER_4 data set, all inputs from Garden ❷ to Income ❸ are suppressed. Customer 4 made the first purchase in **01JAN2011** ❶. Remember that **_T_** = **48** ❺ is the number of months after the first purchase or time on book to the **Currentdate** ❹ **01JAN2015**. Because the model was created using a three-month forecast period, SAS Enterprise Miner computes the hazard for the next three months following the **Today** date—that is, February to April 2015, as seen in Figure 8.32.

Figure 8.32: Forecasting Next Three Months in January 2015

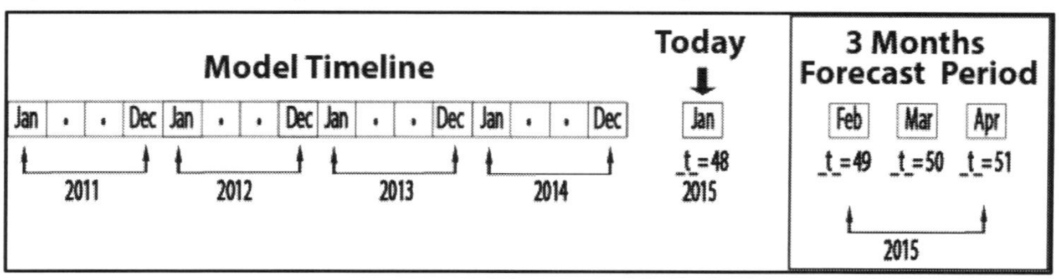

Scoring Customer Id_number = 4 (Future Time 51)

Program 8.10 scores the **ID_NUMBER_4** data set using the optimized score code. This program includes an external file named Optimized Score Code.sas and submits the optimized score code.

Program 8.10: Scoring Customer ID = 4 Using the Optimized Score Code

```
data Id_number_4_Scored;
set  Id_number_4;
%include "Optimized Score Code.sas";
run;
```

After running Program 8.10, you can analyze in detail the ID_NUMBER_4_SCORED data set as seen in Output 8.6.

Output 8.6: Analyzing the ID_NUMBER_4_SCORED Data Set—Part 1

Id_number	Start	Currentdate	_T_	EM_SURVIVAL	EM_SURVFCST	EM_SURVEVENT	EM_HAZARD
01-Customer Unique ID Number	02-Day of the First Purchase	Currentdate	_T_	Survival Probability at Censoring Time	Survival Probability at Future Time	Event Probability before or at the Future Time	Hazard Function at Censoring Time
				❶	❷	❸	❹
4	01JAN2011	01JAN2015	48	0.78164	0.77684	0.006152296	0.002134

In the first and second row, you see the variable name and labels created by SAS Enterprise Miner, respectively.

- **EM_SURVIVAL ❶** is the **Survival Probability at Censoring Time**—that is, at the censoring date January 2015.
- **EM_SURVFCST ❷**is the **Survival Probability at Future Time**—that is, April 2015.
- **EM_SURVEVENT ❸** is the **Event Probability before or at the Future Time**. In other words, it is the probability of repurchase before or at April 2015.
- **EM_HAZARD ❹** is the **Hazard Function at Censoring Time** in January 2015.

Output 8.7 shows the remaining variables created by the optimized score code.

Output 8.7: Analyzing the ID_NUMBER_4_SCORED Data Set—Part 2

EM_HZRDFCST	T_FCST	EM_SUBHZRD1	EM_SUBHZRD0	EM_SUBHZRD1_SURV	EM_SUBHZRD0_SURV
Hazard Function at Future Time	Number of Time Units in Future				
❺	❻	❼	❽	❾	❿
0.002016	51	0.002134104	0.99787	0.002016	0.99798

- **EM_HZRDFCST ❺** is the **Hazard Function at Future Time** in April 2015. It is of major importance because it is the key output variable.
- **T_FCST ❻** is the **Number of Time Units in Future**—that is, 51 = _t_ (48) + 3 units as was explained previously. The score code creates 51 rows for the customer Id_number = 4, but it creates only the last one. Recall the words of the analytical expert in data mining, Jimmy Hosang: "If you fail to understand the score code, you have failed everything in predictive modeling or data mining in general."
- **EM_SUBHZRD1 ❼** and **EM_SUBHZRD0 ❽** are the Subhazard functions for repurchase and non-repurchase at censoring time. Observe that because the subhazard has two levels, the value of EM_SUBHZRD1 + EM_SUBHZRD0 is always 1.

Why is SAS Enterprise Miner reporting the same variable twice? (That is, it's reporting EM_HAZARD ❹ and EM_SUBHZRD1 ❼.) In more advanced models such as competing risk, the subhazards have more than two levels. But, SAS Enterprise Miner keeps consistent names for variables independent of the number of levels in the target. These variables are not important for time-to-next-purchase models because you have just two levels. But, they are fundamental in competing risks. The same analysis is valid for the variables EM_SUBHZRD1_SURV ❾ and ❿ EM_SUBHZRD0_SURV. Observe that these variables do not have labels because they are less significant in terms of analysis. However, they are critical to the scoring process.

Scoring Customer ID = 4 (Future Time 49 to 51)

The final output result created by the optimized score is delivered in a unique row per customer. The information is brilliantly summarized so that a modeler can find in one row almost everything that is needed.

Unfortunately, the reality of the financial world and marketing campaigns demands that each set of customer results be exported in such a way that the modeler can observe how the probability of repurchase changes over time for many months and, in the case of IFRS 9 models, for many years. In Output 8.8, the desired output for Customer ID = 4 is presented, where hazard for the months 48 to 51 is included.

Output 8.8: Desired Results for Customer ID = 4

Id_number	Start	Currentdate	_T_	EM_SURVIVAL	EM_SURVFCST	EM_SURVEVENT	EM_HAZARD	EM_HZRDFCST	T_FCST
01-Customer Unique ID Number	02-Day of the First Purchase	Currentdate	_T_	Survival Probability at Censoring Time	Survival Probability at Future Time	Event Probability before or at the Future Time	Hazard Function at Censoring Time	Hazard Function at Future Time	Number of Time Units in Future
				❶	❷	❸	❹	❺	❻
4	01JAN2011	01JAN2015	48	0.78164	0.78164	.	0.002134	0.002134	51
4	01JAN2011	01JAN2015	49	0.78164	0.78001	.	0.002134	0.002094	51
4	01JAN2011	01JAN2015	50	0.78164	0.77841	.	0.002134	0.002055	51
4	01JAN2011	01JAN2015	51	0.78164	0.77684	0.006152296	0.002134	0.002016	51

To achieve this task and create the table in Output 8.8, you need to modify the original optimized score code.

In Program 8.11, you create an expanded data set named Id_number_4_Scored_expanded ❶.

You must modify a part ❷ of this program. You need to add an **OUTPUT** statement after the **END** statement, which is part of the **DO-END** statement. The OUTPUT statement tells SAS to write each observation to the expanded SAS data set immediately, not at the end of the DATA step.

Program 8.11: Modifying the Optimized Score Code

```
data Id_number_4_Scored_expanded; ❶
set  Id_number_4;
*************************************;
*** begin scoring code for regression;
*************************************;

length _WARN_ $4;
label _WARN_ = 'Warnings';
.
Other lines here……
.
*************************************;
***** end scoring code for regression;
*************************************;

EM_SUBHZRD1_SURV = P__g_1;
EM_SUBHZRD0_SURV =1-(EM_SUBHZRD1_SURV);
EM_HZRDFCST=EM_SUBHZRD1_SURV;
```

```
EM_SURVFCST=EM_SURVFCST*(1-EM_HZRDFCST);
if _T_=_T0_ then EM_SURVIVAL=EM_SURVFCST;
if EM_SURVIVAL >0 then do;
if _T_=t0_fcst then EM_SURVEVENT=(EM_SURVIVAL-EM_SURVFCST)/EM_SURVIVAL;
end;
else do;
if _T_=t0_fcst then EM_SURVEVENT=(EM_SURVIVAL-EM_SURVFCST)/0.00001;
end;
OUTPUT; /*included output statement*/ ❷
 _t_+1;
 end;
_T_ = _T0_;
;
end;
run;
```

Output 8.9 shows the variables created using the OUTPUT statement.

Output 8.9: Scoring Using the OUTPUT Statement

Id_number	Start	Currentdate	_T_	EM_SURVIVAL	EM_SURVFCST	EM_SURVEVENT	EM_HAZARD	EM_HZRDFCST	T_FCST
01-Customer Unique ID Number	02-Day of the First Purchase	Currentdate	_T_	Survival Probability at Censoring Time	Survival Probability at Future Time	Event Probability before or at the Future Time	Hazard Function at Censoring Time	Hazard Function at Future Time	Number of Time Units in Future
				❶	❷	❸	❹	❺	❻
4	01JAN2011	01JAN2015	0	.	0.97975	.	0.002134	0.020246	51
4	01JAN2011	01JAN2015	1	.	0.96173	.	0.002134	0.018395	51
4	01JAN2011	01JAN2015	2	.	0.94753	.	0.002134	0.014769	51
4	01JAN2011	01JAN2015	3	.	0.93676	.	0.002134	0.011359	51
4	01JAN2011	01JAN2015	4	.	0.92826	.	0.002134	0.009083	51
4	01JAN2011	01JAN2015	5	.	0.92079	.	0.002134	0.008039	51
4	01JAN2011	01JAN2015	6	.	0.91366	.	0.002134	0.007743	51
4	01JAN2011	01JAN2015	7	.	0.90652	.	0.002134	0.007820	51
4	01JAN2011	01JAN2015	8	.	0.89929	.	0.002134	0.007977	51
4	01JAN2011	01JAN2015	9	.	0.89212	.	0.002134	0.007968	51
.	.	.	.	.	.	.	.	.	.
.	.	.	.	.	.	.	.	.	.
.	.	.	.	.	.	.	.	.	.
4	01JAN2011	01JAN2015	39	.	0.79805	.	0.002134	0.002531	51
4	01JAN2011	01JAN2015	40	.	0.79607	.	0.002134	0.002483	51
4	01JAN2011	01JAN2015	41	.	0.79413	.	0.002134	0.002437	51
4	01JAN2011	01JAN2015	42	.	0.79223	.	0.002134	0.002391	51
4	01JAN2011	01JAN2015	43	.	0.79037	.	0.002134	0.002346	51
4	01JAN2011	01JAN2015	44	.	0.78855	.	0.002134	0.002302	51
4	01JAN2011	01JAN2015	45	.	0.78677	.	0.002134	0.002259	51
4	01JAN2011	01JAN2015	46	.	0.78502	.	0.002134	0.002217	51
4	01JAN2011	01JAN2015	47	.	0.78332	.	0.002134	0.002175	51
4	01JAN2011	01JAN2015	48	❶ 0.78164	❷ 0.78164	.	❹ 0.002134	❺ 0.002134	51
4	01JAN2011	01JAN2015	49	0.78164	0.78001	.	0.002134	0.002094	51
4	01JAN2011	01JAN2015	50	0.78164	0.77841	.	0.002134	0.002055	51
4	01JAN2011	01JAN2015	51	0.78164	0.77684	❸ 0.006152296	0.002134	0.002016	51

In the **EM_SURVIVAL** column ❶, you find the **Survival Probability at Censoring Time**. If you carefully analyze the value **0.78164** ❶, you see that the values are constant for each month after January 2018 (_t_ = 48). This is not the same for **Survival Probability at Future Time** ❷. These values change every month. The same conclusion is valid for the **EM_HAZARD** column ❹ and **EM_HZRDFCST** column ❺, where you find the variable of major interest: the **Hazard Function at Future Time**. The Hazard Function at Future Time ❺ is the final objective of this chapter.

The **EM_SURVEVENT** column ❸ **Event Probability before or at the Future Time** has no importance in time-to-next-purchase models. This is the conditional probability that a repurchase occurs in February, March, or April, given that no repurchase occurred prior to February. This seems to be a suitable score to rank cases for a promotion activity. If the current time of December 2014 was used, this would be the probability of an event occurring in January, February, or March, given that no repurchase occurred before January.

Using PROC COMPARE for Validation

To validate the score approach using Base SAS as shown in Figure 8.33, you need to compare the data set created by SAS Enterprise Miner ❶ with the data set created by a SAS DATA step using the optimized score code ❷.

Figure 8.33: Comparing the Data Set from SAS Enterprise Miner with the Data Set from Base SAS

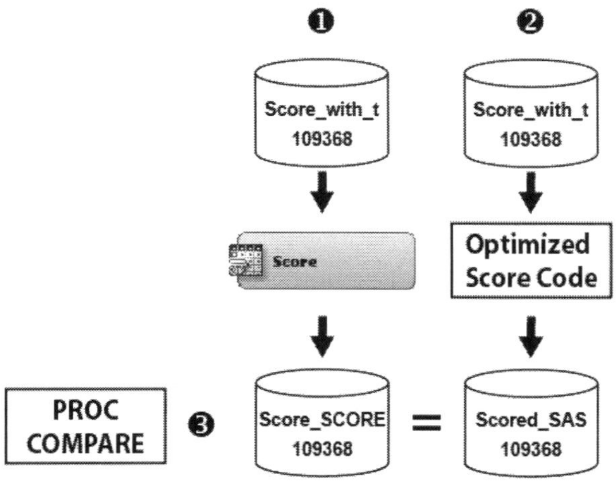

If there is any difference across both SAS data sets, then you made mistakes that must be investigated and remedied. This task of comparing two data sets can be achieved using PROC COMPARE ❸.

First, copy the tables that you want to validate and score to the **Work** library using **PROC COPY**. The reason for working in the Work library is that there is no need to save the output result.

Program 8.12: Comparing Scoring Data Sets

```
proc copy in = chap out=work;
select score_score      ❶
       score_with_t_;   ❷
run;
```

❶ The table scored by the Score node in SAS Enterprise Miner.

❷ The table that you want to validate and that will be scored using the optimized score code.

Score the SCORE_WITH_T_ data set using the optimized score code. In this step, you create the data set **SCORED__SAS❸** to be validated.

```
data SCORED_SAS ❸;
set  SCORE_WITH_T_;
%include "Optimized_Score_Code.sas";
run;
```

Compare the scored data sets using PROC COMPARE.

```
PROC COMPARE BASE    = ❹ SCORE_SCORE
             COMPARE = ❺ SCORED_SAS;
RUN;
```

PROC COMPARE compares two data sets: the base ❹ data set and the comparison ❺ data set.

The results appear in Output 8.10.

Output 8.10: Results of Running PROC COMPARE on Data Sets from SAS Enterprise Miner and Base SAS

```
                              The COMPARE Procedure

            Comparison of WORK.SCORE_SCORE with WORK.SCORED_SAS

                                 (Method=EXACT)


                                Data Set Summary


   Dataset                          Created          Modified        NVar    NObs


 WORK.SCORE_SCORE      ❹       19JUL16:08:23:18  19JUL16:08:23:18     38   109368

 WORK.SCORED_USING_SAS_BASE ❺  19JUL16:08:42:13  19JUL16:08:42:13     38   109368


                                Variables Summary

                        Number of Variables in Common: 38.


                               Observation Summary


                          Observation      Base   Compare


                          First Obs           1         1

                          Last  Obs      109368    109368

    Number of Observations in Common: 109368.

    Total Number of Observations Read from WORK.SCORE_SCORE: 109368.

    Total Number of Observations Read from WORK.SCORED_SAS:  109368.


    Number of Observations with Some Compared Variables Unequal: 0.

    Number of Observations with All Compared Variables Equal: 109368.

    NOTE: No unequal values were found. All values compared are exactly equal. ❻
```

This default output of PROC COMPARE for these two data sets gives all the information that you need. In summary, you are interested in seeing the following:

- whether scored variables have different values
- whether one data set has more observations than another
- what variables the two data sets have in common
- how many variables are in one data set but not in another
- whether scored and input variables have different formats, labels, or types

The information ❻ tells you that PROC COMPARE judged all variables to be equal.

Business Situation 2: Calibrating Scoring Results

This book has demonstrated that the most important business and practical consideration in data mining is scorability (that is, how the model is implemented in old or new customers). The second is forecast performance (that is, how the model performs between Actual x Calibrated Forecast), which is linked to the calibration process.

The calibration of survival models can be seen as a method of adjustment. Calibration tunes the forecast of a new data set using the proportion of actuals in the model data set. Calibration compares measurements with known accuracy with measurements that you want to be as close to the measurements with known accuracy.

This section addresses the practical implementation and aspects of calibration of a data set by using prior information obtained from another data set. The process of calibrating to the total number of repurchase by months is discussed. A SAS macro is used and is available from the author's web page at https://support.sas.com/authors. The intention is to present a practical strategy and not spend time explaining macro code. Macros are part of modeling development, but are not the primary focus of this book.

Figure 8.34: Calibration Strategy

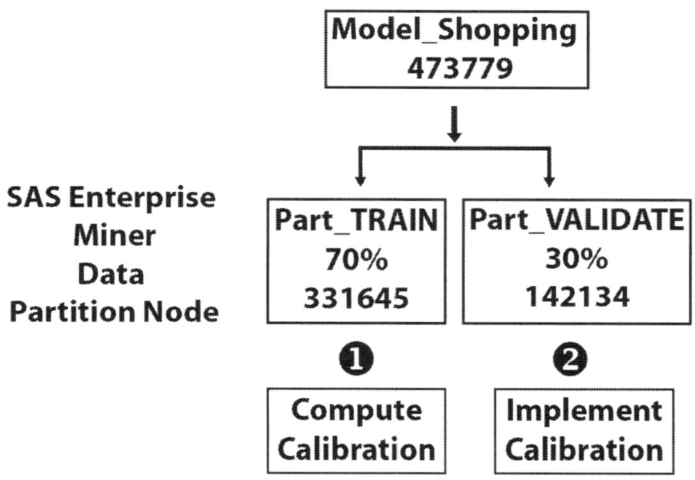

For example, you have the results from Part_TRAIN ❶, and you want to calibrate the model on the Part_VALIDATE ❷ data set. In other words, you want to calibrate a result that predicts the repurchase sales by month on the Part_VALIDATE data set.

You look at past data (Part_TRAIN) of the model, compare the given output to the actual value, and alter the model output to accurately predict the Part_VALIDATE data set.

If the calibration process succeeds, the same proportion found in the Part_TRAIN data set should be found in the Part_VALIDATE data set. The rationale is that any other sample should behave as the modeling sample behaves. If the sample process was correctly designed, the calibration should be successful.

These data sets are used as examples for the calibration process, but the technique can be applied to any data set that you want to score or validate. For this reason, in this book, calibration is presented after the scoring process.

In Figure 8.35, the actual graph ❶ and the desired output graph ❷ are calibrated.

Figure 8.35: Desired Results after Calibration of Survival Analysis Models

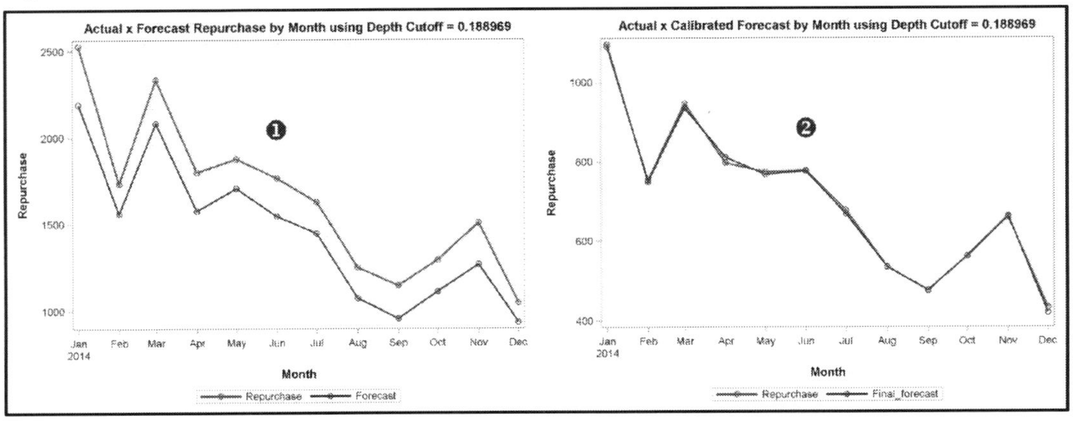

Observe that the model reproduces the pattern of seasonality in demand. This is the most important characteristic when you are analyzing demand forecast.

The principal reason that you need to calibrate the model is that no model is 100% error-free, and you want the forecast number as close as possible to reduce the cost of stock and maintenance of products.

A time series graphic as shown in Figure 8.35 ❶ 0provides a dynamic display of model behavior, while the model is used to forecast in each month. Any sudden changes in this graph indicate a possible lack of performance that should be investigated. You can see that the model performs very well using depth = 0.188969 as the cutoff because the Actual x Calibrated Forecast follows the same monthly seasonality. This proves that the model is a reasonable representation of the actual business demand. The graphic shows that the model is invariant. This graphical check is a way of increasing the confidence placed in the model and providing support for its validity and stability over time.

A good survival model must be able to tackle the seasonality effect of each month. The philosophy behind having multiple months is based on the fact that each month can have a different pattern, such as Christmas holidays, Mother's Day, Go Back to School, and so on.

The calibration process is implemented using the steps in Figure 8.36.

Figure 8.36: Calibration Using Prior Information

Step 1	**Compute the Actual and Forecast for a full year (2014), using the Modeling data set (PART_TRAIN) with depth (0.188969) at max Benefit.**
Step 2	**Plot a time series graph to assess the difference between the Actual and Forecast.**
Step 3	**Compute the calibration (the Prior proportion for each month).**
Step 4	**Compute the full year (2014) Forecast, using the SCORED data set (PART_VALIDATE) or any other data set.**
Step 5	**Apply the calibration to adjust the FORECAST of (PART_VALIDATE) data set .**
Step 6	**Plot a time series graph to assess the final forecast numbers to be delivered.**

Step 1: Compute Actual and Forecast of Part_TRAIN

The first step is computing the actual and forecast number of repurchases by month as seen in Output 8.11.

Output 8.11: Actual Purchase and Forecast for Training Data Set (January to December 2014)

Month of the Repurchase	Actual Repurchase Full Table ❶	Total at Risk ❷	Forecast Repurchase (Depth = 0.188969) ❸
Month	Repurchase	Total_at_Risk	Forecast
JAN2014	**2527**	145500	**2192**
FEB2014	**1733**	143767	**1560**
MAR2014	**2335**	143165	**2082**
APR2014	**1799**	143701	**1575**
MAY2014	**1876**	143624	**1707**
JUN2014	**1765**	143735	**1544**
JUL2014	**1627**	143873	**1446**
AUG2014	**1249**	144251	**1072**
SEP2014	**1145**	144355	**955**
OCT2014	**1293**	144207	**1112**
NOV2014	**1505**	143995	**1267**
DEC2014	**1046**	144454	**933**

The idea is easy: you count how many customers repurchased in the validation period, and you compare the actuals to the forecasts as seen in the **Repurchase** column ❶ and **Forecast** column ❸. Any divergence between both variables indicates that the forecast must be calibrated.

The two variables of major interest are the following:

❶ **Repurchase**: the actual repurchase number of customers.

❸ **Forecast:** the forecast of the repurchase number of customers was obtained from a confusion matrix in Chapter 7, which was computed using the depth = 0.188969 value at the maximum benefit. In practical terms, you run the validation process for each month of the year 2014 to obtain the forecast.

In Figure 8.2, you saw that the sample size of the Part_TRAIN data set was 331,645 customers. But, the **Total_at_Risk** variable indicates that in the first month (JAN2014), there are only 145,500 ❷ customers.

The explanation is that every customer who already repurchased is dropped from the scoring process. For the first month, the customers who repurchased before January 2014 were excluded, and the remaining customers total 145,500.

Why did the Total_at_Risk increase between March 2014 and April 2014? Because some customers started after January. This situation is called *delayed entry*.

Step 2: Plot an Actual and Forecast Graph—Part_TRAIN

You can present the actual and forecast data in many ways. But, a critical issue is to ensure that the graph type selected is the most appropriate for the calibration process. For this reason, the second step is to graphically display the plot in a time series format designed for identifying patterns and trends in the data, such as seasonal effects, large changes, and turning points in sales as seen in Output 8.12. The time series graph is used for comparing different variables in absolute value terms and over multiple periods.

The graphical process focuses on monthly issues that should be addressed when sales demand for different audiences, including financial and marketing, are an issue. The process highlights ways to maximize presentation impact, ensuring that the graphics are easy to read and interpret. Both the actual and forecast time series are included in the same graph. This is particularly useful for analyzing and comparing trends and seasonality.

Output 8.12: Actual x Forecast Repurchase by Month Using Depth Cutoff = 0.188969

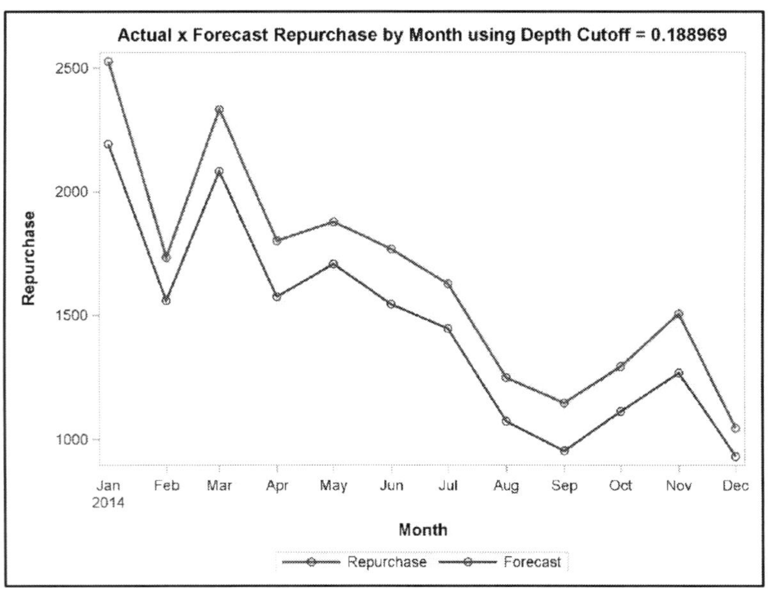

After scoring the Part_TRAIN data set, you realize that the model follows the seasonal demand well. The graphical representation of the two lines showing a parallel pattern makes it particularly clear to you that the forecast is underestimating the demand for every single month of the year. This is deemed normal behavior in terms of survival data mining, which is not a time series technique. This is an indication that the sales numbers must be calibrated to reflect reality as closely as possible. This process is sometimes called *adjustment*.

Keep this relationship in mind: the model was underestimated in the Part_TRAIN data set and, *ceteris paribus* (holding all other things constant), will underestimate in any other data set.

Step 3: Compute the Calibration (Prior Proportion—Part_TRAIN)

The third step is to calculate the **Calibration** variable as shown in Program 8.13.

Program 8.13: Calibration Variable

```
data actualrepurchase_training;
set  actualrepurchase_training;
Calibration  ❹ = Repurchase ❶ / Forecast ❸;
run;
```

To calculate the **Calibration** variable ❹, divide the actual **Repurchase** ❶ by the **Forecast** ❷.

Output 8.13 summarizes the results.

Output 8.13: Calibration from Training Data Set (January to December 2014)

Month of the Repurchase	Actual Repurchase Full Table ❶	Total at Risk ❷	Forecast Repurchase (Depth = 0.188969) ❸	Calibration ❹
Month	**Repurchase**	**Total_at_Risk**	**Forecast**	**Calibration**
JAN2014	2527	145500	2192	**1.15283**
FEB2014	1733	143767	1560	**1.11090**
MAR2014	2335	143165	2082	**1.12152**
APR2014	1799	143701	1575	**1.14222**
MAY2014	1876	143624	1707	**1.09900**
JUN2014	1765	143735	1544	**1.14313**
JUL2014	1627	143873	1446	**1.12517**
AUG2014	1249	144251	1072	**1.16511**
SEP2014	1145	144355	955	**1.19895**
OCT2014	1293	144207	1112	**1.16277**
NOV2014	1505	143995	1267	**1.18785**
DEC2014	1046	144454	933	**1.12111**

The result for the month of January 2014 is easy to understand: because the forecast underestimates the actual repurchase, the calibration value is **1.15283** ❹. This suggests that you should increase the **Forecast** value ❸ (**2192**) in this month by 15.283% to achieve the actual **Repurchase** ❶ value (**2527**). If you have another data set to score in January of every year, then you multiply the results by 1.15283 to increase the forecast accordingly.

Step 4: Compute the Full-Year Forecast—Part_VALIDATE

Once the calibration is calculated using the Part_TRAIN data set, the fourth step is computing actual and forecast numbers of repurchase by month for the Part_VALIDATE data set. You simply apply the same macro, replacing the Part_TRAIN data set with the Part_VALIDATE data set as seen in Output 8.14.

Output 8.14: Actual and Forecast of Part_VALIDATE Data Set (January to December 2014)

Month of the Repurchase	Actual Repurchase ❶	Forecast Repurchase (Depth = 0.188969) ❷
JAN2014	1090	951
FEB2014	754	675
MAR2014	947	835
APR2014	797	710
MAY2014	774	699
JUN2014	778	680
JUL2014	678	595
AUG2014	536	459
SEP2014	476	398
OCT2014	562	484
NOV2014	660	558
DEC2014	433	375

Notice that Part_VALIDATE contains only 30% (142134) of the data rows. Therefore, the **Actual Repurchase** ❶ and **Forecast Repurchase** ❷ numbers are smaller in absolute numbers. To better visualize this, both variables are shown in Output 8.15.

Output 8.15: Actual x Forecast by Month Using Depth Cutoff = 0.188969

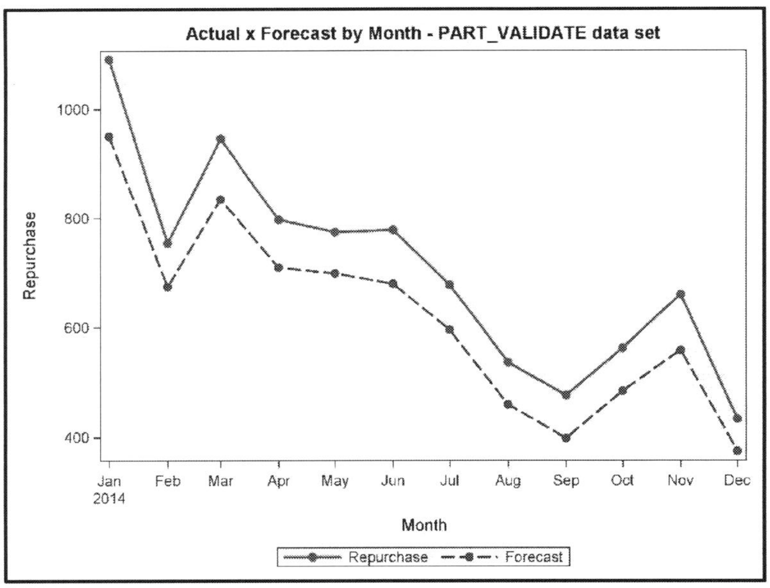

In practical terms, the scoring process applied to the Part_VALIDATE data set underestimated in the same proportion as the Model data set (Part_TRAIN). This is a good indication that the calibration will succeed. You are ready to apply the calibration in the next step.

Step 5: Calibrate the Forecast of Part_VALIDATE

The general assumption is the following: if the forecast underestimates in the model data set, it will underestimate in the sample data set. To apply the calibration and to consequently verify the underlying assumption, you need to merge the results from the model and scoring data sets. This task is executed in Program 8.14.

Program 8.14: Calibrating the Forecast of the Part_VALIDATE Data Set

```
data Calibrated ❶;
merge actualrepurchase_training ❷ actualpurchase_validate ❸;
by month;
Final_forecast  ❻ = round (Forecast ❹ * Calibration ❺);
run;
```

You created the final **Calibrated ❶** data set by merging the **actualrepurchase_training** data set ❷ and the **actualpurchase_validate** data sets ❸ by month. The final calibrated forecast of repurchase number ❻ is achieved by multiplying **Forecast ❹** as calculated in the Part_VALIDATE data set by **Calibration ❺** as calculated in the Part_TRAIN data set. Apply the **ROUND** function, rounding the result to the nearest integer.

Results of the calibration are shown in Output 8.16.

Output 8.16: Calibrated Forecast for Part_VALIDATE Data Set (January to December 2014)

Month of the Repurchase	Actual Repurchase Full Table	Forecast Repurchase (Depth = 0.188969) ❹	Calibration ❺	Calibrated Forecast of Repurchase ❻
Month	**Actual**	**Forecast**	**Calibration**	**Final_forecast**
JAN2014	1090	951	1.15283	**1096**
FEB2014	754	675	1.11090	**750**
MAR2014	947	835	1.12152	**936**
APR2014	797	710	1.14222	**811**
MAY2014	774	699	1.09900	**768**
JUN2014	778	680	1.14313	**777**
JUL2014	678	595	1.12517	**669**
AUG2014	536	459	1.16511	**535**
SEP2014	476	398	1.19895	**477**
OCT2014	562	484	1.16277	**563**
NOV2014	660	558	1.18785	**663**
DEC2014	433	375	1.12111	**420**

Step 6: Plot an Actual by Calibrated Forecast Graph

After the computation of the calibrated forecast, the last task is to create the graph to present the repurchase and final calibrated forecast. Output 8.17 shows that calibration has been achieved.

Output 8.17: Calibrated Forecast for Part_VALIDATE Data Set (January to December 2014)

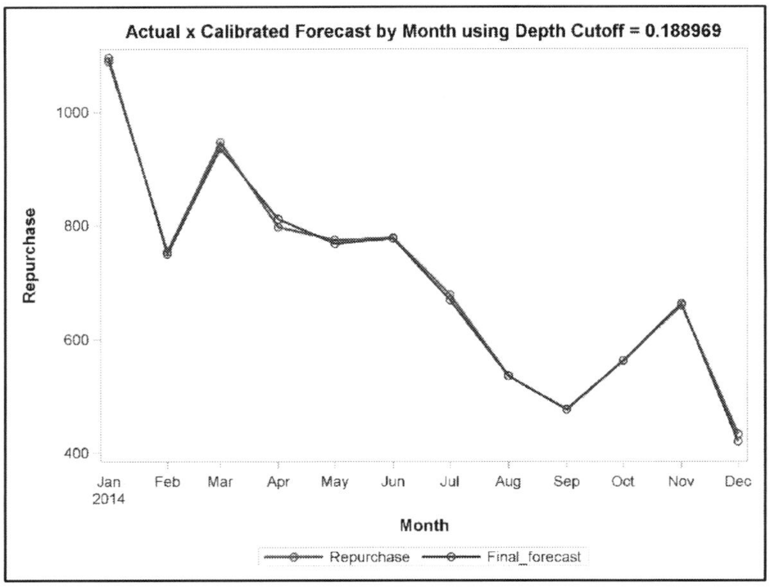

In this section, one possible strategy is presented to show the impact of a calibration forecast number and its implications for the business.

Scoring customers to compute a probability of an outcome is probably the most difficult task in the area of financial modeling. In mortgage IFRS 9 models, the customer needs to be scored for the full lifetime of the contract, sometimes amounting to more than 25 years, by months or quarters. Usually, the business implementation of advanced models can take 30 to 90 days. For this reason, the scoring process presented in this chapter has demonstrated how to accomplish three fundamental tasks:

- Create the score data set.
- Compute the posterior probability, Survival function, and Hazard function.
- Calibrate the scoring results by adjusting the numbers based on historical information.

References

Allison, Paul D. 2010. *Survival Analysis Using SAS: A Practical Guide*, 2nd ed. Cary, NC: SAS Institute Inc.

Basel Committee on Banking Supervision. 2001. *The New Basel Capital Accord.* Available at http://www.bis.org/publ/bcbsca03.pdf.

Basel Committee on Banking Supervision. 2005. *Studies on the Validation of Internal Rating Systems.* Working Paper No. 14. Available at http://www.bundesbank.de/Redaktion/EN/Downloads/Tasks/Banking_supervision/working_paper_no_14_studies_on_the_validation_of_internal_rating_systems.pdf?__blob=publicationFile.

Berglund, Patricia, and Steven Heeringa. 2014. *Multiple Imputation of Missing Data Using SAS.* Cary, NC: SAS Institute Inc.

Blossfeld, Hans-Peter, Alfred Hamerle, and Karl Ulrich Mayer. 1989. *Event History Analysis: Statistical theory and Application in the Social Sciences.* Hillsdale, NJ: Erlbaum.

Collett, David. 1993. *Modelling Survival Data in Medical Research.* New York: Chapman & Hall.

Elandt-Johnson, Regina C., and Norman L. Johnson. 1980. *Survival Models and Data Analysis.* New York: Wiley.

Harrell, Frank E., Jr. 2001. *Regression Modeling Strategies: With Applications to Linear Models, Logistic and Ordinal Regression, and Survival Analysis*, 2nd ed. New York: Springer.

Hosmer, David W., Jr., and Stanley Lemeshow. 1999. *Applied Survival Analysis: Regression Modeling of Time to Event Data.* New York: Wiley.

Hosmer, David W., Jr., and Stanley Lemeshow. 2000. *Applied Logistic Regression*, 2nd ed. New York: Wiley.

Kalbfleisch, John D., and Ross L. Prentice. 2002. *The Statistical Analysis of Failure Time Data*, 2nd ed. Hoboken, NJ: Wiley.

Klein, John P., and Moeschberger, Melvin L. 1997. *Survival Analysis: Techniques for Censored and Truncated Data.* New York: Springer.

Kleinbaum, David G., and Mitchel Klein. 2010. *Logistic Regression: A Self-Learning Text*, 3rd ed. New York: Springer.

Lee, Elisa T., and John Wenyu Wang. 2013. *Statistical Methods for Survival Data Analysis*, 4th ed. Hoboken, NJ: Wiley.

Liu, Xian. 2012. Survival Analysis: Models and Applications. Chichester, UK: Wiley.

Löffler, Gunter, and Peter N. Posch. 2011. *Credit Risk Modeling Using Excel and VBA*, 2nd ed. Wiley Finance Series. Chichester, UK: Wiley.

Mills, Melinda. 2011. *Introducing Survival and Event History Analysis.* Thousand Oaks, CA: SAGE Publications.

Molinari, Nicolas, Jean-Pierre Daurès, and Jean-François Durand. 2001. "Regression Splines for Threshold Selection in Survival Data Analysis." *Statistics in Medicine*, 20 (2):237–47.

Pintilie, Melania. 2006. *Competing Risks: A Practical Perspective.* Hoboken, NJ: Wiley.

Refaat, Mamdouh. *Data Preparation for Data Mining Using SAS.* 2007. San Francisco: Morgan Kaufmann, Elsevier.

SAS Institute Inc. 2007. SAS Institute white paper. "Comply and Exceed: Credit risk management for Basel II and beyond." Available at http://ger.na.sas.com/Marketing/contentbase/Shared%20Documents/RI_WP_Comply_and_Exceed_-_Credit_Risk_Management_for_Basel_II_and_Beyond.pdf.

Singer, Judith D., and John B. Willett. 2003. *Applied Longitudinal Data Analysis: Modeling Change and Event Occurrence.* Oxford: Oxford University Press.

Smith, Peter J. 2002. *Analysis of Failure and Survival Data.* Boca Raton, FL: Chapman & Hall/CRC.

Stone, Charles J., Mark H. Hansen, Charles Kooperberg, and Young K. Truong.1997. "Polynomial Splines and their Tensor Products in Extended Linear Modeling." *Annals of Statistics*, 25 (4): 1371–1425.

Svolba, Gerhard. 2006. *Data Preparation for Analytics Using SAS.* Cary, NC: SAS Institute Inc.

Tableman, Mara, and Jong Sung Kim. 2003 *Survival Analysis Using SAS: Analysis of Time-To-Event Data.* Boca Raton, FL: Chapman & Hall/CRC.

Therneau, Terry M., and Patricia M. Grambsch. 2000. *Modeling Survival Data: Extending the Cox Model.* New York: Springer.

Verbeke, Geert, and Molenberghs, Geert. 2000. *Linear Mixed Models for Longitudinal Data.* New York: Springer.

Index

Printed in Poland
by Amazon Fulfillment
Poland Sp. z o.o., Wrocław

49582655R00134